THE TRAGEDY OF LYNCHING

THE TRAGEDY
OF LYNCHING

By

ARTHUR F. RAPER, Ph.D.

*Research and Field Secretary, Commission on
Interracial Coöperation*

NEGRO UNIVERSITIES PRESS
NEW YORK

HU
6464
.R3
1969 c

Originally published in 1933
by The University of North Carolina Press

Reprinted 1969 by
Negro Universities Press
A DIVISION OF GREENWOOD PUBLISHING CORP.
NEW YORK

Library of Congress Catalogue Card Number 69-16568

SBN 8371-1145-5

PRINTED IN UNITED STATES OF AMERICA

INTRODUCTION

THE LYNCHING PROBLEM is of high national importance. Until America can discover and apply means to end these relapses to the law of the jungle, we have no assurance that ordered society will not at any moment be overthrown by the blind passion of a potentially ever-present mob.

But the quest for a preventive can be undertaken only after we have an understanding of what it is that is to be prevented. This necessary analysis of the lynching, its background, circumstances, and meaning, introduces many baffling elements. Is lynching a group response to general factors? Is there a sufficient common pattern to crimes committed a thousand miles apart to enable us to isolate definite contributory causes? What parts do poverty, ignorance, racial emotions play in these mob-deaths? What is the social pathology, the emotional history, of a lynching mob? Could these things be learned, or any moiety of them, a real beginning toward diagnosis would be made, and prescription would swiftly follow.

With the marked increase of lynchings early in 1930, the Commission on Interracial Coöperation requested a number of men of both races to undertake a thorough study of the lynching phenomenon. Thus was created the Southern Commission on the Study of Lynching, which began its work in June 1930. This Commission was fortunate to secure, as its chief of research and investigation, Dr. Arthur F. Raper, of the staff of the Commission on Interracial Coöperation. In our general field investigations and researches, Dr. Raper was ably assisted by Professor Walter R. Chivers, of the Sociology Department of Morehouse College, Atlanta, who also visited the scenes of each of 1930's lynchings

and secured valuable data. These two investigators in turn are greatly indebted to Mr. R. B. Eleazer, for his study of the lynching at Walhalla, South Carolina; to Mr. N. C. Young, for a report of the lynching at Tarboro, North Carolina; to Dr. and Mrs. J. J. Rhyne for their assistance, and to Mr. Orland K. Armstrong, for an intimate picture of the lynching at Maryville, Missouri. The coöperation of Dr. W. W. Alexander and Mr. R. B. Eleazer of the staff of the Commission on Interracial Coöperation has been of inestimable value in this work. Miss Emily H. Clay and Miss Myrtis Johnson have been most helpful in the preparation of the manuscript for publication.

For two years, Dr. Raper has worked upon the problems, patiently, unflaggingly, in scientific spirit. He and his associates dissected the social anatomy of each of 1930's lynchings. Their observations and conclusions have been carefully debated, tested, and appraised by the members of the Commission. Two reports have already been published: *Lynchings and What They Mean*, an eighty-page pamphlet containing our general findings and recommendations, and *The Mob Murder of S. S. Mincey*, a twenty-five-page pamphlet presenting two of our case studies. In its first chapters, the present volume incorporates much of the data presented in our former publication; the remainder of the volume is devoted to case studies, two of which appeared in the smaller pamphlet.

The Commission feels that the presentation of these more detailed and embracing materials is warranted by the researches of Dr. Raper and his associates, and will afford students of social phenomena an opportunity to study the causation of these examples of group sadism and, finally, will be welcomed by the ever-increasing number of Southern men and women who abhor mob-murder and expectantly look forward to the day when it will be no more.

GEORGE F. MILTON, *Chairman*
Southern Commission on the Study of Lynching.

TABLE OF CONTENTS

PART FIVE

MOB OUTBREAKS IN NORTH TEXAS AND CENTRAL OKLAHOMA, 317

PART SIX

LYNCHINGS OUTSIDE THE SOUTH, 384

PART SEVEN

FOILING THE MOB, 441

PART ONE

THE TOLL OF THE MOB

THE TOLL of the mob reckons not alone the victims but the lynchers themselves and the economic, social, and cultural meaning of their lawlessness. Three thousand seven hundred and twenty-four people were lynched in the United States from 1889 through 1930.[1] Over four-fifths of these were Negroes, less than one-sixth of whom were accused of rape. Practically all of the lynchers were native whites. The lynching rates have been highest in the newer and more sparsely settled portions of the South, where cultural and economic institutions are least stable and officers of the law are farthest apart, poorest paid, and most dependent upon local sentiment.

Of the twenty-one persons lynched in 1930, many were captured after extended man-hunts organized by undeputized armed men who used bloodhounds and conducted some type of mock trial before the lynching. Though two of the victims were unaccused, and there is grave doubt as to the guilt of many more, the findings of these mob trials were the lynchers' assurance that their victims were guilty of the crimes of which they were accused. The fact that a number of the victims were tortured, mutilated, dragged, or burned suggests the presence of sadistic tendencies among the lynchers; herein lies one of the most baffling phases of the mob situation. Though there were a few notable exceptions, most of the lynchers, chiefly young men between their late teens and twenty-five, were from that unattached group of people which exercised least public responsibility and was farthest removed from the institutions and agencies determining accepted standards of conduct. A

---

[1] See "Negro Year Book, 1931-1932," and earlier editions of Year Book for sources of quantitative data on lynchings appearing in this volume.

number of middle-aged women figured prominently in some of the outbreaks; children, too, were present, making more difficult any effective resistance by officers.

Of the tens of thousands of lynchers and onlookers, the latter not guiltless, only forty-nine were indicted and only four have been sentenced. Chief among the factors rendering the courts ineffective was the prevalent indifference of peace officers and court officials and the apathy of the general white public concerning matters affecting Negroes. With but rare exceptions, leaders and members of the local religious and civic organizations were maneuvered by the pro-lynchers into a position of silent acquiescence.

And so the lynchers went unpunished and the communities paid the bills. Hundreds of thousands of dollars worth of property was destroyed with no insurance collectible; indirect financial losses accrued from the unfavorable publicity. Labor was disorganized and racial antagonisms were accentuated, forming the basis for further racial exploitation. The local and state governments were openly defied; the officials along with the general public, by winking at the lawlessness, rendered more difficult the realization of a community where the basic rights of human beings are respected.

CHAPTER I

SALIENT FACTS ABOUT 1930'S LYNCHINGS

In 1930, twenty-one persons were lynched in the United States. Six of these were in Georgia; four in Mississippi; three in Texas; two in Indiana; two in South Carolina, and one each in Oklahoma, Alabama, North Carolina, and Florida. The Florida victim was a foreign-born white; the other twenty were Negroes.

PERSONS LYNCHED AND COUNTIES INVOLVED

Some Facts About Persons Lynched. The ages of the mob victims ranged from the late teens to seventy, with over two-thirds of them less than twenty-five, and only three over forty-five. Ten of them were married, and twenty children, many of them quite young, and all dependent, were left without support.

Sixteen of the victims had never been before the courts. Of the five with court records, two had been charged with rape, two with theft, and one with concealing stolen goods by painting a black mule white.

Four of the mob victims were property owners; the remaining seventeen paid no direct taxes on real estate or other productive property. Most of them had come from homes where father and mother separated when the victims were small boys; for many of them life had been hard and unattractive from the outset. Of the background of some nothing was learned except that they were seemingly without family. When the lynchings occurred, the fathers of two of the victims were serving road sentences. Scarcely half the victims were identified with any church or lodge organization. The Negroes lynched at Union, Bryan, Ocilla, Cartersville, and the first one at Thomasville, were considered "outsiders" by the local Negroes.

The mob victims had but little formal education. Not one had had high school training, and only one had gone beyond the fifth grade; three were illiterate and eight nearly so. The mental status of the victims covered a wide range. S. S. Mincey, though without formal education, was unusually capable and had attained considerable prominence as politician and lodge leader. Allen Greene also was regarded as highly intelligent. Others of the victims, notably Henry Argo and George Hughes, were termed "half wits" or "crazy," and Hughes was said to be subject to "spells." Will Roan, James Irwin, and others were little better; local Negroes termed them "thick skulls."

These data are comments on the South's failure to provide sufficient educational opportunities and adequate institutional care for her population. Adequate provision for the confinement and treatment of imbeciles, insane persons, and certain types of feeble-minded and hopelessly defective persons would have prevented the crimes leading to several of 1930's lynchings.

Alleged Crimes and Probable Guilt of Mob Victims. The alleged crimes which caused the twenty-one lynchings of 1930 were: murder, five; rape, eight;[1] robbery or theft, three; attempted rape, two; bombing a house, one; no crime alleged, two.

All of the alleged crimes of the nineteen accused mob victims were against white people, one of whom was foreign-born. In eight instances the mob victims were accused of crimes involving women; in four, involving men and women; in seven, involving only men. In four instances, the alleged crimes were against members of small farm-owning families; in three, officers of the law; in three, farm tenants; in two, farm wage hands; in two, farm overseers; in two, factory workers; in two, motorists en route; and in one, a filling station operator. Ten of the lynched persons and three of their accusers had used guns or other concealed weapons in the altercations which precipitated the lynchings.

Two of the 1930 mob victims were innocent of crime (they

---

[1] The proportion of mob victims accused of rape was higher in 1930 than for any year since definite records have been kept.

were not even accused), and there is grave doubt of the guilt of eleven others. In six of these eleven cases there is considerable doubt as to just what crimes, if any, were committed, and in the other five, in which there is no question as to the crimes committed, there is considerable doubt as to whether the mobs got the guilty men.

By their very nature, lynchings made it practically impossible to get at the exact facts of the alleged crimes. In practically every community with a lynching a tradition of the absolute guilt of the person lynched sprang up immediately and cut off all further legal investigation. Had the Negroes at Huntsville and Norfolk been lynched, it is highly probable that their guilt would never have been questioned, though their innocence was later established and the blame placed upon their white accusers by the courts.

Location and General Characteristics of Counties Involved. Five of Georgia's six lynchings of 1930 occurred in the southeastern part of the state, the newest and poorest section. Here churches, schools, and a stabilizing tradition are less powerful than in the older communities. In the last decade, this section has been the scene of numerous floggings, with white as well as Negro victims. It is a belated frontier, and one lacking the virility of the typical American frontier. The sixth lynching in Georgia along with South Carolina's two, occurred in the Piedmont section where the textile industry is concentrated. Scarcely any Negroes are employed in these cotton mills.

Other lynchings occurring in communities characterized by open antipathy to Negroes, or by lack of economic need for Negroes, include Brazos, Grayson, and Fannin Counties, Texas; Grady County, Oklahoma, and Grant County, Indiana. No specific background condition appeared as a factor in the lynching of the foreign-born white near Plant City, Florida.

Seven lynchings were in Black Belt counties: Bolivar, Hinds, and Kemper—with two lynchings—Mississippi; Sumter County, Alabama; Brazos County, Texas; and Edgecombe County, North Carolina. In these counties the Negroes live principally in the open country as tenants or wage hands on large plantations. The domination of the plantation system roots back into the master-slave régime. Negroes are considered valuable only in proportion as they are productive. As a corollary, to all practical purposes, the sheriff and other peace officers are the planters' agents.

Two-thirds of the lynchings occurred in the open country or in towns of less than 2,500 population; in five of these counties there were larger towns, but in no case was the actual lynching within six miles of it. Four lynchings were staged in towns of 2,500 to 15,000 inhabitants, and three in towns of 15,000 to 25,000. Sherman and Marion, in the 15,000 to 25,000 population group, are relatively regressive towns of Texas and Indiana and in many respects fall below the average of their respective states.

Poorer Counties the Scene of Most Lynchings. The measures available show that the counties where lynchings occurred in 1930 were economically below the average. In approximately nine-tenths of them the per capita tax valuation was below the general state average as was also the per capita bank deposit. In three-fourths of the counties the per capita income from farm and factory was below the state average, in many cases less than one-half; in nine-tenths, fewer and smaller income tax returns were made per thousand population than throughout the state. In over two-thirds, the proportion of farms operated by tenants was in excess of the state rate; and in nearly three-fourths of the counties, automobiles were less common than in their respective states. As would be expected from their poor economic rating, the educational facilities in many of these counties were far below the state average. Baptists and Methodists account for over three-fourths of all church members in nearly three-fourths of the counties, and two-thirds of them regularly poll Democratic majorities.

MOBS AND MOB MEMBERS

The Extremes of Mob Action. Mobs are capable of unbelievable atrocity. James Irwin at Ocilla, Georgia, was jabbed in his mouth with a sharp pole. His toes were cut off joint by joint.

His fingers were similarly removed, and his teeth extracted with wire pliers. After further unmentionable mutilations, the Negro's still living body was saturated with gasoline and a lighted match was applied. As the flames leaped up, hundreds of shots were fired into the dying victim. During the day, thousands of people from miles around rode out to see the sight. Not till nightfall did the officers remove the body and bury it.

The Sherman mob also went to extreme lengths. The courthouse was fired. Many of the court officials and four Texas rangers escaped by second-floor windows. The accused Negro was placed in the second story of a large vault, where he remained while the courthouse burned to the ground. Members of the mob cut the water hose and thwarted the fire department's attempt to save the building. With evening, a small group of militiamen was driven from the courthouse grounds to the county jail. A little later, a larger unit of militiamen, just arrived from Dallas, was forced to retire to the protection of the jail. Shortly before midnight, with an acetylene torch and high explosives, a second-story vault window was blown open and the Negro's body was thrown to the crowd below. It was greeted by loud applause from the thousands who jammed the courthouse square. Police directed traffic while the corpse was dragged through the streets to a cottonwood tree in the Negro business section. There it was burned. Soon Negro business properties valued at between $50,000 and $100,000 were fired, and the fire department was not allowed to throw water on them, though the mob permitted a hose to be trained on a white man's dwelling within fifteen feet of a burning Negro residence.

At Honey Grove the body of George Johnson was fastened by the feet to the back of a truck to keep the face down. In this position the corpse was dragged for five miles in and out of town, and later burned in front of a Negro church.

In most of the 1930 lynchings, there were evidences of a madness similar to that at Ocilla, Sherman, and Honey Grove. The roots of mob psychology might well be given extended study by competent scientists.

Characteristics of the Mob Mind. One of the most obvious things about the mental make-up of the lyncher or pro-lyncher was that he tended to accept unqualifiedly any and all reports which fitted into certain preconceived notions about Negroes and the kinds of crimes which warrant lynching. The active lynchers and those who sympathized with them wove into a unit all sorts of unfounded rumors arising from many persons and many situations widely separated as to time and place. The avidity with which the general white populace of Sherman received each new bit of gory detail accounts for the staggering magnitude of the disorders there. Though informed physicians refuted many of the bloody stories which motivated the mob, once the excitement was aroused, facts made no difference.

Another obvious mental characteristic of the lyncher was his dogmatic assertion that the right person was lynched. The lynchers or pro-lynchers built up a complete case against their victims. One of the methods of placing greater guilt upon the intended victim was the mob's mock trial immediately before the lynching. While some of these mob trials were little more than tortures, others were conducted with the semblance of regular courts. In cases where there was no conclusive evidence of the victim's guilt, there developed, nevertheless, immediately after the lynchings were consummated, a tradition of absolute guilt, based in part on the mob trial.

The credulity of the lyncher or pro-lyncher in taking at face value all rumors, and the development of the tradition of the absolute guilt of the mob's victims are both phases of the inability of the mass of white people to deal dispassionately with situations involving actual or potential racial conflict.

Many white people—particularly in the open country—assume that Negroes are prone to crimes against women and that unless a Negro is lynched now and then the women on the solitary farms are in danger. These assumptions have been kept alive by certain types of politicians who keep themselves in office by appeals to racial fear and antagonism. In a few cases church leaders have appealed to the same race fears in religious controversies.[2]

The Man-Hunt Tradition. These assumptions underlie the traditional practice of Southern white men in arming themselves unofficially and hunting down an accused person. This method of mutual aid in policing an area, evolved on the frontier, persists in localities where police power is least adequate, or where the populace, for whatever reasons, insist upon dealing directly with crime and criminals. By its very nature the man-hunt operates through a highly selective process. In the first place, people who have regular work-hours and routine responsibilities are precluded from participating in all-day and all-night hunts. Again, those who have faith in the peace officers and courts, are not likely to take part. And, finally, the man-hunt tradition, an important element of which seems to be the lure of the chase, brings together the people who find lynching attractive.

The man-hunt provides an opportunity for carrying and flourishing firearms with impunity, a privilege which appeals strongly to the more irresponsible elements. Moreover, man-hunts and lynchings make it possible for obscure and irresponsible people to play the rôles of arresting officers, grand jurors, trial jurors, judges, and executioners. An added attraction is that they often afford an avenue of emotional escape from a life so drab and unilluminated that any alternative is welcomed.

Man-Hunters and Bloodhounds. Before a half dozen of 1930's lynchings had been investigated, it became obvious that the man-hunt tradition rests on the assumptions of the unlimited rights of white men and the absence of any rights on the part of an accused Negro. Simply by being accused of some crime, the latter—so the man-hunters feel—has forfeited every claim upon society. With men of this mind scouring the woods and fields, it is little wonder that the Negroes lynched near Rosedale, Bryan, and Union never came into the custody

---

[2] See especially the arguments presented in the Methodist controversy over unification appearing in both secular and religious press.

of the sheriff or other peace officers.

Even when the accused was captured by peace officers, the presence of man-hunters militated against his ever getting before the courts. Usually the man-hunters rather than the officers dominated the situation throughout. At Emelle, Honey Grove, and Ocilla they wreaked vengeance on their victims in the presence of the sheriff and his deputies. In each of these cases, the man-hunters felt that the captured Negro was their prey. They had caught him, and consequently it was rightfully within their province to decide whether they would turn him over to the sheriff and the courts, kill him on the spot, or torture and mutilate him and then let a slow fire do the rest.

To facilitate the capture of the accused, man-hunters often resorted to the use of bloodhounds. Although these man-tracking dogs and their managers were usually brought to the scene by the officers, in practically every case their use was determined by the man-hunters who were on the scene when the officers arrived. Presently the sheriff and other peace officers would be in the gallery watching the dogs, which after prolonged indecision usually led off, with the eager crowd following, greatly impressed by the dogs' baying but annoyed by their frequent halts.

After the first hour or so of this tedious trailing, which afforded the followers ready opportunity to exchange all they knew, had heard or believed about the guilt of the accused, the crowds became impatient with the slow progress being made and discussed the capture and future treatment of the pursued. The result was that by the time the hounds had reached a farm-house the man-hunters had agreed upon a course of action. It will be observed in the case studies which follow that the only evidence against several of the persons lynched in 1930 was that of the bloodhounds' halting trails, a fact symbolic of the primitive elements in man-hunts and their logical issue—lynchings.

Some Facts About Known Lynchers. The identification of lynchers can usually be accomplished without great difficulty. The Commission's field workers secured fairly definite information about many of the persons who took an active part in 1930's lynchings. With the exception of the case at Plant City, where a foreign-born white man was presumably lynched by other foreign-born whites, practically all of the lynchers were native whites. The majority of persons known to have taken an active part in the lynchings were unattached and irresponsible youths of twenty-five or less, many of them not yet out of their teens. Among them were older men who encouraged the youngsters. Drinking was in evidence in most of the mobs.

Only one of the known active lynchers had a technical or college education. He was a professional man who had been released from the State Insane Asylum but a few months before his mob participation. Few of the lynchers were even high school graduates. About half of them were not identified with any church, with many others inactive as to contributions and attendance. Most of the lynchers read but little, and were identified with but few or no organizations. In short, they were least susceptible to the ameliorating influences in the community.

As to the ownership of property, the known active lynchers were generally propertyless. In the majority of cases they were unemployed, rambling, irresponsible people, many of them with court records. In the rural communities, the more shiftless types of white farm tenants and wage hands were most in evidence. Being without property to tax or collect legal damage from, mob members recklessly destroyed property at a number of places. More than one of the Sherman rioters remarked when looking at the burning courthouse: "Let 'er burn down; the taxpayers'll put 'er back."

It would be erroneous, however, to leave the impression that all the lynchers were of the shiftless, irresponsible, propertyless type. At Scooba, Mississippi, where a double lynching occurred, the two men reported to have organized and engineered the mob from start to finish were leading people in the community and prominently identified with the local church, school, and other community activities. Generally speaking, the more backward the community, the more likely were the "best people" to participate in the actual lynching.

Onlookers Not Guiltless. Of course, the persons who participated actively in the lynchings were primarily responsible, yet those sympathizers who stood by shared in the lawlessness, and curious onlookers who rushed in merely because something unusual was happening were not without guilt. This last named element, made up of the "better people," provided the active mobbers with a semblance of decency and no small measure of immunity from official interference.

At Sherman, Honey Grove, and Marion, thousands stood by while a few score men did the work. Hundreds were present at Ocilla, Darien, Union, Walhalla, Rosedale, and Chickasha. The onlookers as individuals may not have been in sympathy with what was going on, but their very presence rendered the task of the peace officers more difficult. Consequently they are morally and probably legally responsible for the outrage against law.

Women and Children in Mobs. Women figured prominently in a number of the outbreaks. After a woman at Sherman had found the men unwilling to go into the courtroom and get the accused, she got a group of boys to tear an American flag from the wall of the courthouse corridor and parade through the courthouse and grounds, to incite the men to do their "manly duty." Later in the afternoon and evening, women joined in the throwing of missiles which resulted in the militiamen's retreating to the protection of the jail. Other women held their babies high over their heads and dared the soldiers to shoot. At Marion, several women were close in with the men who knocked down the jailhouse door and seized the accused Negroes. In several instances, mothers with children in arms were in the midst of the mob. Expectant mothers were also in evidence. It is reported that at Honey Grove the wife of one minister ran to the home of another minister and called to his wife: "Come, I never did see a nigger burned and I mustn't miss this chance." At Darien, Ocilla, and Thomasville the part played by the women seemingly inspired the mobs to greater brutalities.

At Sherman a grandmother called her two small grandsons out of bed and took them some blocks away to see the victim's body roasted. Not all of the children in the mobs, however, were taken there by their elders. Children of all ages rushed in everywhere to see what was going on. The presence of women and children incited the men to action and at the same time made peace officers and militiament less inclined to shoot.

Most of the women in the mobs who chided the men into action and shouted approval of what was going on were of middle age. Darien, where the sheriff's teen-age daughter became hysterical, was the single exception. In no mob were women in their twenties reported.

PEACE OFFICERS AND COURTS

County Sheriffs and Their Deputies. "Do you think I'm going to risk my life protecting a nigger?" This remark, by a sheriff, typified a common attitude of peace officers. In most cases the sheriff and his deputies merely stood by while the mob did its work, and later reported that the mob had taken them by surprise, or that, though aware of the impending danger, they were unwilling to shoot into the crowd lest they kill innocent men, women and children.

The sheriff of McIntosh County, Georgia, where George Grant was shot to death in his cell, represents still another type. Here the sheriff stated that he was glad that the "damn nigger" was dead. "Except for my oath and bond," he added, "I'd have killed him myself as soon as they brought him within shooting distance of the jail." At Honey Grove, Texas, the sheriff boasted, "No innocent persons were killed; and not one cent of property was destroyed!" The sheriff of Thomas County, Georgia, reported with satisfaction how he "saw to it" that the lynchers got the "right man."

In Bolivar County, Mississippi, a deputy rode out to the place where the man-hunt was under way. When he was assured that the Negro would be caught, he returned to his courthouse office, quite content with the way the thing was being handled. In two other plantation counties—Brazos, Texas, and Sumter,

Alabama—the officers deliberately left matters in the hands of the local people. In Union County, South Carolina, the sheriff trudged along with the mob for half a mile without gaining control of the accused Negro.

At Marion, Cartersville, Scooba, Tarboro, and Plant City, the sheriffs or other peace officers were either in connivance with the mob or else extremely stupid. In each case the mob took possession of the accused in the presence of the officers, who did not fire a shot or make any other real effort to protect the accused.

However, not all sheriffs reacted in this fashion. At Walhalla the sheriff was dangerously wounded. At Ocilla when the sheriff disobeyed the instructions of the mob who had permitted him to "take charge" of the prisoner, his car was fired upon, and a bullet hole in the car's gas tank caused it to empty immediately.

As will be seen in the case studies, most of the sheriffs along with their deputies and the municipal officials not only failed to resist the mob effectively but later reported under oath to the grand jury that they did not recognize a single member of the mob.

Influence of Political Consideration. It can hardly be doubted that political considerations were largely responsible for the neglect and indifference characteristic of officers and courts in these cases: The members of the mob were nearly all actual or potential voters;[3] the victim and most of his race, disfranchised by social pressure or other means, were politically impotent.[4]

"Outside" Peace Officers a Problem. To all practical pur-

---

[3] In over three-fourths of the counties where lynchings occurred in 1930, less than two-fifths—in four counties less than one-fifth—of whites of voting age took part in the 1928 presidential election, which brought out one of the largest votes ever polled in national or local elections, including "white" primaries. Nevertheless, being white men they could vote by meeting residence requirements, paying poll taxes, and registering, and consequently had to be reckoned with by men desiring office.

[4] The Negro has had a profound influence on American politics from the framing of the Constitution to the present, but largely by reason of the efforts of whites to deal with him rather than his own participation.

poses, the sheriffs and other peace officers who rushed into the communities with threatened lynchings merely increased the size of the mob. Their presence militated against whatever efforts local peace officers might otherwise have made to keep order, for the man-hunters from adjoining counties were naturally emboldened by the sight of their own sheriffs and deputies standing round but taking no part in the defense of constituted authority. Scores of "outside" officers were at Marion and Sherman, and a half-dozen at Ocilla, Honey Grove, and Emelle. In some instances, county stockade guards and other petty officers took active parts.

National Guard Not Always Effective. Although the National Guard in most instances rendered admirable service in preventing threatened lynchings, it was of questionable value in Darien, where a small unit of poorly disciplined militiamen was on hand when George Grant was captured, placed in the jail and shot. Machine guns were mounted and other precautions were taken at the jail only after the lynching. At Sherman, four of the far-famed Texas Rangers and two small detachments of the state guard left the scene of the rioting without any show of determined resistance. Had a large number of militiamen been on hand earlier, or if those who were there had fired to kill, wound, or frighten, they doubtless would have been taken more seriously by the rioters. At Maryville, Missouri, early in 1931, a mob of thousands intercepted the prisoner on the way from the jail to the courthouse, marched him on foot several miles down a country road to a schoolhouse, the scene of his alleged crime, chained him on the roof and burned the building. During the entire time the National Guard was in Maryville and ready for action. The officer in charge of the Guard reported that his instructions were to act only upon the request of the sheriff, and that the sheriff refused to request his services.

The effectiveness of the National Guard in preventing mob outbreaks is greatly hampered by the traditional theory and practice of "county rights," which holds the county virtually self-sufficient. In some cases the sheriff and other county officials deliberately chose not to request the aid of the Guard, and in others, where the Guard was used its presence was looked upon as "outside interference." Many sheriffs and other county officials stated that they disliked to call for the Guard because it often aroused the lawless element and wounded the pride of the better element of the whites. Moreover in most cases the kinsmen and friends of the injured person demanded that the accused be tried in the local court, and protested the presence of any "outside" influence, whether militiamen, lawyers, or organized interest, because they feared these would delay trial, sentence, and execution.

It is clear that the state will have to exercise more power over the county before the full effectiveness of the National Guard can be used to prevent threatened lynchings, for the county sheriff and the district prosecuting attorney—the state's chief local representatives—are elected by the local people and usually conform their official acts to the expressed desires of the local electorate.

Lynchers Usually Go Unmolested by Courts. In six of the twenty-one lynchings of 1930—Sherman, Thomas County, Walhalla, Chickasha, and Marion with its double lynching—grand jury indictments were returned against a total of forty-nine persons. In the other fifteen instances, the coroners reported that the lynched persons came to their deaths "at the hands of parties unknown" to them. The grand juries in turn failed to fix responsibility. Of the forty-nine persons indicted only four have been convicted. At Sherman, two received sentences of two years each, being convicted of arson and rioting rather than of murder. Only in the case of the two whites charged with murdering Lacy Mitchell of rural Thomas County have the sentences approximated the seriousness of the crime. These two were given life sentences. All those indicted at Walhalla were acquitted. The cases in Chickasha have never come to trial. In Marion, a local jury acquitted the two persons with the most evidence against them, and the others were never tried.

In a number of cases state officials offered their coöperation to local officers for the purpose of investigation and prosecution, but the results were negligible. The Attorney General of Texas went to Sherman, and stated that his office was at the service of Grayson County officials for the prosecution of those guilty. The Indiana Attorney General, who has power to bring proceedings of impeachment against a sheriff, announced that the sheriff of Grant County would be made to answer for his failure to protect the two Negroes from the mob. Nothing ever came of his promise. The Attorney General of Oklahoma announced that his office would coöperate in the prosecution of the lynchers of Henry Argo at Chickasha. But here, as elsewhere, the handling of the case was left in the control of the local prosecuting officer and nothing has come of it.

To Union County, South Carolina, and Edgecombe County, North Carolina, the governors of the respective states sent personal investigators, but no arrests or indictments resulted.

Proceedings by Alabama Governor Against Officers Who Permitted Lynching. In the case of Emelle alone did the State authorities do anything of consequence. The Governor of Alabama, with power to bring proceedings against any sheriff who has allowed a person to be lynched in his county, sent members of the State Enforcement Department into the community, and subsequently ordered the judge of the district court to call a special session. The local people were not greatly disturbed, for, as they said, "We still have our *own* sheriff and prosecuting attorney."

But when the special court was convened, the local people found a special judge on the bench and members of the State Enforcement Department[5] performing the usual duties of the sheriff, and the local district prosecuting attorney displaced

---

[5] This department, a chief reason why there was but one lynching in Alabama during Governor Bibb Graves' administration, was abolished by Governor Miller as one of his first official acts, in accordance with campaign promises.

by another sent in by the Governor. By the end of the second day of the special session the sheriff and the district prosecuting attorney had resigned.

The treatment of the Emelle disorders by the special court was a very partisan vindication of justice, however. Two ineffective officers were forced to resign. A score of Negroes were indicted and some of them were given death sentences for killing two white men, but no white men were even so much as arrested for lynching one Negro and killing three more, one of them an innocent woman.

Some Reasons Why Lynchers Go Unpunished. Some factors which make courts ineffective are: Divided responsibility between peace officers, judges, and grand and trial juries; the indifference of some court officials; the widespread feeling that white women should be shielded from court testimony; the disinclination of local jurymen to indict and convict their neighbors, and promises made the mob by officers and leading citizens in order to prevent further outbreaks.

This insistence that white women should be protected at all costs from testifying in open court in the trial of a Negro, in part a rationalization to conceal available evidence from the court and the public, is often used as an argument to justify the acts of lynchers: The accused was guilty and would have gotten the death sentence any way; by lynching him a white woman was spared the humiliation of appearing in court.

The attitude of jurors toward lynchings is often modified by the tradition that it is the duty of one family to another to protect it from violence. Solitary farm dwellers, with little police protection, feel responsible for the protection of their neighbors. A clever lawyer for the defendant lyncher is often able to demonstrate that if the crime had been committed against a member of the juror's own immediate family, he naturally and rightfully would have done what the lyncher did, and if in turn he shares in the larger community responsibility, he would have done the same thing to help protect his distant neighbor. Under this type of reasoning the lyncher becomes a protector of society rather than its enemy.

In the efforts to prevent a lynching, or to prevent further mob outbreaks after a lynching has occurred, peace officers and leading citizens often make to mob leaders promises which virtually preclude impartial court procedure. It is not incorrect to call a death sentence secured under such circumstances a "legal lynching." Except in rare cases, the presence of a mob defeats the ends of impartial justice, either by lynching the accused person or by forcing the courts to summary and perhaps unjust convictions.

The lynching ensued at Cartersville when the trial procedure there violated the general agreement between the mob leaders, officers and citizens, that the accused Negro would be sentenced to death without delay. Attorneys for the defense from Atlanta precipitated this lynching, local people claim, by filing exceptions to the judge's ruling against a change of venue, and thus delaying the trial. On the other hand the attorneys point out that the lynching proves that they were justified in demanding a change of venue.

INDIVIDUALS AND INSTITUTIONS LOOK AT LYNCHINGS

Apologists for Lynching. In every community where lynchings occurred in 1930, there were some people who openly justified what had been done. All walks of life were represented among the apologists—judges, prosecuting attorneys, lawyers, business men, doctors, preachers, teachers, mechanics, day laborers, and women of many types.

Most apologists for lynching, like the lynchers themselves, seemed to assume that the Negro is irredeemably inferior by reason of his race—that it is a plan of God that the Negro and his children shall forever be "hewers of wood and drawers of water." With this weighty emphasis upon the essential racial inferiority of the Negro, it is not surprising to find the mass of whites ready to justify any and all means used to "keep the Negro in his place." It is largely because of this that nothing will get larger headlines in the rural press, receive more discussion at cross-road stores, or draw a larger trial crowd, than some major conflict situation between a Negro and a white person. The vehemence with which the Negro's inferiority is declared is probably an indication that many of the whites base their claims on emotion rather than reasoned thought.

A Vicious Protection Dogma. Regardless of the cause of a particular lynching, there were always those who defended it by the insistence that unless Negroes were lynched, no white woman would be safe, this despite the fact that only one-sixth of the persons lynched in the last thirty years were even accused of rape. Regardless of the accusation, an example must be made of the accused Negro for the sake of womanhood. Thus the apologist for lynching doubly betrays the Southern woman, first, in making her danger greater by exaggerating her helplessness, and second, in undermining the power of police and courts, her legitimate protectors.

The Pressure for Conformity. In practically every community with a lynching in 1930, there were some people who were heartily opposed to what took place; but after a time, even the "best citizens" usually came to feel that "it is all over now, and the sooner it is forgotten, the better for the community." The general public either justified or condoned the lynching, and any individual or group who disagreed was made to suffer. Merchants, bankers, lawyers, and preachers faced a public boycott—or thought they did—should they take a stand in defense of law and order.

No determined community-wide effort for the conviction of the lynchers was made in any community where a lynching occurred in 1930. The nearest approximation was in Montgomery County, Georgia, where a mass meeting was held in the courthouse, with both whites and Negroes present. Scathing denunciations were heaped upon the dozen masked men who had beaten S. S. Mincey to death and a vigilance committee was set up, with chairman and secretary. Yet nobody subscribed or underwrote any money to be used in apprehending and prosecuting the guilty persons. At Sherman, a group of leading citizens passed resolutions denouncing the mob leaders and pledged themselves to the preservation of law and order, including coöperation with the courts. This action may have been influenced in part by the fact that the town was under martial law and it was necessary that local citizens assume responsibility in order to secure the return of control to the local civil authorities.

At Thomasville, Cartersville, Darien, Union, Tarboro, Sherman, and Bryan, property-owning, educated Negro citizens thoroughly disapproved the lynchings. Yet in much the same way as the white anti-lynchers, they too were compromised into the position of saying nothing about what had happened. Only in Marion with a small but active branch of the National Association for the Advancement of Colored People, did Negroes publicly voice a protest. It was not surprising that the leading Negroes should have remained quiet about the lynching when the few white people who might be expected to speak out were afraid to do so. Leading Negroes were further silenced by the fear lest a protest from them might result in things being made harder for the mass of their race dependent upon the whites for employment and accustomed to leaving matters of this kind solely in the hands of the whites. Not infrequently one heard a white man or woman boasting that a particular Negro agreed heartily with the action of the mob, saying that he himself, if he had had an opportunity, would have joined in the lynching. It was found that most of these statements were of the "bread-and-butter" variety, the Negro having said what he knew was expected of him. Where leading white and Negro citizens alike are maneuvered into the position of silent acquiescence, it is inevitable that convictions will be few and far between.

Nominal Opposition to Lynchings by Many South-Wide Organizations. Nowadays there is hardly an important Southern religious conference or convention which does not make a pronouncement on some phase of race relations. Most of these point out that lynching is barbarous and unnecessary. In spite of this fact scarcely any of the local units of these organizations had a word of condemnation for the lynchers in their several communities.

Generally speaking, preachers and church officers, like other citizens, were compromised into letting things take their course. The most common view expressed by ministers was that the lynching, though unfortunate, was inevitable. The ministers, and especially the Southern Methodists and Southern Baptists, usually felt that they would be faced with a serious division among their members should they actively support indictment and conviction of the lynchers.

Attitudes of Large and Small Churches. Within each denomination, however, there was a marked difference between the attitude of the ministers of the larger churches and that of those serving the smaller ones. This is an aspect of the wide difference which exists between the cultural and economic status of the leadership of these two types of churches. The most influential white people were identified with the largest Baptist and Methodist congregations and with the Episcopal and Presbyterian churches, which usually, however, had smaller memberships.

The different attitudes of the larger and the smaller churches are clearly set forth in several of the case studies, particularly that of Sherman. There the pastor emeritus and the pastor of the First Presbyterian Church, along with the pastor of the Disciples Church, stood out uncompromisingly in condemnation of mob rule. The pastors of the largest Methodist and Baptist congregations expressed disgust with what had happened, while nearly all the ministers of the smaller outlying churches of these denominations expressed sympathy with the mob.

The Church's Opportunity. The most fundamental way in which the church is related to mob violence is that, not infrequently, the local church leaves unchallenged the general assumption that the Negro is innately inferior and of little importance. Upon this assumption ultimately rests the justification of lynching. A Southern churchman, recently discussing the responsibility which rests upon the church in the prevention of lynching, said:

"In the absence of passion and excitement, the preacher should instill into the minds of his hearers the danger and crime of mob rule. People should be fortified in the quiet time against the crisis which may arise. There is a marked absence of any feeling of social responsibility in much of our preaching and church teaching of today. The individualistic theology of a large element of the Southern Baptist, Southern Methodist, and Presbyterian churches, must be corrected. A large class of our preachers should be constantly reminded to let the Egyptians and Israelites have a good long rest, and also the sins of the ancient Amalekites, and to deal in a Christian way with our own social and racial problems.

"Preachers and church leaders have their responsibilities for the eradication of lynchings: in normal times, by instilling reverence for human life and personality; in an emergency situation, by co-operating with other exponents of law and order to keep the mob from its murderous goal. On account of their superiority of numbers, a heavier responsibility rests upon Southern Baptists and Southern Methodists than upon any other denominations."

The Southern church papers for the most part are definitely opposed to lynching. The editors of many church papers have taken determined stands against it, in many cases courageously denouncing lynchings near at hand. This has sometimes met with the serious disapproval of the editor's constituents. But the church paper, like the church itself, may well take care lest, by failing to take a stand against injustice to Negroes in general, it leaves intact the views which provide a justification for lynching and other expressions of racial antagonisms.

The Press on Lynching. The daily papers of the large Southern cities almost always denounced a lynching whether near at hand or far away—in a few cases, however, the nearer at hand, the less vigorous the denunciation.

The county weeklies and dailies of the smaller cities throughout the South were inclined to condemn lynching in general, but often justified it in particular instances. To all practical purposes, the Thomasville *Enterprise* justified the lynching there. The papers of Ocilla, Chickasha, Bryan, and Honey Grove indirectly condoned the local lynchings, while the papers at Cartersville, Tarboro, Scooba, and Emelle frankly expressed satisfaction with them. The lady editor of the weekly paper at Rosedale made no mention of the lynching, saying that since such things always result in hard feelings she felt it best to leave them out of her paper. Both dailies at Marion, while pointing out that they thought Marion was the last place in the world where a lynching would take place, looked upon the occurrence as inevitable in view of what had happened.

The editor of the Union (S. C.) *Sentinel* distinguished himself by denouncing the mob. The small weekly at Darien looked upon the lynching there as inexcusable. The Sherman *Democrat* is unique in that it alone of the papers in communities where lynchings occurred in 1930 condemned the mob from first to last and insisted that the courts punish its leaders.

Whereas the Negro press in practically every case assumed that the person lynched was innocent, or that he was guilty of some crime less serious than that of which he was accused, the white press usually accepted as true all the rumored details of guilt. This tended on both sides to accentuate racial fear and antagonism. Both the white and Negro press could render a greater service by carefully confining their reports to facts.

CHAPTER II

GENERAL ASPECTS OF LYNCHING

THAT THE reader may better understand the historical trends of the lynching phenomenon in the United States, the next few pages are devoted to a general treatment of mob murders in recent decades.

RACIAL AND GEOGRAPHIC FACTORS

Racial Factors More Evident as Lynchings Decrease. The number of lynchings has decreased markedly during recent decades. From 1889 through 1899, the average number of persons lynched each year was 187.5; from 1900 through 1909 the average was 92.5; from 1910 through 1919, 61.9; from 1920 through 1924, 46.2; from 1925 through 1929, 16.8.

In the forty-one year period under consideration, 787, or 21.3 per cent of all persons lynched, were white. Between 1889 and 1899, 32.2 per cent of all persons lynched were white; in the first decade in the new century, 11.4 per cent were white; in the second decade, 8.9 per cent; between 1920 and 1924, 10 per cent, and from 1925 through 1929, 13.2 per cent. In 1930 only one, or 4.8 per cent of the twenty-one persons lynched, was white. If Texas, Arkansas, and Oklahoma be excluded, states where many Mexicans have met death at the hands of mobs, the percentage would be nearly ninety-five per cent Negro. Among the remaining small number of white persons lynched in the South were several foreigners. It is obvious therefore that lynching is becoming more and more a Southern phenomenon, and a racial one. In the typical lynching the victim is a Negro and the lynchers are native-born whites.

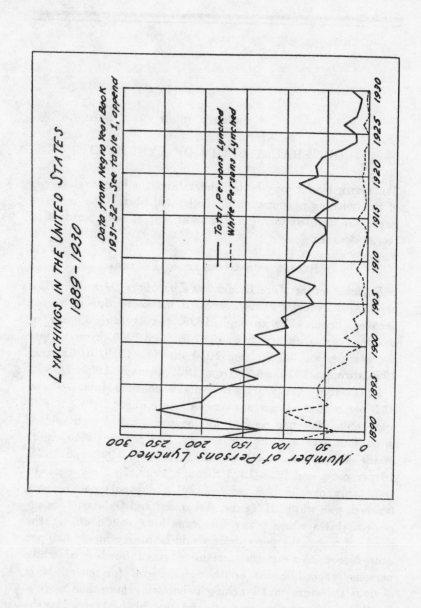

LYNCHINGS IN THE UNITED STATES
1889–1930

Data from Negro Year Book
1931–32 — See Table 1, append.

—— Total Persons Lynched
----- White Persons Lynched

Number of Persons Lynched

300 250 200 150 100 50 0

1890 1895 1900 1905 1910 1915 1920 1925 1930

The decrease in the proportion of white persons lynched is a corollary of the fact that lynchings are decreasing more rapidly outside of than in the South. From 1889 through 1899, approximately eighty-two per cent of all lynchings in the United States were in the fourteen Southern States (in which are included the border states of Virginia, Kentucky, Missouri, and Oklahoma); during the first decade of the new century, 91.9 per cent were in these states; during the second decade, 94.4 per cent; from 1920 through 1924, 95.3 per cent; and for the five-year period ending with 1929, 97.4 per cent.

Of the Negroes lynched outside the South ninety-three, or more than two-thirds, were in the six states—Maryland, West Virginia, Ohio, Indiana, Illinois, and Kansas—which lie immediately north of the Southern States, and throughout the years have received from the South large numbers of white and Negro migrants.

Negroes Safest Per Thousand from Mob Death in Old Black Belt Counties. Statistically, per ten thousand population Negroes are safer from mob deaths in the old Black Belt, where more than half of the population is Negro, than anywhere else in the South. They are relatively less safe in counties with from one-fourth to one-half Negro population, while per ten thousand Negro population they are in the greatest danger from mobs in counties where the proportion of Negroes is less than one-fourth.

In the Black Belt race relations revolve about the plantation system, under which Negro tenants and wage hands are practically indispensable. Here the variant economic and cultural levels of the mass of whites and the mass of Negroes are well defined, and far removed. Another factor is the purely statistical logic that the heavier the Negro majority the fewer the whites, and thus the fewer the occasions for conflict and the fewer the whites to take part in mobs.

The lynching rate per ten thousand Negroes for the fourteen Southern States for the thirty-year period, 1900-1930, was 1.84. The rate was 1.64 for the 235 Black Belt counties; 1.71 for the 345 counties with one-fourth to one-half Negro population, and 2.44 for the 848 counties with less than one-fourth Negro population. To put it another way, the Black Belt counties, with 38.1 per cent of the total Negro population of the South, had 33.8 per cent of the lynchings; the counties with between one-fourth and one-half Negro population with 39.5 per cent of the Negro population, had 36.6 per cent of the lynchings; while the counties of less than one-fourth Negro population, with 22.4 per cent of the Negro population in the South, had 29.6 per cent of all lynchings in the South.

Florida, with its phenomenal population growth in recent decades, shows a lynching rate of 4.5 per ten thousand Negro population during the 1900-1930 period, a rate nearly twice as high as that for either Mississippi, Georgia, or Louisiana, more than three times the rate for Alabama, and six times the rate for South Carolina. Other Southern States where the Negro's life has been least secure from the mob include the newer states of Oklahoma, with a rate of 3.9; Arkansas, 2.9; and Texas, 2.5.

Lynchings Relatively Most Common in Sparsely Settled Areas. Within each of these fourteen states, persons are in greatest danger from mob death in the sparsely settled rural counties. There is an inverse correlation between the population per county and the rate of lynching, the rate being highest in the counties with the fewest inhabitants and lowest in the most populous counties. Note the following data which indicate the number of lynchings per ten thousand population in fourteen Southern States over a thirty-year period:[1]

Counties of less than 10,000 population...........3.2
　　　10,000- 20,000 population.....................2.4
　　　20,000- 30,000 population.....................2.1
　　　30,000- 40,000 population.....................1.7
　　　40,000- 50,000 population.....................2.4
　　　50,000-100,000 population.....................1.0
　　100,000-200,000 population.....................0.6

[1] See Earle F. Young's article in "Sociology and Social Research," March-April, 1928 (Vol. XII, No. 4).

200,000-300,000 population.....................0.3

300,000 and over..............................0.05

It will be observed that an inhabitant in the South's most sparsely populated two hundred and fifty counties is in sixty times as much danger of mob death as a person living in or near one of the South's half-dozen largest cities.

The higher lynching rate in the sparsely populated counties seems due to inadequate local police protection, and the disclination of peace officers, court officials, or citizens to request outside assistance. Moreover, southern rural communities are generally known to be least policed of any communities in the United States. The general public accepts and relies upon the man-hunt tradition and the lynching custom. The meagre political responsibility of the white tenant and the Negro's political impotence in most rural counties merely aggravate the governmental inadequacies inherent in small populations and limited taxable resources.

Lynching Contagious. Not infrequently the lynching mania spreads from one community to another, as is illustrated by 1930's lynchings. The four lynchings west of the Mississippi River occurred within a radius of less than two hundred miles and within a period of less than six weeks. The last three of these demonstrations were to no small extent outgrowths of the outbreak at Sherman. Within a month after the fourth mob death several threatened lynchings were frustrated in Texas and Oklahoma, studies of which revealed that they were in part due to the unrest accruing from the earlier mob outbreaks.

A second concentration of lynchings occurred in Georgia. With no lynchings between 1926 and 1929, this state had six in 1930. The first was at Ocilla on February 1. The other five, four of which were within 120 miles of Ocilla, occurred in the ten weeks' period ending with October 1.

But while lynching clearly appears to be contagious, it seldom strikes successfully in the same spot. One lynching in a community seems to provide an opportunity for all so inclined to share in it, whether through taking an active part in it or through the vicarious participation of justifying or condoning it. Furthermore, the best elements in a community are often shocked into a sense of responsibility for the prevention of further outbreaks; and thus a lynching tends to produce its immediate local immunity. The real problem is how to induce officials and private citizens to exercise the same precautions to prevent the beginning of an epidemic of lynching as they will take to stop it after it is under way.

Lynchings in Unexpected Places. Though the number of lynchings has been decreasing, no community seems free from the danger of mob murder. The public has come to expect lynchings in Southern counties where Negroes are most numerous. But lynchings are by no means limited to these counties. Between January 1, 1930 and September 1, 1931, eleven lynchings occurred in counties which had had no lynching in this century. Four of these were in counties outside the South with less than five per cent Negro population and three were in Southern counties with less than one-fifth Negro population. These facts suggest that mob murder may take place almost anywhere. Many of 1930's lynchings would not have occurred had not local peace officers, court officials, and leading citizens failed to sense the probability of mob violence in their several communities.

Value of Cotton and Number of Lynchings. The accompanying diagram, the data for which were compiled by T. J. Woofter, Jr., shows a rather high relationship between the per acre value of cotton and lynchings in the nine cotton states from 1900 through 1930, omitting the three abnormal years affected by the World War. It will be noted that as a rule whenever the per acre value of cotton is above its trend the number of lynchings is below its trend. In other words, periods of relative prosperity bring reduction in lynching and periods of depression cause an increase. Mathematically, this relationship is shown by the correlation of -.532.

In 1931, however, with the lowest per acre value of cotton in years, there were scarcely half as many lynchings as in

1930. Nevertheless, in many communities the organized efforts of the whites to displace Negro laborers with unemployed whites may be expected to aggravate racial animosity to the level of open conflict and violence.

VALUE OF COTTON AND NUMBER OF LYNCHINGS IN THE
NINE COTTON STATES[2]

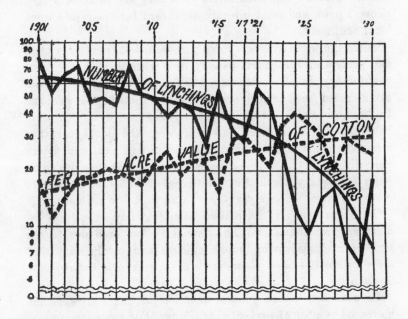

Peace Officers and Courts. Of the 254 persons lynched from 1921 through 1929, 112 or 44.1 per cent never came into the custody of the law. An additional seventy-four, or

---

[2] The scale on the left begins at 4 and runs to 100, the unit being one lynching in the lynching curve and $1 per acre in the cotton curve. The cotton-price year, November to November, was used. For example, the year 1930 in the diagram was November 1, 1929, to November 1, 1930. Because of the abnormal conditions during and immediately after the World War, the years 1918-1920 are omitted. The data presented here were compiled by T. J. Woofter, Jr.

29.1 per cent were taken from peace officers outside of the jail, while the remaining sixty-eight, or 26.8 per cent were taken from the jails. In sparsely settled counties the accused were more generally lynched without having come into the custody of the law; in the counties with good-sized towns the victims were more often taken from the jail. This emphasizes the inadequacies of police protection in the sparsely settled areas, where as suggested already, officers are farthest apart, poorest paid, and most directly dependent for their jobs upon local sentiment.

Although a few lynchers have been indicted, tried, convicted, and sentenced, the courts usually deal with them in the most perfunctory fashion. Between 1922 and 1926, grand juries investigated seventeen lynchings and indicted 146 persons. In 1922, ten were sent to the penitentiary; the next year, two. In 1924, five were given jail sentences; the next year, five received suspended sentences, one was put in jail, and fifteen were given indeterminate sentences of six months on the chain gang to eight years in the penitentiary; in 1926, eight were given sentences of four years, and a ninth, a life sentence.

Thus far lynchers have been comparatively safe from indictment and conviction. This immunity has been due to the lack of a disapproving public opinion and to the fact that state authorities have seldom made effective efforts to prosecute in such cases.

In contrast to the general inaction of the courts is the increased number of prevented lynchings. For the sixteen years ending with 1929, five hundred sixty-nine threatened lynchings were prevented, nearly eighty-five per cent of these being in the Southern States. Between January 1, 1930 and October 1, 1931, eighty-eight threatened lynchings were prevented, more than five-sixths of these in the South. In most cases this was done by the removal of accused persons to distant strong prisons; in other instances, the National Guard was called out to protect the prisoner; and in a few cases, the sheriffs and other peace officers protected their prisoners with no outside assistance. It must not be overlooked that in preventing threatened lynchings the peace officers, court officials, and the general public sometimes made promises to the mob which precluded an impartial trial for the accused. A "legal lynching" is little, if any, improvement over an extra-legal lynching. The fact that most threatened lynchings were prevented in the states where most lynchings occurred is commented upon in the following chapter.

LYNCHINGS AND THE GENERAL CRIME SITUATION

Crime and Criminals by Race. Of the larger population groupings in the United States, the highest crime rates occur among the Negroes, although some elements of the Negro population are more law-abiding than native born whites in general. Throughout the South there are Negro rural and urban communities known for their relative freedom from crime[3] while others are notoriously criminal.[4]

In 1921-22, the homicide rates in Atlanta, Birmingham, Memphis, and New Orleans per 100,000 Negro population were 103.2, 97.2, 116.9, and 46.7 respectively, while the corresponding rates for the white population were 15.0, 28.0, 29.6, and 8.4.[5] The geographic distribution of homicides in each of these cities showed marked concentrations in certain communities, with others practically immune. The highest crime rates among

---

[3] For example, see T. J. Woofter's *Black Yeomanry*, (Henry Holt, 1930) for facts about paucity of crimes among the inhabitants of St. Helena Island, S. C.

[4] It will be observed in H. C. Brearley's *Homicide in the United States*, (U. N. C. Press, 1932), that the homicide rates are highest in the States with the highest lynching rates. Even though the Negro homicide rates in these states are uniformly higher than the homicide rates for the whites, the white rates in most of them are in excess of the white rates in any other states.

[5] "A Study of Violent Deaths Registered in Cities of Atlanta, Birmingham, Memphis, and New Orleans for the years 1921-22," by J. J. Durrett and W. G. Stromquist. According to detailed data presented by the National Commission on Law Observance and Law Enforcement in its Report Number 10, the Negroes of Detroit, Los Angeles, Cincinnati, Cleveland, Buffalo (Table V, p. 116), and other places both North and South are much more lawless than native-born or foreign-born whites.

both Negroes and whites usually occur at the lowest economic levels.

Studies of the prison populations, court records, and jail commitments in Georgia, North Carolina, South Carolina, and other Southern States provide evidence that whereas crime is increasing among the native white element, it is decreasing slightly among the Negro element.[6]

Some Environmental Reasons for High Crime Rate among Negroes. In hundreds of counties in the South, from ten to twenty—and in some instances more than forty times—as much money is allocated for the public education of the white as for the Negro educable child.[7] Suggesting the Negro's greater economic insecurity are the figures on unemployment, which indicate that the proportion of Negroes unemployed is higher than that of the whites, in most places, South and North, being two or three times that of the whites.[8]

The political situation, which does not encourage and often prevents the Negro's participation in local government inevitably affects his crime rate unfavorably. First of all, the states have generally made inadequate institutional provisions for Negro dependents, delinquents—especially juvenile offenders—feeble-minded, and mentally deranged. The proper care of the hopelessly defective Negroes in the Southern States is an essential part of any practical program for lessening Negro crime there.

The generally more adequate police protection afforded whites when molested by Negroes than afforded Negroes when

---

[6] See especially studies made by Hugh Fuller for the Georgia Department of Public Welfare and the University of Virginia; H. C. Brearley's *Homicide in the United States;* J. F. Steiner and Roy M. Brown and Associates, Institute of Research in Social Science at the University of North Carolina, and the reports of Public Welfare Departments and State Prison Boards of the Southern States.

[7] See "Financing Schools in the South," by Fred McCuistion, the Rosenwald Fund, Nashville, Tenn., and *The Annals of the American Academy of Political and Social Science,* Philadelphia, November, 1928, Publication No. 2199.

[8] See reports of Russell Sage Foundation, Urban League, community chests, and business commissions.

molested by whites seems to be another condition which contributes to the Negro's high crime rate. Not infrequently Negroes reported that they, feeling that the authorities would not protect them, had provided for their own protection, oftentimes resulting in a ready use of firearms in trivial matters. Moreover, Negroes are often allowed without interference from police, to commit crimes on one another, which, when committed against white people, result in severe court sentences, if not death at the hands of a mob. Many Southern leaders, white and Negro, feel strongly that the inadequate police provided within the Negro communities virtually breeds crime.[9] The poor police protection provided in most Negro communities seems to be due in large measure to the Negro's virtual political impotence and his consequent inability to command or demand ample police protection.

Various phases of the general racial situation affect the Negro's higher crime rate. The public's low estimate of his worth and indifference to his fate, the ready assumption of his guilt, his ignorance of court procedure, his frequent lack of money and friends and political influence, all make his arrest and conviction easier than that of the white man. In a large measure these are the same factors that produce lynchings.

Courts Not Lenient With Negro Criminals. Data secured from the superintendents of state prison systems and wardens of penitentiaries of Southern States for the eighteen-month period ending July 1, 1931, demonstrate conclusively that Negro criminals brought before the courts are not dealt with leniently. In ten Southern States,[10] of the eighty-one executions, thirteen were white—all convicted of murder—and sixty-eight were Negroes: fifty-seven murderers, eight rapists, and three

---

[9] The homicide figures of Atlanta in 1931, compiled by the Atlanta School of Social Work, show 106 Negro homicide victims and 24 white homicide victims. Seventy-six of the Negroes were killed by members of their own race; 11 were killed by policemen and 9 by other whites. In ten other cases the slayer was not given.

[10] Detailed information on death sentences was not available for Louisiana, Texas, Tennessee, and Missouri.

burglars. During the same period, in twelve states,[11] of 669 life sentences imposed, 199 were whites: 192 murderers, six rapists, and one burglar; of the 470 Negroes, 425 were convicted of murder, twenty of rape, and twenty-five of burglary and other offenses. For minor offenses, too, the sentences for Negroes were often greater than for whites.

Lynchers and their apologists cannot justify their actions on the grounds that unless they dispose of accused Negroes the courts will likely dismiss their cases or treat them lightly. It should be observed, too, that any group which can execute a lynching could place the accused in the custody of peace officers.

Accusations Against Persons Lynched. Of the 3,693 mob victims between 1889 and 1929 in the United States,[12] 1,394, or 37.7 per cent, were accused of murder; 214, or 5.8 per cent, of felonious assault; 614, or 16.7 per cent, of rape; 247, or 6.7 per cent, of attempted rape; 264, or 7.1 per cent, of theft; sixty-six, or 1.8 per cent, of insult to white person; and 894, or 24.2 per cent, of all other offenses.

The following accusations appear among the "all other offenses" for which persons were lynched: Inciting racial troubles, bringing suit against white men, frightening school children, operating house of ill-fame from which two white girls were taken, trying to act like a white man, refusal to pay note, seeking employment in restaurant, forcing white boy to commit crime, expressing sympathy with murder of white men, participating in fight between white and Negro, denouncing sailor's part in Chicago Race Riot, member of Non-Partisan League, strike-breaker, alleged disrespectful utterances against President Wilson, using offensive language, kidnaping, implicated in larceny, stealing hogs, horse-stealing, poisoning mules, jumping labor contract, suspected of killing cattle, keeping a gambling house, boastful remarks, as-

---

[11] Information on life sentences not available for Texas and Tennessee.

[12] Whereas Tuskegee records show 3,703 persons lynched between 1889 and 1929 when reporting lynchings by years, but 3,693 are shown when lynchings are reported by causes.

sisting accused Negro to escape, expressing sympathy with lynched Negro, and accused of conjuring.[13] It will be observed that only one-sixth of the mob victims between 1889 and 1929 were accused of rape. The accusations of rape and attempted rape combined accounted for less than one-fourth of the lynchings, and investigations after the lynchings often proved these accusations to have been unfounded. Many Negroes accused of rape or attempted rape, and saved from mobs by courageous peace officers or other means have been acquitted by the courts. In some cases, girls and women who had posed as victims acknowledged that they made these charges to cover their own derelictions, to divert suspicion from some white man, to reconcile their parents, to attract attention, or "just to have a little excitement." Also numerous cases are on record of white criminals who have blackened their faces to disguise themselves.[14]

In recent months the most sensational case of "framing" a Negro occurred in Norfolk, Virginia, where a white woman accused a Negro of criminal assault. A few weeks thereafter the Negro received a death sentence. Before the execution, however, the judge granted a new trial on the basis of reported "newly discovered evidence." The new trial resulted in the acquittal of the Negro on evidence that the woman had accused him of the assault in order to conceal her illicit association with a white man.

The Contributions of Whites and Negroes. Since police protection, public school facilities and other public welfare services, demonstrably factors affecting crime rates, are controlled at present almost entirely by white people, it is obvious that the primary responsibility for the lessening of Negro crime, the reduction of mob formations, and the eradication

---

[13] One of the most unique lynchings on record was at Pine Level, Johnston County, North Carolina, January 12, 1908, when a Negro was lynched by other Negroes "for giving poor entertainment."

[14] The leaflet "Burnt Cork and Crime" compiled in January, 1931, by R. B. Eleazer from press reports of 1928-30 contains many interesting cases. Sample copies of this leaflet can be had from the Commission on Interracial Coöperation, 703 Standard Building, Atlanta, Georgia.

of lynchings rests with the white people, and especially upon the white element which votes and thereby controls the collection and utilization of public funds. Furthermore, white people chiefly determine the types of work available to Negroes, a regulation of economic opportunities which limits the Negro's ability to raise himself by his own boot straps.

Negroes can contribute much to the eradication of lynching, by demonstrating the ability, character, and good citizenship of the race; by seeking individually and through their churches, lodges, schools and newspapers to allay interracial fear and hostility; by consistently disavowing all disposition to condone crime and to shelter criminals; by reporting to officials and influential white friends when mob danger threatens; and by using their political influence wherever possible in the interest of honest and competent local government.

Mobs and lynchings eventually can be eliminated if the irresponsive and irresponsible population elements can be raised into a more abundant economic and cultural life. To accomplish this there is the need, first, for an equitable allocation of public funds for education and other public welfare as between the whites of urban and rural communities and as between the whites and Negroes, second, for greater economic opportunities for the Negroes and poorer whites, and third, for the general sharing of community responsibilities. To achieve these goals should be the province of the joint efforts of the leaders of both races. The present situation, which does not encourage and often prevents the Negro's participation in local government, inevitably handicaps him in his efforts to improve educational conditions and to curb lawlessness. Undoubtedly three score years of public education, the amassing of considerable wealth, and the establishment of cultural institutions have prepared a goodly number of Negroes for a larger responsibility in the local and larger community affairs, and their constructive contribution should no longer be lost to the community and nation because of discriminatory legislation and party practices. Furthermore, to lessen crime and eradicate lynching, the controlling group of white people will need also to prepare the voteless, propertyless, unattached whites—over half of the Southern white population—for an intelligent participation in citizenship.

CHAPTER III

THE TRAGEDY OF THE MOB

THROUGH FINANCIAL LOSS, through aggravated racial antagonisms, through open defiance of organized society, and in other ways the United States, and especially the Southern States, pay dearly for mobs, threatened lynchings, and lynchings. But, beyond these costs of the actual mobs are the costs of the ever-present potential mobs.

THE PRICE OF LYNCHING

Citizenship Debased. The most obvious results of lynchings include the untimely death of unconvicted people, the crucifixion of law and government, and the barbaric and depraved behavior of the lynchers.

The after effects of lynching affect citizenship. Leading citizens are compromised into letting the matter alone, thus affording the lynchers virtual immunity. The few indictments and fewer convictions of 1930 lynchers indicate that the courts are either grossly insincere or ineffective. "A lynching makes a lot of otherwise good people go blind or lose their memories," was the way one outspoken anti-lyncher put it. In several cases, the accused persons were taken from the sheriff or other peace officers in broad daylight by unmasked men. These officers later swore in grand jury hearings that they could not identify a single member of the mob. In other instances, leading local citizens were onlookers; they likewise gave no convicting evidence to the court. Thus, lynching makes mockery of courts and citizenship. The state itself has been lynched.

Ethical Standards Lowered. This lynching of the state rests immediately upon a widespread dishonesty. When a thousand people, as at Ocilla, or five or ten thousand, as at Sherman and Marion, stand for hours and look at victims done to death and then later come into court and refuse to place the guilt, the moral structure of the community has broken down. When such a situation exists, either the courts are insincere or stupid in handling the case, or jurymen disregard their oaths, or citizens swear falsely. One or all of these elements in the community thus share in the responsibility for the crime of the mob.

Such a disregard of an individual Negro's right to trial naturally diminishes the faith of Negroes in their white neighbors and in the government. This loss of faith was expressed again and again in the communities where lynchings occurred in 1930. On the other hand, by its very nature the justification of lynch-law encourages white people to assume that arbitrary force is the only way to deal with Negroes. Whatever Negro exploitation already exists in the community can readily be exaggerated.

The typical after effects of a lynching put human relations on a lower plane. Barbarism and deception are translated into virtues. Civilized countries everywhere require that death sentences be executed by some quick means. Mob deaths by slow fires, mutilations, and tortures are indicative of a group sadism.

Direct and Indirect Financial Loss. Another obvious aftermath of 1930 lynchings was the direct financial loss. At Sherman, the courthouse, valued at over $65,000, and Negro properties at over $75,000, were completely destroyed, with no possibilities of collecting insurance, due to riot clauses in the policies. In Marion and numerous other places, jail house doors were broken down and other expensive equipment of prisons destroyed.

The indirect financial loss was even greater. The damage done to labor conditions, investment of capital, reputation of the community, and the like is inestimable. The lynchings focused attention on these communities, not as places where labor conditions are settled and life and property are safe, but rather as places where human relations are unstable and life and property are subject to the whims of a mob. Every lynching gives unfavorable publicity not only to the immediate community involved, but to the whole section.[1]

Extensive Lynching Area. Only New York, New Jersey, and the six New England States have had no lynching in this century, and in four of these states earlier lynchings are

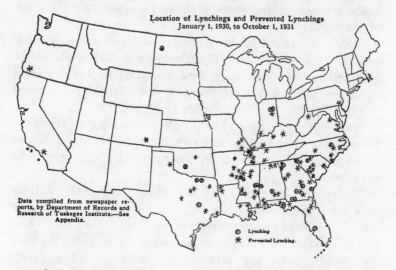

Location of Lynchings and Prevented Lynchings
January 1, 1930, to October 1, 1931

Data compiled from newspaper reports, by Department of Records and Research of Tuskegee Institute.—See Appendix.

◉   Lynching
✳   Prevented Lynching.

recorded. In the light of such facts, no community in the United States can assume that it is without danger of a mob outbreak.

The presence of colleges and universities in a community is no guarantee against a lynching. In 1930, one of the lynchings occurred near the largest land-grant college in the Southern States; one in a town with three denominational colleges; five others in counties with denominational or state colleges. Strong churches are no guarantee against mob violence—witness Sherman, Marion, Cartersville, and Thomasville. Negro suffrage was of no avail toward preventing the lynchings or punishing the lynchers at Chickasha and Marion.

---

[1] Lynchings in the United States have done much to discredit American missionary efforts in Asia and Africa.

Lynchings have occurred in all types of communities, from the capital city of Tennessee, with more than 150,000 inhabitants, numerous denominational headquarters and strong local churches, many well-known colleges and universities, and well-organized police force, to McIntosh County, Georgia, with less than six thousand inhabitants, weak churches, poor schools, and only two peace officers. In the latter case, the Negro was shot to death in his cell; in the former, he was taken from the public hospital. Recent mobs in Atlanta and Shreveport almost succeeded in taking mortally-wounded Negroes from their hospital beds. At Shreveport, the intended victim died in the hospital while the mob hammered at the doors. In Atlanta, a police captain held the mob in check while the accused was secretly removed to a nearby prison.

Parallel Location of Lynchings and Threatened Lynchings. Forty-four reported threatened lynchings were prevented in 1930, and a larger number in 1931. It will be observed from the map that the states with the greatest number of lynchings in the twenty-one months ending with October, 1931, also had the greatest number of lynchings prevented. The eleven states with lynchings had sixty-five preventions. The remaining thirty-seven states had but sixteen, and of these ten were in Arkansas and Kentucky, states with relatively high lynching averages in recent years. To put it another way, the fourteen Southern States, including Missouri and Oklahoma, which had eighty-five per cent of the lynchings between 1882 and 1930, had ninety per cent of the lynchings and ninety-two per cent of preventions in the twenty-one month period ending with October, 1931. Threatened lynchings, no less than consummated lynchings, are products of the mob phenomenon.

ACTUAL AND POTENTIAL MOBS

Size and Intensity of Mobs Vary with Community Conditions. Since the Negro's danger from mob violence is nearly forty times as great as that of the white man,[2] one naturally

[2] From the Negro element, constituting but 10 per cent of the total population, come approximately 80 per cent of all persons lynched in the United States from 1889 to 1931.

looks for a racial element as one of the underlying causes of mob phenomena. While the usual immediate occasion of mob violence against the property and persons of Negroes is the report of some specific crime, the size of the mob, along with the type and extent of its lawlessness, will depend more upon the community situation than upon the type of crime reported. For example, the lynchings in northeast Texas were characterized by tremendous mobs which dragged and burned their victims, while to a lesser degree the same type of mob prevailed in southeast Georgia. Over against the large and desperate mobs in these two relatively new and frontier-like areas, the lynchings in the old plantation counties of the various states were carried out by small and relatively well-organized mobs which did their victims to death with dispatch, without torture before death or burning afterward.

Mob Precipitants and What They Signify. It has been indictated already that many lynchings occurred as the logical sequence of the man-hunt: A crime is reported; excited armed men set out and capture the accused, and the hunters claim the catch.

But many lynched persons were taken from the custody of peace officers. In these cases, the typical situation was something like this: Upon the report of the alleged crime and subsequent arrest, curious people gather about the peace officers or jail. As the crowd grows and discusses the case, the details inevitably are exaggerated. These exaggerated reports, in turn, further excite the excited people who exaggerated them. After a time, the various stories of the crime take on a sort of uniformity, the most horrible details of each version having been woven into a supposedly true account. This milling process continues until an inflammatory speech, the hysterical cry of a woman, the repetition of a slogan, the accidental firing of a gun, the waving of a handkerchief, the racing of an automobile engine, the remarks of some bystander, or some other relatively trivial thing, throws the group into a frenzy and sets it on a career of arson, sadistic mutilations, and murder.

In most cases, the mob precipitant was a mere incident,

for the original crowd of curious persons had been transformed into a tense and demanding crowd—a mob. One precipitant was effective because of the symbolism involved, as at Thomasville, when the mother of the alleged victim frantically inquired: "Are you men going to let that nigger go?" Another was effective simply because an incident suggested a procedure, as at Sherman when a pebble, accidentally thumbed against the tax collector's window pane by a nervous bystander, was followed by larger pebbles and then by stones, cans of gasoline, a match, a burning courthouse, fleeing Texas Rangers, retreating militiamen, burning houses, and a roasting corpse—twelve hours of unrestrained lawlessness. The trivial incidents which precipitate mob outbreaks signify that the mob's greater motivation is from within rather than from without. A mob is a mob, not because of what it does, but because of what it is.

The Mob's Characteristic Discharge. Tense emotional situations have a tendency to resolve themselves by means of action: A spontaneous fight ensues, a house is set afire, a duel is arranged, a shot is fired from ambush, one woman slaps another, or a man stands up before a crowd and abuses his adversary.

The reaction to any particular situation will tend to vary from country to country, and to a lesser degree from one community to another within a country, and no further explanation is needed than "That's the way it is done here!" For example, one man's calling another a liar in France may call forth only a slap with the glove, while on the American western frontier or in an eastern mountain cove, it may be the signal for deadly gun fire. Of course, the immediate emotional discharge depends in part upon the particular individuals involved, for while some are always seeking insults, others have a saving sense of humor and refuse to be insulted. The fundamental consideration is not the particular emotional discharge, but that its nature is largely determined by public opinion and traditional practices. For example, there are communities where a grand jury will exonerate a man for having killed another who had called him a liar or some vile name to which the people of that community expect no self-respecting man to submit.

Groups under emotional tension, like individuals under strain, act in conformity to local attitudes and practices. And throughout a vast part of the United States, these community attitudes readily encourage the formation of mobs, with their characteristic defiant violence to man and property. Mobs are not only violent but reckless. They are seemingly without capacity or inclination to take any deliberate steps either to learn the truth of the accusations or the identity of the accused. That almost no lynchers have ever been punished by the local courts further suggests the degree to which the mob's characteristic discharge of reckless violence is locally accepted. In a very real sense a lynching is but a product of community standards, and consequently will not be condemned by that community.

A Mob Is a Mob. Though since 1920, nearly twice as many reported threatened lynchings have been prevented as have been consummated, these preventions, while saving the lives of the accused persons, have done nothing more to the mobs than forcibly to restrain would-be murderers from becoming actual murderers. And usually, after being kept from the overt act of killing, the mob members have successfully demanded of public officials that the accused person be tried in the local county, that the death sentence be imposed, and that no delay of execution be sought by the defendant's counsel—in most cases a local lawyer appointed by the court. This means that when the mob cannot have its murderous way in defiance of law, it openly attempts to force the constituted authorities to do its bidding. Mobs do not loiter around courtrooms solely out of curiosity; they stand there, armed with guns and threats, to see that the courts grant their demands—death sentences and prompt executions. Such executions are correctly termed "legal lynchings," or "judicial murders."

Since the beginning of 1930, foiled mobs have exercised this sort of influence in cases at Beaumont, Scottsboro, Elberton, and other places. By their insistence that the courts accept their assumptions of absolute guilt, they make the court the agent of the mob, instead of leaving it to mete out justice on the basis of the evidence in the case.

If the mob becomes impatient of the court's procedure, it may take the accused out and lynch him, as at Cartersville. In this particular case the defense lawyers had not only halted the trial, but opened up the possibility of providing a trial place where some sentence other than the death penalty might be given.

What the Mob Is. A Weighty Consideration. In terms of social pathology, the mob itself is a great tragedy. The mob's murder characterizes its negative and destructive nature. The mobs of 1930 had about 75,000 members—men and women and children who went out to kill, or to look on sympathetically while others killed. And not one of these so-called onlookers is morally or legally guiltless: Their very presence directly complicated the task of the peace officers, and emboldened the active lynchers by reflecting to them the community's general approval.

While these seventy-five thousand people were members of actual mobs but one day in the year, they were most probably mob-minded every day in the year. Millions of others were mob-disposed, and under provocation would have joined a mob, killing or standing sympathetically by while others killed. Mobs do not come out of the nowhere; they are the logical outgrowths of dominant assumptions and prevalent thinking. Lynchings are not the work of men suddenly possessed of a strange madness; they are the logical issues of prejudice and lack of respect for law and personality, plus a sadistic desire to participate in the excitement of mob trials and the brutalities of mob torture and murder.

The anti-social and inhumane desires which find expression in lynchings often serve as socializing forces within the white group. Not infrequently more unanimity can be had on a lynching than on any other subject. Lynchings tend to minimize social and class distinctions between white plantation owners and white tenants, mill owners and textile workers, Methodists and Baptists, and so on. This prejudice against the Negro forms a common meeting place for whites, adds to race antagonism,

and further reveals the essentially negative and craven character of the lynchers and their apologists.

A most baffling aspect of the situation is suggested by the
fact that the lynchers often are not content with the death
of their victims. They torture, mutilate, and burn. One is
forced to the conclusion that their deeper motivation is a
desire not for the just punishment of the accused so much
as for an opportunity to participate in protracted brutalities.

Static or Potential Mobs. Thus far the discussion has been
limited to active, or kinetic mobs. There are also potential,
or static mobs. And of the two, the latter is the greater menace
to society; its persistent qualities and semblance of decency
make its eradication exceedingly difficult. The forces that occasionally burst into the aggressive lawlessness of mob violence
are always present, though perhaps unrecognized. They exist as "social pressures," which express themselves in traditional attitudes and practices. They find expression, for instance, when a planter assures the outsider that the propertyless Negroes in his community are wholly satisfied with their
working and living conditions—with their close supervision and
small pay, their one-teacher schools and plantation-unit
churches, and their chronic economic and political dependency.
The query, "But, are they really satisfied?" is answered
quickly and firmly: "Well, if they're not, they'd better be!"

This same pressure finds expression when a sympathetic
white man, asking a Negro why he withheld from the grand
jury certain information about a white murderer, receives the
disarming reply, "This is Terrell County, and I'm a Nigger!"
Other illustrations may often be seen when a Negro questions
a white man's statement at settlement time, when his car col-
lides with the white man's car, when he demands the ballot, or
organizes to hold his job against white men organized to take
it, or does any one of a hundred lesser things which run counter
to the community's traditions.

"The Negro must stay in his place" is a common phrase,
and the white people who have defined "his place" may be
expected to react violently if they think he is either getting
out of it or showing dissatisfaction with it. Thus the potential

mob controls most situations and is accepted without question by most communities. Under shock or sustained emotional tension, it tends to become active.

Cultural Exploitation Plays a Part. The Negro's cultural exploitation, effected in numerous ways, operates to perpetuate his political impotence and economic helplessness. Whatever of humor there is in most of the white man's popular stories about the Negro is based primarily on some open or veiled allusion to him as an amiable simpleton, lacking alike in intelligence, sensibility to pain, and moral aspiration. The black-faced characters common in vaudeville, in grade and high school entertainments—and sometimes in those of the church—are good drawing cards for white audiences primarily because white people enjoy seeing servile and docile Negroes in ridiculous rôles. The exploitative phases of the jokes about Negroes and black-faced characters are all the more insidious because of their superficially convincing realistic touches.

Back of this cultural exploitation is the assumption that the Negro, by divine design, is irredeemably inferior. To the popular mind—steeped in the theology and philosophy which justified slavery, the permanent disfranchisement of Negroes and the present discrimination against them in public expenditures—the Bible provides the explanation of the Negro's economic and cultural predicament no less than his color. Though it says nothing of the sort, the Scriptural story of the cursing of Canaan in the latter part of the ninth chapter of Genesis is popularly construed as depicting the creation of a black-skinned race to be the servants of the other races.

Supporting the white man's theology and philosophy of slavery and subsequent Negro exploitation has been his experience with Negro farm tenants, domestic servants, and casual day laborers. Here he has dealt with persons living on a scant ration, crowded with others into small quarters, accustomed neither to bathing nor clean clothing. Hence asserts the popular white mind: "Negroes are unclean by nature; they stink." They are unclean morally, also, according to the usual insistence; this, too, cannot be helped, for they have within themselves no basis for morality; they are essentially shiftless, care-free and irresponsible. They can scarcely profit by their experiences of yesterday or anticipate their needs for the morrow; consequently they will work only when they are hungry; and if regular "hands" are wanted, the employer had best pay a small wage, for as soon as Negroes get a little ahead they will quit work. Furthermore, according to the popular estimate, all Negroes are essentially alike and are inclined to commit certain crimes, chief of which is the rape of white women. Despite their knowledge of many individual Negroes who are not of this stereotype, most white men proceed upon the assumption that all other Negroes are of this type—and thus implicitly justify mob violence against any accused Negro.

The majority of white people, assuming that Negroes are something less than normal human beings, logically treat them accordingly: To be sure, Negroes should have justice as human beings, but in the light of the kind of human beings they are. Out of this philosophy naturally grow lynchings and other forms of exploitation of the Negro's property, labor and life.

Political and Economic Exploitation as Related to Lynchings. By laws and practices regulating the Negro's working possibilities and limiting his educational and vocational opportunities, the white man has done much to keep the Negro in his relatively low economic status. In the states where most lynchings have occurred, white people generally justified slavery; they bitterly resented and, when possible, openly defied the Reconstruction governments; they justified the methods of terror employed to intimidate and disfranchise the Negroes; they later enacted laws and perfected party procedures to restore and preserve "white supremacy." These historical backgrounds have given rise to many repressive practices and to much discriminatory legislation.

State, county, and municipal governments, like planters and industrialists, have developed their own methods of sharing in this exploitation. To illustrate, the Negro's educational opportunities and hospital facilities are limited; he receives poorer police protection and usually a smaller grocery order from the public charities; he may not sit on a jury or have any voice in the allocation of public funds. A "white man's government" is imperative where three to sixty times as much public money is to be spent for the education of the white child as for that of the Negro child, and where other public services are administered on a similar basis.

These discriminations, of course, are simply the crystallization of public attitudes. The bases of lynch law reside in these same attitudes which find expression in the cultural, political, and economic exploitation of the Negro. Another irresistible conclusion is that lynching is an evidence of the white man's fear of the Negro and lack of faith in his "own" government.

A Few Suggestions

Because of the direct and indirect money losses from mobs and lynchings, the adverse publicity which they bring, their deadening effect upon citizenship and government, and their anti-social implications, the intelligent leadership of every community should be eternally on guard against them. Mobs and lynchings will ultimately fade from the scene with the general rise of the cultural level, which alone can provide the basis for the development of a public which will discard these crude methods of group expression. It is a matter of major importance to stimulate this cultural advancement. In the meantime, however, certain steps offer hope of immediate amelioration, as well as of steady progress toward the eventual goal.

Additional Legislation. The Commission on the Study of Legal Problems in Lynching, made up of deans of the Southern law schools, is now engaged in a thorough survey of this field and is soon to report its findings and recommendations. We do not deem it necessary or advisable to anticipate their conclusions.

It should be said, however, that our study of the 1930 lynchings clearly indicates the need of additional laws to insure the protection of prisoners and to facilitate the apprehension and conviction of mob members. The lynching of twenty-one victims in 1930, many of them taken out of the hands of the law, and the fact that of thousands of persons participating in these group murders, many of them openly, less than fifty were indicted and but four convicted and sentenced, forcibly suggest the need of certain legal expedients. Among those most worthy of consideration may be mentioned (a) compulsory removal of prisoners in certain types of cases; and (b) arbitrary power in the hands of the State authorities to extend protection and, if necessary, to investigate and prosecute in case of mob violence, to change the venue in the trial of lynchers, and to suspend officers who yield their prisoners to mobs.

Practical Measures for Preventing and Dispersing Mobs. Our case studies suggest, among others, the following needs:

Securer jails to keep out mobs, and adequate equipment to repel them—machine guns, gas bombs, etc. The consolidation of small, poor counties into larger and wealthier units would doubtless help greatly to this end. In 1930 there were in the Southern States over 250 counties with less than 10,000 population each, sixty-one of which had less than 5,000 population. Many of these counties are too poor to provide effective local government.

Sheriffs and other peace officers should cease fraternizing and temporizing with mob leaders—a habit that has often encouraged them in their lawlessness. Officers of rural counties might, with great advantage, form working agreements to assist each other in times of crisis. Citizens of influence may be called in to help prevent the formation of mobs and turn them from their purpose, or if necessary they may be deputized to resist them.

Experience indicates that no American community is immune from the danger of mob violence. Therefore, in every community, particularly in rural areas and small towns, a few good citizens should associate themselves in a compact to watch for threats of mob violence and to act together for its prevention. In many of the cases in 1930 such a committee, adept and active, might easily have foreseen and prevented the threatened tragedy.

The relatives and friends of those against whom crimes have been committed may, and sometimes do, greatly help in the prevention of lynchings by urging that the law be allowed to take its course.

Public Opinion the Ultimate Deterrent. It need not be urged that laws at last are of little avail unless supported by public opinion. The various expedients suggested above may help to prevent the formation of mobs and reduce the number of lynchings, but they will contribute to the final end of "lynching" only as they help build a public opinion that will outlaw it.

The growth of such a public opinion—which can come only with the development of a more deliberate and saner public—is a matter of education, working through many agencies. In this process, the churches perhaps have major responsibility, as the traditional arbiters of moral standards and the conservators of human values. In their official pronouncements, the larger church bodies have gone on record with statements that are entirely satisfactory. The practical results will be meager, however, until both ministers and laymen generally take these declarations seriously and begin to mediate them to their congregations. This, of course, is but one phase of the church's mission to teach the sacredness and value of human personality.

Public schools, colleges, and universities should play an important part, through definite courses in race relations and by the inclusion of factual material in courses in history, literature, sociology, civics, and other subjects. Thus the rising generation may be afforded the basis for intelligent, fair-minded racial attitudes which it will hardly secure in any other way.

The press, a third great educational agency, has already demonstrated its value in the anti-lynching campaign. The editorial leadership, it is confidently expected, will continue to render this service till the goal is reached.

In Conclusion. Lynching can and will be eliminated in proportion as all elements of the population are provided opportunities for development and are accorded fundamental human rights. Whether in the field of religion, education, economics, jurisprudence, or politics, anything which looks toward this end is a factor in reducing mob violence. For fundamentally lynching is an expression of a basic lack of respect both for human beings and for organized society.

PART TWO

LYNCHINGS IN BLACK BELT COUNTIES

In 1930, seven lynchings occurred in Black Belt plantation counties where over one-half the population is made up of Negroes: Emelle, Sumter County, Alabama; the double lynching at Scooba, Kemper County, Mississippi; Rosedale, Bolivar County, Mississippi; Raymond, Hinds County, Mississippi;[1] Tarboro, Edgecombe County, North Carolina, and Bryan, Brazos County, Texas.[2] These counties are predominantly rural; nearly all the Negroes and propertyless whites live in the open country, while the plantation owners are concentrated in the county seat towns.

Four of these seven lynchings—those at Emelle, Scooba and Rosedale—occurred in central Mississippi and extreme western Alabama, the newest part of the Black Belt. This area, occupied by the Choctaw Indians, was opened for white settlers only after the 1830 Treaty of Dancing Rabbit.

With the single exception of Brazos County, Texas, where there is a considerable element of European and Mexican immigrants, the white people of these counties are practically all native-born; most of the Negroes are the direct descendants of the slaves who lived there. Both groups, directly or indirectly, are dependent upon cotton alone, except in Edgecombe County, North Carolina, which is in the cotton-tobacco belt. It is literally a cotton-ridden civilization: In good years the

---

[1] Since the case studies of the other three lynchings in Mississippi plantation counties are presented, that of the lynching at Raymond is omitted.

[2] Though with slightly less than fifty per cent Negroes, it is correct to present the Bryan case study in this section, since numerous Mexicans occupy the same place in this plantation county that Negroes do in most Southern plantation counties.

plantation owners and their families buy new cars and make extended trips, and the propertyless farm folks make purchases generally beyond their means; in lean years, the landlords bear the losses with a fitting stoicism, and the tenants patch their old clothes and carry home smaller sacks of corn meal and fewer pieces of "fat-back." Most of the Negroes are farm tenants or wage hands, with a few overseers and farm owners. While there are many white tenants and a goodly number of white overseers, the majority of the white people have proprietary interests in plantation farming. Many of the larger planters are interested also in banks, mercantile establishments and cotton oil mills. Practically all doctors and lawyers secure part of their livelihood from farm operations, for most local people invest their savings in land.

In these Black Belt counties public school funds are allocated least equitably between the races; in some instances forty times as much public money is spent for the education of the white child as for that of the Negro child. The churches of both races are generally weak, especially in the rural areas. In some of these counties, because of the unchurched farm tenants and wage hands, less than one-half the people over fifteen years of age are church members.

Practically no Negroes vote either in national or local elections; Democratic majorities are unusually large. In some of these counties the 1928 presidential election, which registered noticeable inroads into the "solid South," showed a greater increase of Democratic votes than of Republican votes, which serves to emphasize the well-known fact that the rural counties constitute the backbone of the "solid South." Some of the county officials receive unusually large salaries and incomes; the office of the sheriff of Bolivar County, for example, is ten times more remunerative than that of the Governor of Mississippi.

In these Black-Belt plantation areas, where modified slave-time patterns still persist, any crime which occurs among the propertyless Negroes is considered a labor matter to be handled by the white landlord or his overseer. This is accepted

by public officials and civic and church leaders, no less than
by the general public. To all practical purposes the local
peace officers function as agents of the plantation owners
and overseers, rather than as impartial referees to see that
justice obtains between the plantation management and
Negro workers.

With respect to race relations, the minority white element
considers it imperative that the Negro be kept in "his place,"
which means not only that he must refrain from participating in politics, but that he must accept the white man's unqualified right to arbitrate any question which arises between
Negro and white. No movement will be tolerated among the
Negroes which remotely threatens to disrupt the present
system.

No lynching in a Black Belt county occurred in a town,
although in two instances the victims were taken from towns
to the open country to be lynched. None of the victims was
mutilated and none of the bodies was burned. In no case
was there any wide-spread hysteria such as characterized
other lynchings of the year; in every instance the mob was
small, the largest not more than two hundred. In each case
the mob proceeded in routine fashion, in two instances, at
Scooba and Tarboro, with almost clock-like precision. At
Emelle the outbreak took the form of a determined and
extended man-hunt.

The chief reasons why these mobs were smaller and more
direct in their procedure were that there are relatively fewer
whites in these counties, that lynching is a well established
custom, that the mob leaders—when measured by ownership
of property, education, and community standing—were of a
relatively higher type than those who took the leadership
in the other lynchings. The Black Belt lynching is something
of a business transaction, and as noted above, Negroes are
in least danger in these plantation counties. The whites, there,
chiefly of the planter class and consciously dependent upon
the Negro for labor, lynch him to conserve traditional landlord-tenant relations rather than to wreak vengeance upon his

race. Black Belt white men demand that the Negroes stay out of their politics and dining rooms, the better to keep them in their fields and kitchens.

CHAPTER IV

"BLUE-EYED NIGGERS"
EMELLE, SUMTER COUNTY, ALABAMA

ALTERCATION OVER a second-hand auto battery occasioned the killing of two white men and four Negroes in and near Emelle, Sumter County, Alabama, on July 4-5, 1930. One of the six, Esau Robinson, Negro, was lynched on the night of July 4. He was a member of a large landowning family which was characterized by certain distinctive physical features, including greyish-blue eyes. They were referred to by many local white people as the "blue-eyed niggers."

THE LYNCHING AND OTHER KILLINGS

The Victims, White and Colored. Six people, two whites and four Negroes, including one woman, were killed: Grover Boyd, white planter of Emelle community, was killed by the Robinson Negroes; Esau Robinson, Negro, was lynched by a mob; John Newton Robinson, farmer-preacher, and uncle of Esau, was shot to death on the porch of his house when he refused to surrender his gun to mob members; Charlie Marrs, white overseer, was shot to death by a fellow mob member when John Newton Robinson's house was burned; Winston Jones, Negro, was shot to death by a member of the searching party at Narkeeta, Mississippi, ten miles northwest of Emelle; and Viola Dial, Negro woman, was shot to death just across the Mississippi line by undeputized men who fired into a passing auto.

Events Immediately Preceding the Outbreak. In April, 1930, Clarence Boyd, filling station operator at Geiger, seven miles north of Emelle, sold a second-hand auto battery to Esau Robinson for $3.50. On several occasions Boyd had approached Robinson for the money. On July 4 a large number of Negroes had gathered at an Emelle Negro church for a picnic. Clarence Boyd was in Emelle, and again demanded payment. When Esau did not pay for the battery, Boyd lifted it out of his car, placed it in Cobb's store at Emelle, and refused to let Esau have it back until he paid for it. Esau left Emelle saying he was going home for the money. This occurred shortly before noon.

At four o'clock that afternoon Esau Robinson, accompanied by his father, Tom, two brothers, Ollis and King, and a cousin also named Robinson, rode into Emelle. The Negroes were armed and drinking. They filed through each of the stores until they found Clarence Boyd. Motioning him outside the store, Esau hit him over the head with a bottle, momentarily dazing him. Other members of the Robinson crowd rushed in. Boyd called to his uncle, Grover Boyd, for help. As the latter approached, Tom Robinson, father of Esau, picked up a stick about the size of a mattock handle and started toward the struggling parties. Grover Boyd then ran to his automobile nearby, secured a pistol and began firing at Tom, who, though wounded, made his escape. While Boyd was still shooting at Tom, either King or Ollis Robinson came up behind him, took deliberate aim and fired. Grover Boyd fell dying. One of the Robinson party stood immediately over the fatally wounded white man, and fired several shots into him. Boyd's seven-year-old son was the first to reach his lifeless body.

Shortly after the trouble arose between Clarence Boyd and Esau Robinson, a number of white people rushed out and seized all but two of the Robinson Negroes. When the shooting began there was great confusion and with the exception of Esau, all the Negroes made their escape. A white merchant held on to Esau, and tied him to a post to await the coming of the sheriff.

A Reported Underlying Cause. Certain Negroes, conversant with the Emelle community, reported that the altercation over the battery was the immediate but not the real cause of the outbreak. According to these Negroes, the trouble grew out of the insistence of certain white men upon "running with" the Robinson and other Negro women. The sources of this report, though few, are of such character as to warrant its appearing here. On the other hand, many well-informed local Negroes and leading white people expressed complete ignorance of any such underlying cause.

Sheriff Left Esau Tied to Post. After arming themselves, a few white people started in pursuit of those who had killed Grover Boyd. The sheriff, notified soon after Boyd was killed, arrived in Emelle about sundown. When told that the Negro held was not the one who had killed Boyd, the sheriff left him tied to the post in charge of two white residents of Emelle, and went in search of the crowd pursuing the other Robinsons.

Some time before midnight Esau Robinson was released from the post and shot to death by a mob of less than fifty people from Alabama and Mississippi. An informed official stated that only four of the lynchers were residents of Emelle, and that more than half of them were from nearby Mississippi communities. A rope was then placed about the neck of the corpse and it was pulled into a half-suspended position by the roadside so that passing Negroes could see it. The grim warning remained in this position until Saturday noon, July 5. It is reported that when the sheriff ordered the body taken down several white men rushed forward for souvenirs and that one cut off an ear.

Negro Farmer-Preacher and White Overseer Killed. Bloodhounds from Meridian employed by the searching party followed tracks with some difficulty and delay to the home of farmer-preacher John Newton Robinson, brother of Tom and uncle of Esau. The armed man-hunters found John on his front porch with a rifle on his knees. Somebody teased him about borrowing his rifle. He not only stated that no white man could have his gun, but objected to his house being searched. In the resulting quarrel John Newton Robinson was shot to death. Shortly afterward, one of the mob leaders, Charlie Marrs, a local white overseer, was killed, probably unintentionally, by a member of the mob. It is said that Marrs was drunk at the time.

Seeking to place all the blame upon the Negroes, some claim that he was shot by one of the Robinsons. The evidence, how-

ever, seems to indicate that it was a shot intended for the
Robinson house that hit Marrs, who, against specific instructions, insisted on rushing ahead.

Sheriff Orders Negro Dwelling Fired. John Newton Robinson and Charlie Marrs were dead when the sheriff arrived
shortly before midnight. Members of the mob remained at
the house believing that several Robinsons were inside. To run
them out, the sheriff shot at an oil lamp inside the window.
He hit the lamp but it did not fire the house. Under his orders,
gasoline was applied and the house was fired. The flames leaped
up, but no Robinsons were seen. As the dwelling crackled and
crumbled, the dead bodies were dragged back together toward
the darkness lest they get too hot.

While the house burned hundreds of cartridges exploded
within. Numerous 45-cartridge shells and two shotgun barrels
were found in the ashes. About one month before the Emelle
disorders, there had been a schism between the Robinsons and
another faction in the local Baptist Church; John Newton
Robinson, the pastor, had been accused of burning the church.
It is reported that he laid in a stock of ammunition upon being
warned that his church enemies had been threatening personal violence. The station agent at Emelle reported that the
Negro preacher received a case of cartridges during the latter
part of June. Others discount this explanation and contend
that the firearms were for an attack which Negroes had planned
on the whites.

Excited Strangers Everywhere. The searching party became
larger; by noon the next day the countryside was filled with
strangers from nearby and distant communities. Excitement
ran high; armed men in cars chased madly throughout the
countryside. Automobiles were stopped indiscriminately; any
and every Negro was a Robinson until he had proved himself
otherwise.

"Better Stay at the House Tonight." Feeling responsible for
their tenants and Negro friends, many white planters advised
them to stay in their cabins. On the evening of July 4, a
white planter near Emelle said to one of his tenants, "You
had better stay at the house tonight." Twenty minutes later

the planter was surprised to see his Negro families coming in from all directions. The planter meant for the Negroes to stay at their own houses. When he explained this, some returned to their cabins, but several did not. On that and succeeding nights the cook's cabin and other servant houses near "the big house" were filled to overflowing.

A few years ago a white planter near Emelle sold a small farm to an aged Negro couple. On the late afternoon of July 4 the planter's eighteen-year-old son expressed concern about the fright of "Uncle" Ike and "Aunt" Mary; and went down to their house to assure them that they were in no danger if only they stayed inside until the excited strangers left the community. The planter related with feeling how, a few minutes later, "Uncle" Ike followed closely by "Aunt" Mary came in at the back gate. Upon nearing the planter, in his usual place on the spacious back porch with the daily paper, "Uncle" Ike, with tears streaming down his face, said "I des knowd you'd 'member me. An' des as soon as I hears dat mercheen er coming I sez to de ole 'oman, sez I, 'Dey's comin'! I des know dey's come right down heah." And the planter was glad to have them remain at his house until the trouble was over.

Two More Negro Victims. The man-hunt continued through the night of the fifth. The homes of Negroes were searched and all types of firearms were taken—and never returned. It is reported that a Negro still was broken up, the whiskey consumed, and that the owner of the still was robbed of $500.

On the night of the fifth, Winston Jones, Negro, received a fatal shot at Narkeeta, Mississippi, just across the state line. The newspapers reported that he was killed by Clarence Bush, cousin of Guy Bush, the famed Chicago baseball player, and that Bush said he shot the Negro because, when asked to halt, the latter had fired on him, wounding him in the arm. Jones was sought by Tuscaloosa authorities for the recent shooting of a Negro woman there.

A second casualty on the night of the fifth was that of a Negro woman, Viola Dial, who was in a car with her husband and three other men. Man-hunters ordered the car to stop; when it did not they fired upon it, killing the woman; the men

jumped from the car and escaped. Some think the husband in
fright had not understood the command to halt. This was the
sixth and last casualty of the Emelle disorders.

Late Arrival of State Enforcement Officers. Information of
the affair did not reach the office of Governor Graves or that
of the State Law Enforcement Department until ten o'clock
on the morning of July 5. State officers were sent to the scene
at once. They placed the chief blame for the lynching on the
sheriff. The Negro man and woman killed on the night of July
5 came to their deaths after the state officers were in the Emelle
community, but both fatalities occurred in Mississippi, outside
the jurisdiction of the Alabama officers.

For some weeks state enforcement officers continued the
search and apprehended Tom Robinson, the father of the
lynched Negro, and his sons Ollis and King, who were taken
to Kilby Prison at Montgomery. Others of the Robinson family, including women and children, were also confined in Kilby
for safe keeping and as witnesses. Only Negroes have been
arrested thus far.

Months afterwards state enforcement officers stated that it
would be practically impossible to get convictions of the white
offenders, even if they were indicted. The following statement
from one of them indicates his feelings: "After the state law
enforcement agents arrived on the scene there were no more
lynchings and no more deaths in Alabama. The guilty parties
have been apprehended, fair trials have been given and now
one, Tom Robinson, is under sentence of death, and othe·
members of the Robinson family are awaiting trial." Tor
Robinson's overt acts, it will be remembered, consisted onl
of being drunk and picking up a stick to hit Clarence Boyd.
Presumably he was convicted on the ground that he had in-
stigated the affair.

Blue-Eyed Industrious Negroes. The Robinsons formed a
large and very industrious Negro family. The father, Tom
Robinson, was a landowner, having purchased 160 acres some
years ago from the leading white planter of the community.
Esau, about twenty-five years old, unmarried, had finished the
local one-teacher school. None of fifteen children in the family

had ever attended high school. It was the policy of their father to put the children to work on the farm as soon as they had finished the local school. A number of Esau's first cousins, children of John Newton Robinson, who was also a farm owner, finished high school at the Sumter County Training School, some of them being exceptionally good students. None of them ever attended college.

The elder Robinson brothers, John Newton and Tom, were very thrifty, as were also their children, most of whom have always lived in the Emelle community. None had court records prior to the Emelle trouble. The family was active in church matters.

The lynching of Esau, the shooting of John Newton, the death sentence of Tom, and the court trials against others have scattered the family. A well-informed local Negro expressed the belief that county officers know that several of the Robinson men have been "sold" to operators of Louisiana plantations. This report, however, is generally denied by other leading people of both races.

The Robinsons are distinguished by their blue eyes, though otherwise decidedly negroid in type. Several of the white people stated that this family of "blue-eyed niggers" had been back of all the trouble between the races in that part of the county during the last quarter of a century. However, they generally bore a good reputation among the whites prior to July, 1930. The local Negro leaders still speak well of them.

Nothing is known about Winston Jones, killed by the man-hunters at Narkeeta, Mississippi, except that he was a fugitive from justice. It is reported by local Negroes that Viola Dial, killed by man-hunters when they fired into a passing auto, was with child, and that the baby was born shortly after she was shot.

REACTION OF THE COMMUNITY TO THE EMELLE DISORDERS

The fact that every effort has been made by local and state authorities to apprehend and punish the Negroes guilty of killing Grover Boyd and that scarcely any has been made to apprehend and punish the whites who killed four Negroes is indicative of the reaction of the local community and the state.

"Chicago Gangster" Explanation of Sumter County Weekly.
The disturbance at Emelle was generally referred to as a race
riot by the leading dailies of the South. It is more accurate
to speak of it as an extended man-hunt.

In Sumter County's only newspapers, *Our Southern Home*
and *Sumter County Journal,* weeklies, with a combined circulation of less than two thousand, sketchy news stories and ex-
planatory editorials appeared. *Our Southern Home,* on July
9, the first issue after the disorders, carried a news story
featuring the deaths of the two white men, and barely men-
tioning the deaths of the Negroes.

An editorial in the same issue of the paper, captioned "No
Race Riot," is an obvious effort to make all look well for the
whites, and absolve Sumter County and Alabama by resorting
to the "Chicago gangster" explanation:

The talk of a "race riot in Sumter" is unjust to the county. It
may be due to misunderstanding the condition, and probably to
the disposition of some daily papers to "spread-eagle" things into
sensations, and make them appear at their worst. Citizens of Emelle
and others tell us that the Negroes of their neighborhood were
willing to coöperate with the whites in capturing the criminals
in the recent trouble, and offered to do so.

The Robinson family that started the trouble over the small
debt for a motor car battery is composed of blue-eyed mulattoes,
a class that do not have the sympathy and coöperation of the full
blooded Negroes. One of the Robinsons recently took a trip to
Chicago where he became acquainted with gangster operations,
and later returned home with the evident intention of putting them
in practice.[1]

The only other space devoted to the Emelle disorders by
the local county paper was a brief news item lamenting the
"Tragic Death of Mr. Grover Boyd."

Just as the local Sumter County paper made a perfect case

---

[1] As a matter of fact, none of the Robinsons, the investigator was assured,
had ever been in Chicago.

for the white people, a widely published Negro press release over the name of James Higgings made an equally *ex parte* case for the Negroes.

No Outside Help Needed. On July 7 the Tuscaloosa *News* had a lengthy news story, from which the following is quoted:

Although several white men were at the scene of both the recent slayings, residents of the section would not talk of the affair to newspapermen who spent two days in the isolated hamlet on the A. T. & N. Railroad. "What the hell are you newspaper men doing here?" one of the possemen asked a Tuscaloosa *News* representative who was sent to Emelle. "We're just killing a few negroes that we've waited too damn long about leaving for the buzzards. That's not news," the writer was informed.

The Birmingham *News* of July 9 had an editorial on the situation which evoked the following letter from an Emelle citizen:

"To the Editor The Birmingham *News:*

"In the *News* of July 9 is an editorial article on the Emelle race trouble.

"You make the reported observations of Gov. Graves, that he 'will go to the bottom of our trouble' your keynote.

"He will find on the real bottom, if he will go there, not only the prime factors of this trouble, but of almost all others that result in violent deaths nation-wide; whisky and concealed pistols. . . .

"Liquor and concealed pistols given a squad of blue-eyed Negroes, a plot forms to do a white man to death because he asked payment of a small debt.

"Where in the South is the community that would not do as was done here?

"If those who will that this should not recur will remove the liquor and the pistol from the Negro, the possibility will be taken away.

"W. L. MURRAY,
Emelle, Alabama."

Forced Resignation of Sheriff and Circuit Solicitor. The coroner's jury which investigated the Negroes' deaths "found" that they had been killed by unknown persons. Had it not been for the interposition of Governor Bibb Graves on the basis of information secured through the State Law Enforcement Department, the court proceedings would doubtless have been equally ineffective.

Two weeks after the Emelle disorders, Judge B. F. Elmore, of the 17th Judicial Circuit, of which Sumter County is a part, was directed by the Governor to hold a special session of the court in Sumter County "as quickly as practicable." In the next issue of *Our Southern Home* there was notice of a special session of court called for August 18, 1930.

From the outset Gov. Graves expressed concern about the affair: State enforcement officers were sent there immediately; rewards of $300 each were offered for the arrest and conviction of the persons responsible for the deaths of the Negro woman and the Negro man on the night of July 5. Rewards of $300 each were also posted for the capture—dead or alive—of Tom, Ollis, and King Robinson, alleged instigators of the trouble.

The people of Sumter County resented the Governor's attitude and generally did not coöperate with the state officers sent there. Governor Graves stated that many people of the county were displeased with his "meddling in their affairs," and reminded him that though he might call a special session, they had their "own" sheriff and circuit solicitor.

Shortly before the special session began, however, this complacency was disturbed, when state enforcement officers reported to issue subpoenas, and Solicitor Bart Chamberlain of Mobile came into court by order of the Governor to conduct the grand jury investigation. Sheriff Scales and Circuit Solicitor W. R. Kimbrough were very much disconcerted, and before the end of the second day both had resigned. It was the Governor's expressed intention, under his power in such cases, to impeach the sheriff and solicitor for failure to perform their official duties. Anticipating this they resigned. The Governor made appointments for the unexpired terms.

The impeachment of the circuit solicitor, who was running

for re-election, would have made him ineligible to hold office again. Because of his resignation, his election on the following November 4 was regular, and consequently, since January 1, 1931, Sumter and other counties of the 17th Judicial Circuit of Alabama have had for circuit solicitor a man who resigned in the face of impending impeachment.

Abolition of State Law Enforcement Department. The State Law Enforcement Department provided the Governor with a means of dealing directly with mob activities. Under this provision there could be no such sorry scenes as the impotence of the militia in the cases at Darien, Georgia, and Maryville, Missouri, which are discussed elsewhere. During his four years in office, Governor Graves used the State Law Enforcement Department at Montgomery, Eufaula, Huntsville and a score of other places to prevent threatened mob violence. During his administration there was but one lynching, and in that case state proceedings were brought against the sheriff and circuit solicitor for failure to perform their sworn duties.

The State Law Enforcement Department was an issue in the 1930 political campaign in Alabama. Numerous interests combined to be rid of it and so, according to promise, one of Governor Miller's first official acts, a gesture of economy, was its abolition.

Reported Mob Leaders and Suicides. It was not definitely ascertained who shot and killed and later hanged Esau Robinson. A confidential report from a state enforcement officer, however, is to the effect that, of the forty-five men in the lynching party, four were from Emelle and more than half of the remainder from Mississippi. It is reported from this same source that the lynchers were representative of the sorrier element of the white people.

It has been observed already that the activities of the sheriff and his deputies differed little from those of the lynchers and man-hunters. There is evidence that an ex-sheriff and members of the Boyd family were active in the mob activities. It is reported that the suicide of a deputy shortly after the disorders came as the result of his brooding over having killed the pregnant Negro woman. The ex-sheriff also killed himself in the courthouse a few weeks after the trouble.

It has been shown already that people rushed to Emelle from widely scattered communities. Unusually large numbers went from York and other points in the southern part of the county where the poorer whites are most numerous. On July 5 frantic appeals for help came to York from Emelle, and an attempt was made to get the Alabama, Tennessee and Northern Railroad officials at York to run a special fare-free train to Emelle. The railroad officials, however, persistently refused the request.

White Murderers Unmolested by State and County. The grand jury, in session three days, returned indictments for murder against three Robinson Negroes. No white men were indicted for their part in the affair. In the case of the lynching of Esau Robinson, the grand jury said, "We have been unable to ascertain from any of the witnesses who appeared before us any evidence which would warrant the returning of a true bill." The grand jury, however, did do the justice of requesting that the unaccused Robinson Negroes held in Kilby prison be released.

"What Else Could One Expect?" One person summed up the situation when he said: "Well, what else could one expect?" Doubtless he was thinking of two things, first, that a group of armed Negroes had killed a white man, second, that in the last few years several Negroes accused of killing white people in Sumter County had been given penitentiary sentences rather than the electric chair.

The general run of merchants, bankers, business men, planters and professional men apparently felt much the same way. Negroes cannot kill a prominent white man in Sumter County without taking the consequences. In view of the whole situation the people in the community express surprise that so few Negroes were killed. The attitude of women was not unlike that of the men: The incident might be sad, but nevertheless it was inevitable. It is sufficient to state that no white person was located who seemed to feel that anything very bad had happened other than the deaths of Grover Boyd and Charlie Marrs; no evidence was found which indicated that any effort was made to keep Esau Robinson from being lynched; and, except the advice to stay in their houses, nobody around Emelle attempted to save the Negroes from the imminent danger caused by the armed and excited outsiders who overran the country-side.

Indifference of Church Leaders Charged. Ministers at Livingston commented upon the "unfavorable and unwarranted" publicity given them and their county by J. D. Burton, Alabama-Tennessee Interracial Secretary—on the scene in the later stages of the disorder—in his statement to the press charging the church people with indifference. Burton's exact statement, appearing in the Montgomery *Advertiser* on July 18, was:

"Goodwill between the races should be fostered by the church world. At one of the places we visited in the disturbed zone, we could not locate a single minister. One was on his vacation, the second was holding a revival in the country, and one was out at the swimming hole. No churchman at this place was making any definite effort to stop hostilities. No religious leader seemed perturbed over what was happening. Mobs were organized, using telephone and other means of communication, but the church forces were not actively at work to combat the mob influence. At one place where we called, the minister could not give us the initials of two fellow ministers who lived in the small town, representing different denominational groups. The three ministers had lived here for some time. It is a pity that the various denominational groups cannot get together in emergencies of this kind in behalf of law and order."

The Methodist minister at Livingston took the position that he and the other ministers could in no wise be held accountable for either the outbreak or the duration of the trouble at Emelle; it was a dozen miles away. Moreover, preachers are not policemen anyway. The minister stated that he was about his church duties—holding a revival in a rural church near Livingston—and that it was most unjust for a man to run into the community "between trains" and then give the church people and the preachers a bad name. Evidently the Interracial Secretary assumed that church people and ministers have a special responsibility toward the underprivileged, regardless of color, and that they should have been endeavoring to restore law and order in the community; the local ministers and church people in conformity with the local racial situation obviously felt no such responsibility.

Increased Dissatisfaction Among Best Negro Element. Realizing that the county and state officers while hunting down every Robinson have arrested no whites, the Negroes have borne the situation in silence, fully aware that their immediate security lies within the shelter of the landed white element.

A few days after the Emelle disturbance one of the leading Negro landowners went to a white planter, from whom he had bought his farm several years ago, saying that he would like to come back on his place as a cropper. After being reassured by the white planter, he decided to remain for the time at least on the farm which he owns. This case illustrates the feeling of insecurity prevalent among the landowning Negroes in this community. Several families have gone away and others are considering a move. Negro tenants are but little less apprehensive.

In view of the fact that Sumter County has more workers than opportunities for making a good living, it might be a fine thing for the county if many of the least productive Negroes would move away. On the contrary, the Negroes leaving are of the better element. This selective population movement can only be harmful to the county.

Fear of Negro Retaliation. The most direct and immediate result of the Emelle outbreak was that the mass of whites were fearful that the Negroes would retaliate. On every hand they said that the Negroes were arming themselvs and going by pairs or threes or fours. The Emelle trouble merely aggravated an already insecure feeling on the part of the white people in the plantation area. They told with alarm of a recent case where two Negroes went to the home of a sawmill operator, and in the face of his wife's pleadings for mercy, robbed and murdered him.

A few weeks after the Emelle trouble a serious outbreak was barely prevented at York, in the southern part of the county. A Negro working in the railroad shops there went into the storeroom and whistled the attention of a white attendant from whom he wanted some article. The overseer happened to be nearby and called to the Negro, "You know those are white men in there; when you want one of them you call him by name. Don't be whistling around here!" The Negro answered, "Well, I didn't want to come in here anyhow." "Make none of your insulting remarks, Mr. Nigger," retorted the overseer, as he started after him. The Negro rushed out. Upon leaving the shops he passed close by a car under which were some white workmen, and they claim to have heard him mumbling to himself: "Well, d—— it, I'll get my gun!" The white workmen immediately reported this threat to the overseer; within a few minutes a score of men were armed and searching for the runaway. Negro workmen on the outskirts of the railroad yards, knowing what was going on, saw the threatened Negro returning and advised him that he would be killed if he went back to the shops. Taking the advice of his fellow-workmen, he fled for safety. In the meantime, although positively asked to refrain from doing so by the enraged workmen who wanted to kill the Negro, the superintendent of the shops got in touch with the mayor and marshal of York and asked them to arrest the Negro at once, which they did. The superintendent was frowned upon in no uncertain terms by many, some of them his own employees, for interfering with "their nigger." Excitement was high, and in running here and there to get guns one man ran into a store and picked up an unloaded gun; when the trouble was over, much to the embarrassment of the determined gunner, the owner demanded that his unloaded gun be put back where it belonged.

White Supremacy and Negro Boycott. Situations similar to the one just pictured are very much more likely to result in mob activities now than prior to the disturbance at Emelle. White people are generally conscious of the fact that to maintain "white supremacy" they are forced to take no chances with Negroes. As a part of this control, Negroes are kept economically and otherwise dependent upon them; and even now, when most Negro tenants in the county are barely able to pay the rent promised, one hears not infrequently that the chief trouble with the Negroes is that they are making too much money. And so one of the after effects of the Emelle trouble is that white people in general will further justify whatever steps are necessary, regardless of their ethical implications, to keep the Negro dependent and powerless.

The Negroes in the Emelle community are using the boycott as a weapon of revenge. Silently but certainly they do practically all their cash trading in Livingston and York. Two stores at Emelle were closed within six months after the trouble, and the volume of business in the others has fallen off. As gestures of friendliness the white people of Emelle have given three barbecues for Negroes, but the latter have stayed away pretending to believe that the white people are now trying to poison them.

FACTS ABOUT THE COMMUNITY

Sumter County, Alabama, is on the extreme western border of the state, midway between the Gulf and the Tennessee line. It is within the Gulf Coastal Plain, is generally level, and has a mean altitude of less than two hundred feet above sea level. The county is drained by a system of small streams which empty into the Tombigbee River, navigable for small river craft, flowing along the entire eastern boundary of the county from northwest to southeast. All of the streams have Indian names, except two, Factory Creek and Tom's Creek. The latter commemorates an Indian-Negro family, and the former received its name from an Indian trading post, or factorage.

Emigration of Indians. Prior to the treaty of Dancing Rabbit in 1830, this section was occupied by Choctaws, but in accordance with that treaty the Indians trekked westward in 1831.

Concerning their departure, in his *History of Alabama*, Thomas M. Owen wrote: "On the banks of the Bodaka Creek, there are two or three high hills, and all of the Choctaws rendezvoused on these hills just before their emigration. Here they remained for three days, lifting their voices in wailing lamentations, performing their religious rites, and here from the summits of the hills, they took their last look over the beautiful country which they were to see no more."

A Wealthy Indian-Negro Family. When the first white settlers arrived in this area to take up lands, according to Owen, "they found a wealthy Indian-Negro family, owning Negro slaves, living on Factory Creek. Sallie Tom, the widow of an Indian who had secured a large tract of land under the stipulation of the Treaty of Dancing Rabbit, was head of the family. She had several sons and two married daughters. None of the family followed the Indians west. Jack Tom, one of the sons, was a well educated man. After the death of his mother he sold fifteen or twenty slaves to Major John C. Whitsitt, and about six thousand acres of land to Mr. Gerry Brown. Tom's Creek, a tributary of Factory Creek, commemorates the name of this early free Negro family."

White People from Everywhere. Upon the heels of the departing Indians came white people by thousands to take up the fertile lands. In 1832, a new county was laid off; it was named Sumter in honor of the South Carolina general of Revolutionary fame. The county seat, located near a large spring which had been frequented by the Indians, was called Livingston to honor Edward Livingston of Louisiana.

Between 1831 and 1840 the white and Negro population of Sumter County rose from a dozen or so to 29,937. Only one census, 1900 with 32,710, showed a larger total population than 1840, the first census year.

Temporary Haven for Poor Whites. Poor whites, pushed off the land to the east of the Tombigbee River by the development of plantation farming there, rushed into the newly opened territory. At the same time wealthy planters from South Carolina, North Carolina, Virginia, and Tennessee were leaving their exhausted plantations for the rich black soil of Sumter County.

The poor whites stayed on the rich soil but a short time, however, for they were soon pushed off by new slave planta-

tions, just as they had already been pushed off the best lands
in central Alabama. The Negro element, which outnumbered
the whites five years after the Indians left, continued to be
increasingly more evident until 1900 when 82.7 per cent of
the county's population were Negroes. Since the turn of the
century, when plantation farming reached its zenith, the number of Negroes has been on the decrease and the number of
whites on the increase. At no time since 1860, however, has
the white population been half what it was in 1840. There
have been scarcely any foreign-born whites in the county's
population—in 1930 less than one-tenth of one per cent as
compared with six-tenths of one per cent for the entire state.

Fertile Soil and Big Plantations. The Negroes are concentrated upon the rich black lands in the northern half of the
county where the area is taken up by big plantations. In the
post oak flats and sandy knolls regions, small farms are inter-
spersed with swamp lands and pine barrens. Less than forty
per cent of the land in the county is in farms, as compared with
over fifty per cent for the entire state. The population density
is but 28.2 per square mile as against the state average of 48.8.

Emelle, a small trading center, has only five residences, a
half-dozen stores, two garages, a postoffice, and a cotton gin.
It is located in the plantation area where Negroes outnumber
the whites almost twenty to one.

Negro Gang Laborers and Croppers. In some instances the
plantations are cultivated by gangs of field hands working
for wages under overseers; other large tracts are cultivated
by share croppers under the direction of the plantation owner
or his "riding agent"; occasionally a large tract is rented
for a stipulated amount of cotton to some frugal white or
Negro family who works part of it and sub-rents the remainder.
In 1925, seventy-one tracts of five hundred acres and over—
approximately one-fourth of the cultivated land in the County
—were worked by gang labor. This is typical of no section of
Alabama outside the black soil belt. Of the remaining 2,824
farms in the county, 2,311, or eighty per cent, were operated
by tenants, mostly of the cropper type. All the gang labor

plantations utilize Negro workers, and approximately ninety-five per cent of all tenants are Negroes.

With the partial disintegration of plantation farming since 1900 a few of the large plantations have been sold, and the number of Negro owners has increased. In 1925 there were 296 Negro farmers on their own land. Some of these had secured their farms from resident planters, but most had bought land from big sawmilling interests operating on land least attractive to white planters. Several Negroes, including the Robinson family, had bought farms from an estate adminis-tered by the leading white planter.

In the entire county there are but six Negro business enter-prises, chiefly at Livingston, and with the exception of two grocery stores, none is of any consequence. In and around Emelle Negroes operate no business of any kind. Except for untrained and poorly paid preachers and teachers, professional Negroes are lacking in the county.

Cotton and Corn. The crops of Sumter County are cotton and corn, about 30,000 acres being devoted to the latter and 50,000 to the former. The average yield of corn is between twelve and fifteen bushels per acre. The annual cotton crop ranges between fifteen and twenty thousand bales. The next largest acreage, less than one-fifth of that of corn, is devoted to legumes and wild hay. Less than a thousand acres is used for sweet potatoes and all other vegetables.

There is practically no dairy or poultry industry in the county. Livestock farming is limited to a few beef herds and to scrub pigs and cows kept by the farm families, four-fifths of whom are tenants without facilities for the care of more than a few pigs and a cow-on-a-chain. Besides, cotton farmers usually find livestock a bother at chopping and picking time.

County's Low Economic Rating. Economically, Sumter County ranks much below the average for the state. In 1925 the value of farm crops and manufactured products was $152.31 per capita in Sumter and $286.93 in Alabama; the re-lation was similar in 1919 with each one-fourth higher. The per capita amount of bank deposits in 1929 was $41.07 in the county and $107.07 in the state. In September of 1930 the county's largest bank, at Livingston, closed its doors and the depositors do not hope for more than part settlement.

While the great mass of people are propertyless Negro farm tenants on big plantations, the landowners themselves are not generally wealthy, though some few are well-to-do as Southern farm owners go these days. In 1924 there were 154 income tax returns made in the county, or one for each 162 persons, as compared with one return for each 56 persons throughout Alabama; by 1927 the number in Sumter had fallen to one return for each 283 persons, while the state rate was one to each 98 persons. The county's returns were also smaller than the general state average.

A Rural County With Impassable Winter Roads. Six-sevenths of Sumter's people live in the open country and the remainder in six towns. The largest of these is York with 1,796; then follow Livingston with 1,072, Gainesville with 329, and Cuba, Geiger and Epps. These are mere farm trading centers with the exception of York, where the railroad junction and shops offer employment to a number of people, and Livingston, which besides being the county seat is the site of the Livingston State Normal School for Girls with a faculty of twenty-eight and a resident student body of less than four hundred.

There are small banks at Livingston, York, and Cuba, and at all of the towns the usual stores and garages, hotels or boarding houses, cafes and lunch stands, cotton gins and cotton warehouses. As in other Southern rural communities, practically all the professional men in the county, most of whom are also plantation owners, live in the towns.

North and east of Emelle, in the heart of the plantation area, several large plantation owners live in manorial homesteads built before the War Between the States. The Negroes looked to this landed gentry for protection during the disorders of July, 1930.

The county is served by the Southern Railroad and the Alabama, Tennessee and Northern Railroad. An improved state highway, part of which is hard surfaced, parallels the

Southern main line. The remainder of the county is served by a system of county roads, rough in dry weather and in wet weather slick and full of ruts. In winter, many of the roads—even that between Livingston and Emelle—become impassable for autos.

Public Schools. Public school conditions in Sumter County are much better than a decade ago, due to the efforts of the present county superintendent. Recently a new brick plant was built at York for white children, other white schools have been improved, and all but three of the one-teacher white schools have been consolidated. Negro schools, too, have been improved: A Negro school supervisor is employed by the county; a half-dozen Rosenwald schools have been built, one of which is the Teacher Training School, located on the paved highway a mile north of Livingston. In 1930 this school had a total enrollment of 443, with 119 and 52 in the junior and senior high school departments, respectively.

By its superior work and better equipment, this Training School is having a wholesome influence upon Negro education throughout the county. Many of its graduates are employed in the county schools, usually supplanting older and less well trained teachers.

A Sordid Contrast. According to the 1928 school census, there were 1,889 white children and 10,191 Negro children of school age in Sumter County. The term for Negro high schools was 137 days, and for Negro elementary schools 86 days; that of the white schools was 176 days. A white teacher was provided for each thirty-two children, a Negro teacher for each 110. There were in the county fifty-nine one-teacher Negro schools, eight two-teacher, and four three-teacher, while only the County Training School had more. In the 1928-1929 scholastic year, the total current expense per school age white child was $53.75, while that for the Negro child was but $2.41. The white child state average was $34.89, the Negro child state average $9.39. Sumter County's white teachers received an average annual salary of $1,187, while the Negro teachers received $217; the state average for white teachers was $872 and for Negro teachers $368. The eighty-six elementary

Negro teachers in Sumter averaged $171 per year, in Alabama $323; the sixteen high school teachers in the county $445, in the state $741.

The value of Sumter County's school property was $345 per white child and $8.35 per Negro child; nevertheless, during the scholastic year (1928-1929), $162,761 of public funds were used by the county school board for new buildings and equipment for the less than two thousand white children, and only $210 for improvement of buildings and equipment for the ten thousand Negro children. For the transportation of less than six hundred white students, the sum of $17,666 was spent by the county, while for all Negro educational purposes the county spent but $24,848, which sum included $1,017 of the county superintendent's salary, $163 for the school board, $271 for compulsory education, $1,490 for the Negro supervisor, and $210 for buildings and equipment. The total educational outlay of county and state funds in 1928-1929 was $150.03 for each white child, and $2.44 for each Negro child of school age.

Dogmatic Landlords, Indifferent Parents, Uninspired Children. Most landlords and a goodly proportion of the Negro parents seem satisfied with this situation. In this plantation county all hands, little and big, are needed for chopping cotton in the spring and picking it in the fall. It is common to find big planters who see Negroes only in terms of their profitable use as hired hands or tenants, who assert that education is ruinous to them. Sorry schools, poorly paid and poorly trained teachers, indifferent parents, uninspired children and dogmatic landlords have contributed to an abnormal rate of illiteracy and near-illiteracy among the Negroes.

In 1930, 32.5 per cent of Sumter County's Negroes over ten years of age were illiterate, against 1.0 per cent of the whites; for Alabama 26.2 per cent of Negroes and 4.8 per cent of whites. In 1928, there were in the county 1,545 illiterate Negroes between the ages of seven and twenty-one. Near-illiteracy is almost as great a problem. Of 10,191 Negro children of school age, only 5,204 were enrolled in 1928-1929 and of this number 46.4 per cent were in the first grade, as compared with 11.6 per cent of the white enrollment.

A smaller proportion of Negro boys than of girls were in school, and the boys made the slower advancement. Boys outnumbered girls in only the first and second grades; from the third grade through the sixth, boys made up but 42.6 per cent of the enrollment, and in the high school grades, only 28.6 per cent; of 1929's fifteen Negro high school graduates only two were boys.

Church Membership Unusually High. In 1926, the proportion of church membership in the county was unusually high. A little more than three-fourths of the whites of fifteen years and over were members, as compared with sixty-two per cent throughout the state, and over ninety per cent of the Negroes over against eighty-two per cent for the entire state.

The county's white church membership of 3,703 was divided as follows: Methodist Episcopal South 1,820, Methodist Protestant seventy-three, Southern Baptist 1,178, Primitive Baptist eight, Presbyterian 596, and Episcopalian twenty-eight. The Southern Methodists are members of churches belonging to either the York, Livingston, or Gainesville Circuits, each of which is made up of one town and four rural churches. There are nine Southern Baptist churches, the largest ones—York with 400 members, Cuba with 219 and Siloam with 203—are in the southern part of the county where the land is poorest and the proportion of whites is greatest. The Baptist Church at Livingston has a membership of 153 and the pastor's salary is $1,375, the largest preacher's salary in the county. Four of the Baptist churches have a membership of less than seventy each and five pay less than $300 pastor's salary. The Baptist and Methodist denominations are strongest in the southern part of the county, and the Presbyterian and Episcopalian in the plantation area to the north. Six of the eight Presbyterian churches, including the one near Emelle, have less than fifty members each.

Of the 13,088 Negro church members in 1926, 10,780 were Missionary Baptists, 154 were Primitive Baptists, and the others were Methodists; A. M. E. Z., 1,383; C. M. E., 494; M. E., 142; and A. M. E., 135. It is estimated that there are well over a hundred Negro churches in this county, nearly seventy of which are Baptist.

In July, 1930, when the killings were going on—one white man and two Negroes, and then another white man and two more Negroes—what responsibility did all these churches assume? None whatever beyond this: The two white men were buried from white churches, crowded with their kinsmen and friends humiliated that death should have been dealt them by "niggers"; and the four Negroes, one a preacher, were buried from their churches amid the numb silence of the inarticulate black folk who dared not curse or shout lest the landed white gentry cut off their rations or the man-hunting whites cut off yet other lives. Like the school authorities and other public officials, the ministers and church members conform fully to the social and economic situation which dictates, above everything else, that the rule of the white minority be complete and unchallenged.

Four-fifths Black—Nine-tenths Democratic. Sumter County, with four-fifths of its population Negro, always goes Democratic by about ten to one. The total vote in the 1924 presidential election was 837 Democratic, twenty-eight Republican, and nineteen Progressive; in 1928, 1,011 Democratic, and 118 Republican. Since the state came near going Republican, it is obvious that Sumter is not a typical Alabama County. The white people look upon the Democratic party as the champion of white man's government; no Negroes vote in local or state elections, and but few in national elections. In 1928, the total number of votes cast was slightly less than one-third of the county's white population of voting age.

The welfare agencies of Sumter County are limited to the schools and churches described above, and to white and Negro county farm agents and a white home demonstration agent. There is no public library, hospital, or Red Cross organization, and no public health officer or social worker in the county.

Slave Time Patterns. In the Emelle community white people do scarcely any manual labor, most of them being of the landed families or doing business as cotton gin owners, small town merchants, and gas station operators. Slave-time patterns are evident. Instances like this are not uncommonly reported: A Negro tenant rented a farm for two bales; he made an extraordinarily large yield and at settlement time the landlord took three bales, saying, "Well, even after you pay me the three bales you will have plenty left to pay all your other expenses." A few planters get laborers from the courts by paying their fines, but this provides opportunity for the exploitation of only a few. The custom of taking no tenant, except with the consent of the plantation owner whose place he is leaving, makes it possible for unscrupulous landlords to hold their tenants in virtual peonage year after year.

This practice they justify on the ground that only in this way can Negroes be controlled.

As in slave times, many white men in the plantation area feel that they have certain privileges with Negro girls and women. Near Emelle there is at present a landed white man who lives with a Negro woman, and by her has several children. It is reported that a prominent citizen of Livingston virtually lived with a well-known Negro woman. The following from Fleming's *Civil War and Reconstruction in Alabama* suggests backgrounds: "In Sumter County (in 1868) one Prince, who had a Negro wife, was registrar, superintendent of schools, postmaster and circuit clerk."

The relation between the races at present precludes any great exercise of independence on the part of even Negro landowners. Within the past quarter century several of the large planters have sold land to Negroes. Some were personally interested in certain Negroes having homes of their own, others found the successful Negro tenants the best available market for their less valuable tracts. The Negro purchasers are very conscious of their dependence upon the white men who made ownership possible for them; and, though not as servile as the landless Negroes, they are far from being independent farmers. Their avenue into ownership, as well as their security in ownership, was and is contingent upon their being acceptable; and being acceptable in this Black Belt county means that they will be punctiliously servile to the whites and find no fault with existing educational, social, political, and economic conditions.

CHAPTER V

"DECENT BURIAL" FOR LYNCHED PAIR
SCOOBA, KEMPER COUNTY, MISSISSIPPI

Mid-morning of September 10, 1930, "Pig" Lockett and Holly White, Negroes, were taken from two Kemper County deputies and lynched. The masked mob came upon the officers while they were taking the Negroes, accused of robbery, from the county jail at DeKalb to Scooba for preliminary trial. In ater afternoon one of the mob leaders bought coffins so the ynched pair could have "decent burial."

THE LYNCHINGS

Reports of the Alleged Crime. Shortly after ten o'clock on the night of September 6, the little town of Wahalak, a flag station on the M. and O. Railroad in north Kemper County, was all astir. A young couple, said to have been recently married, had been brought to the local store by a passing motorist. They reported that about ten o'clock, just before reaching Wahalak, three Negroes halted them by waiving a flashlight, and took forty-five dollars from the man and a wedding ring from the woman. After having secured these valuables, one of the Negroes, they reported, looked at the man and said, "I've a good notion to kill you and throw you in a ditch. We will not kill your wife; we can use her." The man plead for his life. In the meanwhile, to effect an easy escape, the Negroes had thrown away his car keys. At this juncture an approaching automobile, the one which carried the couple to Wahalak, caused the Negroes to make a hurried escape.

When the couple reached Wahalak the few white people there became very much excited. They called to DeKalb, the county seat, for the sheriff, to Scooba, the nearest town, for help to

capture the Negroes, and to Meridian for the Jenkins' bloodhounds. The town clerk and other Scooba citizens rushed to
Wahalak.

After a few hours the bloodhounds from Meridian arrived.
Haltingly they followed a trail from the scene of the alleged
robbery to a Negro cabin where "Pig" Lockett and Holly
White were arrested. The two Negroes had attended a revival
meeting at Scooba on the night of the alleged robbery, and
had left about 9:30, before the service was over. Two nights
previous at the mourners' bench Lockett and White had been
the center of much shouting and emotional confusion.

When the Negroes were arrested a considerable number of
the man-hunters expressed the desire to make short work of
them. The man who professed he had been robbed, though
greatly excited, finally agreed that the officers might take
the Negroes to the county jail at DeKalb. No ring or money
was found on the Negroes and they made no confession. Since
their route home from church led past the scene of the alleged
robbery, the fact that bloodhounds picked up their trail did
not necessarily incriminate them.

*Negroes Lynched in Presence of Officers after Unique Third
Degree.* The Negroes remained in jail at DeKalb until the morning of September 10, when Marshal Guy Byrd of Scooba and
Constable J. J. Dotson of the eastern district of the county
started with them toward Scooba for a preliminary trial. The
officers left DeKalb about nine in the morning, driving leisurely.
When about six miles out, where the road passed through a
wood, the mob is reported to have come upon the officers and
caught them so completely off their guard that not a shot was
fired in defense of the prisoners. The masked members of the
mob, twenty or thirty in number, made known their wishes
to the officers in no uncertain terms, assuring them that they
would not be harmed so long as they made no attempt to protect their prisoners.

The officers were tied, backs together, to a tree, and within
their full view the two Negroes were hanged, but not until the
mob had tried to secure confessions from them. Ropes were
fastened around their necks; when they persisted in denying

their guilt they were lifted off the ground, and then let back down to talk; again they were pulled up, and again let down. Steadfastly refusing to implicate himself, one was finally strangled to death; the other, it is reported, at last gasped out a confession of the robbery. After this he also was hanged.

According to a professed onlooker, the following method was employed by the mob in each case: A small tree was pulled over by a dozen or so lynchers; a short rope, tied to the bent-over tree, was fastened immediately around the Negro's neck. In trying to get a confession they allowed the tree to spring up enough to raise the Negro off the ground. When everything was ready, all let go the tree and the Negro was jerked up "like a kitten."

Traveling Salesman's Protest Resented. While the Negroes were being tortured, two salesmen from Meridian came along the road. Recognizing some of the lynchers, one of the two suggested that maybe the Negroes were not guilty, and that even if they were guilty severe punishment would certainly be visited by the courts. His interference was resented, and he was curtly told to move on up the road if he did not want to see what was going on. When he persisted, his mob acquaintances warned him to get away, and that right quick, or he would be strung up, too. The salesmen left immediately and reported the affair at Scooba.

The lynchings occurred in the middle of the forenoon. During the remainder of the day people from DeKalb, Scooba, and other parts of Kemper and surrounding counties rode out to see the two limp warnings.

Fourth and Fifth Grade Mob Victims. "Pig" Lockett, twenty-one years old, and Holly White, nineteen, were born and reared in Kemper County. In the local one-teacher school, they had reached the fourth and fifth grades, respectively. Both were unmarried. Neither had a court record: White was not known ever to have been involved in any disorderly conduct; Lockett's single offense, which did not come into court, was that of shooting at another Negro. Both had the general reputation of being very good farm laborers, though dull and slothful.

"Decent Burial" Arranged by Mob Leaders. When evening came, a reported member of the mob, a planter, went to Scooba and bought two cheap coffins. This planter, active in the local church, felt that it would be sacrilegious not to give the victims a "decent burial."

On September 9, the day before the Negroes were lynched, two men said to be leaders of the mob had been in Scooba and had secured from Marshal Byrd and Constable Dotson information concerning the exact time of next day's trial and the movement of the prisoners from DeKalb to Scooba. With this information, it is said, they returned to Wahalak and organized a mob. A message to Tennessee brought three loaded cars.

What became of the third Negro accused in the case? Though nothing definite is known, it is reported that some of the young white men around Wahalak found him shortly after Lockett and White were taken to the DeKalb jail, and disposed of him in their own way. On several occasions, it is said, white boys around Wahalak when drinking, have said: "Ah! that third nigger won't never bother nobody no more."

REACTION OF THE COMMUNITY TO THE LYNCHINGS

What the people of Scooba and other communities in Kemper County felt concerning the lynchings can be judged by the fact that the local papers carried only brief mention of it, the preachers did not mention it, a woman's organization refused to have it discussed, and people in general, although not convinced of the Negroes' guilt, found no fault with their fate.

Action of Courts. The courts have done nothing. Although a brief grand jury investigation was conducted, no indictments were brought.

Local Paper Devoted Two Sentences to Two Lynchings. The Scooba weekly paper, *Kemper Herald*, carried only this two-sentence news item concerning the affair:

"Pig Lockett and Holly White, Negroes accused of holding up and robbing Mr. and Mrs. Thomas McCoy and threatening their

lives on highway 45 several nights ago were taken from officers
Dotson and Byrd Wednesday morning when they were being
brought to Scooba for preliminary trial, and hanged. The officers
were tied to trees and their guns taken from them."

The editor stated that it was his policy to give matters of
this kind only the briefest mention. It should be pointed out,
however, that most of the space of the four-sheet *Kemper
Herald* is taken up by advertisements and plate matter. It was
from the editor of this sheet, who is the mayor of Scooba, sometime Presbyterian preacher and undertaker, that the coffins
were bought. The county's other weekly paper, the DeKalb
Sentinel, carried only a brief mention of the lynching.

The Meridian *Star* devoted considerable space to both the
alleged robbery and the lynchings. Both stories were carried
under full page headlines, "Negroes Rob and Threaten to
Kill Couple," and "Lynched—Two Blacks." These reports were
detailed and for the most part accurate. The policy of this
paper is decidedly anti-lynching.

Press Releases Generally Misleading. Other Mississippi
papers, along with the leading dailies of the Southern States,
carried Associated or United Press releases. The United Press
release seemed to overstate the anti-lynching sentiment of
Scooba citizens:

"Scooba, Miss.—Lynching near here yesterday of two Negroes
charged with highway robbery brought open condemnation by
citizens of Scooba today. Altho officials remained silent, it was
believed an investigation would be conducted to determine the
leaders of the mob.

"Doubt was manifest by both citizens and authorities as to the
guilt of the Negroes."

No evidence was found of more than a half-dozen Scooba
white people who were dissatisfied with the lynchings. The
release is correct, however, in its statement as to doubt of the
Negroes' guilt. The Associated Press release stating that
they took forty-five dollars from the man and threatened his

wife could well have used the introductory phrase, "According to local reports."

Statements of Scooba Officials. Scooba's mayor, from whom the coffins were bought to provide a "decent burial," stated that he knew nothing whatever about the lynchings other than as generally reported. He accepted at face value the story told by the couple. Others, however, expressed doubt concerning the whole affair, pointing out that no positive evidence had been found against the Negroes other than the bloodhounds' halting trek to the cabin. The opinion was expressed also that the couple might have hatched up the story of robbery in order to enlist sympathy and get money with which to continue their motor trip. It is a fact that they stayed in the community till they received in donations an amount of money equal to that of which they claimed they had been robbed.

One of Scooba's town officials rushed to Wahalak soon after the alleged robbery. According to his statement, he is convinced that Lockett and White were guilty. He stated that he had talked with the man and woman separately and that their stories were identical. This official reported with alarm an increase of intimate relations between white women and Negro men and advocated the establishment of a red light district, with white and Negro women, in which only white men would be allowed.

The modern hotel situation, so he stated, encourages the consorting of lewd white women with Negro bell boys through whom they secure patronage. Curiously enough, while damning the bell boys in scathing terms, he found no fault with the white women who consort with them.

Captain Jack's Explanation of Officers' Deaths. The one person in Scooba who wholeheartedly denounced the lynchings was Guy Jack, referred to later in this report as the author of *Captain Guy Jack's Iconoclast.* He stated that he believed Town Marshal Byrd, Deputy Sheriff Dotson, and another officer most certainly knew that an attempt was going to be made to lynch the Negroes. Two of these officers died shortly after the lynchings: One was killed by a bootleg runner, and the other died of sickness. Captain Jack stated that every time he saw the surviving member of the trio he inquired solicitously about his health, implying that he is expecting him, too, to die ere long. The officer was said to have become somewhat depressed. The Captain stated that members of the recent mob were nearly all young roustabouts, the same kind of white people who had made up every Kemper County mob he knew about.

No Church Pronouncement Against Lynching. The resident white ministers of the Methodist and Baptist denominations stated that nothing was said in either of their churches about the lynchings. Any reference to the matter, they felt, could have resulted only in dissension, for while some would certainly have joined in a protest against mob violence, the majority would have resented any mention of it.

When Captain Jack's daughter, who lives in Scooba and teachers school in Meridian, mentioned the lynchings at a missionary meeting she was told very definitely not to hurt their campaign for missionary funds by discussions of mob violence and the racial situation.

The president of Scooba's other woman's missionary society, at a meeting shortly after the lynchings, expressed doubt of the Negroes' guilt and the opinion that the lynchings were a disgrace to the county and should be soundly denounced. The society, however, did not support her in these statements. Here, as in most rural Black Belt counties, it is assumed that it is the business of the church to "save" people and that it has no obligation in matters of this kind.

FACTS ABOUT THE COMMUNITY

Similar to Sumter County, Alabama. Kemper County, along with more than a score of other counties in eastern Mississippi and extreme western Alabama, midway between the Tennessee State line and the Gulf of Mexico, was laid off from territory secured from the Choctaw Indians by the Treaty of Dancing Rabbit in 1830. The adjoining county on the east, Sumter County, Alabama, where the Emelle lynching occurred a month earlier, was formed from this same tract of land. Since the two counties lie side by side, and are much the same in background and in social and economic conditions, the Emelle case study will generally suffice as a picture of past and present conditions in Kemper County, Mississippi.

The principal differences between the Mississippi county and its Alabama neighbor are matters of degree rather than kind, and in every instance the Mississippi county trails: It has poorer railroad connections, fewer miles of improved highways, smaller towns, poorer schools, weaker churches, worse political records, and cruder human relations. The poor conditions of the Alabama county, already presented, are exaggerated in the Mississippi county. In so far as inadequate institutions and unwholesome human relations are concerned, Kemper County is just like Sumter County—only more so.

"Captain Guy Jack's Iconoclast." This is the name of a suppressed pamphlet which purports to be "an exposure of hypocritical Christians and corrupt Jews," setting forth the crimes in high and low places which earned for the county the name of "Bloody Kemper."

The author describes how the merchants on Scooba's one business block have burned themselves out at intervals to cash in on their fire insurance. Some of the most horrible crimes exposed were charged to a triumvirate—a lawyer, a doctor, and a life insurance agent—which developed a murderously novel way of securing money from life insurance companies. The procedure was described as follows: The three would decide upon some person who "needed" insurance, and unknown to that person a policy would be written. The medical blank, filled in by the doctor, and the papers signed by the "contracting parties" were sent in with the first premium. Not infrequently the "insured person" was chosen because of some fatal malady which promised an early demise. As the legal representative for the estate of the deceased, the lawyer would get a settlement from the life insurance company and divide with his confederates. In other instances simple white folks and Negroes were insured. The doctor provided the poison—sometime administering it through his own medicines—and filled in the death certificate; the victim was buried by ignorant, unsuspecting kinsmen; the lawyer "administering the estate" got the insurance money; the doctor, lawyer, and life insurance agent shared the profits.

A few of Captain Jack's thirty chapters are as follows: "Scooba's First Great Fire," "The Devil Riding the Insurance Companies," "White and Black Victims of Poison," "Persecuting the Widows and Orphans," "The Devil's Den in Kemper County," "Mob Violence and Its Damnable, Destructive Influence," "Shyster Lawyers, Dastard Life Insurance Operation—Bribery and Confessions," "Exposure Kemper County, Mississippi, Jew Bank President of Murder, Arson, and Robbery, Life and Fire Insurance Companies," and "Dramatic Trial and Acquittal of Captain Guy Jack of Charges of Criminal Libel Preferred by Ex-Mississippi Officials." He presented names and dates of the crimes attributed to his neighbors, and was arrested and jailed on charges of criminal libel. He was acquitted, and several of the persons he accused, including a banker, were given penitentiary sentences.

As might be expected, Kemper County has had more than twice as many lynchings as the average Mississippi county.

CHAPTER VI

"IMPERIAL BOLIVAR" AND WHAT IT MEANS
ROSEDALE, BOLIVAR COUNTY, MISSISSIPPI

ABOUT MID-MORNING of April 23, 1930, Dave Harris, Negro, was lynched near Waxhall, seven miles north of Rosedale, Bolivar County, Mississippi. He had killed Clayton Funderberg, a seventeen-year-old white tenant, the evening before.

THE LYNCHING

White Tenant Killed in Altercation with Negroes. Dave Harris, hostler on the Scott plantation near Waxhall seven miles north of Rosedale, sold liquor. There are two stories, differing only in details, as to the events leading up to the trouble. That accepted by the Negroes of the community was that Funderberg was one of Harris' customers and was shot in an altercation about his unpaid liquor bill. With two of his friends he had gone to Harris' cabin where, according to this version, he made demands for more liquor. On being refused, he threatened Harris, who retaliated with a shot that killed Funderberg.

The story told by the white people agrees with the above as to the visit of Funderberg and his friends, but holds that they had gone to remonstrate with Harris because of the alleged theft of some of Funderberg's groceries. The Negro denied the theft and killed Funderberg in the altercation which developed.

Assured of Man-Hunter's Success, Deputy Returns to Courthouse Office. Funderberg's two friends reported the affair immediately. A searching party was organized. After some time, news of the killing was received by the deputy sheriff at Rosedale, who immediately went to Waxhall. Upon being assured that a large number of people were close on the Negro's trail, the deputy sheriff expressed satisfaction with the way the affair was being handled, and returned to his office in Rosedale. The sheriff at Cleveland was also called, but was engaged in court and did not respond.

Aided by bloodhounds, the man-hunters, about two hundred in number, kept on Harris' track throughout the night and captured him the next morning about eight-thirty, when his hiding place in a corn crib was revealed by another Negro. He was carried directly to the Mississippi levee, a short distance away, where he was tied to a tree, hands behind him, and his body was riddled with bullets. A plantation owner reports that he heard the fusillade, and is certain there were no less than two hundred shots.

The Victims, Black and White. Dave Harris, forty years old, had a wife and several children. He was generally known as a bootlegger and a fighter. But according to a local planter, on whose place he lived for several years, he was an excellent worker. He had no court record.

Clayton Funderberg, seventeen-year-old, unmarried, white tenant, had come to Waxhall a year earlier from Calhoun County, in north central Mississippi; he was from the same locality as most of the other Waxhall tenant whites. Though generally known as a hard drinker, he had been in no previous trouble in Bolivar County.

It is reported that the Negro who revealed Harris' hiding place was "gotten rid of" shortly after the lynching. It was said that he was associated with competitive liquor interests, and that the Harris crowd avenged his betrayal of their confederate.

The mob which lynched Dave Harris was composed almost exclusively of tenant whites living in the Waxhall community; most of them were from the white-tenant plantation, having come into Bolivar County within the past five years.

REACTION OF THE COMMUNITY TO THE LYNCHING

As one would expect from what has been said already, the lynching caused little excitement, and no one has been indicted.

Not News for Local Paper. Rosedale's weekly, the *Bolivar County Democrat*, made no mention of the lynching, seven miles away. The editor, a woman, explained that she did not know anything about the matter until some time afterward; besides, it was her policy not to mention things of this kind, since publicity on such matters merely results in a lot of adverse criticism by outside papers. The only reference ever made to the lynching in the Rosedale paper was the reprinting of an editorial, "No Criticism Deserved," from Cleveland's *Bolivar Commercial:*

"We have noted in the press several severe criticisms of Bolivar County officers on account of the lynching near Gunnison a short time ago.

"Those who are making these criticisms do not know that at the time of this unfortunate occurrence the entire force of deputies in the county was concentrated here at Cleveland to protect from imminent violence the lives of two other poeple. The peace-officer of the county cannot be expected to be in all places at once, an. we think that they have done an exceptional piece of work in preventing violence here. . . .

"That the lynching occurred in the First Judicial District is to be deplored. To investigate the matter, however, would be entirely futile. No hope of conviction could be entertained, in view of local sentiment. Such occurrences are reflections on the citizenship, rather than on the small force of peace-officers."

The Cleveland *Enterprise*, Bolivar County's third weekly, carried this brief item:

"Dave Harris, Negro, who mortally wounded Clayton Funderberg, a white tenant on a farm near Gunnison Monday, was shot to death yesterday near the scene of the trouble with young Funderberg. The demand of the officers of the law that he be given into their custody was ignored by the 200 men who had been hunting him, and he was handcuffed and tied to a tree. It is said that not less than 200 shots were fired at him."

But few other news items, and these very brief, appeared in the white dailies of the South. The Memphis *Commercial Appeal*, with detailed reports, was the one exception. A news release by the Associated Negro Press was carried by practically all the larger Negro papers. This report, though wrong in a few details, was for the most part accurate.

No Court Investigation for Six Months. Most of the Negro papers commented upon an alleged report from a deputy sheriff that it was very doubtful if any inquest would be held over the body, and even more doubtful if a special investigation would be made of the lynching. The Norfolk *Journal and Guide* put it this way:

"According to beliefs expressed here (Rosedale) following the brutal lynching of Dave Harris, 40 year old father, not even the customary perfunctory investigation of the mob murder will be conducted until the next session of the court which convenes in about six months."

The investigation held at Rosedale six months after Harris had been lynched was disposed of as routine business; no one was surprised that no indictments were drawn. The investigation amounted to nothing more than an entry on the court records that a lynching had been investigated.

Leading Whites Had Forgotten About the Lynching. Before Dave Harris had been dead a year, many of Rosedale's leading white people recalled with difficulty the most general facts concerning the lynching. A resident minister, along with many others, had forgotten whether it occurred in the spring of 1930, the fall of 1929, or at some other time. While the white people of Rosedale looked upon it as an outside affair, and, therefore, of little local interest, those of Waxhall, many of whom were directly or indirectly involved, look upon the matter as their own business.

The Negroes were not greatly disturbed by the lynching, being already inured to the undisputed domination of the whites. In Bolivar County, with an average of one lynching every four years, such occurrences are a part of the normal picture.

FACTS ABOUT THE COMMUNITY

On the Banks of the Mississippi. Bolivar, second largest county in the State of Mississippi, and one of the most fertile and most populous rural counties in the South, has earned the name of "Imperial Bolivar" by reason of its wealth and prestige on the one hand and its political self-sufficiency on the other. It is, so to speak, a nation within itself.

It is in the northern half of west Mississippi, with the great river forming its western boundary. The white man's first public claim to this territory was established early in the nineteenth century when Andrew Jackson and Thomas Hines were commissioned by the United States government to secure from the Indians a tract of more than 5,000,000 acres in the fertile Yazoo Valley. Later, in 1830, by the Treaty of Dancing Rabbit,[1] the Choctaw Indians relinquished certain other claims to this territory.

Bolivar County was settled from the Mississippi River eastward; its population has increased regularly up to the present. After 1850 the fertile lands immediately along the river were opened up rapidly by the issuance of land script, in payment for the construction of levees. This work was begun during the presidency of Zachary Taylor, who was a Mississippi Valley planter and knew the need of flood control.

Three Negroes to One White. In 1890 the population of the county was 29,970; in 1920, 57,669; and in 1930, 71,051. The county's continued increase has been in response to the progressive reclamation of the low bottom lands. From the outset, plantation farming has been the principal industry, and Negroes have made up a preponderant majority of the total population. In 1890, 89.2 per cent were Negroes; in 1920, 82.4 per cent; in 1930, 74.0 per cent.

Until recently there were hardly any people in the county except landed whites and landless Negroes. Three other elements are now in evidence: A few hundred landless whites from the hill county of Mississippi have come in as tenants; a relatively small number of Negroes have acquired property in the open country or in the towns; the smallest and newest element

---

[1] See case studies of Emelle and Scooba for other 1930 lynchings in territory ceded to whites by Treaty of Dancing Rabbit.

is composed of Chinese merchants in Rosedale and other river towns.

In 1930, the county's proportion of foreign-born was 0.7 per cent of the total population, nearly double the state average of 0.4 per cent. As will be seen, each of these groups has had some effect on the general racial situation.

Cotton—Nine Farm Tenants to One Owner. This is Mississippi's banner cotton county; not infrequently one-tenth of the state's entire crop is from "Imperial Bolivar." Over 200,000 acres are planted to cotton each year; the annual crop for the five-year period after 1925 was 145,714 bales. The second most important crop is corn. Here, as elsewhere in the South, however, it is a support of the cotton system rather than a competitor.

In 1930, the county had 15,949 farmers, an increase of 24.5 per cent during the decade; the state's increase was 14.8 per cent. The use of additional white tenants during the decade raised the proportion of white farmers from seven to ten per cent of the total. The antagonism which has developed between these newcomers and the Negro tenants has been noted. In 1910, ninety per cent of all farmers were tenants; fifteen years later 93.4 per cent were tenants, this being 96.3 per cent of all Negro farmers and 74.8 per cent of all white farmers.

Negro Farmers and All-Negro Towns. Twelve or fifteen years ago, when fabulous prices were being offered for labor in the Northern industrial centers, some Bolivar County planters began using Negro overseers. This aided them in retaining their laborers. Many Negro overseers are still used, not to retain labor, for now there is plenty of it, but because they are relatively less expensive. One can ride for miles along the river from Greenville toward Rosedale without seeing a white man.

At least 95 per cent of the Negro population is directly dependent upon agricultural pursuits. There are nearly five hundred Negro farm owners, more than a hundred overseers, a few commissary keepers, hundreds of farm hands, and more than ten thousand Negro farm tenants. The county virtually lives on the labor of Negro tenants and wage hands. Here, as in most of the older cotton counties, the crop is produced with a minimum of tools and a maximum of human labor, the typical equipment being limited to hoes, one-mule bull-tongue plows, and other similarly crude implements.

Negro towns have developed in these areas. With a population of 775, Mound Bayou, in the eastern part of the county, is perhaps best known. Its uniqueness as an all-Negro town is passing, due largely to the chain stores and other national organizations which are rapidly reaching out into the small communities. A second all-Negro town in this county is Chambers, with about two hundred people.

An Experiment with White Tenants. An interesting landlord-tenant experiment is now under way at Waxhall, where a leading white planter is using white tenants. Last year he had on his plantation 125 white families and one Negro family. Ten years ago he was using only Negroes. This year, he will use fewer than 100 families, because of the greater acreage each family will cultivate. These white families are encouraged to raise their meat and bread at home, and to "furnish" themselves; the planter proposes to sell them farms as soon as they so desire. This experiment is of significance for several reasons: It has brought additional tenant whites into this Negro tenant area, immediately complicating the race situation; it is based on a type of farming which makes possible a cash surplus for tenants; and it is making small farm ownership available to white people, thus affording the possibility for the development of a middle-class white element.

Decadent and Booster Towns. Just as Bolivar is the biggest cotton producing county in the state, it is also one of the most rural. In 1930, 86.4 per cent of the county's people lived in the open country and the remainder in one of eight farm trade center towns, Cleveland with 3,240 people, Rosedale with 2,221, and Shelby with 1,811 being the three largest. The county's industries are limited to cotton seed oil mills, cotton compress, a few sawmills and lumber yards, a box factory, and other smaller industrial concerns. The remainder of the townsfolk are plantation owners, professional men, bankers and merchants, shopkeepers, mechanics, domestic servants, and casual laborers.

Rosedale, on the bank of the Mississippi River has for decades remained about the same size and until recently was the largest town in the county. Everything looks old; an air of complacency pervades the once-ambitious little town. Many of the other older towns share this appearance of decadence.

In the past ten years, on the contrary, Cleveland's population increased from 1,674 to 3,240 and Rosedale lost its place as largest town. In reporting the reaction of Cleveland's mayor to the first count of the census enumerators, the Cleveland *Enterprise* said that the mayor "had a hunch that they were wrong, and immediately got in touch with the supervisor's office and in so doing added nearly one hundred to our population figure. . . . So you see after all it pays to have a mayor. . . . There is no city in the state that can boast of better advantages for residency. In the heart of the staple cotton center of the entire world, with a college and school standing that is unsurpassable, with every convenience that contributes to the comfort of the home and its occupants and with a citizenship without 'knockers,' there is just no telling what the next census figures will do for us. . . ." Cleveland boasts that it is the best city in the delta, regardless of size; that it has small but substantial growing industries, a proud citizenry, one of the state's best teacher training schools, and the largest consolidated school in the world.

In May, 1930, when Cleveland was drunk with its census report, three young men opened up the "Playmore" bowling alleys and indoor golf course. It was advertised as the only resort center of its kind between Memphis and New Orleans. With alleys equipped with automatic pin setters and comfortable settees for the players and on-lookers, the "Playmore" was up to date in every respect. Before six months had passed, however, the "Playmore" was deserted and its promoters were in bankruptcy.

Cheap Cotton and Failing Bank. Economic conditions have been at a very low ebb in Bolivar County for some years, and particularly since the fall of 1930, due to the low price of cotton. Early in 1931 Rosedale's leading bank failed as a result of the community's general financial condition. The cashier, brooding over the failure of the institution, committed suicide.

Some measures of the county's economic rank in 1930 as compared with that of the state were: There was one automobile to every 9.9 persons in Bolivar County and to 9.7 throughout the state; the estimated per capita value of taxable property was $406.28 in the county and $385.96 in the state; in bank deposits the county fell far below the state average, with $46.44 per capita, against $121.10. Almost none of the tenants have bank accounts. In 1928 there were 586 income tax returns made in the county, which was one for every 114.9 persons, while for the state there was one for every 118.2. From the above it is evident that, whereas there is a considerable element of fairly well-to-do people in the county, the great mass of the people are poor. Compared with the present, Bolivar was wealthy a decade ago. But then as now, the rural landless masses were merely making a living.

Forty-two Dollars for the White School Child to One for the Negro. On its white public schools, the county expended $45.55 a year for each white child of school age, and $1.08 for each Negro child. In the scholastic year 1928-1929, the county board of education received from the state school fund $99,-368.24 on account of its 35,708 Negro children, or $2.78 each. Of this sum, $38,765.64 was used for Negro schools. The remainder of this sum, $60,703.60, was diverted to the white schools, which received also all the county's school taxes, amounting to $113,059.10; all special local district taxes, amounting to $92,117.37; and the state funds for the whites, $17,280.48. This makes a total of $283,160.55 spent for 6,216 white children, against the $38,765.64 which was spent for the 35,708 Negro children. The Negroes made up 88.2 per cent of the school population and received 16.8 per cent of public funds; the whites with 11.8 per cent of the school population received 83.2 per cent of the public school funds.

The 1930 census reported 364 native white illiterates, 2.8

per cent of the population ten years old and over; and 11,276 Negro illiterates, or 27.1 per cent of this age-group. The state average was 2.7 per cent of whites and 23.2 per cent of Negroes.

The only Negro school with rating is the Bolivar County Training School at Cleveland; the Rosenwald Fund shared in the construction of this plant, and has made a small donation for its library. The Rosedale Negro school, second best in the county, has five teachers and a term of eight months, of which the county provides five, and the district one, while two months' expenses are borne by the Negro patrons. The present enrollment is 360. Though nominally giving instruction through the tenth grade, in 1930 there were no students enrolled above the eighth grade. The faculty consists of a principal and four assistants. The principal receives $85.00 a month; the domestic science teacher, $50.00; and the other three, $40.00 each.

Cotton-Ridden White Churches. As is typical for Southern Black Belt counties, most of the white church members are affiliated with the Southern Baptist and the Southern Methodist denominations. Of the county's 7,462 white church members in 1926. 2,298 were Southern Baptists; 1,809, Southern Methodists; 912, Roman Catholics; 351, Presbyterians; 259, Disciples of Christ; 153, Protestant Episcopalians, and 78, Jews.

The white churches in Rosedale and environs are very weak; no church has preaching every Sunday. When cotton sells well, plantation owners and their families buy expensive cars, make trips to Europe, and tune in with new radios; farm tenants and wage hands come into town and buy second-hand cars, showy clothes, brass bedsteads, and a few choice viands beyond their normal purchasing power. When cotton prices are low, the landlords and their families are depressed; the tenants go to town and return with small portions of "fat back" and corn meal. In neither situation do landlords or tenants pay very much attention to the church. When times are bad, they have nothing to give; when times are good, they go on a spree. The churches exercise the conventional functions of public worship and provide facilities for weddings, baptisms, and burials.

Unchurched Plantation Negroes. More than two-thirds of the county's 9,158 Negro church members are Baptists and nearly all the others are Methodists. The Negroes of this delta county, however, have not identified themselves with the church to the extent that they have in most Southern rural communities, nor in most Mississippi counties. In 1926 only 23.5 per cent of the county's Negro population over fifteen years of age held church membership, while in Mississippi as a whole their church membership was equal to 47.8 per cent of this age group. The county's white church membership, on the other hand, was unusually high, 89.5 per cent of the population over fifteen years of age, compared with the state average of 72.7 per cent.

$40,000 a Year to Sheriff of "Imperial Bolivar." Political affairs have always been of great concern to the minority white element. The sheriff of Bolivar County last year, so his deputy at Rosedale stated, made a net cash income, after all deputies' salaries and other expenses of his office were paid, of over $40,000. This is ten times the salary of Mississippi's Governor. In this county the sheriff collects the taxes, for which he receives a commission, and executes court orders, for which he gets fees.

Itinerant Courthouse. Bolivar County's first courthouse was a "little old shanty" twenty feet square and two stories high, built on a flatboat. The lower floor was a court room; the upper floor was used by the judge and the clerk of the court. This courthouse moved up and down the Mississippi River from one plantation to another until 1857, when the seat of justice was definitely located on the McGuire plantation, at a town called Prentiss, where a small brick courthouse was built. The seat of justice was later moved to the Bullah plantation, and finally in 1872 to Floraville, now Rosedale.

Now Two Courthouses. Bolivar County now has two courthouses, one at Rosedale in the western part of the county, and one at Cleveland in the eastern part. The second was built some years ago when the voters in the newer part of the county outnumbered those in the older western half. This, no less than the movement of the original seat of justice from one plantation to another, evinces the adaptation of public matters to plantation demands. The administration of county affairs is divided between the two centers, in accordance with the places of residence of the various officers.

The whole tradition of Bolivar County, accepted by officers, churches, and other agencies and institutions, is that each planter, much as in slave days, shall be allowed complete control of his tenants and wage hands. To all practical purposes a dead "nigger" is just a worker gone, and of no concern to the public. This tradition also determines the prevailing attitude toward Negro education and similar public matters.

Unusually Large Democratic Vote in 1928. The county is more completely Democratic than the state as a whole; in 1928 nearly ninety per cent of its presidential vote was Democratic compared to 82.9 per cent for the state. The county's total number of votes in 1928, which was 2,205, the largest ever polled, was less than six per cent of the county's population twenty-one years and over, and was equal to scarcely one-third of the adult whites. The number of votes in the state was equal to 30.4 per cent of the adult whites. The Negroes in this county, as repeatedly implied, have almost no participation in politics.

Court Sentences and Lynchings. In the June, 1930, term of Bolivar County circuit court at Cleveland, a Negro was given the death sentence for murdering another Negro. Though death sentences are common for Negroes accused of capital crimes against whites, this is said to be the first time that a court of this county ever gave a Negro the death penalty for a crime against a member of his own race. At the same term of court, a second Negro was sentenced to hang for criminal assault on a white woman, while a third received a life sentence on the same charge. Three other Negro men and one Negro woman were given life sentences, convicted of murdering other Negroes. Of the others tried in this term of court, all for less serious crimes, only one was white. He was convicted of burglary, and received a sentence of one year.

Since 1900 seven Negroes have been lynched in the county, six accused of murder and one of rape.

The Gulf Between Whites and Negroes. The lynching of many Negroes, the small expenditures for Negro education, the economic dependence of the Negroes, all measure the gulf between the races. The general relationship is still not far removed from that of master and slave. Both races seem adjusted within this situation. The Negro's traditional improvidence is encouraged virtually to the point of a requirement by nearly all white planters, assuming as they do that empty larders are prerequisite to the consistent application of the Negroes' brawn to plantation tasks. On the other hand, a full or half-filled larder may encourage the desire for more self-expression and self-direction than the plantation system will permit. Dependent Negroes are essential to the delta white man's economic, social, and political demands. This situation accounts for the many conditions of injustice and neglect which Negroes must bear in silence and with such patience as they may.

Midway Racial Position of Chinese. The small Chinese element in Bolivar and other delta counties is racially significant, because it occupies a position midway between the Negroes and the whites, thereby giving rise to unique situations. One of the best grocery stores in Rosedale is owned and operated by a Chinese. They are permitted limited social privileges with the whites in proportion as they do not mingle socially with the Negroes.

Recently in Greenville, thirty miles south, a Chinese boy who married a white girl was forced to leave. This marriage would probably have been permitted to pass, except for the fact that the boy's brother had previously married a Negro. Since that time the white people have held several anti-Chinese meetings, to which Negroes were invited. The Negroes, however, did not attend, and subsequently a white committee waited upon them to ascertain their attitude toward the Chinese. The immediate purpose of the movement was to establish a boycott against Chinese business, in which the coöperation of the Negroes was essential. Somewhat amused and silently unsympathetic with the effort, the Negroes failed to participate.

CHAPTER VII

NORTH CAROLINA SLIPS BACK
TARBORO, EDGECOMBE COUNTY, NORTH CAROLINA

SHORTLY BEFORE one o'clock on the morning of August 20, 1930, Oliver Moore, Negro, was taken from the Edgecombe County jail, hurried to a spot near the scene of his alleged crimes, suspended from a tree, and shot. He was accused of attempting to rape two white girls, aged seven and five.

THE LYNCHING

The Alleged Crime Which Caused Lynching. The alleged crime took place on July 18, at a tobacco barn a short distance from the home of the girls' father, by whom Moore was employed. The older girl went to her parents crying and reported that Moore had hurt her while playing a game with her at the tobacco barn. Moore and the younger girl followed the older to the house, Moore standing at the porch and talking with the girls' father while the girls went inside to their mother. The father demanded from Moore an explanation of why his child was crying, whereupon he is reported to have answered: "We were playing and I guess I scared her." While the father was questioning the Negro, the mother observed on the girl's dress a paste-like substance which suggested to her the nature of the Negro's game. While she was excitedly telling her husband about this, Moore ran away.

A Fruitless Man-Hunt. Shortly after the Negro ran away, the father telephoned the Wilson County sheriff, who, learning that the reported crime had been committed in Edgecombe County, brought the case to the attention of the sheriff of the latter county.

The Edgecombe County sheriff and his son, a deputy, secured

a brace of bloodhounds and reached the scene of the crime about ten o'clock in the evening. Finding a large gathering of excited people there, the sheriff formed them into a posse. Immediately the man-hunt was on. After a fruitless all-night search, the posse disbanded. On the next afternoon, reports came to the sheriff that Moore was in hiding near Sparta. Another posse was formed, and conducted a second fruitless all-night search with bloodhounds. The sheriff stated that "The people were hot for him; and he would have been shot on either night, without a chance to surrender, if the possemen had found him."

Hearing that the Negro had escaped into Virginia, the sheriff sent a blanket warrant over and ordered his arrest. Moore escaped back into North Carolina. In the meantime, the sheriff had offered a $100 reward for Moore's capture, broadcasting this description: "Oliver Moore, dark, 5 ft. 6 in. high, wt. 140 lbs., age 30."

On August 16, a young white man passing the house of Moore's brother, heard voices and upon stopping to listen, discovered that Oliver Moore was within. When the white man entered the house, Moore hid in a closet; but when called upon to surrender he did so without resistance. The white man who apprehended him reported that Moore said: "I am the man you are looking for." Moore was delivered to the sheriff at Tarboro, and placed in the county jail to await trial.

Venereal Disease and Preliminary Trial. Three days after the alleged attack, a doctor in Tarboro examined the two girls thoroughly. He reported that they had well developed, virulent cases of positive gonorrhea. Neither showed any evidence, however, of having been bruised or roughly handled. No examination was made of the parents of the children to discover whether they were infected. Moreover, the doctor suggested that a girl child may easily catch gonorrhea from her nurse or other adult.

The state then requested a Tarboro physician to make an examination of the Negro to discover whether he had gonorrhea. The physician procrastinated, however, and the examination was never made.

On the afternoon of August 19, a preliminary trial was held before the judge of the recorder's court. This evidence was given: A nurse, an aunt of the two girls, stated that both children had gonorrhea and that they were in the hospital in her care. The older child told the story of a "game" the Negro suggested. She said he put them in a tobacco wagon and hurt her, and she ran to the house crying, Moore and the younger child following. The father testified that he asked Moore what the child was crying about and was told: "We were playing and I guess I scared her." The mother also testified as to the indication she had found.

The judge allowed Moore to say nothing during the preliminary trial, and no lawyer took the case when the judge asked for a volunteer. Moore was bound over without bail to await the action of the Superior Court, and the sheriff put him back in the county jail.

Precautions to Prevent Mob Violence. The county sheriff, newly elected and without experience in handling such cases, stated that he was advised there was no need for taking the prisoner out of the county. However, thinking mob violence possible, he slept in the jail both nights preceding the preliminary trial, and as there had been no evidence of a demonstration he felt much relieved. He had arranged with deputies and leading citizens that if any efforts were made to take Moore from the jail the fire alarm would sound a signal for the immediate formation of a posse to prevent it.

On the morning of the preliminary trial, the sheriff suggested to the judge the possibility of a demonstration in the court room, at the same time giving the judge a revolver and promising to be "handy" with his own if trouble started. However, there were only a few people present at the trial, and no evidence of emotion or excitement. The judge felt reassured and told the sheriff that he thought Moore would be perfectly safe in the local jail.

Jailer Surprised and Negro Lynched. Between twelve and one o'clock on the next morning, August 20, a deputy sheriff, acting as county jailer, heard someone knock at the outside door of the jail. Thinking it was one of the city police bringing in a prisoner, the jail keeper explained, he opened the door and saw scores of people outside, some of them masked. He attempted to turn in the prearranged fire alarm, but guns were leveled at him. The leader of the mob quietly told him what they were there for, and that if he would lead them to Moore's cell and unlock it, no one else would be disturbed. The deputy denied having the keys, saying the sheriff had taken them home with him. The leader is quoted as saying, "Come on, then, and we'll go get the sheriff!" They were about to start when one of the members of the mob called out: "He's a d— liar, here are the keys!"

Having unlocked the jail, the leader gave orders to take Moore, tie him, and place him in one of the cars. Working quickly and quietly, this was done, and the fourteen to twenty cars with their sixty to eighty mob members whizzed out of town. Three police were supposedly on night duty at the time the attack on the jail occurred. They stated that they saw nothing, heard nothing, and knew nothing of the mob's activities until after the mob had left town. The chief of police reported that he knew nothing of the affair until he came down town next morning.

Some time passed before the sheriff was notified. Despite the prearranged fire-alarm signal, the acting jailer called the sheriff over the 'phone and reported the matter. The sheriff, after going to the jail and again hearing the deputy's report, as stated above, organized a posse to pursue the mob, but seemed uncertain which way it had gone. At dawn, the Negro's body, riddled with bullets and buckshot, was found swinging from a pine tree, a plow line tied underneath the arms. The lynching had taken place just over the line in Wilson County, in the nearest patch of trees to the scene of the alleged crime.

The mob's victim had little education—was barely literate. He was a tenant farmer, raising tobacco chiefly, was employed as a sort of house boy by the white farm family, and was known as a "white man's nigger." During the winter he had been employed as "shine" boy in Rocky Mount. A rumor was current in Tarboro at the time of the lynching that he had been accused of a similar crime before, but this was not substantiated. He was without court record.

The people of Tarboro contend that the leader of the mob, who was in absolute control of all its actions, was not a local man. Every step was well thought out, every command was given in a low, quiet, firm voice, and was obeyed instantly and without question. The mob was effectively organized for its murderous purpose. Various reports in Tarboro had it that its members came from Wilson, Rocky Mount—in fact, from anywhere except Tarboro and Edgecombe county. Notwithstanding this, the judge of the preliminary trial stated that he was "morally" certain that Tarboro people were in the mob.

REACTION OF THE COMMUNITY TO THE LYNCHING

"A Problem for the Negro to Solve"—Said a Local Paper. One of the few North Carolina daily papers to condone the lynching of Oliver Moore was the Rocky Mount *Telegram*, the daily paper nearest the scene of the lynching. Three weeks after Moore was accused, and two weeks before he was lynched, the *Telegram* had a lengthy editorial captioned "A Problem for the Negro to Solve," parts of which were:

"The increasing number of criminal assaults upon white women in the Southern States, the accounts of which frequently are exaggerated, add nothing to the effort to bring about more harmonious interracial feeling. . . . Because of the inability of officers to cope with situations arising in their territories; because of the seeming indifference among the leading class of Negro citizens; because of the regular recurrence of crimes of such a revolting nature that no man may pass them unnoticed we feel, keenly, the necessity for careful consideration. . . . To discuss the matter frankly, we hold the Negro to blame for the repeated unfavorable publicity he receives.

". . . No people can endure criminal assaults of the nature we constantly have called to our attention. Three cases of the nature to which we refer, have been brought forcibly to our attention within the last two weeks. One of them is so terribly obnoxious that we have a feeling of nausea whenever we consider it. . . . We have looked in vain for Negro leaders in this state to make even the slightest gesture of protest. The responsibility rests with the Negro."

week after the lynching a local Negro's letter to the *Telegram* answered the above editorial position in part as follows:

"The Negroes of Rocky Mount, the State and the Nation think with equal horror and incredibility as the white man upon th recent crime of which Oliver Moore was accused, and for whicl. he was lynched. I say accused, for he was actually proved neither guilty nor innocent. . . .

"First, leading Negroes cannot publicly denounce criminal at tacks on white women, nor on any woman, unless it be known ii they were positively committed, and by whom. One wouldn't knov where nor how to begin denouncing. Secondly, attacks on white women are not always at the bottom of lynching. A Negro was recently lynched in a southern state for being accused of shooting a white man. Thirdly, Negro leaders would wonder how publicly denouncing attacks on white women could possibly be a remedy for the lynching disease. For, in all probability, Oliver Moore, if guilty or not, in his depraved mind never heard of Negro leaders, much less of their denouncing anything."

Lynching Virtually Condoned by Local Paper. On the afternoon of the lynching, the *Telegram*, in an editorial, "Mob Violence Takes Its Toll," pointed out:

"The *Telegram* has always opposed mob violence. Such an action is contrary to good government; is a violation of the principles of government; is in the final analysis, a reversion to the primitive in man. Consequently, we find it imposible, regardless of the motive, to approve of or condone the action of masked men who in the night take prisoners from jails and lynch them. . . .

"That the feeling of a people should be aroused is natural and we find ourselves, despite our views on lynching, not too greatly disturbed. . . . But the regular recurrence of this sort of. crime and the seeming failure of the courts to combat it is responsible for the action of the Edgecombe mob last night. If Negro leaders are as active in teaching their people the futility of the crimes accredited to them as they are in adding publicity to lynchings more good will result. Just as long as members of one race attack members of another race, or, to put it more frankly as long as Negro men attack white women, it will be exceedingly difficult to persuade white men that lynching does not have its virtues.

"There is little likelihood that the Edgecombe County officials will conduct an investigation. And while we are opposed to this sort of solution to a crime we find ourselves calmly accepting the crime last night as inevitable."

On August 22 the *Telegram* had a column editorial replying to criticisms of other North Carolina papers and further condoning the lynching and defending the officers.

Mob Death Justified by Few Papers. A half-dozen other smaller papers in eastern North Carolina took a position similar to that of the *Telegram.* The one striking statement in the Tarboro *Southerner's* story of the lynching was that a nurse at the local hospital said that she had expected the lynching to take place a night earlier. The Williamston *Enterprise,* on August 20, had an editorial stating, "Assaults, murders, and crimes of various sorts are becoming too numerous, and the law is too dilatory in the punishment of crime. To this, we believe, is due lynchings, and an effort to take the law into the hands of the mob, that swift and sure vengeance shall be met." The day following, August 21, the Lillington *News* contrasted the pictures of the alleged assaulted girls and the lynched Negro, and also commented upon the tragic results of white and Negro boys pitching horseshoes together:

"Over against the gruesome picture of the mangled body of the black man is presented the terrible picture of two little girls suffering from an act unmentionable in polite society. The weight of the outrage will follow them through life. . . .

"If some white people were not so prone to be familiar with Negroes and socialize with them, allowing them reasons to suppose their presence among white people is acceptable, there would still live in the heart and soul of the Negro the fear and dread of swift and sure punishment in case of his wrongdoing.

"Oftentimes we have thought of this very thing. We have seen white boys and Negroes socializing right here in this community—pitching horseshoes together and engaging in many other pastimes—a practice that will inculcate in the mind of the Negro that he is acceptable company in white society. There is a way to treat Negroes and yet be kind to them. They should be given all that rightfully belongs to them—in material things as well as in rights and privileges. With that the border line should be drawn and they should be sternly schooled in the laws of segregation. We fear that the Edgecombe-Wilson tragedy was brought about by lack of enforcement of this law."

The Washington *Progress* most outspokenly said: "If the evidence relative to the identity of the Negro was absolutely conclusive, then we have no criticism to make of the action of the mob. We commend them for what they did." To this, the Greensboro *News* replied that, while there might be some chance of a mob making a mistake, "There is no if or and about the low mental and spiritual state into which a community has fallen when it sets aside duly constituted authority and commits a collective crime to avenge an individual."

Among the weekly papers in this section condemning the lynching vigorously were the Albemarle *Press*, the Laurinburg *Exchange*, the Nashville *Graphic*, the Kings Mountain *Herald*, and the Lexington *Dispatch*.

Lynching Roundly Condemned by Leading Dailies. The Raleigh *News and Observer* boldly criticised the officers and citizens for permitting the mob death, and published a picture of the swinging dead body with these comments:

"It was quite the thing to look at the bloody, dead nigger hanging from the limb of a tree near the Edgecombe-Wilson County line this morning. . . . Whole families came together, mothers and fathers, bringing even their youngest children. It was the show of the countryside—a very popular show. Men joked loudly at the sight of the bleeding body . . . girls giggled as the flies fed on the blood that dripped from the Negro's nose."

In answer to the storm of criticism which came down upon the veteran editor of the *News and Observer* for publishing the picture and criticizing the officers and community, on August 28 he wrote an editorial asking, "Who Lynched the Negro?" He stated that while there was a considerable sentiment in Raleigh as in Edgecombe County "which gave tacit approval to the lynching on the basis of the Negro's guilt, the evidence of guilt, though strong, was by no means conclusive, and that the admission that, despite a question of the Negro's guilt, there is anywhere approval of the mob's action brings North Carolina sharply to the point of a necessary self-scrutiny."

The Concord *Tribune* on August 23 had an editorial, "People Probably Don't Want a Solution," pointing out that the handling of the Edgecombe County case "indicates strongly enough that a majority of the people in the community of the lynching don't want any solution to the mystery. . . . There must be scores of persons, innocent themselves, who through various 'grapevine' sources, have learned the identity of at least a few of the mob members, but they are not talking. They are giving approval to the act of the mob by making no effort to apprehend those making up its membership."

The High Point *Enterprise* on August 20 carried a forceful editorial, "A Sheriff Whose Fitness Seems Questionable," part of which was: "Isn't it reasonable to doubt the fitness of a sheriff for his job in circumstances like these? The precaution ordinarily taken now in this state in similar cases would have prevented the lynching." The Durham *Herald* expressed the opinion that law violaters are punished only in accordance with the demands of the local people. The Wilmington *Dispatch* said: "North Carolina's record as the foe of mob violence received a severe setback early this morning when lynchers forced their way into the Edgecombe jail, removed a Negro accused of attacks upon white girls, and riddled him with bullets. . . . This outbreak should be dealt with to the fullest extent of the law."

On August 20 the Greensboro *News* expressed the opinion that the officers' claim that they were completely surprised was a decided challenge to public credulity. Two days later the *News* pointed out that the mob always "Picks on the Weak": "A white man who has the ability to make a fight—friends and money—may escape his just dues; sometimes does. But mobs don't go after those who are likely to escape that way. . . . It picks on the weak and helpless; those unable to fight for themselves and who have no influential friends to start something when they are murdered. . . ."

Punishment of Lynchers Demanded by Leading State Papers. In the other end of the state from Tarboro, on the afternoon following the lynching, the Asheville *Times* asked: "How can the might and prestige of North Carolina law be enthroned in the minds of the people when officers, charged with a duty demanding all their vigilance, turn out the lights and go to bed, leaving a potential mob to carry out its plans without intervention?" On the day following, this paper commended Governor Gardner for his assurance that the case would be investigated thoroughly and quickly, reflecting, "Edgecombe County and the State of North Carolina must bring the guilty into court. So-called lynch law is a menace to American democracy and American justice far more imminent than the bogey of Russian Communism which so often excites our sensory systems." Next morning, August 21, the Asheville *Citizen* declared that lynchings are not to be tolerated, and North Carolina "must show now that officers of the law will be held to the standard that has been established over the past eight years."

"Seems about Time to Punish a Mob" was the caption of an editorial appearing in the Winston-Salem *Journal* on August 21. The Raleigh *News and Observer* demanded that "all the legal resources of the state" be brought to bear on the case, and stated that "the will to lynch cannot live in an atmosphere of certainty that the lynchers must pay for it in prison stripes."

The Greensboro *News* on August 23, after saying "An officer who failed to detect any danger, when it seems to have been sensed all around him, could hardly be expected to shine as a sleuth in running down members of the mob which conducted this surprise sortie against law, order, and civilization," echoed the position of many other papers, when it said that for the conviction of the lynchers North Carolina's best citizens must look to the state.

The Charlotte *Observer* expressed the hope that the Governor would not only do his utmost to bring the lynchers to justice but "determine if the sheriff is not guilty of negligence." The Concord *Tribune*, in an editorial, "The State's Shame," declared: "This Negro should have been taken to the State's prison immediately upon arrest, and hereafter officers who refuse to profit by this experience should be summarily removed from office."

Two of the most forceful editorial statements were by the Greensboro Daily *News* and the Raleigh *Times*: The *News* declared, "Blood, spilled by mobsters' bullets, is on North Carolina's hands. Only partial erasure is possible, and that through application of a rebounding law to those who wantonly trampled its majesty beneath their scurrying feet." The Raleigh *Times* said: "It would be a hard but wholesome example if some day a North Carolina white man should be electrocuted for having participated in the deliberate and premeditated murder of a Negro guilty of and held for trial for the commission of a capital felony."

Why the Lynchers Have Gone Unpunished. Further than the finding of the coroner's jury that "Oliver Moore met his death by gunshot wounds at the hands of a mob of masked men whose identity is unknown to the jury" and a similar decision of the Edgecombe County grand jury, no court action has been taken. In spite of Governor Gardner's early statement that he would utilize the full powers of his office to apprehend and punish the lynchers, and of the reputation of the local district attorney as a fearless and effective prosecutor, the murderers have gone unmolested by the courts, due to the general attitude of local officers and citizens that the lynching was inevitable, if not desirable.

The following statements from leading citizens further explain why the lynchers were afforded virtual immunity: "From the standpoint of state and legality it's regrettable," said a

court official, "but, personally I think it was a good thing."
This official added: "Now, I've been perfectly frank with you
and told you everything I know, but I don't think you should
write this up; it's too bestial, too revolting, too inhuman. For
the sake of the children it is better forgotten." Another official
commented: "I hate that this thing occurred on account of
the criticism it has brought. There's no question, however, of
Moore's guilt, and personally I'm glad it happened." "In principle, I'm against lynching," remarked a local newspaper man,
"but this crime was so horrible, I think it was all right—
there's no doubt about Moore's guilt."

"The black son of a b— got what he deserved," was the
reaction of a policeman, who added: "If the crime had been
committed against the lowest white woman in the world he
should have been killed; if I had been there I would not have
interfered, for them folks would a-killed a good man to get
that nigger." "Legally awful; personally admirable," said a
leading white citizen, while a hotel proprietor dismissed the
matter with, "Well, when a Negro touches a white woman in
the South he'll be lynched." The ministers and most of the
school teachers, though not openly condoning the lynching,
did not speak out against it.

The physician who examined the two little girls said: "There
will always be an element of doubt in my mind as to Moore's
guilt. This is the first virulent case of positive gonorrhea I
have ever seen develop in three days. If the Negro had been
examined and found to have had the disease I would not question his guilt. If they got the right man I'm glad of it." The
physician who was asked by the preliminary trial court to
examine Moore explained: "Just failed to get around to make
an examination for gonorrhea. Sent organs to laboratory after
death, however. The pathological examination showed a
violent urethral stricture, which in this case, I'm sure, meant
gonorrhea." When asked what he thought of a virulent case
of positive gonorrhea developing in three days, he said: "It
is not at all unusual. This popular idea that it takes gonorrhea
seven to nine days to develop is all rot. The only regrettable
thing about lynching a Negro is that we sometimes get the

wrong man. In this case there is doubt that we had the right man."

The Negroes generally feel that Moore was unjustly accused and that his mob death was inexcusable. While the lynching, it seems, has resulted in no perceptible overt change in race relations, the memories of the Reconstruction period have been revived, the protection of white womanhood has become something of an obsession, and the Negroes are more often reminded that they are Negroes and must "stay in their place."

FACTS ABOUT THE COMMUNITY

Negro Slaves and Indentured Servants from Virginia. In 1720 a group of Virginians came to the mouth of Town Creek, fifty miles east of Raleigh, and established the first permanent settlement in present-day Edgecombe County. Two years later, to the site of Tarboro, the present county seat, came another group of young Virginians.

From the outset, the settlers on Edgecombe's fertile soil were greatly interested in agriculture. Tobacco, hemp, flax, pork, beef, flour, and indigo were the popular products, with additional income from turpentine, tar, pitch, and shingles from the extensive pine forests.

Slavery, present in the county from its earliest history, was not confined to Negroes, for in a number of cases captive Indians were forced to work in the turpentine industry on Tar River; there were also a goodly number of indentured white servants brought over from England. Both types of servitude were introduced into Edgecombe by the Virginia immigrants, who would have considered it a hopeless task to open new plantations without them. In 1730, Governor Burrington and his council offered each immigrant fifty acres of land for every slave he brought with him. In 1754, there were 624 Negroes and 1,160 whites in Edgecombe County, while twenty-three years later there were 1,060 Negro slaves and 1,200 whites. Adjoining counties, some of which had been formed from Edgecombe, showed a similar increased proportion of slaves.

Many Non-Slave-Owning Whites. In 1790 the county had 6,933 whites and 3,152 slaves. Of the 1,260 heads of white

families only 381 owned slaves: Thirty-seven families owned
twenty or more; seventy-five owned between ten and twenty;
one hundred owned between two and ten; ninety-nine owned
two; seventy owned one, and 879 families owned none.
The 1800 census showed a decrease of 417 whites and an
increase of 753 slaves. By 1830 the numbers of whites
and slaves were approximately equal. During the next
decade the county's Negro population rose to 15,708,
which was more than twice the number of whites. The
tide was shifting by 1850, as many of the largest planters
began to migrate with their slaves to the fertile lands of the
southwest. In 1860 the county had 10,108 Negro slaves, 369
free Negroes, and 6,789 whites.

The county's population increased 26.1 per cent between
1920 and 1930. Negroes accounted for 58.9 per cent of the
total in 1920 and 56.9 per cent in 1930, while foreign-born
whites accounted for but 0.2 per cent in 1920 and 0.1 per cent
in 1930. In both census years 0.3 per cent of the state's
population were foreign-born.

A Town and a Half. The county has ten towns, chief of which
are Rocky Mount—half in Edgecombe and half in Nash—
and Tarboro, the county seat. In 1930 the former had a
population of 21,412 and the latter 6,379; Negroes made up
slightly over one-third the population of each.

The county seat's chief industries include two cotton mills,
a knitting mill, a peanut factory, two cotton oil mills, a veneer
plant, a fertilizer factory, and a milk plant. There are two
banks, eight first-class grocery stores, four drug stores, two
motion picture houses, three well-equipped cafes, a number
of general merchandise and supply stores, and one large hardware store. The town has a good school system, and is well
supplied with doctors and hospital facilities.

Rocky Mount, only one-half of which is in Edgecombe
County, is also a well-serviced town. The other eight towns
in the county are mere farm trading centers in every instance
with less than a thousand inhabitants.

Over Four-fifths of Farmers are Tenants. Edgecombe
County, with its 329,920 acres, is one of the largest counties

in the state. With ideal conditions for farming—natural drainage, a long growing season, comparatively level land, and good soil—the county long has been predominately agricultural. The 1930 census shows Edgecombe with 3,998 farms, an increase of 4.1 per cent over 1920, while the increase for the state was 3.7; of the county's area, 65.2 per cent was in farms, while 59.6 per cent was the state average.

When compared with the state at large, farm tenancy is unusually high in Edgecombe County: In 1910, 42.3 per cent of the state's farmers and 72.8 per cent of Edgecombe's farmers were tenants. Twenty years later, the tenants accounted for 45.2 per cent of the state's farmers and 83.3 per cent of Edgecombe's farmers. In his book, *North Carolina: Economic and Social*, Dr. S. H. Hobbs, ranks Edgecombe next to the lowest in farm ownership. This county's farming is still on the clean culture cash crop basis. The two main crops are cotton and tobacco. It is significant that with 3,999 farms, Edgecombe County has only 1,184 milk cows, less than one-third of a cow per farm. Chickens and pigs, too, are scarce.

Crop Values Unusually High, Wealth Retention Unusually Low. The county's per capita and per acre value of farm crops is usually considerably above the state average; but by the time feed, food, and fertilizer bills have been paid there is but little left for tenants or landlords. Dr. E. C. Branson and others have repeatedly commented upon the fact that while the crop value per acre is unusually high in the eastern Carolina cotton-tobacco belt, the per capita wealth retention is unusually low. Each year this one county sends out more than a million dollars for fertilizers, feeds, and foods. The paucity of livestock increases the fertilizer bills, while the traditional dependence of landlord and tenant solely upon cotton and tobacco has resulted in the home production of but little feed and food. Edgecombe County's bank deposit was $54.39 per capita against the state average of $88.94.

Over Six Thousand Illiterates. In 1930, Edgecombe County spent more than four times as much on the white schools, with a school census population of almost 6,500, as on the Negro schools, with over 9,500. The figures were $141,290.82 for white schools and $33,055.02 for Negro schools, an expenditure of $21.94 for the school census white child as compared with $3.42 for the Negro child. The white school term was one hundred and sixty days, the Negro term one hundred and twenty days; the average annual salary was $996.52 for white teachers and $391.92 for Negro teachers. The county school superintendent has a Negro assistant. She has the confidence and respect of both races and can control not only the Negro schools of the county but almost every Negro gathering or organization in the county.

The 1930 census showed 5,814 illiterate Negroes and 863 illiterate whites in Edgecombe County. Of the county's people over ten years old, 29.7 per cent of the Negroes and 5.6 per cent of the whites were illiterate; the state illiteracy rate among Negroes was 20.6 per cent, among whites 5.6 per cent.

Nearly Fifteen Thousand Unchurched. The white church membership in 1926 was as follows: Methodist Episcopal Church, South, 2,265 members; Protestant Episcopal, 1,458; Southern Baptist, 1,304; Presbyterian, 892. The Negro membership was: Baptist, 4,950 members; A. M. E. Z., 1,237; A. M. E., 876.

Of the county's population in 1926, over fifteen years of age, 5,937 whites and 8,816 Negroes were members of no church. Of this age group only 54.1 per cent of the county's white population were church members, as compared with 64.2 per cent throughout the state; 44.6 per cent of this age group of the county's Negroes were church members, in contrast with 69.7 per cent for the entire state.

The unchurched people of both races are, for the most part, propertyless tenants. While itinerant tenant farmers seldom stay in one place long enough to become a fixed part of the community, other determining considerations are that church attendance implies Sunday clothes, a ready means for riding to church, and something for the collection plate. The frequent movements of the typical tenant virtually preclude his being a leader in the local church, while his limited financial resources

leave him an unattractive prospect for the church in need of
resident supporting members.

Four-fifths of Votes for Democratic Presidential Candidate.
Edgecombe County boasts of the "quality" of its political
leaders. This "quality" consists of being personally acceptable
and liked by the majority of the voters. The sheriff who pre-
ceded the present sheriff, was tried and found guilty of em-
bezzling county funds. Many Tarboro people claim that morally
he was not guilty: "Why he was one of our good folks; the
irregularities of his books were due solely to ignorance of
business technique."

A candidate is usually elected, not because he is qualified to
hold office, but because he is personally popular. The present
sheriff claims to know every man in the county. The number
of votes cast in an election depends largely upon the weather,
transportation, and how "even" the race is. The heaviest
vote is cast in the Democratic primary where the officers are
actually selected. Except in the towns, but few women vote. The
Negroes take almost no part in politics.

Although North Carolina gave the Republican presidential
candidate a majority of over 50,000 in 1928, more than four-
fifths of Edgecombe County's votes were for the Democratic
candidate—4,184 against 977.

In the four years ending June 30, 1926, 629 cases were tried
in the Edgecombe County Superior Court, distributed as follows: Negro men, 372; white men, 206; Negro women, 42;
white women, 5. Among the Negroes, the greatest number of
cases was for larceny and receiving, violation of liquor laws,
housebreaking, and assault with deadly weapon—these four
accounting for nearly two-thirds of the total; among the
whites, the violation of liquor laws, conspiracy, assault and
battery, larceny and receiving, and assault with deadly weapon
were most common, the five comprising a little over half of the
total white cases.

Prior to the lynching of Oliver Moore in 1930, there are
three recorded instances of mob violence in Edgecombe County:

In slave times Jim Hargrave, Negro, was drawn up by his thumbs and almost killed for the murder of Gray Hargrave, a white man; in 1870, the Ku Klux Klan emasculated eleven Negroes; in 1898, a Negro accused of rape was hanged at Tarboro.

Reconstruction and White Supremacy. During the Reconstruction period the Negroes gained political ascendancy in Edgecombe County. According to J. K. Turner and J. L. Bridges in their *History of Edgecombe County*, crimes against white people and their property were very common, but the guilty Negroes went unpunished.

Racial antagonism remained intense until the overwhelming victory of the Democrats in the county in 1897. In 1900 the virtual disfranchiment of Negroes occurred, "white supremacy clubs" having been organized at Rocky Mount and Tarboro. George H. White, Negro congressman from that district, seeing that the white people would control the election, promised the Negroes that if the whites did not treat them right, he and others would see that their cases came into court, and, if the courts did not give them justice, then he would say: "May God damn North Carolina, the state of my birth."

Racial antagonism has died away, on the surface, at least; whites and Negroes now live and work side by side with little or no difficulty. The white people of Edgecombe County are almost unanimous in saying "We've got the best Negroes of any county in the state; they are good workers, and 'they know their place.' "

CHAPTER VIII

"RED-BONED NIGGER FROM LOUISIANA"
BRYAN, BRAZOS COUNTY, TEXAS

ON THE morning of Wednesday, June 19, 1930, Will Roan, Negro, was found dead in a pasture near Benchley, six miles northeast of Bryan, county seat of Brazos County, Texas. His death had been due to gunshot wounds. He was accused of an attempted assault upon a white farm woman.

THE LYNCHING

Report of Alleged Attempted Assault. Will Roan, Negro, wage hand of a white owner-renter who lived near Benchley, was accused by his employer's wife of an attempt to assault her in the late afternoon of Monday, June 17. She stated that her assailant fled only when her screams had attracted an aged Negro man who lived in a cabin nearby. This Negro, coming upon the scene with a gun, wanted to follow Roan and kill him, but the woman would not allow him to leave her.

A Bryan barber, friend of the white farmer, stated that on the day before, which was Sunday, the woman's husband had trouble with the Negro for being "sassy" to his wife, and that after tersely reprimanding him he had taken him to the barn, stripped him, and administered a severe whipping with a wet rope.

The officers of Brazos and Robertson counties were notified of the alleged attempted assault. They took no very active steps, however, seeming to feel that the matter was only labor trouble and that it was the white man's business to settle the affair with his hired hand. From Monday afternoon to Wednesday morning a small group of undeputized people searched for Roan. One member of the searching party was from Bryan, three or four from Hearne, in Robertson County, and the remaining ten or twelve from the Benchley neighborhood.

Corpse Found by Man-Hunters. The man-hunters, while intent upon getting Roan, were not inclined to do violence to other Negroes. On late Tuesday afternoon, a Negro suspect was found and taken before the husband and others. When his innocence was established, he was courteously released.

Shortly after daylight on Wednesday morning, two of the man-hunters, crossing a pasture in an automobile, discovered the dead body, still warm, and brought it in.

Although there were a dozen men looking for Roan, it is reported that he came to his death by gun shots from a man who lives on a farm near Benchley, who alone came upon Roan and killed him, one load going into his arm and another into his left breast. It is generally believed that Roan was apprehended in Robertson County near the Brazos County line, and was either killed there and carried across the line into Brazos County, or else was taken across the county line to be shot.

"Red-Boned Nigger from Louisiana." Will Roan was of the creole type with fair skin and rather light hair. In many respects he resembled a Frenchman. He was spoken of by local white people as "a red-boned nigger from Louisiana," who had come into this section six or seven years before and since that time had been working about as a hired hand. Local Negroes considered him "an outsider."

According to a Negro physician, Roan was of very low mentality and generally irresponsible; a number of white people, including the sheriff, made similar reports. Local farm Negroes say Roan was generally peaceful and attended to his own business; and many of them do not credit his guilt. They think rather that he and his employer got into some personal altercation and that the charge of attempted rape was trumped up as an excuse for getting rid of him.

Efforts to Prevent Lynching. With two exceptions nobody made an effort to prevent the lynching. A leading citizen of Benchley on several occasions went to the group of men looking for Roan and plead with them to "keep their feet on the ground," pointing out the danger of something rash in a moment of excitement. He stated that his suggestions were not taken graciously by the man-hunters, many of whom were youngsters who openly resented his advice. A deputy, employed as an overseer on one of the large bottom plantations, also did everything he could to apprehend the Negro, spirit him away, and keep the case within the bounds of the law.

The Man-Hunters. The man reported to have killed Roan is said to be a "high-strung," excitable landowner, living in Robertson County near Benchley, who has followed the practice of working his land by the use of persons of low mentality over whom he maintains the strictest control, often not even permitting them to leave his farm. After working these unfortunates for a few years, he replaces them with others of the same type. He was referred to by local people as a "labor bruiser."

One of the men active in the man-hunt had attended college for a year or two, but did not graduate. The husband of the woman in the case participated in the hunt Monday night and Tuesday; on Wednesday morning, when the Negro was killed, he was in Bryan, drunk.

One of the men who found the corpse is about forty years old and especially active in the local unit of the American Legion. It is believed that he and his companion knew where the Negro's body was, and had driven out to get it. They claimed, however, that they had only started on a hunting trip and found the body by accident. When this explanation was ridiculed one of the two gave still another—that they were out looking at some mules.

Though nearly half of the people of Brazos and Robertson counties are Catholics, the men who hunted down Roan were not of this group. They were all Protestants or of Protestant families. If the family involved had been Catholic, the situation might have been different; it was generally reported, however, by Protestants of Bryan that the Catholics are not inclined to lynch.

REACTION OF THE COMMUNITY TO THE LYNCHING

The general reaction of the community was that the trouble had arisen between a small white farmer and his Negro hired hand, and that the death of the Negro had settled the affair. The local people do not consider Roan's death a lynching.

Little Newspaper Space Devoted to Lynching. Very little mention was made of the case in the newspapers. The local daily paper, the Bryan *Eagle,* carried a full story of the affair on June 19, but referred to it no further. It is doubtful if any of the state papers made editorial comments concerning it, for, as stated above, it was not generally regarded as a lynching, but rather as merely the killing of an impudent Negro by a justly wrathful white man.

The following story was carried in a number of the Negro papers in Texas and elsewhere:

"Bryan, Tex., June 19—Texas' third Negro mob victim within two months, Bill Roan, who was accused of attempting to attack a white woman, was found horribly mutilated Wednesday in a field. A man hunt had been conducted for Roan since Monday afternoon, when the woman, on whose farm he worked, said he made advances to her. The Sheriff was said to have told a mob seeking Roan that he would attend to the fugitive."

In the last week of June, 1930, the following Associated Press release was carried by a number of Texas papers:

"Bryan, Texas—Evidence indicating the identity of members of a posse that killed Bill Roan, Negro, on June 18, taken by a court of inquiry here, will be presented to the Brazos County grand jury at the September term, A. S. Ware, county attorney, stated Saturday.

"The court had listened to six witnesses and others had been summoned, Ware said."

Investigation, but No Indictments. The coroner's verdict over Roan's dead body was to the effect that the Negro "had come to his death by gun shots at the hands of an unknown person or persons." An investigation was made by a court of inquiry, but no indictments were brought by the grand jury. The county attorney had died a short time before the lynching, and the commissioners had not appointed his successor. Soon after Roan's death an acting county attorney was appointed to fill the unexpired term. At the subsequent November election, this man was elected.

The grand jury investigation of the death of Roan was not begun until about six months later and doubtless would not have been instituted then except for the persistent demands of a few of Bryan's leading citizens. The case was investigated at some length. Most of the witnesses called were residents of Robertson County. The county attorney stated that though he had secured no indictments, and had no hopes of securing any, he had made it uncomfortable for the guilty men. He said he knew Negroes with sufficient evidence to lead to indictments and probably convictions, but for fear of reprisals they would not give their evidence before the courts.

FACTS ABOUT THE COMMUNITY

In the Fork of the Brazos and Nevasota Rivers. Brazos County, far-famed for its fertile river bottoms, in 1840 was laid off from the territory of Washington County by an act of the Texas Legislature. It is in the fork of the Brazos and Navasota Rivers which from the boundaries on two sides.

Recent Population Decreases. In 1850 the county had 594 inhabitants, of whom approximately one-fourth were Negro slaves. As the decades passed the population increased rapidly, the Negroes making up a larger portion of the population with each census until in 1890 slightly more than half of the total of 16,646 were Negroes. But in 1920, when the county's maximum population of 21,975 was reached, the Negroes made up only 41.6 per cent of the total. In 1930, 41.5 per cent of the county's 21,835 inhabitants were Negroes; of the 12,771 non-Negro inhabitants 10,817 were native-born whites, 662 were foreign-born whites, 1,968 were of foreign or mixed parentage, and 1,292 were classified as "other races"—chiefly Mexicans. The proportion of Negroes has declined because of the influx of European and Mexican immigrants. Several hundred Italians, Poles, Bohemians, and Czechs came into the county between 1885 and 1900, and hundreds of Mexicans since that time. The place each race occupies in the economic and social structure of the county is discussed later.

Equally involved in Roan's death were people of Robertson County. Lying immediately north of Brazos County, Robertson is bounded by the Brazos and Navasota Rivers and is the heart of the Texas "Black Waxy Belt," where agriculture is the chief industry and cotton the principal crop. In this section, where the soil does not require commercial fertilizers, "cotton is supreme and the term 'King Cotton' is not a misnomer," writes Nevin O. Winter in her *Texas the Marvelous*. The population of Robertson County, made up of much the same elements as Brazos, reached its highest point in 1900 with 31,480 inhabitants. In 1930, the county's population was 27,240.

Influx of Immigrants from Europe and Mexico. In 1880, two Italians from Southern Italy purchased small tracts of the swamp bottom lands in the northwest part of Brazos County, and demonstrated that this land could be utilized. Within a few years other Italians arrived, coming into the States by way of New Orleans, wheie they worked for a year or so, saving enough money to buy small tracts of land upon reaching Brazos County. The expansion of the Italian community has been on this wise: The older settlers have bought additional tracts of land, paid for them, and in turn sold them to newcomers. This is said to be one of the largest immigrant farm colonies in the United States.

Other immigrant colonies of Bohemians, Poles, and Czechs are located in the Navasota bottoms and upland parts of the county.

The Mexicans, coming into the county in considerable number only since 1900, work as croppers and wage hands on the river plantations under the supervision of paid overseers. They follow the same types of work, live in the same kind of houses, and in general maintain planes of living similar to the Negro croppers and wage hands.

European Newcomers Own Fertile Farms. The Italians,

Poles, Bohemians, and Czech farmers, who live on their small tracts and produce their own food and feed, are located entirely on the most fertile lands in the county, a settlement of Poles on the poorer uplands southeast of College Station being the one outstanding exception. From the outset, these small farmers have used only the best type of livestock, and now as one rides through the fertile bottoms he can identify their farms by small plots of alfalfa, which practically everyone has, and by their small but well-kept dwellings and premises.

Many of the houses are of the same type of construction as those occupied by the Negro and Mexican tenants, the difference being that the late-comers from Europe often have painted their houses and always have well-kept gardens, a few fruit trees, grape arbors, and usually shrubs and flowers. Also, the small tracts immediately around their houses are under fence. It has been the policy of this group for each family to cultivate its own land. Within the last three or four years, improved equipment and diversified farming have enabled these farmers to cultivate larger acreages. As a result, about fifty families from the Steele Store community have pushed on up the bottoms into Robertson County, where they have purchased farms. Not only does each original holding remain intact, but practically all the children stay in this section and in turn become farm owners. It is obvious that if this procedure continues—and there is now no indication to the contrary—the Brazos bottoms will eventually be owned by this group.

Besides these immigrant farmers, probably more than four hundred in all, there are nearly a hundred old-line white and about two hundred Negro families who own small farms, practically all of which are in the upland portions of the county. These farmers, too, follow a more or less self-sufficient farm economy.

The Plantation's Dominance. In spite of the seven hundred independent farmers, the economic life of the county is dominated by plantation farming. Though the European immigrants are making steady gains, the major portions of the Brazos and Navasota bottoms are still cultivated by propertyless

Negro and Mexican tenants. In 1925, sixty-five per cent of all farmers in the county were tenants, there being 619 white tenants, many of them Mexicans, and 1,179 Negro tenants. During the last decade the county's farms have decreased 17.5 per cent. This decrease has occurred almost wholly by tenants being discontinued on the marginal lands of the large plantations.

Soon after the Civil War, parts of the bottoms were cultivated by hired convicts. The after effects of the use of this enforced labor are still seen in the attitudes toward Negro and Mexican croppers and wage hands. The plantation owners and overseers, rather than the police and courts, virtually administer "the law" in the plantation areas.

One Large Town and a Few Small Ones. Bryan, county seat of Brazos, with 7,813 people in 1930, had 31 per cent of the county's population. It is the largest town in the two counties, and is the only urban community of consequence in this area. Robertson County's largest town has only 2,956 dwellers, and the combined population of this and smaller towns make up but 18.5 per cent of the county's population. The early development of the two counties was much the same.

Although the population of Brazos County was a little less in 1930 than ten years earlier, the population of Bryan has almost doubled. It has a cotton mill and lumber plants, but it thrives mainly as a trading center of a large agricultural section. All banks and wholesale houses and most retail businesses of the county are locaed at Bryan.

While most of the European element, as stated above, are small landowners, in recent years several of this group, particularly Italians, have gone into business at Bryan, conducting eating places, meat markets, and grocery stores. Realizing that English names make business opportunities better for them, many are doing business under such ordinary names as Luke's and Charlie's Store, the K. & T. Store, Humpty Dumpty Shop, and the like.

Negroes own several small enterprises in Bryan, located almost entirely in a block of new brick buildings on Main Street just north of the main business section. A number of small shops kept by Italians and other whites are in the same block. Two Negro insurance companies have local offices here and both are reported to be doing a good business. "The True People of America," a Negro lodge, maintains a district office which does a monthly business of $1,200. Other Negro concerns are barber shops, shoe shop, tailor shop, two funeral parlors, auto repair shop, four grocery stores, and a number of cafes. The town has a small Negro hospital, three Negro physicians and two dentists. A goodly number of Negroes own their homes.

An Unusually Large Proportion of Poor People. Brazos County has an unduly large proportion of poor people. In 1930, there was in Texas an automobile to every 4.2 persons, with a one per cent increase between 1929 and 1930; in Brazos County, there was an automobile to every 4.6 persons, with a decrease of one per cent between 1929 and 1930. The per capita valuation of farm products in Brazos County was $128.91, against $219.80 for the state; the value of manufactured products in Brazos was $51.37, as compared with $214.04 for the state. The combined values of farm and manufactured products was considerably less than one half of the state average. In 1930, the total assessed per capita value of taxable property was $507.84 in Brazos County and $743.07 throughout the state. In this same year the county's bank deposits per capita amounted to $176.30 in contrast to the state average of $206.05. The income tax return figures further indicate not only that the people are generally poor, but that the more prosperous element is less numerous than in the general population, there being an income tax return in the county for each 67.6 persons, as compared with one for each 51.9 persons throughout the state, with the proportion of returns for income of more than $5,000 smaller in the county than in the state.

Largest A. & M. College and First-Rate Military Academy. The Texas A. & M. College, with an enrollment of over 2,000, is located five miles southeast of Bryan. This institution, the largest of its kind in the United States, is of considerable economic and cultural benefit to the county. Allen Academy at Bryan, a military school, offering first-year college work, has an enrollment of 230 and ranks among the best military schools in the state. The heads and faculties of these schools, while not in sympathy with the mob activities of June, 1930, did not feel any responsibilty for preventing them. Bryan has a small Carnegie Library.

Schools for Native-whites, Immigrant Whites, and Negroes. Except for one Mexican school, there are only white and Negro schools provided. Due to the European colonization certain of the white schools are patronized almost exclusively by Italians, while others have enrolled only Bohemians or Poles or Mexicans or native whites.

Adequate high school facilities are provided for white children by each of the urban comunities in Brazos and Robertson Counties. Several of the larger centers of rural population, such as the Italian settlement at Steele Store, have junior high schools.

Just now a high school plant for Negroes is being completed at Bryan at a cost of $45,000, of which the Rosenwald Fund provided $4,000. The remainder was secured from city bonds. This is the only high school for Negroes in the county. The Negro county nurse has her headquarters at this school. Near Benchley, in Robertson County, is a two-teacher Rosenwald school, teaching seven grades for eight months.

Although considerable progress in white and Negro education has been made in recent years, at present Brazos County has thirty-six one-teacher Negro schools and fifteen one-teacher white schools. The county superintendent hopes to have all the small white schools consolidated within a few years. He does not feel that consolidation of the Negro schools is feasible.

White Schools Better and Negro Schools Poorer Than Texas Average. The average annual salary per Brazos County white teacher was $1,239.52 or $122.58 above the Texas white teacher average, while the average annual salary of the Negro teacher was $498.53, or $136.33 below the state average; in Brazos County a white teacher is provided for each 26.9 enrolled pupils, as compared with the state average of 28.6; a Negro teacher is provided for each 43.5 enrolled pupils in

Brazos, as compared with 39.6 throughout the state. Illiteracy rates are higher for all population elements: In Brazos, 2.8 per cent of native-born whites over ten years old are illiterate as compared with Texas' 1.8 per cent; of foreign-born whites, 31.6 per cent against 7.3 per cent; of Negroes, 20.6 per cent against 13.4 per cent. The aged county school superintendent is proud of the improvement of white schools in recent years. He looks upon the Negro schools as something of a side issue, but points with pride to his $60.00 per month minimum salary for Negro teachers.

Roman Catholics Most Numerous. There are many Roman Catholics in Brazos County. From point of numbers, they lead with 2,380; the Southern Baptists come second, with 2,210; then follow the Southern Methodists, with 996, Presbyterians, 350, Protestant Episcopalians and the Disciples of Christ with 185 and 164 respectively. The relative strength of the denominations among the white element of Brazos County is almost identical with that of the state. The chief difference is that the number of white church members in Brazos County is equal to 85.6 per cent of the total population of fifteen years and over, whereas the total number of white church members of the state is equal to but 59.4 per cent of this age group.

The Catholic churches, one for the Central Europeans and another for the Southern Italians, are at Bryan; the resident priests have been men of influence and have enjoyed the respect of all the people in the community, Protestants as well as Catholics. A few years ago when there was an active Klan organization in Brazos County headed up at Bryan, Father Gleisner of the Catholic Church which serves the Central Europeans, was taken into its counsels. While most of the members of the Catholic churches live on farms, and many at a distance of five to fifteen miles, they are very loyal and attend church services regularly.

Unlike the Catholics, who are members of two strong churches, the 2,210 Baptists are members of small, weak churches scattered all over the county, particularly in the upland portion. The Southern Methodists also belong to small scattered churches. The few Episcopalians are for the most part members of the old landed families. The membership of the Disciples Church is composed largely of the poorer whites.

Out of the county's 5,784 Negro church members, 5,055 are Baptists, while the A. M. E. has 386 members, and the M. E., 343. In 1926 86.4 per cent of the Negro population of fifteen years of age and over belonged to churches, whereas throughout the state but 53.7 per cent of this age group were church members. The Negro churches with the best equipment are located at Bryan.

But Few Votes. In 1928, when Texas fell into the National Republican column, Brazos County's vote was overwhelmingly Democratic; 1,480 votes for the Democratic candidate and 738 for the Republican. The county vote in this election equalled nineteen per cent of the county's white voting population; the state vote equalled 27.8 per cent of the total white voting population.

In state and county elections, voting is limited largely to the native whites and Central Europeans. Except when some local issue arises, such as a school tax or road tax which concerns their particular community, the Italians express little interest in the ballot. When they vote on local matters, they usually vote as a unit.

The Negro vote is comparatively small, being limited to home-owning Negroes in Bryan and a dozen or so farm owners. The younger Negro men and women seem to lack interest in politics, it is said, and at the same time the whites have discouraged Negro participation. Because of their potential voting power, however, Negroes are sometimes called into conference in regard to bond elections and in this way have been able to secure some public consideration.

"A Dead Nigger Was a Bad Nigger." The following case will illustrate how crimes are cared for within the plantation regime. In the spring of 1930, a Negro tenant and a white overseer had an altercation. The overseer threatened the Negro boy, whose mother standing nearby called to him to run in the house and get the gun. The overseer, however, outran the boy, got the gun, wounded the mother, and killed the boy.

The sheriff, coming down next day to investigate the affair, was told by the overseer that it was all over and the matter was dropped. A Bryan lawyer voiced the general attitude with the statement that "a dead nigger was a bad nigger, and a live nigger is a good hand."

Contrary to popular opinion, the Italians have a record of almost no homicides in Brazos County. They come into the courts very rarely, except for the violation of the prohibition law, which they do not regard as a crime. For example, when one of their group is in prison for this cause, his farm work is carried on by his neighbors; when he gets out he is welcomed back to the community as though he had been away on a visit and is usually presented with monetary gifts to make up his loss.

Brazos County's Triple Lynching of 1896. Lynchings have been common in Brazos and Robertson counties. In 1896 three Negroes were hanged at one time on the same tree. Tuskegee records show two lynchings in the county since that time. In Robertson County five Negroes have been lynched since 1913.

Welfare Agencies and Activities. Bryan has practically all organizations of a civic and religious nature found in any Southern community of less than 10,000; the remainder of the county like most Southern plantation areas is lacking in organizations other than poor schools and weak churches.

Two county nurses, one of each race, do case work in connection with the administration of the local charity fund, and add much to its effectiveness.

A Good Example of a "Legal Lynching." There came near being a lynching in Brazos County March 23, 1929; a Negro was accused of assaulting a white school teacher at Millican. The uncle of the girl doubtless prevented the lynching by agreeing to leave the case in the courts upon the promise of officers and leading citizens that the Negro would be electrocuted. Suspicion fell upon a colored man who was subsequently arrested and questioned. When his old clothes were examined, two strands of blonde hair were found on a sleeve, which to the sheriff was ample proof of the Negro's guilt. He was taken to Bryan, and thence immediately to the Franklin jail. On the way, so the sheriff reports, he asked the Negro to acknowledge his guilt. When he persisted in maintaining his innocence, "Let's stop," the sheriff stated he said to his deputy, "if he won't tell us the truth, we will let the mob have him." The sheriff stated that the Negro hurriedly said: "Yes-suh, you got the right nigger."

The mob which reached the Bryan jail shortly after the sheriff had left with the Negro, secured the keys from the jailer's wife and searched the jail.

A leading attorney of Bryan stated that he guaranteed to the uncle of the school teacher that the Negro would receive the death sentence and be electrocuted without delay if the law were allowed to take its course. The lawyer stated that this was one of the most distasteful tasks he ever performed, but that he considered it the only way to prevent a lynching. The judge gave the case the earliest possible hearing.

Within a few days the Negro was brought to trial. The case was called late Saturday afternoon. The eager crowd in the courthouse insisted that it be finished that night. Court officials feared to refuse; the case went to the jury at ten o'clock, and a half hour later a verdict of guilty was brought in. Immediately the death sentence was imposed. The defense attorneys were at first inclined to file the usual appeal, but, after consulting briefly with other lawyers and citizens, decided that to do so would result in an immediate lynching. A month and three days later the Negro was electrocuted.

The head of Allen Military Academy expressed the feeling of the community when he said, "Well, it is good there was no appeal, for he would have been lynched, and I do not think anybody would have cared much." Had the appeal been taken and the Negro lynched, the outcome would have been much the same; for there is only a superficial difference between an extra-legal execution and a mob-dominated court execution.

PART THREE

LYNCHINGS IN SOUTHEAST GEORGIA

OF GEORGIA's six lynchings in 1930, five were within a seventy-five mile radius in the southeastern part of the state: Ocilla, Irwin County; Ailey, Montgomery County;[1] Darien, McIntosh County; Thomasville, Thomas County; and one in rural Thomas County.[1] The sixth lynching was at Cartersville, Bartow County, in the Piedmont section.

The inland counties of southeast Georgia, commonly referred to as the Wire Grass section, constitute the newest and poorest one-fourth of the state. Seventeen of Georgia's twenty-four counties formed since 1900 are in this part of the state, as are also twelve of Georgia's twenty-four counties with less than 7,500 population. In 1930, more than a score of southeastern counties had taxable wealth of less than two million dollars each, while in 1929, in each of thirteen of them, the combined value of all farm crops and manufactured products was less than a million and a half dollars. The largest towns of this area have been relatively hard hit, Waycross and Brunswick, being Georgia's only towns of over five thousand inhabitants which lost population between 1920 and 1930.

The inland counties of southeast Georgia have been a sort of eddy between the population movements through central Georgia from northeast to southwest, along the Georgia coast from north to south, and across northern Florida from east to west. The generally poor soils, requiring constant application of costly fertilizers, and the swamp's "bad air," resulting

---

[1] The deaths of S. S. Mincey, Ailey, Montgomery County and of Lacy Mitchell, rural Thomas County, listed as lynchings by the Tuskegee Department of Records and Research, were not typical lynchings, for in each death but a few people participated, and these few employed private and secret means to evade the law, whereas 1930's remaining nineteen lynchings were effected publicly and in open defiance of the law.

in much chills and fever, have made and kept this area relatively undesirable for farmers and manufacturers. Decades ago many of the white people of small means, who were pushed out of central Georgia by the expansion of Negro slave plantation farming, settled in this area of cheap lands. With the partial disintegration of the central Georgia plantations within the past decades, numerous Negroes have drifted aimlessly into this area, as did the whites decades earlier. Here the masses of whites have always been in competition with Negroes and antagonistic toward them. The recent low prices of tobacco, melons, and peanuts have destroyed the hope that these new crops would restore the short-lived prosperity of earlier years based on the exploitation of the virgin pine forests.

In this newest and poorest part of Georgia, governmental and cultural institutions are least well-established. With Montgomery and Toombs Counties as the center, floggings by the score, with white as well as Negro victims, have characterized the past decade. In the extensive rural areas, there are more "five-point" Methodist circuits for whites than elsewhere in the state, while Baptist ministers are poorest paid; and the white public schools are least adequate. Eleven[2] of the state's two dozen counties in which six per cent or more of the whites are illiterate lie in a body, including Montgomery and McIntosh counties. Twenty-one of the state's forty-two counties paying rural white teachers less than five hundred dollars a year are in this newest fourth of Georgia, and include the counties of Montgomery and Irwin. As one would expect, Negro churches and schools are also relatively weak in this area where the Negro has but little economic attachment.

While the lynchings at Darien and Thomasville were not in the midst of these southeastern Wire Grass counties, it is correct to include them here, for, as we shall see presently, the racial disturbances at both of these places attracted people in large numbers from neighboring Wire Grass counties. Further than this, a large portion of the poorer whites of both counties have come but recently from the Wire Grass counties.

---

[2] The names of all of the counties involved in this and subsequent categories appear in the Ailey case study below.

CHAPTER IX

LYNCHED AFTER AN ALL-NIGHT MAN-HUNT
OCILLA, IRWIN COUNTY, GEORGIA

On the last day of January, 1930, in a rural community southeast of Ocilla, Irwin County, Georgia, the dead body of a sixteen-year-old local white girl was found in a puddle of water by the side of the road. Circumstantial evidence and suspicion pointed to James Irwin, a Negro of a nearby community. He was captured next morning and taken to the place of his alleged crime. There he was tortured and mutilated, and then burned. Great crowds rode out to see the body during the day.

Irwin County is of historical interest chiefly because at Irwinville, its earliest county seat, Jefferson Davis was captured. Some of the local people are hoping that a monument will be raised to mark the spot.

The Lynching

A Double Capital Felony. Shortly after noon on January 31, 1930, a sixteen-year-old white farm girl, living a few miles south of Ocilla, went down the road to another farm home with a letter, which, by mistake, had been left in her father's mail box. On her return, as she neared a stream about half way home, James Irwin, seated on a load of corn, drove past her and stopped, pretending to be making repairs on the harness. When the girl came alongside the wagon he grabbed her. In her efforts to escape him a struggle ensued in which he stabbed her severely about the throat and breasts and knocked out one of her eyes with a dull knife. He raped her, threw her body in a puddle, got back on his wagon, and, laying the whip to the mules, hurried away.

The above story, according to the county sheriff, was the confession Irwin made when captured the next morning. While his reported confession agreed with the known facts about the crime, and while it is generally believed that Irwin was guilty, his guilt has never been conclusively established. The evidence against him was his reported confession, plus the fact that he had passed along the road shortly before the body was found.

When the crime was discovered, suspicion immediately fell upon Irwin. An automobile took up the chase and when it came close behind him, a little distance from the Lax community, Irwin left his wagon and ran down a small stream. The sheriff was notified and at once got in touch with officers in other counties for bloodhounds. The report spread rapidly, and by late afternoon several bloodhounds were on hand. In the meantime a host of armed and excited men had gathered. Automobiles rushed in from widely scattered communities. A man-hunt of huge proportions began.

An All-Night Man-Hunt. With more than a thousand men participating, the hunt lasted all night. Except for short intervals when the track was lost, the dogs trailed the Negro continuously. About three o'clock, he ran out of a cabin in the Lax community. The mob gave chase but a volley of shots failed to stop him. The dogs took up the trail again. Shortly afterwards the sheriff went home to get a little rest, returning to the chase about four-thirty in the morning.

Near daylight the dogs bayed before a farm cabin in the Mystic community. The Negro who lived there told the searching party that Irwin was not inside. The sheriff, however, found Irwin crouched in the kitchen safe. Members of the mob wanted to do violence to the Negro who had shielded Irwin, but the sheriff prevented them.

Several Ocilla business men who participated in the all-night hunt report that when the sheriff captured Irwin they returned home for breakfast and then went to work. Certainly law and order gained nothing when those who had work at offices and shops withdrew and left the situation in the control of those who had nothing to do.

Sheriff Fired on and Ordered About by Mob. No sooner had the sheriff captured Irwin than members of the searching party filled the cabin and took complete control of the situation. The sheriff no less than the suspect was subject to the mob's orders: Irwin was left in his hands only on condition that the sheriff follow their instructions. With the prisoner and two deputies, he was permitted to get in a car and follow close behind a truck carrying fifteen armed men. Behind the sheriff's car were seventy-five or a hundred cars.

Reaching the edge of Ocilla, the sheriff endeavored to get away from the mob by going straight ahead when the truck had made a right-hand turn. As soon as he veered from the route, however, his car was fired upon. A bullet pierced the gasoline tank, emptying it immediately; a second passed through the hood of the car and the radiator, and a third pierced the top. The sheriff got out of the car and with profuse profanity accused those who fired upon him of being the lowest kind of cowards, emphasizing the fact that his own life had been endangered. In commenting upon his narrow escape, the sheriff later stated that anybody was mistaken who thought he was going to jeopardize his life to save a "nigger brute" —that he wouldn't do it and he thought any other white man with good sense would feel the same way. It is evident that the mob meant to have Irwin regardless of what happened to the sheriff.

After this attempt to escape, the sheriff, so he stated, maintained as before the custody of the prisoner, but only within the will of the mob, which with suspect and sheriff passed by the county jail in Ocilla on its way to the place where the girl's body had been found the afternoon before.

Protracted Tortures, Followed by Fire and Bullets. Upon reaching the place where the body of the girl was found, Irwin was tied to a tree with chains. The tortures began. Approximately a thousand people were present, including some women and children on the edge of the crowd. Members of the mob cut off his fingers and toes, joint by joint. Mob leaders carried them off as souvenirs. Next, his teeth were pulled out with wire pliers. Whenever he expressed pain or tried to evade the approaches of his sadistic avengers, he was jabbed in the mouth with a pointed pole. Because of their nature, the remaining mutilations and tortures will not be described. Suffice it to say that they were indecent and brutal beyond belief.

After these mutilations, which lasted more than an hour, Irwin's mangled but living body was hung upon a tree by the arms. Logs and underbrush were piled beneath. Gasoline was poured on. A match was struck. As the flames engulfed the body, it was pierced by bullets.

James Irwin was dead. All day his body, burned past recognition, hung in the tree by the public road. Thousands of white people, including women and children, rode out to see the spectacle. At nightfall the county authorities took the body down and buried it.

The Mob's Victim. James Irwin was working as a wage hand for the uncle of the murdered girl. Until three years before, he had lived in Pulaski County, fifty miles north of Irwin County on the lower edge of the old Georgia Black Belt. The sheriff stated that Irwin had served a sentence in Pulaski County for raping a Negro woman, and that a few months before the lynching he found him prowling about a white home at Ocilla. The evidence in the latter case, however, warranted only a severe reprimand from the court. Following the lynching it was reported about town that Irwin had been treated for a venereal disease by an Ocilla physician in the fall of 1929.

The mob's victim, practically illiterate, had always worked as a farm wage hand. He was married and had one child. The majority of the white people who had known him referred to Irwin as a well-behaved Negro, and expressed surprise that he should have been accused of such crimes. Local Negroes reported that Irwin bore a good reputation, and was a hardworking field hand.

A Close-up on One Lyncher. One of the Commission's investigators, traveling by auto, happened upon one of the mob members, herein called "Sandy," and transported him from Irwin County to Atlanta, a distance of over two hundred miles. According to "Sandy's" statement, he was there from first to last; he cut off and now has a joint of one of Irwin's toes;

he took part in the later tortures, and put three bullets through Irwin's suspended body just as the flames flared up from the gasoline-soaked rubbish. The details of the tortures described by him parallel those given by others, including a college professor who was in the vicinity. By several statements "Sandy" implied that the immediate kinsmen of the murdered girl took prominent parts in Irwin's slow death.

"Sandy" was 21 years old; he was recently married, and is a Primitive Baptist. He attended high school for two years. "Sandy stated that he drank some, but was never drunk beyond consciousness except one time, and that was when he was married. He told in detail how the morning after his marriage he awoke and demanded an explanation: "What are you doing here?" He could scarcely believe it when told by the girl that they were husband and wife.

The first year after his father moved to Irwin County, "Sandy" worked at Ocilla and Fitzgerald. The second year (1930) he share-cropped a farm, and hardly broke even. Without money he decided to hitch-hike to a Texas ranch, where he had worked for a few months two years before. He left his wife behind.

"Sandy" is about six feet tall, weighs near 175 pounds, and his posture is a bit slouched. His coarse blond hair curls a little, and occasional freckles emphasize the blueness of his eyes. When last seen he was dressed in soiled overalls and denim jacket; his right shoe sole was flapping; he had on no socks or hat. In his left hand he clutched a wad of clothes about the size of a ten-cent watermelon, while with his right hand he hailed approaching motorists for passage to Texas.

Reaction of the Community to the Lynching

Attention of State and Nation Focused on Lynching. The Ocilla lynching was the first in the United States in 1930;[1] it was first in the southeastern states, excepting Florida, since the triple lynching at Aiken, S. C., three years earlier; it was the first in Georgia since 1926, when Dave Wright, a white

---

[1] In January a Negro, Jose Hernandez, had been lynched on the accusation of cannibalism at Yatepec, State of Morelos, Mexico.

man, was taken from the jail in Douglas, county seat of Coffee County, which borders Irwin County on the southeast. In this last case sixteen members of the lynching party were indicted, tried, and given penitentiary sentences of from one to twenty years. A precedent had been set; Georgia lynchers had been punished, and in the three years following, there had been no lynching in the state.

The Ocilla lynching was spot news for all papers in Georgia, particularly the county weeklies. The nature of the reported double capital crime tended to inflame the weeklies and to dampen the ardor of most of the metropolitan papers which usually condemn lynching. The daily papers in Georgia and the southeast, excepting the Macon *Telegraph*, devoted but little space to it. The Northern Negro papers carried the report with box letter headlines.

Local Weekly Defends Mob Members. The Ocilla *Star*, Irwin County's weekly, comes from the press Thursday. The lynching occurred on Saturday; and consequently, the first local report was nearly a week later. The news article of February 6th featured the horror of the crimes committed and the record of the Negro lynched. The lynching was dealt with in a matter of fact way, as though it was as it should have been:

"Negro burned by Angry Mob for Brutal Crime. James Irwin gets swift justice for assault and murder of sixteen year old girl.

"Swift punishment was meted out to James Irwin for the commission of the most dastardly crime ever committed in Irwin County, when a crowd of enraged citizens from this and surrounding counties, early Saturday morning, after binding him with chains to a tree where he had attacked and murdered a 16 year old white girl of the county the afternoon before, burned him to death and later hung him to a black gum tree near the public highway.

"After being captured, Irwin confessed to the crime, giving the details substantially as has been related. He also stated that he was an escaped convict serving a ten year term in Pulaski County.

"He lived for the last two years at the home of Mrs. J. M. Willis near Mystic, where he had worked about the house. He was caught last year prowling about a house at Ocilla and locked up, but the charge was not pressed against him.

"Irwin was carried to the spot where he had committed the most heinous crime in the history of the county and soon a fire snuffed out his life."

The editorial in this number of the local paper was an open attack upon the "unfavorable publicity" given "Irwin County's own lynching" by the Macon *Telegraph*:

"Some of those who have criticised us most severely for the lynching that occurred in our county last Saturday seem to have almost lost sight of the fact that a most heinous crime had been committed the afternoon before by the man who was lynched. They lose sight of the fact that one of our pure lovely young girls just budding into attractive young womanhood was attacked and slain by the wanton brute who was the victim of the mob's summary punishment. They write chiefly of the quivering flesh of the burning victim, and not at all of the grasp of the foul beast, or of the deep sorrow that has settled down in the stricken home from which she was so ruthlessly snatched.

"It is one thing to sit behind a mahogany desk a hundred miles away when one knows none of the persons concerned and write scathing editorials on the abstract subject of lynching and its evils. It is quite another thing when it comes close home to us as did last Friday's crime. When it is some other man's daughter or wife, especially if she is far removed from the moralizer, it is easy to see what ought not to have been done. When it is one's own wife or daughter or the wife or daughter of one's neighbor, it is quite a different matter.

"It is unfortunate that the law was not allowed to take its course. There was not a chance that the brute would escape prompt conviction and death at the hands of the law if the mob had permitted his trial.

"But it is to be expected. When this kind of crime is committed, whether it be in Georgia or in Maine, men are going to see that the offender gets his punishment without waiting for the courts. Wrong, of course, but it will nearly always be done. This paper does not condone lynching, but so long as this crime is committed, so long may criminals expect mob violence. . . .

"Let us all hope that there will never be another lynching in Irwin County and that there will be no crime like the one that caused this one."

In this same editorial the following comments on race relations appeared:

"And it is not a question of race. Had a white man been guilty of the crime that James Irwin committed last Friday afternoon, he would have been lynched just as surely as the Negro was. It is noteworthy that in the all night hunt for this criminal several negroes joined in the search, and many of them have expressed the conviction that Irwin got just what he deserved. While on the subject of race, it is to be noted that this crime was not committed by one of our Irwin County Negroes. He was an escaped convict from another section. Our Negroes are a much better class than was this man."

"The Macon Telegraph Flops," Says Local Editor. In the following number of the Ocilla *Star*, February 13, were two editorials, the first, "An Appreciation":

"The editor would be less than human if he did not appreciate the many kind things that have been said to him since the editorial on the lynching appeared last week. One commendation is especially appreciated, and that is the assurance that has come to him that the editorial played some part in reassuring the law abiding negroes of the county that no harm to them was meant. The relations between the negroes of Irwin County and the white people have always been agreeable. . . ."

And then this for local consumption:

"The editor of the *Star* hangs his head in shame. W. T. Anderson calls into question his character."

And then a jubilant comment entitled "The Macon *Telegraph* Flops":

"The always virile, but sometimes wrong editor of the Macon *Telegraph*, alone among the daily editors of the state, just simply turned over his can of vituperation and spilled the contents over the people of this county and section who lynched the negro James Irwin on February 1st.

"Following this up a few days ago he took a column and a half of his editorial space to pay his respects to the editorial that appeared in the Coffee County *Progress* and the Ocilla *Star,* which he says condoned the lynching. He reviews the case and finally reached the same conclusion the *Star* reached in its editorial last week, that is that the lynching is deplorable, but to be expected whenever such a crime is committed.

"Mr. Anderson admits that if the crime were committed upon a member of his family he, too, would kill, but adds that he would probably write a strong editorial against his act, and then humbly kneel down and pray over it. Maybe so, hardly more than two-thirds of what he says he would do would likely be done."

Two Revealing Open Letters. On the editorial page of the Ocilla *Star* appeared two open letters which perchance say other things the editor wanted his subscribers to get:

Arp, Ga.

"Editor of The *Star,* Ocilla, Ga.
"Dear Sir:

"I have just read your editorial in the *Star* in regard to the recent lynching in Irwin County.

"You have expressed my sentiment in regard to the matter and I believe that your attitude will be admired by Irwin County citizens and others outside the county. . . .

"My father moved to Irwin County about 43 years ago when I was a small boy.

"I believe that we can measure arms with many other Georgia counties when it comes to a matter of good citizenship, especially

Fulton and Bibb counties, from which has come two scathing editorials. One from a Methodist preacher, editor of *The Wesleyan Christian Advocate* and the other from Mr. Anderson editor of the Macon *Telegraph*.

"No doubt some of the mob who participated in the lynching of Irwin were of the lawless element.

"On the other hand I believe that some of our most law-abiding citizens during the heat of passion and without due consideration in an unguarded moment took the law into their own hands.

"And as you say Mr. Editor just so long as such diabolical crimes are committed, we may expect mob violence."

(signed) A. V. YARBOROUGH.

"Editor of the *Star*.

"To merely imagine a dead human burn at the stake is horror itself, but on the other hand—

"To see that little girl in death with the half smile upon her lips. One clear eye half closed, the other stabbed out by a dull knife, her breast slit by the same dull knife, great gashes on either side of the throat and the whole of the body mutilated by brute force and brute lust, our viewpoint seems to change as to the justice that the brute deserved. That little girl who had just begun to realize that life is worth living went through more hell in the last minute of her existence than James Irwin could have gone through in twenty years of torture.

"Furthermore it has been said that James Irwin could have received more justice but the idea mocks itself. He tried himself when he passed the little girl on the road and jumped off the wagon to go back and kill her. He tried himself and lost the case, it seems. He confessed his guilt by running twenty miles through the night with the howl of that lonely pack of hounds on his heel and he committed himself for execution when he forgot to kill himself just before they caught him. Compared to the crime he committed James Irwin spent his last two hours in paradise contrasted with the justice he deserved."

(signed) JIMMIE FULLER.

Court Action Limited to Judge's Charge. The courts have done nothing. The coroner's inquest "found that the deceased

came to his death by burning and gunshot wounds at the hands
of parties unknown."

The judge of the Superior Court gave a lengthy charge to
the grand jury in which he stressed the supremacy of the law
as the only means of safety. These paragraphs are taken from
his charge:

"Law is not civilization, but it is the only barrier against the
onrush of anarchy and barbarism; the only safeguard against an
eye for an eye and a tooth for a tooth, blind chaos and the rule
of the club and the claw.

"In taking upon himself the right to identify, try, condemn
and punish law violaters, or in calling upon others to do so,
is he not, in a manner, playing traitor to a government patriots
have died to establish and to defend? Is he not with his own
hands striving to tear down the only bulwark of civilization and
only defense—the law?

"Crimes are committed that blind with horror and blast the reason
of man. This has been going on since the race began its early
pilgrimage. Those who commit such crimes deserve the punishment of death; the law so decrees. Let us say that they deserve
death at the hands of him who first overtakes him. Even so,
should those who have made the law, who have ratified the law,
who live under the protecting shadow of the law violate and slay
the law as the criminal has violated and slain his victim? Is there
nothing sacred about the form and spirit of the law? Should its
chosen agents and representatives be driven from their places,
shot at, battered or maltreated while they are striving to do the
duty they are sworn to perform? Let your common sense and your
patriotism answer this question.

"I am of the South and of these people. I know of the dangers
of the remote farmhouse and the lonely road and the silent terror
that lingers there. . . . It is not for me to say that I would not go
from the shadows of my broken home to seek and to slay; it is not
for me to denounce; it is not for me to condemn; but is for me
to pronounce the judgment of your own laws, our own laws, the
laws of which and for which I am but the humble spokesman.
That judgment is:

" 'We will not hold him guiltless who slays not to prevent, but to punish, not to defend, but to revenge.'

"Grand jurors are sworn. The oath you take is far-reaching and all embracing. Under that oath there is no violation of the law, known to your members or capable of ascertainment through your diligence, that you may honestly ignore. . . . Hard, yes, it is hard, but a judge can understand.

"You, as a grand jury, are not to concern yourself with punishment, the nature or extent thereof. The law leaves that with judge and trial juries.

"Your duty is fully performed when an honest and legal indictment is found. . . .

"If grand juries fail, prosecutions fail; if prosecutions fail, malefactors go unpunished; if malefactors go unpunished, justice will fail; if justice fails civilization must fail."

The crowded courtroom listened attentively to the judge's lengthy and forceful charge. But no indictments were brought, and nobody was surprised.

Governor's Request Amounts to Nothing. The part played by the state authorities is limited to Governor Hardman's request for a report on the lynching. In his request for the report from the local authorities the Governor virtually promised not to interfere with the matter when he said: "Any action of the state will depend upon what the sheriff and the solicitor general report to me." The solicitor general reported to the Governor that he found no information to warrant an indictment. Commenting upon the failure to indict, the Eastman *Times-Journal* remarked: "Foy said he reported to the governor he had talked with a score of persons about the incident, and that, as usual, those who knew anything would tell nothing, and those who would tell, knew nothing."

No Local Condemnation of Mob Death. No preacher, teacher, public official, or other individual—except the judge in his charge to the grand jury—voiced sentiment against the lynching. No organization made any protest. The ministers, while not proud of the mob's activities, have said nothing and plan to say nothing, reasoning that since there is so much pro-lynching feeling in the community it is best to leave the matter be. While a few white people apologize for the lynching, the masses of white people frankly justify it; and Negroes accept it—probably a condition of continued residence in Irwin County.

Not only is the public generally satisfied with the lynching, but little or no fault is found with those who during the man hunt fired into a car full of innocent Negroes, wounding some of them. The possemen claimed the Negroes would not stop when told to. The Negroes said nothing. The grand jury ignored the incident. The lynching was considered a local matter by the local people, and Editors W. T. Anderson, A. M. Pierce, and anybody else who found fault with it were damned.

In an adjoining judicial district, a Superior Court judge stated to one of the Commission's investigators that he knew personally many people of his own home town who were at Ocilla and participated in the lynching there; he stated further that no indictments had been brought or would be brought, and that if indictments were brought nobody would be convicted. The above statements were made in the presence of the district prosecuting attorney and the district court stenographer. This judge doubtless has not and will not communicate his evidence concerning the lynchers to the proper court officials of the adjoining judicial district.

And With What Results? The local people have given complete immunity to the lynchers, and are mightily pleased with the futile efforts of the press and the courts. What effects will the whole affair have upon Irwin County? What will the economic consequences be? How will it affect the allocation of public school funds as between urban and rural children of both races? What will be the influence upon ethical and moral standards?

A wide range of attitudes prevailed throughout the State, as reflected by the press.

"They Lynched Justice," Says Macon Telegraph. While other dailies called attention to Georgia's broken record, the

Macon *Telegraph*, the only daily with any considerable circulation in south Georgia, came out with an editorial captioned "Justice Lynched," parts of which were:

"The mob of a thousand white men who yesterday morning mutilated and burned James Irwin did more than send into eternity the brutal soul of a black. They lynched justice in Georgia. . . .

". . . It was the ferocity of the pack turned loose in a supposedly civilized community. On no other basis can the lawlessness of the lynchers be explained. . . .

"It was the average man who took the vicious Negro, James Irwin, from the sheriff and mutilated and lynched him. For their crime there is not the shadow of excuse. . . . By their deed they wiped their bloody feet on society's rule of law. By their deed they lynched justice in Georgia and did almost as terrible a thing to society as did the Negro."

The suggestion that those who lynched Irwin "did almost as terrible a thing to society as did the Negro" angered the people of Irwin County, and later when one of the *Telegraph* reporters went there for news he was warned to leave town at once; and the local report is that he did. The Ocilla *Star's* editorial of February 6th, given above, was Irwin County's answer. The Coffee County *Progress* also had a scathing editorial closing with ". . . when he (editor of the Macon *Telegraph*) stated that those who participated in the killing of James Irwin are quite as guilty as the Negro himself he denotes himself a low thinker, and in the minds of a great many people, a vicious liar." A number of people on the streets of Ocilla and Fitzgerald said Anderson's life would not be safe in Irwin County.

The "Flop" of the Macon *Telegraph*, referred to above, was editor Anderson's acknowledgment: "I do not undertake to say what I should do if the horrible thing were perpetrated upon a member of my family or one of my neighbors. I do not see how I could restrain myself from doing just what was done by the beast's victims in Irwin County the other day." He continued by saying how he might write editorials denouncing his own rash actions, and then "I should go to God on my knees and acknowledge my error" and "ask Him to make me clean if it could be done . . ." closing with: "I have done many things that were wrong. I knew it was wrong when I did it. My only virtue was in not contending afterwards that it was right, and perhaps that is the only difference between myself and these two editors and the people who composed the Ocilla mob. Who knows?"

A second exceptionally forceful editorial appears in *The Wesleyan Christian Advocate* in which Dr. A. M. Pierce pointed out that two heinous crimes had been committed—one by the Negro, the other by the mob. This drew several adverse replies, the most virulent of which appeared in the Butler *Herald*.

"The editor of *The Wesleyan Christian Advocate* ought to stick his head in a hole and hide after ranting over the lynching of the Irwin County brute at Ocilla. There is more for which many Methodists will blush at the editorial expressions of the *Advocate* than the doings of the mob. No right-thinking person in the state upholds lynchings, but there are some crimes that good southern blood will not stand for and the Irwin case was one of them. Therefore, why shed tears. If the *Advocate* editor is ashamed of his state there's plenty of room elsewhere for him. He is not chained here so far as we know."

Only Brief Mention in Other State Dailies. The leading dailies throughout Georgia carried news of the lynching, but except in the Macon *Telegraph* only brief editorials appeared. The Savannah *Press* of February 1, after briefly rehearsing the facts, commented editorially that, "so we are not surprised to hear that a crowd of several hundred persons took by force from the sheriff the man suspected of the crime and put him to death. . . . Of course, we cannot defend the crime of lynching. . . . But it is wasting breath in a time like this to censure an indignant people. . . . The whole thing is deplorable—tragic." Next morning the Savannah *News* pointed out that two white boys in Oconee County were sentenced to die in the electric chair for killing an aged Negro couple on the same day that Irwin was lynched at Ocilla, and that "both events indicate

factors in the relation of races in the state," and "we would
be glad if northern critics would study both of these stories.
. . ." On the same day the Albany *Herald* had an editorial on
"Judge Lynch Returns to Georgia," lamenting the affair, but
pointing out that "when crimes like the one which threw Irwin
and adjoining counties into a frenzy are committed, ordinarily
sane men are going to do that which they can be expected to do
when they 'see red.' "

Nearly two weeks after the lynching the Atlanta *Independent*,
a Negro weekly, came out with an editorial captioned "Eloquent
Silence," pointing out that "so far as the crime goes, the culprit
was an incident and the wrong is the lynching of the majesty
of the law," with this about the "silence" of Atlanta's three
white papers:

"But the sad thing about it is, the metropolitan press of the
state is notoriously lacking in editorial condemnation of the crime.
If either of our great city papers have said a word in condemnation
of mob law on this occasion it has escaped our attention.

"This is to be deplored for the reason the public accepts the
silence of the press as acquiescence in the crime."

A Few County Weeklies Denounce The Lynching. The weeklies throughout Georgia commented at length upon the lynching. Some editors termed it deplorably inexcusable; others considered it deplorable but inevitable, while still others saw in it a
much-needed object lesson for Negroes who will not voluntarily
stay in "their places." All were aware that Georgia's three year
record had been broken.

The Folkston *Herald* lamented the broken record, and acknowledged the Negro's horrible crime, "yet it would have been
better to have let the law take its course and save our state
the name of still having a barbaric nature." The Dalton *Citizen*
pointed out that regardless of the crime of the Negro, "it
would have been better to let the law take its course. When a
mob mimics a crime it, too, is guilty of a crime. That is in-
escapable." The Elberton *Star*, Sylvester *Local*, Commerce
News and other of the small papers carried a reprint of the

Savannah Press' editorial referring to the whole thing as "deplorable-tragic." The fact that two white boys had been sentenced to death for killing an aged Negro couple in Oconee County on the same day of the lynching was discussed by the Summerville *News* and the Cordele *Dispatch*, the latter's editorial concluding, "But we can hold up the majesty of the law and defend it against all crises in both mob rule and wilful murder." "An aroused public conscience," said the Cairo *Messenger*, "checked lynch law in this state a few years ago and sent quite a number of members of one mob to the penitentiary for punishment. Is the public conscience dead?" "It is not a matter of race resentment," explained the Cedartown *Standard*, "when such terrible tragedies occur, for as a race the Negroes are no more prone to such crimes than whites of the same grade of intelligence as those who commit such bestial crimes. Regardless of color all should be educated sufficiently to lift them above the brute level." The Statesboro *Times and News* felt that while the Negro got what he deserved, "the commonwealth of Georgia deserved better treatment than was meted out to her by the people comprising that mob. Georgia laws deserve respect."

Many Weeklies Justify Lynching. The Sandersville *Progress* is an illustration of how the press dragged out the arguments of dead politicians to defend the lynching:

"The late Senator Thos. E. Watson, in reply to a question whether he considered mob violence justifiable, stated that the only way to stop them is to stop committing such crimes. The late Senator Mrs. Rebecca L. Felton,[2] when asked her opinion on this subject, replied that she was in favor of lynching when such crimes were perpetrated, as she believed if this was not done there would be many more of them committed."

The Butler *Herald* expressed sympathy with the Irwin County lynchers and "any censure that is placed upon that good county's name will be shared willingly by the people of the

---

[2] A Negro accused with murder was lynched in Mrs. Felton's home town, Cartersville, on Oct. 1, 1930.

state as a whole." "The murder of the young girl," reflected
the Adel *News*, "was a most atrocious one and called for speedy
justice." The Greensboro *Herald-Journal* and others were
certain that "lynchings will occur anywhere in the country
under similar circumstances," while the Ringgold *Record* disposed of the matter by saying "it is just our way of giving
base criminals their just deserts." "These fiends," said the
Homer *Journal*, "often cost counties many thousand dollars . . .
if the defense happens to have money 'alienists' are hired.
Then the state hires more alienists. An alienist has always been
a strange bird to us. If the defense hires him the subject is a
nut. If the state hires him the subject is a brilliant man."

And then this from the Metter *Advertiser:* "I, like any
average Georgian, under normal conditions, oppose lynchings,"
but, "had this same crime been committed in our county of
Candler the papers would have hailed Candler for staging the
first Georgia lynching after more than three years." "Georgia
has one lynching to her credit this year," commented the
Crawfordville *Democrat*, "and the sob sisters will get busy."
Several papers pointed out "the slow process of the law,"
and held that the possible delays based on technicalities and
appeals partially or wholly justified the lynching. The Douglas
Progress of February 6th had this statement which leans toward a theological justification, ". . . it is not so sure a thing
that the Deity looks with such disfavor on the merits of justice
as does the editor of the Macon *Telegraph*."

Lynching has "become a custom," said the Sylvester *Local:*

"There won't be anything done about the lynching of the brute
in Irwin County, fuss and talk about investigating, and all that,
to the contrary notwithstanding. That brute met his just fate.
He wasn't worth honoring with a court trial. It is right that he
was disposed of like a mad dog. Other brutes, committing like
crimes in Georgia will meet with the same fate. It is the unwritten
law of the land. It is unfortunate that such drastic means for dis-
posing of a brute of this kind has become a custom but it is a
fact and there is no way in which to get around it."

Editors Ridiculed Prosecution of Lynchers. That court investigations of the Ocilla lynching would amount to nothing was generally expressed by the Georgia rural press. The Crawfordville *Democrat* concluded that "lynchings will never be stopped in this state so long as such crimes are committed, and officers may investigate as much as they please but nothing will ever be done about it. And that's that." The editor of the Bainbridge *Post-Searchlight* became the spokesman of those who justified the lynching.[3] His editorials were copied widely by the county papers. In his first editorial after the lynching, reference was made to Georgia's broken record in this fashion: "As for us we don't care a darn thing about the record when such an offense causes the breaking of that record. Let all the fawning hypocrites weep over the murdered rapist, our tears are for the poor little girl." The next week came an editorial on "Furnish Governor Dope," which was in part: "The governor wants a report on the lynching at Ocilla. Well, that is easy. Negro attacked and then killed a fourteen year old girl, threw her body in a hog wallow. Folks rose up and lynched the negro that did it. That is all there is to it and that is all there is going to be to it. So just cuss around a little about it and shut up for that is all that can be done about it." This editorial was copied in the Ringgold *Record* with the following comment: "You tell 'em Pat. A little cussing is all they can do about it and we think your report on the lynching over at Ocilla is correct and should be sufficient for the governor." The third week after the lynching some of his choicest lines were: "There is no use in shedding crocodile tears over this thing . . . we would rather see a dozen brutes lynched than one good woman or girl raped and that is that so far as we are concerned."

Now and then some reference was made to federal legislation on lynching, and in every case the opinion was expressed that the South could attend to its own business. "Investigations

---

[3] And interesting enough, a lynching was prevented in his home town a few months later and he was one of the leaders in protecting the Negro and dissuading the mob from its purpose.

may be made," remarked the Pelham *Journal*, "men convicted
and sentences served but so long as women are attacked just
that long will lynching occur regardless of Mr. Dyar's (Sic)
opinion." The Cedartown *Standard* pointed out that "Both
the murderous rape and the lynching are most unfortunate,
but the jackasses who are now about to bray about it in
Congress should bear in mind that if there had been no crime
there would have been no lynching."

Facts About the Community

Inland Southeast Georgia a Population Eddy. When Irwin
County was laid off by a lottery act in 1818 its territory em-
braced nearly a score of present-day south Georgia counties,
including Thomas,[4] Wilcox, Lowndes, Brooks, Colquitt, Worth,
Turner, Tift, Cook, Ben Hill, Berrien, and others. It was a pine
woods frontier; in 1820 the whole area had but 411 inhabitants.
From the outset, this unproductive land attracted men of small
means who wanted to lead a free and independent life.

With the development and spread of slave plantations in
central Georgia, lands were concentrated into fewer and fewer
hands. Farmers with small tracts of land tended to sell to
the big planters and then do one of four things: move on ahead
of the big planters to the rich lands at the wilderness' edge;
move northwest into the hill country; move southeast into the
pine barren region where land was cheap and unproductive;
or remain within the plantation community as "poor whites."
Some of those who moved on ahead of the expanding plantation area amassed enough property to become planters themselves; many of those who went into the hill country to the
northwest pushed on across the mountains into Tennessee and
beyond to become economically secure in the rapidly developing country.

For those who moved into the pine barren section of southeast Georgia there were no rich lands in the wilderness ahead
as in the southwest, no fertile river bottoms and prairies beyond
as in the northwest. Beyond them were thickets and the

---

[4] This County was organized from Irwin County territory in 1826. A
lynching occurred in it on September 25, 1930.

swamps' "bad air," then believed to be the cause of the chills and fever which tormented the inhabitants of this region. The area along the coast was already settled, as were also the uplands of northern Florida. Irwin and adjoining counties were an "eddy" between the main currents of population movements. Historically, into the eddy have gone, for the most part, men who lacked the vision or the courage to push on. Inland southeast Georgia has had no beyond—it has been and is an "eddy" for drifting poor people.

Independent Farmers and Timber Trailers. Stock raising was the first principal means of making a living. Scrub cattle and "razor-back" hogs were allowed to run free to find subsistence in the coarse grass of the upland forests and the tender new growth of the swampy thickets.

The whole area was covered with a heavy growth of long leaf yellow pine, the earliest settlers having cleared only sufficient ground to grow such crops as were needed for their own use. Later timber trailers came in, and some of the local people found employment cutting logs, getting them to the river, and then rafting them down the Ocmulgee and Altamaha rivers to sawmills at Darien.[5]

In 1850 there were more than seven whites to one Negro: 2,884 whites, 1 free colored male, and 450 Negro slaves. With the introduction of commercial fertilizer after the Civil War, farming in Irwin and surrounding counties showed some increase; commercial fertilizers were expensive, however, and did not prove to be very popular with these self-sufficient independent farmers.

As late as 1866, G. G. Smith in his *Story of Georgia* wrote, "The writer, passing through this county, rode seventeen miles on the public road without seeing a house." The section referred to by Smith may have been in territory since that time organized into a new county. The statement is pertinent here, however, for people from all the surrounding counties participated in the lynching of James Irwin.

With the development of the turpentine and sawmill in-

---

[5] Darien, in McIntosh County on the coast, had a lynching on September 8, 1930.

dustries during the last quarter of the past century, the
Negro element increased to approximately one-third of the
population; in 1890 there were 4,241 whites and 2,075 Negroes,
most of the latter being little more than transient laborers
living in shacks about the turpentine stills and logging camps.

A Flourishing Colony of Yankee Soldiers. In 1896 the northern part of Irwin County was in the throes of a boom. P. H.
Fitzgerald of Indianapolis, and other Northern men had established a colony to which 7,000 people, mostly Northern
pensioned soldiers, came within a year. In 1906 a county was
laid off from Irwin; it was named Ben Hill in honor of the
Georgia statesman. The new town was called Fitzgerald to
commemorate its founder; east of Main the streets were named
for Federal generals; to the west they were named for Confederate generals. A large hotel was built; it bears the unusual
name of Lee-Grant. Northern soldiers came by the thousands;
pension checks to the value of over ten thousand dollars were
cashed each month.

There was an influx of laborers, white and illiterate, to
help build the fast growing town, to cut firewood for the 200
fireplaces in the Lee-Grant Hotel. With the growth of the
town, additional lands were put into cultivation.

Within a few years Fitzgerald lost its glamor for the immigrants from the North, and the local people began to turn to
other sources for a livelihood. The A. B. & A. Railroad had
shops there employing 1,200 men at one time. Sawmills developed. With the passing of the tourist trade and the falling
off of employment in the sawmills and the A. B. & A. shops,
cotton mills were built and now give employment to a goodly
number.

From the start Fitzgerald has not been a normal community. At first it was a colony of soldiers in the wilderness,
with over 40 per cent of the people 55 years of age and above.
Then came the poverty-ridden rural white dwellers into town
for the cash wages paid for day laborers and domestics. Next
were the sawmills, then the railroad shops, and finally the cotton mills. Fitzgerald is less than ten miles north of Ocilla and
has been given special consideration here because the two towns

are connected by a hard surfaced road and many of the people in the mob that tortured and burned James Irwin were from Fitzgerald and other parts of Ben Hill County.

Recent Population Decrease. The population of Irwin County increased rapidly during the first two decades of this century. The exhaustion of the soil in the central Georgia counties by the clean culture crops of cotton and corn had made the pine barren section relatively more desirable. Then, too, the use of commercial fertilizers had become general. Georgia's newer crops—tobacco, watermelons, pecans, and peanuts—when sufficiently fertilized, thrive in southeast Georgia's sandy loams.

The 1930 census shows a population of 12,199 for Irwin County, which is a decrease of 3.7 per cent since 1920. Of the 2,553 inhabitants of the three incorporated towns, Ocilla, the county seat, has 2,053. The white people of the county are of early Georgia stock. In 1930, less than one in a thousand was foreign-born, as compared with the state average of six.

The Negro element increased regularly until ten years ago. In 1850, about one-sixth of the population were Negroes; in 1890, nearly one-third; in 1920, approximately 45 per cent. In 1930 but 37.2 per cent were Negroes, there being 1,175 fewer Negroes and 670 fewer whites in the county in 1930 than in 1920. The recent population decrease has been a concomitant of the low prices paid for cotton, tobacco, melons, and pecans. The one person out of five who lives in town earns a livelihood as plantation owner or turpentine operator, storekeeper or banker, public official or lawyer, doctor or preacher, auto mechanic or gas station keeper, and most of his money comes directly from the rural folk. The cotton seed oil mill at Ocilla has but a few employees. Florida tourists in transit leave but little money in Ocilla, for the town has only one attractive tourist stop, and it can accommodate but a few guests.

The turpentine and sawmilling interests have declined markedly in the past few years. Between 1920 and 1925 the landowners were faced with the necessity of securing an income from their lands in spite of the pestiferous boll weevil, which had caused the abandonment of 250 farms. The land owners naturally cashed in on their timber, and now there is scarcely any of the original long leaf yellow pine left; the second growth is too small for sawing. If the price of resin products warranted it, the turpentine industry would doubtless be extended.

Increase of Tobacco Acreage and Decrease of Negro Farmers. By 1925 the inroads of the weevil made new crops imperative. The 1924 cotton crop was but 5,375 bales. The yield in 1929 had gone back up to 7,288, which is nearly a thousand bales in excess of the yearly average between 1925 and 1929, but more than 10,000 bales below the normal pre-weevil crop. Except for the introduction of tobacco, Irwin County would have lost still other hundreds of farmers. In 1924 the county had 541 acres in tobacco; in 1927, 1,300 acres; in 1929, 2,750 acres. Nevertheless, cotton is still the chief source of income for the vast majority of farmers; for in 1929 nearly seventy-five thousand acres were planted in cotton. An acre of tobacco, however, involves more work and a much larger money outlay than an acre of cotton and in turn brings an income of from three to six times as much. In terms of labor required, expense of production, and income the 2,750 acres of tobacco were equal to more than 10,000 acres of cotton.

Tobacco growing has increased as cotton farming has decreased. The partial shift from cotton to tobacco has resulted in a decrease of Negro farmers and an increase of white farmers. Between 1920 and 1930 the number of white farmers increased slightly while the number of Negro farmers decreased more than one-fourth.

An Expensive Year-Round Crop. It is possible to produce a cotton crop between March and November, and with the minimum equipment of a mule and plow, some commercial fertilizer and a little weevil poison, enough hoes and bags for each member of the family at "choppin" and "pickin" times, and a wagon to haul the cotton to the gin. The tobacco farmer, on the other hand, has a year-round job and an expensive one. This has resulted in tobacco's being a white man's crop in Irwin and adjoining counties. To produce tobacco a farmer must either own his own land or be furnished the expensive equipment by a landlord. Only under strictest supervision is tobacco growing on a plantation scale possible in this area, unused as it is to its cultivation. The propertyless tenants with the cotton culture tradition of nothing to do in winter and again in mid-summer look with disfavor upon tobacco or any other continuous farm industry. When a plantation owner is experimenting with tobacco he usually uses only white tenants. The bulk of the tobacco, however, has been produced by small owners, and there are less than forty Negro farm owners in Irwin County.

The type of white people who settled and developed this county, the physical factors of topography and soils, the coming of the weevil and the subsequent development of the tobacco industry have all functioned in making chronically unattached transient laborers of the vast majority of Negroes. The fact that there were practically no slaves in the county and that the Negroes have never been an indispensable part of the economic fabric of the community leaves them without "their own white folks," doubtless a fundamental reason why the torturing and burning of James Irwin has been so universally condoned or justified by the local white people.

Low Economic Rating of County. In 1924 Irwin County's value of farm crops was $101.94 and of manufactured products $69.45, making a total of $171.39 per capita; the state average from these two sources was $310.78 per capita. Other indices are as follows: Bank deposits in Irwin County in 1929 were but $33.54 per inhabitant as compared with $155.89 for the state at large: eighteen income tax returns were made for the county in 1924, which is one return for every 700 people, while throughout the state there was a return for every forty-six people; there were but seven returns in 1929, or one for every 1,743 as compared with one for every ninety throughout Georgia for the same year; exclusive of corporation taxes, the tax valuation was $218.93 per inhabitant in the county and $348.03 throughout the state. In spite of the small amount of money, the number of persons per auto in Irwin County decreased from 25.4 in 1925 to 9.7 in 1930, when there was an auto to every 8.4 persons in Georgia. Money invested in autos by poor people makes it easy for them to get away from their sordid rural dwellings, but at the same time reduces the amount of money they have for other things. Thus the ownership of an auto, while making the road more attractive to the poor man, not infrequently makes his home less comfortable.

Small Expenditures for Public Education. The expenditures for schools in Irwin County are far below the average in Georgia. Not only is less spent on white schools, but the proportion of the county's public funds going to Negro schools is much below the state average. The figures for 1928 by race were: For each white child of school age $29.72 was spent in the county, as against an average for the state of $36.88; for each Negro child $2.85 in Irwin and $5.07 in the state. The Georgia Legislature appropriated approximately $5.20 to the Irwin County Board of Education for each school-age child regardless of race. The Negroes not only failed to share in the county school tax, but received little more than half the amount allocated for them by the state.

These lower expenditures mean poorer paid and generally poorer trained teachers, and also poorer schoolroom equipment, than for the state as a whole. Some concrete comparisons will demonstrate this conclusively: In 1928, the average white teacher in Irwin County received $526.85 per year against the state average of $792.32; the average Irwin Negro teacher received $143.72, as compared with the state average of $306.76. In 1928 the County School Board spent nothing for Negro public education other than for teachers' salaries. Nearly thirty-seven per cent of all Irwin white teachers were in one and two-teacher schools, in contrast with but 21.2 per cent in the state; 89.4 per cent of the county's Negro teachers were in these small schools, as compared with 66.1 per cent throughout the state. In the county's Negro schools there was a patent desk to each 11.8 pupils in average daily attendance, while for the state at large there was a patent desk to each 4.3 A. D. A. pupils. In 1930, of Irwin County's white people ten years old and over, 5.4 per cent were illiterate against 3.3 per cent throughout the state; the Negro's illiteracy rate for the county was 19.8 per cent and for the state 19.9 per cent.

Differences in School Expenditures by Race Were Least Where White Schools Were Best. The above is not the whole story, for while the schools in Ocilla are better than these figures suggest, the schools in the open country are poorer. For example, the average annual salary of the thirteen white teachers in Ocilla was $915.00 while the average for the thirty-eight rural teachers was $422.46; the average salary of the four Negro teachers in Ocilla was $423.75 and of the twenty-one rural Negro teachers $138.00. The data presented here indicate that inadequate educational facilities are provided for all rural children, and especially for rural Negro children. The situation in this county illustrates a condition which is generally true throughout the South, namely, that the differences between the white and Negro schools are least where the white schools are best and greatest where the white schools are poorest.[6] In Ocilla where white teachers were best paid, the average salary of the Negro teacher was nearly half that of the white teacher, while in the remainder of the county it was but a little more than one-third.

A Strong Primitive Baptist Influence. Church organizations are weak in Irwin County. In 1926, the white church membership of 1,856 was but forty-two per cent of the white population over fifteen years of age. The total Negro church membership of 1,526 was forty-one per cent of the Negro population over fifteen. For the state at large more than sixty per cent of the population over fifteen were church members.

The Primitive Baptist denomination has a strong following in this county; it is properly called "Primitive," for ignorance is one of the things its members boast; its ministers are advertised as unschooled, and in this sect it is considered sinful to use musical instruments in church services. They have nothing to do with foreign missions, Sunday schools, and farmers' organizations, much less the lately developing programs of public health and general public welfare. In fact, they are "agin" nearly

[6] This thesis is presented more fully in my *Two Black Belt Counties*. (Ph.D. dissertation, University of North Carolina, 1931.)

everything, and by their persistence have invited their critics to dub them "Harshells." And the "Hardshells" are hardest where the people are poorest and farthest removed from the center of things. Irwin County, historically a population eddy because of its poor soil and geographic location, might be expected to have some very unusual examples; and so it has, as was indicated in an earlier section of this report.

The Primitive Baptists are such chronic opposers of organizations that here, as in other communities where their ideas dominate, there are no strong churches, for many people find this philosophy a reason for staying out of all organizations, including the Primitive Baptist Church itself. Their following is not limited to whites, for here, as elsewhere, the Negroes have taken over the white man's religious forms.

Weak Methodist and Baptist Church Organizations. The Presiding Elder of the Methodist Episcopal Church, South, for the district in which Irwin County is located, formerly pastor at Ocilla, in discussing the prevalence of unchurched people in the county writes: "The reason is that it is a Primitive Baptist stronghold and it always has been exceedingly difficult to get a foothold for Methodism in that county. Missionary money has been spent in the county for years and much work has been done. Our Methodist people are poor and few." There are three white Methodist churches in the county with a total membership of less than 400, three-fourths of whom are members of the church at Ocilla, which has preaching every Sunday and is equipped for and conducts a departmentalized Sunday school. The other two churches have preaching but once a month; one has only twelve members.

Scattered over the county are seven white Missionary Baptist churches. More than one-third of their total membership of 1,425 is in Ocilla. The church at Ocilla is valued at $39,500, which is more than five times the combined value of the other six. The Ocilla pastor receives a yearly salary of $1,800, while the combined salaries paid by the six other churches is but $1,035, $645 of which is for the churches at the small incorporated towns of Mystic and Irwinville. Ocilla has preach-

ing every Sunday, Irwinville and Mystic twice a month, and
the other four once a month.

Eighty per cent of the Negro church membership of 1,526
is identified with the Negro Missionary Baptist Convention,
the remaining membership being about equally divided between
the Negro Primitive Baptist, A. M. E., and C. M. E. Churches.
The Corresponding Secretary of the General Missionary Baptist Convention of Georgia reported thirty Negro churches
in Irwin County. These churches have an average of but forty
members each. With Negroes as poor as they are in Irwin
County, this inevitably means weak churches with sorry buildings and poorly paid and uneducated men who come once a
month. These once-a-month ministers are preachers rather than
pastors.

Irwin County is a Baptist County. Other than Baptists
and Methodists there are but eighty-four church members of
both races in the county.

A Segment of the "Solid South." The 1928 presidential
election brought out 1,079 voters in the County, nearly nine-
tenths of whom voted the straight Democratic ticket. The
Democratic vote alone was nearly three hundred more than
the total number of votes cast in any previous presidential
election. Voting is limited almost entirely to whites, and not
nearly all of them vote; a little more than one-third of the
adult whites voted in the 1928 presidential election, one-
fourth in 1920, one-ninth in 1924. This lack of interest is not
explained by the fact that Irwin County always goes Democratic anyway, for in the State Democratic primary on September 10, 1930, after four popular candidates for governor
used every known means of getting people to vote, but 611
votes were cast in the county. This is less than one-fourth,
whereas approximately one-third of the adult whites throughout
the state voted.

The relatively large vote in the 1928 presidential election,
especially since there were fewer Republican votes than in
1920, suggests how loyal the general public is to the Democratic party. The rank and file of white people in Irwin and

adjoining counties are descended from non-slaveholders and are ardent supporters of the doctrine of "white superiority," always most virulent among the less privileged whites, who cling to the Democratic Party for protection from "nigger-lovin' " administrations in Washington and for a guarantee of "pure white" rule at home. This doubtless means that a considerable proportion of the white people feel the need of legislation to keep the Negro down, no less than to keep themselves up. The most "solid" portions of the "solid South" are to be found in this county and similar areas.

Jail population by race in Irwin County in 1921 and 1929 suggest that lawlessness is increasing among the whites and decreasing among the Negroes. The white jail population rose from twenty-six in 1921 to forty-four in 1929, an increase from 4.0 per thousand population to 6.9 per thousand. During this same period the Negro jail population decreased from seventy-two to fifty-eight, a decrease from 12.4 to 10.0 per thousand. For the state as a whole, in 1929 the white jail population was 12.5 per thousand and the Negro jail population 25.4 per thousand. Not only were jail commitments lower for each race in this county than for the state as a whole, but the number of felons in the penitentiary per thousand population was 1.08 as compared with 1.64 for the entire state. There is the possibility, of course, that a low rate of jail commitments and of felons may merely indicate unpunished lawlessness.

Scarcely Any Welfare Agencies. Irwin County is about as poor in welfare agencies and institutions as it could be. It has no health officer, no county nurse, social worker, recreation worker, tuberculosis clinic, county-wide library, city library, or Red Cross chapter. In the nature of welfare agencies and institutions it has only a Home Demonstration Agent, a small hospital at Ocilla, and schools and churches which, as has been shown, are far below the state average.

Neither the State Department of Public Welfare nor the State Board of Health has been able to get satisfactory co-operation from officials or the general public in this county. Early in 1930 when an epidemic of septic sore throat broke out in Ocilla a specialist was sent from the State Board of Health. He traced the seat of the infection to a dairy, and reported his findings to the local authorities with certain recommendations. The local officials, as well as the general public, expressed resentment of this outsider's "meddling."

Poor Race Relations and No Signs of Improvement. In terms of race relations, as in many other ways, Irwin County is typical of the newer counties of the South. In the early days there were no large slave owners; now there are hardly any whites who have the paternal attitude toward Negroes which characterizes the whites in many of the old Black Belt counties. The poorest whites and Negroes, working as farm wage hands, propertyless tenants, and at sawmills, are in daily competition for the necessities of physical existence. The few employers of labor, however, get the most labor they can for their money, and so the Negroes eke out a living along with the poorer whites.

As an illustration of the organized determination of the whites in this part of Georgia to keep themselves apart from the Negroes, the charters fo Fitzgerald and Tifton expressly provided that no person of African descent might own property inside the corporate limits. This ruling is still in effect at Tifton.

Irwin County's economic outlook gives little hope for relief. Available farm lands are largely utilized now, large tracts of the poorest uplands are devoted to turpentine, and immense areas are still in swamps. The population density is less than thirty-three to the square mile, as compared with the state average of nearly fifty. The county seat town is served only by a spur line railroad from Fitzgerald.

Without any permanent place in the economic life of the community, the Negroes are thoroughly cowed, meek, humble and generally silent. Of course, Negroes can and do adjust themselves to the situation. One Negro storekeeper had accumulated a fair bank account, while a local preacher said, "The white people are very nice to me; I've been here twenty-four years. They always contribute to my trip to the National Baptist Convention."

CHAPTER X

HE ANGERED THE "LILY WHITES"
AILEY, MONTGOMERY COUNTY, GEORGIA

SHORTLY after midnight on July 29, 1930, a truck containing a group of masked men drove up a farm road, one mile north of Ailey, to the home of S. S. Mincey, prominent Montgomery County Negro. The men forcibly entered the house. Then Mincey, a veritable giant and active for his seventy years, was "quieted" by blows over the head, thrown into a waiting truck, and hurried away into the night. Early next afternoon he died of cerebral hemorrhage.

THE FLOGGING AND SUBSEQUENT DEATH

Envy a Reported Cause of Flogging. S. S. Mincey was active and influential in the Republican organizations of the county and state, and had been a delegate to National Republican Conventions. He was also prominent in Negro fraternal circles, having been elected Secretary and Treasurer of the Widows and Orphans Department of the Negro Masonic Lodge of Georgia, and in that connection at the time of his death was opening an office at Ailey, with a full-time clerk. Some Negroes believe his murder was caused by envy of the prosperity evidenced by this fact.

About a week before Mincey's death, the records and other properties of his new office had been received from Columbus, accompanied by the clerk. Though this office was inconspicuously located across the railroad track from the white stores and bank, he introduced his clerk at the bank, store, and other places where she would need to do business.

This clerk reports that, while the office was being made ready, it was the object of much curiosity on the part of certain types of white people. After Mincey's death she interpreted this interest as the evidence of resentment and envy of her employer's prosperity. Except for the tragedy which befell Mincey, perhaps she would not have thought the onlookers were other than "curious" loafers.

Negro Leadership of County Republican Committee Favored by Leading Whites. The above, however, is not the common explanation of Mincey's death. Leading citizens of the community are morally certain that Mincey was "taken for a ride" because of his political activities. At the time of his death, he was the leader of the local Republican organization, and had been so for a quarter of a century, except for two or three years, when a schism among the Negro Republicans gave the office to another member of the race. In the spring of 1930, however, it became clear that unless the Negroes stood together, the "lily white" Republicans would gain control. Prior to the County Republican Convention of April 5, 1930, the "lily whites" formed an organization and came to the convention with the avowed purpose of electing white officers.

Shortly before this convention some of the leading whites of Ailey, including a physician and banker, advised Mincey to get the Negroes together and keep the control of the organization out of the hands of the whites who had turned Republican for the "loaves and fishes." The Negroes did get together. They utilized a procedure which allowed the white men to vote in the convention only after signing an affidavit that they would vote only the Republican ticket for one year. Eighty-eight of these affidavits were filled in by white men and filed with Mincey. At the request of the Ailey banker, these affidavits were placed in his hands for safe keeping, and months after Mincey's death, were still in the banker's possession.

There are three evident reasons why some of Ailey's leading citizens offered Mincey advice and assistance: (1) A Negro controlled Republican County Committee would not be a serious competitor for the control of county politics; (2) in contrast with the "lily whites" who were flouting their "Solid South" heritage, Mincey was a well-known and respected Negro whose habitual place in the Republican ranks was part of the accustomed picture; (3) in view of the prevalence of the flogging practice in Montgomery and adjoining counties, these citizens felt that sworn affidavits of "lily white" Republicans were not secure at Mincey's farm house, one mile north of Ailey. On three occasions Mincey's white friends had warned him of the personal risk he ran by having incurred the anger of his political enemies.

Mincey Offends "Lily Whites" at County Convention. When the April convention opened, there were two very differing elements present. On the one hand were the old-line Negro Republicans, the most respected Negroes in the county; on the other were the "lily white" Republicans, recruited in the main from a class of whites usually antagonistic to Negroes. Mincey called the convention to order.

On a test ballot the "lily whites" polled ninety votes, though only eighty-eight had signed affidavits. Confident that the Negroes had voted as instructed, Mincey was considerably angered at the apparent fraud. Expressing himself vigorously, he declared that the best white people in the county had their Democratic primary and were always willing to let the Negroes manage their own affairs, but that the whites present did not belong to this class. This statement caused a commotion. The "lily whites" resented the implication from a Negro that they were "poor white trash." It is reported that one of them retorted, "That's all right! We'll see you later about that!" In fright, some Negro tenants left the meeting and reported to their landlords what Mincey had said. Though fearful of the results of Mincey's cutting remark, the Negro delegates reconvened, outvoted the "lily whites," and elected Mincey chairman of the Montgomery County Republican Committee.

"Lily Whites" Further Angered. Between the April Convention and the date of his death in July, Mincey further antagonized some of the "lily whites" by refusing to support one of them who was applying for a postmastership in the county. Mincey's control of Republican patronage in Montgomery and adjoining counties made his opposition an almost insurmountable obstacle in the way of this "lily white's" appointment. Two weeks before his death, Mincey is reported to have told

a leading Negro politician that he had recently been threatened and advised to refrain from his political activities.

Masked Murderers Mistaken for Friends. Before he died, Mincey told his physician that he heard the arrival of the truck, but thought the occupants were friends come to "celebrate" with him his accession to high office in the Masonic Lodge. Even after they broke into his room and said "Stick 'em up," he still thought it only a joke.

Presently he was struck a terrific blow, and then realizing they were not his friends, he reached to the corner beside his bed to get his gun. It was not there. Then he started across the room to his trunk for his pistol. Another blow knocked him almost senseless. His grandson, in bed with him, awoke and was treated roughly by the night prowlers. About this time, Mincey's wife, sick with a fever and under the care of a physician, appeared on the scene and was threatened by members of the gang.

The masked men told Mincey that he had been entirely too busy in political matters, and they meant to run him out of the county. Before leaving the house, he assured them that with the Masonic job he could make a living without being active in politics, and that he would stop all political activities if they would leave. They did leave, but they took him with them in their truck to a lonely spot near Uvalda in Toombs County and left him there with "his clothing beaten into threads and his skin and flesh torn from his back."

Back to Ailey and Death. Mincey managed to crawl back near the road, and just at daybreak a white farmer of Toombs County en route to Vidalia with a load of tobacco heard someone call from the roadside, and stopped to discover what was wrong. He found a large Negro man, partially clad in torn and bloodstained night clothes, writhing in pain. The wounded man said he was S. S. Mincey, that he lived in Ailey, and would pay seven dollars to be taken home.

This man, with the help of a neighboring white farmer, placed Mincey in the car and, after leaving their tobacco in Vidalia, took him to the office of an Ailey physician. Mincey asked the doctor if his skull was fractured. The doctor, after giving him a hurried examination, said he thought not and asked that he be taken to his home, saying that by the time they had him bathed and dressed he would be there and give him a thorough examination. Two hours later when the doctor arrived, Mincey was unconscious; at two o'clock he died of cerebral hemorrhage, due to a blow on the head.

It seems that fate was against Mincey! He thought the mob who killed him were coming to "celebrate" him. When he found they were not friends, he reached for his gun to find it not there—his wife that afternoon, fearing lest the grandchild play with it, had put it elsewhere. It is generally believed also that his assailants did not mean to render him a fatal blow. "But they did," was the comment of one incensed white woman, "and I hope his hant'll foller 'em as long as they live."

Politician, Lodge Official, and Community Leader. At the time of his death, Mincey was seventy years old. He was born and reared in Ailey, and was said by the oldest white citizens to bear a uniformly good reputation. The only thing which qualified this at all was the statement that he trafficked in Republican patronage. This, however, was taken as a matter of course and did not discredit him locally.

Mincey lived on a farm of about forty acres, which he owned and from which he made his living, except what he is alleged to have secured from those who needed his support to get and keep postmasterships. How much he netted from his political activities is not known. All his children had received a common school education and with one exception had moved away to Macon, Savannah, and other cities. Mincey owned a house in Vidalia, and when he got the lodge office his wife wanted him to move there; he countered that he was under obligation to bring the honor of his new office to his home community.

Mincey was very active and effective in Republican politics— the ranking Republican in the county, several times district chairman, a member of the state organization, and four times delegate to the Republican National Convention. It is reported that he refused a considerable sum at the 1912 Convention when the Roosevelt faction tried to get him to abandon his pledge to Taft. Mincey was a leader in Negro fraternal organizations, and the Masonic office to which he had just been elected carried a salary of nearly $100 per month and a full-time office helper. He planned to devote the major part of his time to this work, and as stated was opening up an office in Ailey.

Mincey was looked upon with favor by the majority of Montgomery County's leading white people, as a man of great common sense and one who did much to quiet disturbances brewing between Negroes and whites. His credit was good at the local bank. At the time of his death he owed the bank $150, $100 of which had been secured by a lien on his crop, the other $50 on his own signature. The Ailey banker stated that he always considered Mincey's note absolutely good. He added that the $100 was repaid two months after Mincey's death and that payment of the remaining $50 would be forthcoming from his insurance money.

Mincey's ability was such that his meager schooling did not seem to handicap him seriously. Astute and clever, he knew how to deal with all kinds of people—in the committee room, on the streets, and in the rurals of South Georgia. His implication that the "lily whites" were "white trash" was evidently the result of heat and not in keeping with his usual restraint.

REACTION OF THE COMMUNITY TO THE FATAL FLOGGING

Unlike the other communities in Georgia where, in 1930, mob deaths occurred and were generally justified or condoned, in Montgomery County one hears people openly condemn the death of Mincey and express the hope that the guilty will be apprehended and punished. Both the weekly and daily press of the state gave considerable attention to the Mincey case.

"... *We Can Assure No Man That He is Safe.*" In the July 31 number of the Montgomery *Monitor*, the first issue after Mincey's death, the leading editorial, "Hail, the Conquering Heroes!" not only openly charged Mincey's death to the "lily white" Republicans, but concluded that in view of the fact that Montgomery County's earlier floggers had gone unpunished "... we can assure no man that he is safe in his liberty or life while in our midst."

"When we learned that the life of a local citizen had been taken by a mob of unknown assailants without the least known provocation we were dumbfounded. We did not believe there to be enough men in this section of such brutal and bloodthirsty temperament as to commit such a horrible crime. But the crime has been committed, right here in our midst. A citizen has been taken from his home in the dead of the night and deliberately deprived of his life by a mob of masked people. It is one of the most brutal crimes we have yet heard of among civilized people in this enlightened age and country.

"S. S. Mincey, the citizen killed by the mob one night this week, was a Negro. He had taken a very active part in Negro social, fraternal and political activities of this section and the state. He had been prominently connected with the Republican party in this county and state for over a quarter of a century. He was considered an important factor in state Republican activities. He was recognized as a Negro citizen of rather unusual abilities and energies.

"It is reported that those who killed Mincey warned him to sever his relations with the Republican party in this county and get out of the county in thirty days. If such be true, these fellows can take delight in the fact that their request has been granted. His relations with the party have been severed and he has left the county.

"These fellows can now come forth and claim their spoils. We shall watch and wait for their arrival. The public will observe as they step into the coveted place of their dead adversary, but we doubt there being anyone to congratulate them on their spendid victory. They are the victors, 'and to the victors belong the spoils.' They laid siege upon the stronghold of S. S. Mincey. They planned the line of battle and were in the thick of the fight. They have won, and to them shall go the laurel wreath of victory. Even now there must be rejoicing in their victorious camp as the jubilant spirit of the Goddess Victory hovers over their forces. The enemy has been conquered. S. S. Mincey is dead. A new leader must be chosen from among the conquering forces. To this fortunate soul will go the heritage of the dead Negro leader. Upon his honored brow will be placed the crown of authority.

"Who will the new leader be? Who is it who so coveted the place held by Mincey that he would take a chance at even murder in order to gain his goal? Let the new chief be chosen! To you who have been so hasty and thorough in battle, we implore you that you not procrastinate in proclaiming your leader! Fill, with haste, the place left vacant when you took the life of your adversary! You kept the public ignorant of your intentions to take this man's life, but now that this obstacle has been removed be courageous enough to announce your newly chosen leader! Advise us as to how you shall improve upon the policies of your dead enemy! Now that you have fought a valiant battle and won a noble fight what shall your next move be?

"We do not know who took this Negro's life or how on earth you reasoned that you or anybody else would be helped in any possible manner by such an act of dastardly cowardice. But we do know that you have upon your hands the blood of a human being which will curse you until your dying day and your children's children yet unborn.

"What shall the law abiding people do about this crime? Or, have we any law abiding people left? There are those left who do not approve of such disregard for human life, but judging from the past we would seem safe in saying that these criminals will go unpunished. It seems almost impossible to bring such men to justice. From the crowded streets of New York and Chicago to the sparsely settled country sections of Montgomery County the gangster who takes a fellow 'for a ride' seems immune from punishment.

"The majority of the citizens of this county do not approve of such things. We speak for the majority when we say that Montgomery County condemns such brutal actions. Yet, we can make no apologies and do not attempt to do so. The minority which indulges in such practices has, so far, gone unpunished, and we can assure no man that he is safe in his liberty or life while in our midst."

These three statements below were taken from the lengthy news report of Mincey's death appearing in the July 31 number of the *Monitor:*

"Mincey was conscious at the time of his arrival (in Ailey) and told briefly of the incident. He is reported to have said that the men warned him that he was entirely too active in Republican affairs in this county and must resign his position as Chairman of the County Republican Committee, a position which Mincey has held almost continuously for over a quarter of a century. They also advised him that if he would leave the county in thirty days they would do nothing further to him. . . .

"On last April fifth a hotly contested election was held by the Republican forces of this county at a mass meeting called for the purpose of choosing a County Republican Chairman. A large number of white citizens as well as over a hundred Negroes attended the meeting. There were two candidates for the place. S. S. Mincey, the Negro candidate, had the support of the Negro citizens and was elected to the place as county chairman. . . .

"S. S. Mincey was seventy years of age and so far as anyone has been able to learn had done no injury to any citizen of this section which would have provoked the brutal flogging and his death. County authorities have investigated the murder but seem to have made little progress toward the apprehension of members of the mob. Local citizens are aroused over the situation and notice of a mass meeting of citizens is run in this issue of the *Monitor*. It is presumed that a reward will be offered for information leading to the identity of those who committed the crime."

Editor's Earlier Position Shifted. A mass meeting denouncing mob rule was held on August 4 in the county courthouse. The next number of the local weekly paper, August 7, carried a full report of that meeting, which had endorsed the editorial position previously taken by the paper. By this time, however, the editorial emphasis had shifted from a thorough condemnation of those guilty of Mincey's death to that of defense of the county against outside critics. Montgomery is a good county, he was now insisting, with only a very small lawless element. The second editorial, captioned, "Citizens Denounce Crime at Mass Meeting," was as follows:

"A representative gathering of citizens of this section at the courthouse Monday morning for the purpose of registering public protest against the recent brutal flogging of a citizen of this county was timely and commendable.

"No doubt the impression has been made on the public that our county is filled with a lawless element and that it is dangerous to live among our people. Those familiar with the situation know better. They know that the big majority of our people are bitterly opposed to such things. They know that our citizens have been very active in an effort to bring those committing such crimes to justice. They know that our people have done much more than have the folks in some other communities to rid our section of this lawless element.

"The public at large did not know these things, however, and we are confident we had, as a body of people, been branded as outlaws on account of the activities of a small group of such folks. This meeting Monday did much to correct this idea. A large number of good citizens were present at the meeting. Many made vigorous talks condemning these things and practically the entire audience gave ample evidence of their approval of such expressions.

"We have plenty of good good citizens in this county. There are hundreds of our folks who are anxious to clear our county of the disgrace which now seems to be ours. There are many who are doing all they can to bring about justice. It seems that we are making very little progress but it is extremely hard to uncover such things. And it seems at times that our courts do not lend the proper coöperation in such matters. In fact many citizens are prone to believe this the weakest link in the chain with which our people are trying to draw these fellows to justice.

"We are glad that the public has in a mass meeting expressed its voice on this matter and trust that others will not be too hasty in condemning all our people for the crimes of a few, especially when such crimes do not have the approval of more than a very small portion of our people, if any."

Comments of Neighboring Editors. In adjoining Treutlen County, the Soperton *News*, the editor of which had been flogged some years ago, carried a unique editorial on August 8, under the title, "He was only a Negro, But—," parts of which were:

"The brutal killing of S. S. Mincey, Negro, who was taken from his home at Ailey by a masked mob of white men one night recently was one of the most atrocious crimes ever perpetrated in this section of Georgia. . . .

"Statements from reliable white men of Montgomery County are to the effect that Mincey was an humble and law-abiding Negro. . . .

"When any man, whether he be white man, yellow man, red man or black man, cannot pursue the even tenor of his way, whether it be political or otherwise, without molestation at the hands of a murderous gang of degenerates, it is high time that a civilized and law-abiding citizenry rise up in arms and protest. . . .

"We had rather be this old worn out Negro, whose body reposes in its bed of clay and whose soul, we hope, rests in peaceful slumber, than to be one of the criminals who caused his death, and who must go through eternity with the blood of their victim dripping from their finger tips. Hell is too good for them and we wonder if the devil won't have a place a little deeper and a little hotter than hell for such as they."

Another striking editorial from a small town paper appeared in the *Madisonian,* of Madison, Georgia, on August 4:

"Georgia will remain at the bottom of the list of illiteracy and in the sisterhood of states—will continue to go backward in the things worth while as long as outrages like that a few nights ago in Montgomery County continue to happen. An aged Negro man was taken from his home at night by a robed and masked band of white men, the skin all whipped from his back, his skull crushed and his body thrown in a ditch. He died next day. His only offense was being a good citizen and a leader of his race. That section of Georgia furnishes a congenial atmosphere for such crimes. The officers of the law want to be re-elected, so nothing will ever be done about the outrage and encouragement will be given to others that will occur. Something should be done about it."

A Vigorous Mass Meeting. The mass meeting of August 4, referred to above was held in the courthouse on the first day of court. Mincey's murder was denounced in vigorous fashion. The chairman of the indignation meeting, Col. L. C. Underwood, leading farmer of Montgomery County, said Mincey had given his life to rid Georgia of floggings and if necessary he himself would do as much. Ministers, physicians, lawyers, and business men expressed their utter disapproval of the wanton murder. Dr. J. W. Palmer, of Ailey, described the bruised and mangled bodies of Mincey and other flogged persons who had been brought to him for treatment. J. M. D. McGregor, one of Ailey's oldest and most respected citizens, denounced the crime and told of Mincey's wholesome work in the community.

Other speakers were W. A. Peterson, Mount Vernon banker, who was secretary of the meeting, A. L. Lanier, M. B. Calhoun, and Rev. L. S. Barrett, pastor of the Ailey and Mount Vernon Baptist Churches and teacher of theology at the Brewton-Parker Institute. The last named speaker, who had been active against floggings and Klan practices in general, made a stirring address in which he is quoted as saying, "It's plain hell to live in such a mess." In addition to these speakers from the county, Ben Grace, W. M. Lewis, and Wimberly Brown, leading citizens of Toombs County, and Solicitor General M. H. Boyer, of the local judicial district, made strong statements decrying Mincey's death and mob rule in general.

Resolutions Adopted. The meeting adopted the following resolutions offered by H. B. Folsom, clerk of the county commissioners, and one of Mount Vernon's oldest and most highly respected citizens:

"Resolutions adopted in mass meeting, Courthouse in Mount Vernon, Georgia, Monday morning, August 4, 1930.

"Whereas, in recent years a number of horrible crimes have been committed within the bounds of Montgomery County, or upon citizens of this county forcibly taken to an adjoining county by masked bodies of white men; the perpetrators of such despicable and cowardly acts, under cover of darkness and their identity unknown, have gone without apprehension or punishment, to the indignation of an enraged citizenship; and

"Whereas, in the early morning of July 29 this county again suffered an unpardonable shock to civil rights and justice, when S. S. Mincey, a colored citizen, was by a masked band of white men dealt a fatal blow in his home, forcibly taken away and tortured to death in an unmerciful and heinous manner, and this without provocation, and unwarranted by any rule of civilization. The murder of this citizen has but forged another link in the chain of violence; it is a tendency toward anarchy and a reign of terror, which, if not summarily checked by enforcement of law, supported by a righteous citizenry, will soon render this county unsafe and unfit for citizenship of character and decency; it is a blot on civilization, a blow at American constitutional rights, and an unsavory record abhorred by the law-abiding element of Montgomery County. Therefore, be it

"Resolved, by the citizens of Montgomery County, Georgia, in mass meeting assembled at the courthouse of said county, August 4, 1930, that their unqualified condemnation of this and similar acts of violence, contrary to law, human instincts, and social order, be expressed in a demand for more direct and definite action by officers of the law charged with the apprehension of criminals and the courts responsible for the administration of justice and the punishment of those so flagrantly defying the law of the land, in the support of which our efforts are hereby openly and freely pledged, that crimes of this nature may be stamped out and a higher and unquestioned standard of citizenship be raised in this section of Georgia.

"Resolved, further, that copies of this declaration be transmitted to the state press, with request for publication in behalf of the law-abiding citizenry of Montgomery County, and a copy be furnished the clerk of the Superior Court of said County, with request for entry on official records, in behalf of public honor and integrity.

"Unanimously adopted by a rising vote in mass meeting assembled at the courthouse in Mount Vernon, August 4, 1930.

"L. C. UNDERWOOD, *Chairman;*

"W. A. PETERSON, *Secretary.*"

Death-Dealing Floggers Unpunished. The coroner's jury implicated no one. The Montgomery County Grand Jury, which convened a few days later, investigated the case without results. That part of the grand jury's presentments relative to the Mincey case was:

"Having investigated very earnestly every source of evidence at our command, we find no definite clues which would lead to the conviction of the party or parties responsible for the death of S. S. Mincey. As members of the Grand Jury, and as individuals, we wish to publish to our fellow citizens that we denounce Mob Law, and urge all law abiding citizens of our country to use their influence to put an end to the practice of flogging, which is an open violation of the law, and so often results in permanent disability and often death.

"Therefore, we heartily recommend and urge our next Grand Jury to continue zealously the investigation which we have begun.

"We wish to thank our Solicitor, Hon. M. H. Boyer, for his thoughtfulness and assistance in the discharge of our duty. We also wish to express our appreciation of His Honor, Judge Eschol Graham, and extend to him our thanks for his faithfulness and business-like administration of the court. Especially, is he to be congratulated for his able charges to the Grand Jury in the matter of Mob Law."

"No Definite Clues"? Though the grand jury stated that it found "no definite clues" the following significant circumstances were generally reported in the community: (1) On the night of the flogging the new International truck used at a county convict camp was credibly reported away from the camp from 9:30 till nearly dawn; (2) the tracks at Mincey's home are reported to have corresponded to the tires of this

truck; (3) the same night a man at Uvalda saw a new International truck filled with hooded men on the road between the camp and Mincey's home. A prominent citizen brought the above reports to the attention of Solicitor-General M. H. Boyer, but for reasons unexplained, neither the persons professing knowledge of the truck nor anyone connected with the convict camp were called to testify.

In addition to the above, there were other facts tending to suggest the guilt of certain individuals well-known to the community, and generally believed to have been involved in the lynching.[1]

Practically all those believed to have taken an active part in Mincey's death are "lily white" Republicans, and reputed former members of the Ku Klux Klan. Some of them have court records for bootlegging, participation in previous floggings, seduction or other immoral conduct. Nearly all are either landless farmers or roustabouts who earn a living as convict guards, making and selling liquor, and so on.

Some Dissatisfaction With Courts. Many of the leading white people around Ailey and Mount Vernon feel that the judge and solicitor general have not done as much as they might to apprehend and convict Mincey's assailants or those guilty of previous floggings. In connection with the flogging of a white man two years earlier, citizens point out that the county commissioners offered a $300 reward for the apprehension of the floggers, the reward to be paid by county warrants. In this case a white man was indicted, tried, and sentenced to serve a twelve-month term on the chain gang, only to have the judge grant a new trial which resulted in his acquittal. Moreover, the same judge ruled that the reward warrants that had been issued by the county commissioners were illegal, and, therefore, of no value.

These four sentences from the Montgomery *Monitor* editorial of August 7 represent the attitude of these citizens: "There

---

[1] "We know almost to a moral certainty who lynched Mincey, but it is a case like that of Al Capone in Illinois. Knowing who did it and proving it are two different things. . . ." Statement by editor of Montgomery *Monitor* quoted in an Associated Press release of Mach 3, 1932.

are hundreds of our folks who are anxious to clear our county of the disgrace which now seems to be ours. There are many who are doing all they can to bring about justice. It seems that we are making very little progress but it is extremely hard to uncover such things. And it seems at times that our courts do not lend the proper coöperation to such matters. In fact many citizens are prone to believe this the weakest link in the chain with which our people are trying to draw these fellows to justice."

In disbanding without returning indictments in the Mincey case, the August grand jury urged its successor to "continue zealously the investigation we have begun." The November grand jury in turn, made no indictments, but suggested that the matter be given serious consideration by the next grand jury. These continued efforts are the direct results of two things: Many people had become outraged at the unfavorable publicity accruing to their county from unpunished floggings of the past ten years; Mincey was a law-abiding Negro of unusual ability, and had many local white friends who desired the punishment of his murderers.

"*Vigilantes.*" This pressure on the courts emanated in large measure from a group of leading white citizens of Ailey and Mount Vernon who, immediately after Mincey's death, formed themselves into a committee which they called the "Vigilantes." The expressed purpose of this committee was to inform the people of the revolting state of affairs, to place before the courts all available evidence, and to raise among themselves and from other sources funds to apprehend and convict those who beat Mincey. So far this committee has succeeded in getting no indictments, has contributed no funds to push the investigation, on the ground that to do so would render its members ineligible to sit on the jury should the case ever come to trial, and has secured no funds from any other source. Their desire to have the county offer a reward was blocked by the judge's previous ruling. Yet these "Vigilantes" still express hope of securing from somewhere enough money to put a secret service man on the job and leave him there until evidence sufficient to convict is secured.

Another and more numerous element of the county's white population is determined that the guilty go unpunished for their part in the flogging of Mincey and others. Some Negroes feel more secure after the wholehearted way in which the best white people have denounced Mincey's murderers; others are reminded by Mincey's death that no Negro, regardless of his relation to the leading white citizens, is secure from the mob. It is reported that Mincey's own pastor was afraid to conduct the funeral and that another minister was called.

What Was Mincey's Worth to Montgomery County? The economic loss resulting from Mincey's death is not negligible. He owned a farm; he was custodian of lodge funds of not less than $6,000 which he was placing in a local bank; he believed in Montgomery County and encouraged Negroes to be industrious and make their homes there; he was instrumental in getting a Rosenwald School for his people; he was a leader among Negroes, was respected among the best element of whites, and was helpful in maintaining peace between the two groups.

Though the county's direct loss from Mincey's death was considerable, the indirect losses will probably be greater. What the county will lose by the brutal way he met his death cannot be definitely measured, but certainly investors will not be attracted to communities where life is not safe from masked mobs who break into houses and take their victims. Then, too, Mincey's death is a powerful argument to the typical Negro cropper that it is best to "have nothing and be nobody." Such an attitude on the part of laborers has a bad influence on any community. Not only Negroes, but some of Montgomery's oldest and wealthiest white citizens, expressed concern for their personal safety in life and property.

Representative Comments of Daily Papers. Editorials were numerous decrying the Mincey murder. The resolutions adopted by the Montgomery County mass meeting were widely published. Commenting upon the call for this meeting, the Macon *Telegraph* said on August 3:

"We said a few days ago that it was not to be presumed that the responsible citizens of Montgomery County would insist that

the Mincey lynching, by a robed and masked mob, should be solved
and the offenders punished, because we have become so accustomed
to having verdicts at inquests, 'Dead at the hands of parties unknown to this jury,' that we take them almost as a matter of
course. We are delighted to find that we are wrong and that the
people of Montgomery County are giving every evidence of their
desire to punish those who outraged elemental decency in taking
an offenseless 70-year-old Negro out of his home and beating him
to death because he had not resigned as the county chairman of the
Republican party.

"A mass meeting is to be held at Mount Vernon Monday night
that will result, no doubt, in the crystallization of sentiment against
such lawlessness and for the punishment of those hoodlums who
are guilty of the crime. We are gratified that there is such a fine
reaction on the part of Montgomery County to this instance of
rank illegality and injustice to a member of that race for which
the white people of the South have a peculiar responsibility and a
peculiar guardianship. . . .

"If hoodlums feel they are immune to punishment when they take
good Negro citizens out and kill them, what is to prevent them
from feeling they will be immune if they take good white citizens
out and kill them? For the protection of all good citizens in this
state, white and black, we hope Montgomery County will solve this
lynching."

"Well Done—Montgomery," was an editorial in the Atlanta
Constitution August 6, parts of which were:

"Reports of the gathering of more than a thousand of the best
citizens of Montgomery County in a great mass meeting to protest
the recent beating to death in that county of an aged and respected
negro, is conclusive evidence of the attitude of the people of
that section towards the activities of hooded barbarians. . . .

"Resolutions decrying in scathing terms all acts of violence,
and demanding direct and definite action by officers of the law . . .
that crimes of this nature may be stamped out and a higher standard of civilization be raised in this section of Georgia, told plainly
of the temper of these good citizens.

"The fact that Montgomery is one of the state's smallest counties make more significant the size of this outpouring of her upright and clean-thinking citizens. At a time when the oratory of political candidates is attracting audiences of only a hundred or so people, this affront to the good name of their county and section brought together a crowd of more than a thousand.

"Such public expressions as those of the people of Montgomery are, thankfully for the good name of the state, causing such depredations, committed by a vicious element, comprising only a small per cent of the state's population, to grow less frequent as the years go by.

"The citizens of Montgomery are to be congratulated on the prompt and emphatic manner in which they have struck at the threat of mob law within the borders of their county."

The Augusta *Herald* had the following editorial:

"The cruel and brutal murder of S. S. Mincey, 70 years old, who was kidnapped at his home in Ailey, Georgia, by a band of robed men Tuesday night is greatly deplored. Mincey was well known in Augusta, having been identified very prominently with fraternal and political and church organizations in this state. . . .

"That a man of the type of S. S. Mincey should have been overpowered in the presence of his family, carried off into another county, unmercifully beaten over the head and back, until his back was cut into threads, and which within a few hours thereafter resulted in his death, will, of course, meet with general condemnation on the part of all who believe in justice, fair play and fair treatment by all citizens, white and colored alike.

"Such atrocities as the wilful murder of Dennis Hubert last June in Atlanta, a divinity student at Morehouse College and the burning down of the home of his parents a few days following; the murdering of Mincey; and the assault and robbery of another, Will Mincey at Walden, Georgia, on Wednesday night, are stigmas upon these respective communities that have silent effect on the entire colored population of the state of Georgia. There is no telling how far reaching the effects have gone or will go in connection with the discontentment already so prevalent in the minds of so many who do not feel that they have full protection of life and property."

FACTS ABOUT THE COMMUNITY

Scotch Highlanders With Native Gaelic. When laid off in 1793, Montgomery comprised the area of several present-day counties, including Tattnall, Toombs, Treutlen, Wheeler, and others. Its area has been reduced until at present the parent county, with but 190 square miles, is one of the smallest in Georgia. The county is about 120 miles from the ocean and has a mean elevation of 125 feet. The Oconee River flows along its western boundary, and at the southwest corner unites with the Ocmulgee to form the Altamaha River. Until the building of the railroads this river was the chief artery of transportation for central Georgia's commerce.[2]

Scotch Highlanders, banished from their native land because of their adherence to the House of Stuart, were Montgomery's first settlers. They came direct to eastern North Carolina, and thence to South Georgia's pine barrens. These Highlanders brought their preacher with them, established a kirk in the pine woods, and had services in their native Gælic. The county's population increased slowly, for the early settlers soon found the land generally unproductive, and the "air not free from malaria."

Plantation Farming Limited by Sandy Uplands. In the first quarter of the nineteenth century, planters of English descent opened up a few large plantations on the fertile strips along the larger streams. Because of the unproductivity of the sandy uplands, which constituted the major part of the county's area, there was opportunity for only a limited extension of plantation farming. Nevertheless, the few planters lived in affluence among their Negro slaves. "The face of the country is

---

[2] On September 8, 1930, a lynching occurred at Darien, McIntosh County; this now decadent town, located on the banks of the Altamaha River about fifteen miles inland, was, in the early decades of the nineteenth century, one of Georgia's thriving seaport towns.

level," wrote George White, in 1850, "the soil is sandy and in some places fertile."

The whites in the sandy upland pine barrens wrung a livelihood from their care of livestock and cultivated patches. An independent, rugged folk, they lived well enough, but made no pretense to wealth or culture. In 1830, Montgomery County was over four times its present size, but had a total population of but 1,259. A little more than one-fourth of this number were slaves, a hundred or so were of the white planter class, and the remainder were independent farmers.

Propertyless Whites From Old Southern Communities. Between 1830 and 1860, the white population of the county was increased by an influx of poor whites who had been pushed out of the counties west and south of Augusta, by the development of slave plantation farming. A considerable proportion of these newcomers had earlier come into the area around Augusta from the pine woods of the eastern Carolinas.

Negro slaves were increasing, also, as a few additional plantations were opened up and some of the older ones were expanded. In 1850, with the same territory as in 1830, the county had a population of 2,154, of whom 613 were Negro slaves.

At the time of the Civil War, the county's population was made up of four distinct classes: the slave-owning group, the propertyless whites from the old slave plantation counties, the descendants of the Highlanders—a very substantial middle class—and the Negro slaves. The propertyless whites were most numerous, the slaves next, then came a goodly number of the middle-class whites, and finally a few score of the planter class.

Since 1870, with the partial disintegration of plantation farming in the plantation counties to the north, many Negroes have drifted aimlessly into Montgomery and adjoining counties. By 1890, the exhausted soils of central Georgia and the common use of commercial fertilizers had made the county relatively attractive. Of the county's total population of 9,248 in 1890, Negroes numbered 3,658.

In 1930, Montgomery County with a little less than one-fourth of its 1890 territory, had a population of 10,020.

Added to the natural population increase, and the coming of ever larger numbers of Negroes from the old plantation counties of central Georgia, there has been a considerable migration of whites of small means from the upper Piedmont and Mountain counties. Other whites of the small farmer or tenant type from the old tobacco belts of eastern and Piedmont North Carolina and Virginia have been attracted into this new tobacco-growing country. In 1830, the Negroes made up 26.6 per cent of the total population, 39.4 per cent in 1890, 47.4 per cent in 1920, and 44.6 per cent in 1930.

The Disintegration of the White Middle Class. Although this increase of Negroes and outside whites has modified the whole social and economic structure, there still remains a vestige of the old class distinctions as between the English planter class, the middle-class whites of Scotch descent, and the poorer whites. These old class lines have been modified further by the virtual disintegration of the white middle class. To all practical purposes, this class has disappeared. A part of it has accumulated property and become identified with the old landed aristocracy; a larger proportion has slumped into tenancy and become identified with the poorer white element. The Scotch descendants who rose into the wealthy class have been friendly to Negroes. From this class came those who insisted upon the punishment of Mincey's murderers. On the other hand, the Scotch descendants who passed into the tenant class tend to justify or condone Mincey's death. Among the Negroes, formerly all slaves two well-defined classes have developed; those with a small amount of property, and those with none. Those Negroes with most property and the whites with least property have been struggling for the leadership of the county Republican organization, and therein, as we have seen, lies one of the major factors leading to Mincey's flogging and subsequent death.

A Poor Rural County. In 1930, Montgomery County's six towns had a combined population of but 2,364, less than one-fourth of the county's total. Mount Vernon, the county seat, is the largest town. Among its 779 inhabitants are a scattering of propertied white people, and many poorer whites, while nearly half of the population is made up of Negroes.

Ailey, one mile east of Mount Vernon, has less than four hundred people, and claims to be one of the wealthiest towns in the United States per capita. Nearly all the people who live in Ailey are white plantation owners, merchants, and professional men. The people who work the large farms, the poorer whites and Negroes, live in the open country. Except for the gas station operators, a few auto mechanics, day laborers, and domestics in these agricultural villages, nearly everybody in the county is directly dependent upon the farm and the farm folk's trade for a livelihood. There are but a few bankers, merchants and professional men, and practically all of these, along with most of the county officials, own farm lands and live in Ailey or Mount Vernon.

The county is rural and poor. The combined value of farm crops and manufactured products in 1924 amounted to only $130.92 per capita, one-sixteenth of which was from manufacturers while the state average was $310.78 per capita, more than three-fourths of which was from manufacturers.

There are many poor people in Montgomery County, and a few wealthy ones. Only thirteen income tax returns were filed in 1929, and only one of these was for an income of more than $5,000. Thirteen returns were made in 1927 and fourteen in 1924. In 1930 the county's bank deposits were $41.33 per capita, as compared with a state average of $155.89. To date, the county has had no bank failures, an evidence of the ability of the men managing them. Montgomery County's per capita valuation (exclusive of corporation taxes) for 1930 was $182.-98 as against the state per capita average of $348.03. Automobiles are relatively scarce in Montgomery County, in 1930 there being one to every thirteen persons as compared with the state average of one to every 8.6 persons.

No Indications of Early Improvement. The county has had river transportation from the outset, and railroad and highway connections comparable to other rural Georgia counties. The Seaboard Air Line Railroad from Americus to Savannah bisects the county from east to west; the Macon, Dublin, and

Savannah Railroad cuts the northeast corner, and the Georgia and Florida Railroad skirts the southeastern part of the county. The county is served by a state highway from east to west, paralleling the Seaboard, and by another leading north from Mount Vernon to Soperton. These roads are not paved, nor is there any pavement in any of the small towns, yet they compare well with the typical rural roads of Georgia. In addition to these state highways, the county maintains a system of roads. With river transportation, railroads, and highways, the county has virtually no manufactures. The flatness of the country, the prevalence of malaria, and the distance from markets all militate against the development or attraction of manufacturers of consequence at any time in the near future.

The chief crops of Montgomery County are cotton and corn, with tobacco and peanuts gaining headway. After 1915 the boll weevil reduced the cotton crop by several thousand bales, and by 1925 the landowners were seriously casting about for new crops. The cotton crop decreased year by year—9,658 bales in 1926, 6,017 in 1927, 5,504 in 1928. It is not surprising that the area devoted to tobacco increased from 150 acres in 1926, to 225 acres in 1927, 1,650 in 1929, and a still larger acreage in 1930. The increased acreage in peanuts was much the same, from 300 acres in 1927 to 1,700 in 1929. The fact that these crops, looked upon by some farmers as possible substitutes for cotton, sold for such low prices in 1930 only further demoralized an already pessimistic rural folk. Many of the landowning whites faced bankruptcy, while a considerable proportion of the landless masses, whether white or colored, faced actual physical privation.

There is room for but little expansion of farming, for in 1925 over four-fifths of the land area was in farms. Whatever advancement is made must be in a shift in agricultural practices, but cheap human labor tends to perpetuate old and crude systems of farming, rather than to inspire the introduction of new crops. The population density of this rural county is slightly more than for the state at large; where land is poor and agricultural methods crude, a dense rural population inevitably means a low plane of living for the masses. The percentage of farms operated by tenants has been increasing rapidly in recent years, 56.3 per cent of all farmers being tenants in 1910, and 69.6 per cent in 1925. Tenancy among white farmers increased from 40.3 per cent to 56.4 per cent from 1920 to 1925; the increase among Negro farmers was from 83.7 per cent to 88.7 per cent. This trend measures both the influx of poorer people of both races from central and north Georgia, and the disintegration of the local middle class white group.

Sorry Plight of Propertyless Rural Whites. The property-less rural whites of Montgomery and surrounding counties are poor indeed. The Klan which they generally accepted as a way out has failed them; cotton is cheap; there are no prosperous cities to run off to at will. Many of these men with their wives and children are emaciated in appearance, and look old beyond their years. One sees mothers with sunken chests and practically no teeth, little babies in arms with scabs on their heads and running sores about their ears, boys chewing tobacco before they are half grown and girls staring and popping their gum. Men, women, and children, dirty and unkempt, seething fatalism and pessimism are not uncommon sights. Now and then an intoxicated fellow breaks the monotony and adds to the sordidness of the picture.

One Saturday afternoon, at a small town between Ailey and Ocilla, a snaggled-toothed white mother was seen carrying a six-months-old baby with a stick of candy in its mouth, stumbling over a half-grown pig just out of a street wallow midway between the bank and the post office. There is much of the frontier in this part of Georgia, without the frontier's typical virility.

Unusually Low Public School Expenditures. The expenditures for public schools in Montgomery County were far below the state average. In 1928, for a school census population of 3,404, the sum spent was $34,264.09, or $10.07 per school census child. The state average was $24.35. The 1928 expenditure per white child of school age was $16.81 in this county and $36.88 in Georgia; for the Negro child of school age, $2.39 in Montgomery and $5.07 in Georgia. The expenditure per white child in average daily attendance was $21.05 in Montgomery and $54.60 in the state, $4.44 for the Negro in this county and $9.90 in the state.

The expenditures suggest the level of salaries, training of teachers, schoolroom equipment, and general educational opportunities provided. In 1928, the county employed 53 teachers with average annual salaries of $518.15—reduced to $450.-84 in 1930—for 1,614 white children, and 24 teachers with average annual salaries of $174.26 for 1,790 Negro children of school age. Of the county's twenty-two one-teacher schools in 1928, eight were for white children and fourteen for Negroes; of the six two-teacher schools, two were for Negroes. There were three other Negro schools, the largest of which, with five teachers, is a Rosenwald School completed shortly before Mincey, one of the moving spirits in its construction, was flogged to death. Three-fourths of the county's Negro teachers and 30.1 per cent of its white teachers were in one-and two-teacher schools. For·the state as a whole, 66.1 per cent of the Negro teachers and 21.2 per cent of the white teachers are in these smallest unit schools.

Surrounded by Georgia's Poorest White Schools. Of the twenty-four Georgia counties in which in 1930 white illiteracy equalled or exceeded six per cent, eleven immediately surround Montgomery County: Johnson, Treutlen, Toombs, Wheeler, Jeff Davis, Appling, Telfair, Bacon, Wayne and McIntosh; in this last there was a lynching in September, 1930.[3] Leaving Wrightsville, one can visit in succession the county seat towns of Soperton, Lyons, Mount Vernon, Alamo, McRae, Hazelhurst, Baxley, Alma, Jesup, and Darien—a journey of over two hundred miles—and traverse no county having less than six per cent of illiteracy in its white population over ten

---

[3] Except two counties, Glascock, in central eastern Georgia and Miller in the Southwest, the remaining counties with the highest illiteracy rates are in the northern mountainous portion of the state: Madison, Jackson, Banks, Stephens, Habersham, Union, Lumpkin, Murray, Chattooga, Pickens, and Bartow—the last of which had a lynching on October 1, 1930.

years of age; the state average is 3.3 per cent. The Negro illiteracy rate for Montgomery County paralleled the state rate,
both being slightly less than 20 per cent.

Montgomery County is also in the midst of the state's largest
concentration of contiguous counties paying white rural teachers an average of less than five hundred dollars per year. One
can make a continuous motor trip from the Florida line through
the county-seat towns of Waycross, Hoboken, Blackshear,
Baxley, Mount Vernon, Soperton, Dublin, Irwinton, Cochran,
Eastman, Alma, Hazelhurst, Douglas, Fitzgerald, Ocilla—with
a lynching on February 1, 1930—Nashville, Valdosta, and
back to Statenville on the Florida line—a journey of over 350
miles—without leaving territory where white rural teachers
salaries average less than $500.00 per year.[4]

A Poorly Supported But Important Institution. Brewton-
Parker Institute, with high school and junior college departments, has a library of only 1,570 volumes and in other ways
is poorly equipped, but it is none the less a distinct educational
asset to the local white people. This school, the property of
the Georgia Baptist Convention, lies midway between Mount
Vernon and Ailey. In 1930, its enrollment was 185, one-third
of which was in the junior college. Besides the regular academic
course, it has a theological department with an enrollment
of twelve, one of whom is a girl preparing to be a foreign missionary, a musical department with 38, and an expression department with 16. Although the cost for boarding students
is less than $300 a year, the dormitory accommodations are not
fully utilized; approximately two-thirds of the enrollment is

---

[4] Of the remaining 26 Georgia counties with white rural teachers' salaries
averaging less than $500 per year, five are in the South Georgia area:
Dooly, Crisp, Marion, Grady, and Long—the last two lying fast by
Thomas and McIntosh counties respectively, with lynchings in September,
1930. The remaining nineteen counties with lowest salaries for rural white
teachers are generally concentrated in the northern counties: Fannin,
Union, White, Habersham—adjoining Oconee, South Carolina, with a
lynching in April, 1930—Banks, Franklin, Lincoln, Walton, Gwinnett,
Milton, Forsyth, Dawson, Lumpkin, Gilmer, Murray, Dade, Gordon, Floyd,
and Paulding—the last three of which border three sides of Bartow County
with a lynching on October 1, 1930.

of day students from Mount Vernon, Ailey, and other nearby places accessible by auto.

Weak and Small Churches. Montgomery is a county of small churches as of small schools. The largest white denomination is the Southern Baptist, with a total membership of 1,169. It has twelve churches, the largest at Ailey and Mount Vernon with 147 and 146 members, respectively. The church at Ailey has preaching twice a month; the other eleven have preaching but once a month. In 1929 these twelve churches paid an aggregate of $2,517 for pastors' salaries. One-third of this total is paid by the Ailey and Mount Vernon churches. The pastor of these two churches has taken an active stand against the floggings and other undercover activities of the Klan and other masked groups in Montgomery and adjoining counties.

The Methodist Episcopal Church, South has a total of 853 members in the county, most of whom are in the Mount Vernon and Uvalda circuits. The latter is made up of six congregations, the former of five. Besides Southern Baptists and Methodists there were, according to the 1926 census of religious bodies, 127 white Presbyterians and 28 white Primitive Baptists. "In the early days," said George Smith in his *Story of Georgia*, "nowhere were there better country churches and schools." With the disintegration of the middle class, many of the old Scotch Presbyterian group have become Baptists or Methodists.

Though the Primitive Baptist membership is small, a portion of the rural folk are inclined toward this denomination, which is conscientiously opposed to foreign missions, church musical instruments and educated pastors. In Montgomery County, as elsewhere in southeastern Georgia where there is a considerable element of the Primitive Baptist persuasion, there are large numbers of adults identified with no church. A little more than one-third of the whites over fifteen years of age, and a similar proportion of the Negroes, are unchurched.

Of 1,848 Negro church members in the county in 1926, 1,389 were members of the Baptist Church, 327 of the African Methodist Episcopal, and 132 of the Methodist Episcopal. The Negro churches are small and weak, there being twenty-three Baptist and more than a dozen Methodist churches. The Negro preachers who hold services at these churches once a month are paid very small sums, and have had practically no training, some even boasting, "Hardshell" fashion, that their "larning' ain't of man."

The custom of having revival services, usually called "big meeting," is well established among both the white and Negro rural churches. Usually in the mid-summer slack-work seasons, after the cotton is "laid by" and before picking begins, a series of revival services is featured. These meetings give the once-a-month-preachers a chance to stay in the community long enough to get new members. Usually an "outside" preacher delivers the sermons, affording some swapping association among the preachers. To the church members, dwelling apart in solitary farm houses, the meetings give an opportunity for entertaining the preachers, mingling of neighbors at church, and neighborly visiting between afternoon and evening services. The subject matter of the sermons at these perennial revival seasons is calculated to arouse people to the need of church membership, and the effectiveness of the series of meetings is usually measured by the "additions to the church." These revival meetings are most in evidence where Sunday schools are weakest.

But Few Voters. The people seem to have but little interest in politics. The total number of votes cast in the presidential election of 1928—337 for the Democratic elector, 43 for the Anti-Smith Democratic elector, and 55 for the Republican elector—was less than one-sixth of the white population of voting age; in the 1924 presidential election, 353 votes were cast for Davis, 87 for Coolidge, and 13 for LaFollette. Although scarcely one-third of Georgia's white people interest themselves in politics, the proportion of white people voting in Georgia as a whole is almost twice as great as the proportion in Montgomery County.

Until recently, the Klan was strong in the county, but never made much headway in Ailey. Now the Klan's control is on the wane; and although one of the county officials was reported to be a Klansman, several others were not sympathetic with the hooded empire. Other than its county and home demonstration agents, and the poor schools and weak churches described above, Montgomery has no welfare agencies. There is no public library, hospital, health officer, social worker, or Red Cross—not even a motion picture show—in the County.

Conspicuous for Floggings. Montgomery and adjoining counties have made themselves conspicuous by their floggings, with white as well as Negro victims. The flogging a few years ago of an editor at Soperton, Treutlen County, immediately north of Montgomery, received nation-wide publicity. Montgomery County's three floggings prior to Mincey's death were briefly as follows:

Three years ago, when a Negro moved from Uvalda, a small town in the southern part of the county, he tried to get a settlement with his landlord who owed him some money. When the landlord would not settle, the Negro filed a suit against him. The Negro was severely flogged. None of the floggers were ever indicted.

The second case was of a young white man who went to court charging another white man with the seduction of a kinswoman. The accuser was severely beaten. Grand jury indictments were brought against the man accused of seduction and another man. At length their trials were held, and the man originally charged with seduction was sentenced to one year's imprisonment for flogging; the judge gave him a new trial, however, and he went free.

The third flogging was that of a Negro boy who operated a pressing club at Mount Vernon. White people across the street from his stand reported that he was very polite, and would not permit any boisterousness about his place. He did good work, and was liked about town. At length a white man from Tarrytown, northern part of the county, came to Mount Vernon and opened a pressing shop; he got but little business. After a few months he died; his widow opened the place for business; she got but little patronage. One night a masked mob broke into the Negro's pressing room and took him "for a ride." They beat him badly and dumped him in Toombs County near the spot where Mincey was later left. The boy moved to Atlanta; more recently he moved again to Dublin. Virtually boycotted, the white woman presently sold out and returned to her people in Tarrytown, where live a number of the "lily white" Republicans who found Mincey a political obstacle.

Other Indications of Excessive Lawlessness. While Montgomery County's floggings have gone virtually unmolested, the county's jail population per thousand inhabitants is unusually high. Between 1921 and 1929, the county's white jail population rose from 7.3 to 18.4 per thousand, the Negro jail population from 29.2 to 36.0. In the latter year the state rate for whites was 12.5, for Negroes 25.4 per thousand.

Montgomery County had four lynchings between 1900 and 1930. Earle Frank, accused of robbery, was lynched on July 25, 1901; B. Clark, accused of murder, was lynched on August 27, 1909, along with Benjamin Clark and John Sweeney, accused of murder and complicity in murder respectively. The last two lynchings were at Tarrytown.

Cordial Relations Between Negroes and Wealthiest Whites. The Negroes are concentrated on the bigger plantations, and within the landlord-tenant pattern there exists a very cordial relation. Many of the larger plantation owners prefer Negro to white tenants. This very fact has resulted in the poor whites looking with disfavor upon both the Negro tenants and the plantation owners.

CHAPTER XI

LYNCHED IN HIS CELL
DARIEN, McINTOSH COUNTY, GEORGIA

SHORTLY AFTER nine o'clock on Monday, September 8, 1930, George Grant, Negro, alleged slayer of the Brunswick Chief of Police, was shot to death in a second floor cell of the McIntosh County jail at Darien, Georgia. He had been placed there only a few minutes before by National Guardsmen and the county sheriff. A member of the Guard was in the jailhouse yard and the commanding officer of the Guard was within hearing distance of the fatal shots; the county sheriff was in a downstairs room of his house which opens upon the narrow corridor leading to the second floor cells.

THE LYNCHING

Night Watchman Shot. During the late summer of 1930, there were repeated burglaries of the bank and stores of Darien. There were indications that the guilty persons were amateurs. All of the burglaries had occurred on Thursday and Sunday nights after midnight. Unknown to anyone except the town night watchman, the mayor deputized Ora Anderson, fifty-five years old, to aid in apprehending the burglars.

About midnight on Sunday, September 7, seeing some men on the street, Special Officer Anderson hid near the bank. These men went on up the street. After a time, however, a Negro man came along on the outer edge of the sidewalk, going in the direction of the bank. There was no evidence that he was planning to rob the bank other than that it was late Sunday night, that the bank had been entered before on Sunday night, and that he was going along the sidewalk in its direction. A few feet behind him came a second Negro, who passed close beside Anderson's hiding place. Anderson stated that the Negro saw him and, pulling a gun, said, "You son of a b—, I've got you where I want you," and began firing. One bullet went through his shoulder, another struck his trigger finger, a third went into his leg, a fourth pierced his gun barrel, and the fifth went wild. Though dazed and wounded, Anderson fired at the Negroes as they turned and ran down the slope toward the river's edge and disappeared in the thicket.

Brunswick Chief of Police Killed. Anderson called to the night watchman who was nearby; and presently the fire bell was rung, and many of the townspeople turned out. Upon learning the cause of the alarm, the Negroes who had responded returned quietly to their homes. The sheriff, who was not well, sent his daughter for his only deputy. He also telephoned Glynn County officers and requested bloodhounds. Citizen guards were stationed at the Altamaha River bridge and along the edge of the marsh.

After a while Chief Freeman and a deputy from Brunswick came, and they with the local deputy entered the marsh with a flashlight. After two hours' searching, they cornered a Negro, later believed to have been George Grant, upon a narrowing point of land between the river and a wide ditch. The Negro fired upon them repeatedly. All three officers were wounded; Chief Freeman died instantly. The pursued Negro escaped farther into the marsh.

Sheriff's Frantic Reports. When the sheriff learned of Freeman's death and the wounding of the two deputies, he called to Statesboro and Blackshear for bloodhounds, and notified the sheriffs of many other counties that a "race riot" was threatening at Darien. During the early morning hours, excited officers and men rushed into Darien from a dozen counties.

Seeing that the situation was fast getting past the control of the local sheriff and his one wounded deputy, the chairman of the county commissioners called upon state officials to send the National Guard. Shortly after daylight eighteen National Guardsmen arrived from Savannah.

George Grant Surrenders. By good daylight bloodhounds

were baying in the marshes, and at nine o'clock George Grant called out "Prisoner surrenders," and came out of the marsh with hands high in the air. The National Guardsmen, several sheriffs and deputies, and hundreds of excited people were along the edge of the old rice field, not far away. Grant surrendered to the sheriff, saying that he had done no shooting, but that he was with "Nigger Freddy Bryan," who had wounded Anderson and killed Freeman. A .32 pistol with three empty chambers was in Grant's possession. Freeman had been killed with a .38. Had Grant thrown one pistol away, or had somebody else killed Freeman? Grant answered Anderson's description of height, weight, and stocking cap of the Negro who walked past his hiding place near the bank shortly after midnight, but not of the Negro who had fired upon him.

When Grant voluntarily surrendered, he was on the opposite side of a deep ditch from the sheriff; in crossing it the Negro fell into the water over his head. As he scrambled out, more than a score of people had guns drawn, and threatened to kill him. Others came, and by the time the Guardsmen arrived to escort Grant to the jail, approximately a hundred armed men were begging the sheriff to let them kill him.

Placed in Jail by Guardsmen. Surrounded immediately by Guardsmen, and then by a couple of hundred hangers-on, Grant was marched through the town to the jail, less than a mile away.

On the way to the jail, while the prisoner was in the custody of the Guardsmen, special officer Anderson and at least one other man hit Grant over the head with the butts of heavy pistols. Along the line of march a big man carrying a rifle, reported to have been a guard at a nearby county camp, threatened three Negro boys innocently standing in a store door; cursing in boisterous fashion, this man persistently urged the crowd to lynch Grant. Others were yelling, "Lynch the damn son of a b——!" "Let us have him!" and the like. The mayor stated that a county commissioner, trying to keep the mob from its purpose, was summarily told by one of the up-country man hunters: "Shut your mouth and keep it shut, and that right quick!" Excitement was at a high pitch.

Upon arriving at the jail,[1] members of the Guard placed Grant in the "bull pen" on the second floor. The sheriff locked the grated door of the cell corridor, leaving Grant free to go through the inner connecting corridor from one cell to another. The sheriff's only key to the solid steel door at the head of the stairs was gone. He told the investigator that he was not disturbed about the missing key, for he knew "some of the folks wanted it, and had taken it." Hence the solid steel door was left open. The Guardsmen who placed Grant in the second floor cells entered by the outside west door, and left the jail by the same doorway, posting a uniformed man there to guard it. However, there were two other entrances which were left unguarded.

Milling Men and Screaming Women. The crowd which had followed Grant to the jail went in and out of the sheriff's yard, porch, and rooms at will. A Brunswick lawyer, the local state senator, and several other people from Darien called attention to this fact, but nothing was done about it.

While people were coming and going through the sheriff's rooms, he was on a cot by the window with a "fainty spell," (his own words). One of his teen-age daughters was on the porch screaming hysterically that the sheriff's only deputy, wounded in the marsh, had just died (which was not a fact; the deputy recovered), and calling for somebody to go kill the "nigger." Her condition was so hysterical that it was brought to the attention of a local physician who was in the crowd. An older woman from Brunswick, also loudly demanded the lynching of the Negro.

Four Shots in Jailhouse. While the women continued to scream, and the crowd within and about the jailhouse kept coming and going, with the sheriff still lying in a stupor, three shots, with a slight interval between were heard on the second

---

[1] The sheriff's quarters and the cells are in a small two-story brick building, and are separated by a narrow hall which contains a stairway to the second floor cells. This narrow hall runs east and west and can be entered from either end by outside doors. The sheriff's living room also opens into this hallway.

floor. After a few moments, a fourth shot rang out. George Grant had been killed in the McIntosh County jail. His blood dripped through into a white woman's cell below.

When the body was brought down for the coroner's inquest, the Brunswick woman was loath to see it go away—she wanted it burned then. It was taken to Brunswick in a truck, and is reported to have been placed before a white undertaker's establishment so the public could "come and see" who killed Chief Freeman.

Nobody in Charge. Even if the sheriff had been wise and courageous, and the Guard had functioned to the best advantage, the presence of so many excited outside people—most of whom were attracted, it seems, by the possibility of a lynching—would have created a very difficult situation to handle. As a matter of fact, however, nobody was in charge. Besides being "sickly," the sheriff seemingly was without executive or administrative qualities; the mayor had been elected shortly before and did not know his duties or powers; the officer in charge of the National Guard had been instructed by acting Adjutant General Oberdorfer to "coöperate with" the local civil authorities. The result was that everybody did about what they pleased.

Lynching Highly Satisfactory to Sheriff. The sheriff's statements to the investigator indicate clearly that the mob which lynched Grant had only carried out his desires. If it had not been for his oath and bond, he stated, he himself would have shot Grant when he came out of the marsh to surrender. He stated further that but for fear of the courts he would have killed him as soon as he came in shooting distance of the jail.

He stated that when he came down after placing Grant in a cell he was "almost struck down" when his daughter, ill-informed, told him that his only deputy had just died of the wounds inflicted when Chief Freeman was killed. He remembered going to a spigot on the porch for a drink of water, and that he was almost strangled by getting the water into his nose. The next thing he knew he was on the bed by the window, with several people standing over him trying to get him "fixed up."

About that time, so the sheriff stated, he heard: "Bang! and a nigger groan; bang! and a nigger groan; bang! . . . no groan." Then he straightened up a bit and said:. "Now, that's all I know; I don't know who killed the damn nigger and I don't care! I'm glad he's dead! Law and order! What's law and order when Mr. Nigger can kill a good white man like Freeman and try to kill a half a dozen more, and then keep him in jail and give him a trial—and cost the county a whole pile of money? I'm glad he's dead; I'd a liked to a killed him myself, damn nigger!"

Ineffective Performance of National Guard Unit. Even though he was proceeding on the theory that he was subordinate to the sheriff, it is difficult to understand why the officer of the Guard should have guarded one entrance to the hallway and left the other two unguarded, when he knew the steel door at the top of the stairs was swinging open for lack of a key. Also, though he was within a few yards of the jail when Grant was killed in his cell, there is no satisfactory explanation of why the Guard officer made no effort to find out who had been upstairs with a gun. Machine guns were not put up at the jail until after Grant had been killed.

It is generally reported that the Guardsmen were poorly disciplined. A city official said that his statement in the newspapers concerning the good behavior of the guardsmen was an effort to "help patch up a mess"; that shortly before giving the article to the press he had told the officer of the Guard that he could see no service the Guard had rendered, and thought things would have been better had it not come. Shortly after the lynching the mayor got in touch with the Governor, and in mid-afternoon martial law was declared with the officer of the Guard in command. Several persons suspected of being Grant's aides were arrested and sent to Savannah or elsewhere under armed escort.

Innocent Negro Killed by Undeputized Men. On Tuesday morning following the establishment of martial law, William Henry Bryan, rural McIntosh County Negro, conceded to be innocent, was shot and killed by three undeputized men from Glynn County. They claimed that he had resisted arrest.

Bryan's mother who saw the shooting stated that her son was unarmed, and that the man who shot him was an ex-policeman of Darien who had been dismissed by the county commissioners. The fatally wounded Negro, who died in Savannah soon after he was taken there in a truck, said the same. However, another of the three man-hunters claimed the gory honor. The National Guard unit ignored the case as outside their sphere; the sheriff made no arrests.

Mob's Ranks Swelled by Outside County Officers. According to a statement appearing in the Waycross *Georgian* on September 12, six police officers, including Sheriff L. C. Warren and County Police Chief O. M. Hiers from Ware County, went to Darien, more than sixty miles, in response to the McIntosh County sheriff's "race riot" call. Officers swarmed into Darien from a dozen other counties. However, outside of the two officers from Glynn County, there is no evidence that a single one of them tried to help preserve law and order. Were they mere onlookers? Or were they numbered among the man-hunters? These same questions should be asked with reference to the lynchings at Thomasville and Ocilla, where equally large numbers of officers from surrounding counties were present.

The Mob's Victim. George Grant was born and reared in McIntosh County twelve miles from Darien near the village of Townsend, where his father still lives. For several years, Grant had been employed by cross-tie cutters operating north of Darien. It is reported that he was not regular at his work, and that on one occasion, when his employer complained of the quantity and quality of his work, Grant, in a very cool and insolent manner, looked at him and said: "Boss, do you carry a pistol?" "Yes," was his employer's quick reply, "and you'll get it if you bother me!" The employer reported that Grant looked as though he would have taken pleasure in mutilating him. The gun found on Grant when he was arrested had two notches in the grip, which was taken by many of the local pro-lynchers as proof that he had killed two people. The fact that the notches might mean something else, or that he may have bought, swapped for, or stolen the gun was overlooked.

Grant had lived in McIntosh County all his life and was
without court record. It is established, however, that some
months before the lynching, Grant had ambushed and shot a
white man for "running with his woman." The man though
seriously wounded and disfigured, did not have him arrested.
It was not learned how much schooling Grant had had or what
his general intelligence level was.

William Henry Bryan, killed by the three undeputized men
from Glynn County, was born and reared in McIntosh County
three miles northeast of Darien. For some years he worked
in Philadelphia, and after his return lived near where he was
born. He had a wife and two children, one of them being born
within a few days of his death. Several items, at first reported
to have been stolen goods found at his mother's house, were
later identified by his mother's former white employers as
things which they had given her from time to time in appreciation of her good services.

Principal Figures in Mob. Just who shot George Grant in
his cell is not definitely established. It was reported about town
that a business man of Darien fired the fatal shot. This report
was contradicted by a large number of people who said that
a Brunswick man did it. Adjutant General Homer C. Parker
implied, as we shall see later, that a local peace officer had
something to do with Grant's death.

Of the three who were present when William Henry Bryan
was killed, one was an ex-police officer of Darien, dismissed some
years before by the county commissioners because he had shown
himself bloodthirsty on several occasions, and had been accused of selling liquor and "planting" whiskey and guns on
people he wished to "frame." After his dismissal he had dropped
out of sight until he came from Glynn County to "help" in the
Grant affair. Another of the three, the one who claimed to be
the killer, was the operator of a filling station in Brunswick,
and several times had been charged with selling liquor. The
third member of the group was also from Glynn County.

REACTION OF THE COMMUNITY TO THE LYNCHING

The reaction of the community to the lynching of Grant can be judged by the fact that both the coroner's jury and the grand jury reported that he came to his death at the hands of unknown persons.

Lynching Condemned by Local Papers. The local weekly paper, the McIntosh County *Herald*, circulation 300, carried a news story and an editorial in its issue of September 12. The news story, entitled "Two Die from Gun Shots in Monday's Affray," gave a summary of the principal facts and closed with the words; "Many wild and conflicting reports and rumors were heard during the trouble, and excitement ran high at times. Many officers of adjoining counties were here." The editor of this paper is a member of one of the county's leading families, and had just served as state senator from his district. His editorial captioned—"Tragic, Indeed" is given in full:

"That an occurrence such as transpired in Darien on last Sunday night and Monday morning in regrettable is to express it mildly.

"*The Herald* regrets each and every incident of the affair, except the capture of the bandit. It regrets the shooting and wounding of R. J. Anderson, a brave officer. It regrets the shooting and killing of Bob Freeman of Glynn County, one of the best officers of the law known anywhere. It regrets the wounding of Mr. Hatch Collins, Deputy Sheriff of this county, and of Mr. John Fisher, a member of the posse. Whether these men acted wisely or whether their desire to apprehend a violator of the law overrode their better judgment is unknown. It is known that they acted fearlessly and bravely.

"That a prisoner after being lodged in jail should be killed by a mob is regretted. Such action cannot do the killed or wounded any good. It can, however, place upon the name of a county or community an insignia of lawlessness, a stain. It helps break down the majesty of the law. It is bad from each and every angle it is viewed.

"It is regretted that the Sheriff and other officers of the law did not prevent what happened after the fugitive was captured. It is regretted that the detachment of the military organization sent here to prevent violence were helpless and did not prevent such an occurrence."

This editorial is representative of the attitude of the educated and most refined element in the county, which is numerically small and made up in the main of descendants of the old aristocratic families.

The Brunswick *News*, published twenty miles south of Darien, carried detailed stories for several days. The fact that a popular Brunswick officer had been killed at Darien naturally caused the paper to give special attention to the disorders there. Throughout the turmoil the paper maintained its usual insistence that lynching cannot be tolerated. On September 10, there was a news item, "Wrong Negro Was Killed at Darien," stating that, according to the Mayor of Darien, William Henry Bryan, the second Negro killed, was innocent.

Fallacious Assumptions of General Press Reports. In a news story in the Waycross *Georgian* on September 12 appeared the following statement:

"Chief Bob Freeman of Glynn County, brother of Henry Freeman of Waycross, is dead, George Grant and Willie Bryan, Negroes, are dead and three officers of the law are wounded, as the result of an alleged attempt to rob the Bank of Darien after midnight Sunday.

"Ora Anderson, night watchman, was shot and wounded when he attempted to stop the alleged effort to rob the bank."

In this story, as in others appearing throughout the state and nation, it is implied that the Negroes killed were in the act of robbing the bank. But it has been shown already that there was no positive evidence whatever that the Negroes were going to rob the bank. It was never established that Grant was one of the two suspected of intent to rob and, as stated above, Bryan's innocence was conceded.

National Guard Scored by Press. Many daily and weekly papers over the state and nation carried long reports of the Darien disturbance. "Why the National Guard?" and numerous other editorials appeared in leading Southern papers, commenting upon the fact that the Guard did not protect the prisoner after placing him in jail. An editorial in the Durham *Sun* (N. C.) on September 9 raised this question:

"What good was it to have the soldiers there if they were not going to discharge their duty? If they were to protect the prisoner, why didn't they do it? They had machine guns. They could have held off the mob. . . . If Georgia doesn't take some sort of drastic action against the machine gun company and against the members of the mob, the state will stand indicted in the eyes of the civilized world."

The Greensboro *News* of September 10 raised similar queries and severely arraigned the National Guard and its commanding officer.

An Extended Three-Sided Controversy. The Macon *Telegraph* and the Atlanta *Constitution* evinced great interest in the case from the outset, and were largely responsible for getting into the open the three-sided controversy between local police officers, the National Guard, and the district solicitor general, a controversy which resulted in the indictment of all three in the eyes of thoughtful citizens.

The Savannah papers might have been expected to find whatever excuse could be made for the Guardsmen who went from Savannah to Darien. The Savannah *Press* said editorially:

"Where people are aroused—infuriated—by tragic events something like this is liable to happen. Color has little to do with it—white men might have shared the same fate. Military and machine guns will not protect such a prisoner. Commander will hesitate to fire upon his neighbors. People may speculate upon drastic military duty. Citizen soldiery are not held up to the same laws that prevail among regular troops. If there is any criticism upon the military in the Darien case it is that they vacated the jail as soon as they delivered the prisoner up to the civil authorities and put him in jail. The work of the military was not finished when the Negro was routed out of the swamps. They were sent there to prevent a lynching and this we are told they failed to do."

In answer to the widespread reports from Darien, based largely upon Sheriff Poppell's statements that members of the mob "crashed into the building" and shot Grant in spite of Colonel Neal's "pleas" and the physical efforts of guardsmen to protect the prisoner, Colonel W. R. Neal, commander in charge of the National Guard unit, said in an Associated Press story of September 9:

"No machine gun was at the jail until afternoon and no speeches were made by any officer or enlisted man of the detachment to any mob or group of citizens.

"At no time were any members of the Savannah National Guard overpowered in Darien. . . .

"I wish to emphasize the fact that at the time the Negro, Grant, was killed by three pistol shots in his cell in the jail there was no National Guardsman in the jail and had not been there after I turned Grant over to the civil authorities after seeing that he was locked in his cell."[2]

When this statement failed to relieve the Guard of criticism, Adjutant General Homer C. Parker, campaigning in the primary for Comptroller-General when the troops were sent to Darien by Acting Adjutant General Oberdorfer, made the following statement in defense of the Guard:

"The press of this and other states has been carrying news stories and editorials with reference to the happenings at Darien that reflect on the name and reputation of the Georgia National Guard and bring into question the efficiency, courage and honor of one of its regimental commanders.

"As head of the military forces of the state I cannot allow such statements to go unchallenged. I hope to be able to vindicate the National Guard. . . .

"I am loath to believe there is an officer or a man in the Georgia

[2] Taken from the Atlanta *Constitution*, September 10, 1930.

National Guard which would shirk his duty in such an emergency as existed at Darien.

"I shall not inquire into the conduct of the civil authorities or other persons not connected with the military service. To do so would be beyond the scope of my duty."[3]

Sheriff and Guard Commander Accuse Each Other. Sheriff Poppell's reply was that no guard was posted at the jail, nevertheless concerning the identity of those who shot Grant in his cell he said: "I don't know who did it and I don't care. If you want to know ask the Savannah National Guard officers who were here." A few days later Colonel Neal's full report was transmitted to Governor Hardman by Adjutant General Parker. This report, as shown by the excerpts below, clearly attempted to pass the responsibility of Grant's killing back to Sheriff Poppell and other local officers:

"I was last to leave the negro's cell, leaving him there alone, and the sheriff of McIntosh county locked the cell door. I asked the sheriff if the negro would 'be safe now' and received an affirmative answer. I saw that everybody except prisoners and the sheriff left the jail building and then left myself by the door which leads into the jailyard. This door was closed and from the sound made apparently was locked behind me. I do not know whether the door leading from the jail into the sheriff's house, which is part of the same building, was locked. Lieutenant Blake remained in the jailyard until after the negro was killed at 9:25 A.M., and reported to me that the door to the jailyard was not opened again during that period. . . ."[4]

Adjutant General Parker endorsed Neal's report:

"I can find no cause or reason to criticize Colonel Neal or any other officer or men of the Georgia National Guard who performed service at Darien on the dates mentioned above pursuant to the orders transmitted to the detachment commander by the acting adjutant general.[4]

---

[3] From the Thomasville *Times-Enterprise*, October 4, 1930.
[4] Taken from the Atlanta *Constitution*, October 11, 1930.

The question of Colonel Neal's instructions upon going to Darien naturally arose. Was he sent there without power? According to statements from Colonel Oberdorfer, who ordered the troops out, the Governor stipulated that any troops should "coöperate" with the local civil authorities, "rendering them the assistance that had been requested." Colonel Neal arrived at Darien at 7:25 A.M.; it was 3.47 P.M. when the Governor declared martial law with Colonel Neal in command. In the meantime George Grant had been captured, placed in jail, and shot to death.

Sheriff, Guardsmen, and Governor Blamed by District Solicitor. While the controversy raged between the sheriff and National Guard, the Solicitor General of the Atlantic Judicial Circuit made an independent investigation at the request of Governor Hardman. Representative sections of the solicitor's report appear below:

"It is impossible to believe that either the civil or military officers would have thought that the prisoner was in no danger, if reports to the effect that at the very time he was locked in his cell there were outside in the yard and on the premises not less than 100 men, many of them showing intense anger and feeling, are true.

"Yet the sheriff, sick and with no deputy, did not call on the military forces to guard the jail, neither did the commander of the military department take charge, or volunteer his services to the sheriff. Why not is something hard to answer. The seeming dereliction of the sheriff may be explained by his physical condition at the time, but I know of nothing that can be said in behalf of the officer in charge of the troops. And in this connection I might add that both the mayor of the city of Darien, and the sheriff of that county told me that they did not ask that troops be sent there, had nothing to do with them being brought there, and did not know that they were coming until after they were there. The sheriff says that the officer in charge of the troops never at any time reported to him for service, nor offered in any way to help him, and he flatly denies a statement of the officer in charge of the military forces, that he told that officer after the negro was locked up that the negro 'would be safe now.'

"The mayor stated to me that while the negro was killed at about 9:30 o'clock A.M., the officer in charge of the troops came and reported to him about 10 o'clock A.M., or at least 30 minutes after the negro was dead, and that this was the first report of any sort that he had from the military.

"*Divided Responsibility.* In my opinion this killing of the prisoner was largely caused by divided responsibility. The military appeared to be in charge, and thus in a way justified the sheriff in leaving them to protect the prisoner, while they were in reality not in charge, and really supposed to be under the control of some civil officer, that they had seemingly failed to locate from their arrival at 7:30 o'clock A.M. until 10 o'clock A.M., when they found Mayor Young. I might add that I understand that after the prisoner was killed and his body carried away, the military authorities took charge and posted a machine gun at the head of the stairs at the jail door, seemingly to prevent entrance into a jail from which the prisoner had already been killed and taken. I am unable to explain the childish gesture.

"Seemingly the law was not followed in calling out the military forces, that is by the proclamation declaring a state of insurrection in Darien, as provided for by the law in such cases, and it is regrettable that the military forces should have been sent there, without being given the authority under which they could act, independent of the civil authorities.

"When considered from every vantage, it would seem that the first error was in sending the troops there with their hands tied, by giving them no authority. Then it is apparent that the officer in charge certainly failed to offer his services to the civil authorities, when they needed it most. Likewise the civil authorities either thinking that the military was in charge, or from indifference, did not avail themselves of the help that they should have obtained from the military. All of which are errors, which in my humble opinion contributed to the death of the unfortunate prisoner.

"I shall report my findings and all available information to the grand jury of that county, which convenes on the first Monday in

December, next, and have a thorough investigation made by that
body, so that if possible the perpetrators of this crime may be
brought to justice.

> "Joseph T. Grice,
> "Solicitor Gen. Atlantic Circuit,
> "Glenville, Ga., Oct. 14, 1930."[5]

"... *Military Authorities Are in Possession of Definite Information.* ..." Adjutant General Parker responded to the
solicitor's report with the statement that "... military authorities are in possession of definite information. ... If Solicitor
General Grice is really in earnest and wants to know who killed
the negro, the military department can give him some very
definite information. Otherwise he had better stay off the
military department. Two or three people have come to Atlanta
recently and have told me who killed the negro in the jail. If
the solicitor general will call on us we will be able to help him,
but he has not communicated with me. If he wants to know,
he can easily find out. Dragging the military in was done in
an effort to muddy the water and becloud the issues."[6]

On the following day, October 31, the Atlanta *Constitution*
again carried a long story about the controversy, in which
appeared a lengthy statement by Adjutant General Parker,
from which the following significant paragraphs are quoted:

"Heretofore, I have not deemed it my duty to charge this
atrocious crime to any one. I felt like it was a matter to be handled
by the civil authorities of McIntosh County. I still think so.
However, as stated to a reporter for the Atlanta *Constitution* on
yesterday, the military authorities are in possession of definite
information that Mr. Grice can have if he desires it.

"If the mayor of Darien can afford to deny that he asked for
the troops, and if the sheriff of McIntosh County can afford to
refer newspaper men 'to the national guard for information' stating
that he knows 'nothing about the case and cares less,' and if the
solicitor-general of the Atlantic judicial circuit can afford to sit

---

[5] Taken from the Atlanta *Constitution*, October 30, 1930.
[6] Taken from the Atlanta *Constitution*, October 30, 1930.

in judgment on the actions of the governor and everyone else connected with the military establishment of the state, then I am inclined to believe that the military authorities can well afford to defend themselves and place the blame for the murder where it rightfully belongs.

"I wonder if Mr. Grice knows who beat George Grant almost to death when he was first apprehended, and as he came out of the marshes, with both of his hands up? I wonder if he knows that his slayer admitted that he had killed Grant and attempted to justify himself because of a pact that he had entered into with a deceased official to the effect that either of them was to avenge the untimely death of the other at the hands of any negro? I wonder if he knows who killed the second negro on the morning of September 9?"

Challenge Verbally Accepted. In reply to Parker's announcement that he knew who killed Grant and would give such information to the grand jury if called upon, the district solicitor by long distance telephone promptly accepted the challenge and declared that he would request all information which General Parker had and would follow it through.

Sheriff Poppell branded as a "lie" the Adjutant General's intimations that as the result of a pact between two local officers one of them had killed Grant. Solicitor Grice made a statement in which he said: "I feel that the Adjutant General must have been misled in some of his information, if I understand his statement. . . . Freeman was killed, Deputy Sheriff Collins so seriously wounded he was believed dying and Fisher wounded. Obviously, from the information I received at Darien when I investigated for the governor, neither of these two survivors could have shot Grant in his cell. I certainly know nothing of his intimations or charges. I must decline to enter a controversy with him, but want to assure him and all others that my duty will be done."[7]

The Sordid Dénouement. The sorry conclusion of this controversy between Adjutant General and the Circuit Solicitor is contained in this one sentence from the Atlanta *Constitution* of December 5: "General Parker stated Thursday that he

[7] Taken from the Atlanta *Constitution*, October 30, 1930.

had not been asked by Solicitor General Grice to testify before the grand jury."

The grand jury made its presentments at the end of the fourth day. No one was indicted for lynching Grant or for murdering Bryan, and the sheriff and National Guard were exonerated in the following statement:

"We severely condemn the killing of George Grant, a prisoner in the McIntosh County jail, September 8. From our investigation we find the sheriff of the county in charge at the time of the killing and proper steps to safeguard the prisoner were not taken by him due to the fact that his physical condition was such that he was unable to cope with the situation, and also that he was further handicapped by the fact that his deputy had been wounded and was in the Brunswick hospital.

"Some party or parties unknown took advantage of the situation and shot George Grant.

"We further want to thank officers and citizens of the surrounding territory for the assistance rendered local authorities during the trouble.

"We have thoroughly investigated the duty imposed on the military called to Darien and find they acted in direct accordance with instructions. They were not negligent. Colonel Neal and his troops are entitled to complete exoneration for all blame and criticism directed at them.

"We want to express appreciation for their services on behalf of the citizens of McIntosh County."[8]

Community Attitudes. A majority of the white people of the community held that Grant should have been killed, and that even if Bryan was the wrong "nigger," the men who killed him thought they were getting the right one. The only fault this element finds with the lynching was that Grant's death robbed them of information concerning his confederate, who, according to their thinking, should have been lynched, too.

"Well, trouble between the whites and blacks has just begun, but things are not so bad yet that niggers need be robbing banks." This statement in Darien's white barber shop

---

[8] Taken from the Atlanta *Journal,* December 4, 1930.

was the investigator's introduction to the local situation, three days after the lynching. The speaker was an unemployed youth of eighteen who, on hearing of the excitement in Darien, had hurried down from Savannah to take part in it. "Well, I'm glad you young fellows are taking an interest in keeping these d— niggers in their place," was the comment of an elderly man in the barber shop. One of the barbers added, "I'm glad you got here in time; it was a good experience for you." The other barber, who had come to Darien a few years ago from the up-country, told how, on Sunday night, he heard the shots and, without changing his "Sunday clothes," joined the crowd hunting for the Negroes.

Another element of Darien's white people are astride the fence. Theoretically they do not approve lynchings, but they find little or no fault with Grant's death. However, they do deplore the death of Bryan, but they have never been inclined to do anything about it other than express regret with it as a closed incident.

A small minority feels that the whole affair was disgraceful. They openly assert that the sheriff erred unforgivably in spreading the riot alarm through a score of counties, when a few good men could have captured the Negroes who shot at Anderson and thus could have disposed of the whole matter with nothing more serious than a charge of assault with intent to kill. After the lynching occurred they hoped that the grand jury would bring indictments against the guilty persons, and especially against those who killed Bryan.

A Closed Incident. The mayor, the resident state senator, the leading lawyer, the city clerk, the resident Episcopal Rector, and the town's oldest retired planter especially deplored the lynching and subsequent murder and desired punishment for the guilty. But, as in most other communities with lynchings in 1930, nearly every one of them expressed the hope that he would not be called to testify. The person who privately denounced the lawlessness most vigorously was the resident Episcopal rector. Being "an outsider," however— an Englishman—he thought it best to say very little publicly, lest it interfere with his work. So within a short time after the lynching of Grant and the murder of Bryan, practically every white person in Darien, whether at the outset justifying, condoning or condemning the affair, looked upon it as a closed incident. Naturally enough, after seeing two of their number killed in open defiance of the law, the Negroes maintained a profound silence about the whole matter. Even the mother and wife of the murdered Bryan did not dare ask for his body.

Facts About the Community

The economic and social structure of this once prosperous coast county has collapsed. Now there are only occasional turpentine stills, small fisheries, a small amount of sawmilling and other woodwork, a little farming of the most primitive type, a small amount of tourist trade, and the business enterprises and professions to be found in any county seat town with a population of a little less than one thousand people.

Early Scotch Settlers. Darien, first known as New Inverness, was settled by the Scotch. John More McIntosh, a Scotch laird, head of his clan, was persuaded by Captain Mackay to lead a colony to Georgia. One hundred and thirty sturdy Scotch highlanders, "with fifty women, took shipping from Inverness for Georgia. They reached Savannah in due time and then went in flat-bottomed boats to find their new home sixteen miles from Frederica, on the Altamaha. Calling their town New Inverness, they established their settlement, built their huts and were just getting settled when the war with Spain began. . . . The settlers were in main very poor peasants, only seventeen, according to General Oglethorpe's Letters, being able to pay their passage across the sea."[9]

Many of the poorer highlanders, soon growing tired of the lonely and Indian-threatened New Inverness in the wilderness, gladly enlisted in Oglethorpe's army. Several other members of the colony went elsewhere, but "John More McIntosh and his immediate family remained, and as he was a man of substance and kept the storehouse of the colony and traded with the Indians, he was well to do." Several of the leading families

---

[9] G. G. Smith, *Story of Georgia and Her People.*

signed a document allying themselves with Oglethorpe, with
headquarters at Frederica, and thus gave permanence to New
Inverness or Darien.

Slave Labor Introduced. The number of people in Darien
and environs remained small for several decades. There was, in
fact, but little increase of population until the second quarter
of the eighteenth century when, upon the recommendation of
James Habersham to the trustees of the Colony of Georgia,
the restrictions against the use of slaves were removed. Habersham argued that Georgia needed cheap labor, thus reversing
the colony's earlier reasoning on this subject which was to
the end that slave labor would be economically unwise in that
it would make labor odious to free people. The trustees were
convinced by Habersham that slave labor would benefit the
colony, and decided to permit importation provided slaves not
be in large numbers on any plantation, that profanity be pro-
hibited, that they be encouraged to marry, that they learn
none of the mechanical arts, that they do no work on the
Sabbath day, that they attend church regularly, and that
they be instructed by the Protestant ministry.

Within a few years, rice plantations were opened up all
along the Altamaha River. Negro slaves did the work. White
people directed their labor. A new county was laid off in 1793
and named McIntosh to honor the leading family.

As the people of means became richer through the use of
slave labor, and the best lands were concentrated into the control of the most wealthy families, the poorer people tended to
push into the country away from the Altamaha River and
the coast, to pasture their livestock. These inland portions
were "thinly settled by plain stock-raisers, who lived hard and
had no social or educational advantages. These people were
many of them the descendants of those Scotch who first fixed
their homes near Darien." In contrast with these humble folk,
along the Altamaha River and the coast were "a number of
rice plantations which were owned by planters who had large
estates and elegant homes. There were found here, as along
all the coast where these planters had their homes, much intelligence, enterprise and hospitality. . . ." As time passed

these two classes of white people remained far apart.

A Prosperous Coast Town. With the settlement of the up-country, Darien became a port of some consequence. Located at the mouth of the Altamaha which is formed by the Oconee and Ocmulgee rivers, Darien was the natural seaport for Athens, Milledgeville, Macon, and a score of smaller places in central Georgia. Smith tells us "the cotton boats from the up-country brought great loads of cotton to this port for shipment to Europe and the North, and Darien was for many years a great lumber market. The timber ranger of the up-country rafted his timber to this little city and found a market for it. It had a small but cultured and wealthy citizenship, and was pleasant and attractive."

The Bank of Darien, chartered by the State Legislature in 1818 with branches at Milledgeville and other points, had a capital of $469,017, and a circulation of $329,942. Only four banks in the state had a larger capital and but two a larger circulation. In 1850 there were several steam sawmills at Darien, and five large gang saws valued at $50,000; more than 50,000 feet of lumber was sawed each day. A considerable number of laborers were used at the sawmills and in reloading the cotton from river craft to sea-going vessels.

Three Negro Slaves to One White Freeman. By 1850, Darien had two sets of rich white people—the planters and the operators of commercial enterprises; and two sets of poor white people—the small farmers and the laborers employed by the cotton and lumber industries. No group was large, for the total white population was but 1,372. The slaves, of course, did part of the work about the sawmills and boats, but they were generally restricted to labor on the rice and sugar cane plantations.

The Negroes outnumbered the whites more than three to one, and were divided into slaves and freemen. In 1850 there were 4,629 slaves, forty-one free colored males and thirty-one free colored females. Though the number of freemen was small, the conditions in McIntosh County after Emancipation might have been incomparably worse had it not been for the steadying influence of these few free Negroes, who had had at least a little experience in self direction.

Excessive Economic Retrogression. A combination of circumstances has disrupted the economic structure of Darien and McIntosh County. Except for the new life which came into it a few years ago with the opening of the coastal highway it would be even worse off than it is. By 1890 the economic structure of the county, weakening from immediately after the war, had crumbled. The first severe shock was the freeing of the slaves. This immediately disrupted the economic order, and subsequently modified the political situation to the extent that Negroes filled practically all political offices during the decades following. This discouraged the influx of propertied white people and probably caused some to go elsewhere.

Next came the gradual decline of Darien as a port; railroad transportation was fast supplanting river boats. The final blow was that rice and sugar cane could be produced much cheaper in Louisiana. By the turn of the century the sawmills at Darien were almost idle; seagoing vessels had practically quit coming in, and the former rice plantations were overgrown with tall marsh grass. The owners of the "big houses" were growing old and dying; many of their children had already established themselves at Savannah and other cities. The tenant houses were no longer kept in repair.

Population Decrease Between 1890 and 1920. The county's population of 6,470 in 1890, eighty-six per cent of which was Negro, inevitably decreased; but the decline has not been so rapid as one might expect, for the crumbling of the economic structure has gone on slowly. The local political situation made the county attractive to Negroes; furthermore, farm lands were almost valueless to the aged plantation owners and could be rented from them for practically nothing, and upon their deaths could be bought at a nominal figure from the heirs, most of whom had left the county. Between 1890 and 1920 the Negro population of the county dropped from 5,212 to 3,803. The number of white people remained constant at 1,258.

Small Increase Since 1920. Between 1920 and 1930 the white population increased by 561, a forty per cent gain, while the Negro element gained but 73. With an increase of 114 during the decade, Darien had a population of 937 in 1930.

The all-weather road has made the turpentine industry and the growing of vegetables a bit more attractive. Most significant, several gasoline stations, garages, quick lunch places, and rooming houses have been opened up along the highway. The increased economic returns, however, have been of no considerable value to the local Negroes, for with these new developments, outside white people have come into the county: The Negroes who drove the turpentine wagon trains have been replaced by white truck drivers; and all the road stands, and most of the Darien stores are now operated by whites. Practically all these newcomers are poor whites, and most of them have come from the inland pine barren counties where whites are traditionally antagonistic toward Negroes.[10]

A Very Rural and Very Poor County. With but one town and it with a population of less than 1,000, McIntosh County, with hardly twelve people to the square mile, is one of the most sparsely settled counties in Georgia, which has an average density of approximately fifty to the square mile. Scarcely one-third of the rural population supports itself by farming. While some of the non-farming rural dwellers earn small amounts of money during the year by irregular work at the few small fisheries, turpentine farms, and sawmills, the vast majority secure the major portion of their livelihood from fishing and hunting and the cultivation of small patches of corn and yams. In the entire county, less than one hundred acres are usually devoted to cotton.

Approximately three-fourths of the county's four hundred farmers are Negroes, four-fifths of whom own farms. After the collapse of the plantation structure, Negroes in McIntosh and other Georgia coastal counties bought farms for practically nothing, simply because nobody else wanted them. Less than one-fifth of the county's land is in farms at present. On their small unproductive tracts, these Negro owners have as little as

---

[10] See case studies of Ocilla and Ailey for detailed facts about the inland poorer whites.

any people in Georgia. Farm ownership here has been of no noticeable economic or cultural benefit.

In 1924 the average value of farm crops per McIntosh farm family was but $113.27 as compared with the state average of $831.75. The income from manufactured products was also far below the state average, being $68.27 per capita in McIntosh and $239.39 in Georgia; the total per capita value of farm, fisheries, and manufactured products was $95.46 against $310.78. In 1929 the bank deposits amounted to $27.84 per capita in this county and $155.89 in the state. The average wealth in McIntosh is low because of the small incomes of the masses, and especially the Negroes. In 1929, twenty-eight income tax returns were filed, practically all for less than $5,000; most of these were returned by lumber dealers or turpentine farm operators. The tax valuation of $263.93 per inhabitant, though $85.10 below the state average, reaches this figure by reason of the county's sparse population, and the certainty that a poor county will tax all lands.

The rice fields and virgin forests of former decades have been supplanted by the valueless silent marsh and scrub timbers. There were scores of vessels along well built wharves in earlier days where now one can hardly make his way through thickets to the bank of the Altamaha. A few light craft come into Darien each year, but largely for small business or out of sheer curiosity. In fact, except for that strip of the county rejuvenated by the coastal highway, the present economic structure of the county is but the vestigial remains of a century ago.

School Expenditures High and Illiteracy Rates Higher. In 1928, the McIntosh County Board of Education provided eighteen teachers for 393 white school census children and twenty-nine teachers for 1,326 Negro children. Even though more than ten times as much is spent upon the white child as upon the Negro, the sum spent for each school census Negro child was, according to the records, far above the state average: $87.28 per white child and $8.13 per Negro child in McIntosh, against the state's average of $36.88 per white child and $5.07 per Negro child.

The county's schools, however, are not so good as these expenditures would suggest, for the smaller the school population the larger the overhead per child. Interestingly enough, in 1928 but twelve county school superintendents in Georgia received a salary equal to that paid the superintendent of this poor county; the relative cost of transporting pupils was higher, also, because of the sparsity of the white population. The sum of $2,695 was paid the county superintendent and $7,126 was spent for the transportation of a part of the 393 white school children. This latter item cost almost as much as the county spent for the education of its 1,326 Negro children. The average annual salary of the white teachers in 1928 was $812.00 in McIntosh and $792.30 in Georgia; the average salary of the Negro teacher was $299.82 in McIntosh and $306.76 in Georgia.

The principal of the Negro school at Darien, the leading colored man in the county, receives a salary of approximately $1,500, and his four assistants get much better than the county average. Just recently a new schoolhouse was erected at Darien, with the Rosenwald Fund coöperating. Besides this five-teacher public school, which does junior high school work, there is at Darien a one-teacher grade school operated by the Episcopal Church. In the remainder of the county there are ten one-teacher schools, five two-teacher schools, and one three-teacher school for Negroes. There is a patent desk to every 1.8 Negro child in average daily attendance throughout the county, which is much above the average of the state at large, with a desk to every 4.3 Negro pupils. The prevalence of patent desks in this county may be a hang-over from former decades when the Negroes controlled local politics.

There are five white schools in the county. The one at Darien with nine teachers is an accredited high school, housed in a small brick building and two or three temporary buildings put up to care for a recent consolidation. One of the other four schools has four teachers, one has three, and the remaining two are one-teacher schools.

In spite of its relatively higher expenditures for both races, McIntosh County's illiteracy rates in 1930 were 6.1 per cent of whites over ten years of age in contrast with the state average of 3.3 per cent, and 23.1 per cent of Negroes while the Georgia average was 19.9 per cent. It is inevitable that a large proportion of school expenditures and other funds for county services be consumed by overhead expenses in a county with a total population of less than six thousand.

Weak Churches of Many Denominations. The county's white church membership is divided as follows: Southern Baptists, 145; Primitive Baptists, 15; Southern Methodists, 144; Presbyterians, 74; Roman Catholics, 14; and Protestant Episcopalians, about fifty. In the county there are four Missionary Baptist Churches for whites, and of necessity all are small and weak. The Southern Methodist churches in McIntosh County are a part of the Brunswick Circuit, which has a total of but 315 members in five churches. There is a Protestant Episcopal Church at Darien with a resident rector, an Englishman, who serves three other churches, two of which are for Negroes and located in McIntosh County; his fourth church, white, is at Jesup, fifty miles away. The major part of his salary is from the mission board of his denomination. The Presbyterians, too, have a small church at Darien. When the early settlement at Darien was weakened by the enlistments in Oglethorpe's army, the Presbyterian minister, who had established at Darien the first kirk in Georgia, departed. For some years there was no church. Later, Episcopal missionaries came into the county. With the recent opening up of the paved coastal highway, a few additional Southern Baptists and Methodists have come in from the inland counties.

Of the county's total Negro church membership of about two thousand, 1,408 are Missionary Baptists, 364 are members of the African Methodist Episcopal Church and over a hundred are Protestant Episcopalians. The county has more than thirty-five Negro Baptist churches, and all but a few are very weak. The Negro First Baptist at Darien has played an important part in the history of the county, especially between the Civil War and the end of the century when Negroes were in control of local politics.

Negroes Disfranchised by Special State Legislation. Social and political changes in McIntosh County have been no less phenomenal than the economic changes discussed above. Immediately following the Civil War, and to a marked degree to the beginning of the twentieth century, the Negroes controlled political affairs. From the end of the war to the end of the century the local state legislator, the Darien marshal, and some of the county officers were colored. Negro office holding ceased only when, shortly before 1900, special state legislation was enacted for McIntosh County, making all county officers the direct or indirect appointees of the district judge of the superior court, who was white. The special legislation empowered the judge to name a jury commission to appoint the grand and petty juries; the grand jury in turn appointed the county commissioners, and the mayor and aldermen of the town of Darien.

The popular vote still sent a Negro to the state legislature until about 1900, when by state laws voting was limited to the sons of war veterans, to people with $500 of taxable property, and to persons who could read and explain satisfactorily a passage from the Constitution. The Negro vote was at the mercy of the white examiners. While the first two requirements disfranchised most Negroes, the third provided an opportunity to disfranchise the others at will, for, according to statements of resident elderly politicians, even those who could read often were unable to give a "satisfactory" explanation of a passage from the Constitution. Since that time no Negro has sat in the state legislature in Georgia. The Negroes, thus made politically powerless, have been losing interest in politics. At present but few take part in any except presidential elections, and in these less than fifty usually vote.

Few White Voters and Few Negro Criminals. In the 1920 presidential election a total of 119 Democratic and 39 Republican votes were cast; in 1924 there were 127 Democratic and 44 Republican votes. Here, as elsewhere, the 1928 election brought out additional voters: A total of 321 votes were cast, 141 for the Democratic electors, 26 for the Anti-Smith Democratic electors, and 154 for the Republican electors. In the 1930 Democratic primary, 269 votes were cast for governor.

Since the Negroes have been legislated out of local politics, there is no great interest taken among the ruling white minority. County offices are not generally sought after. A leading citizen made this comment in defense of his vote for the present sheriff: "Well, I voted for him because he does not drink. He is no good as a police officer, but then he has but little to do and gets nearly nothing for it. Of the possibilities, I thought he was the best." The fact is, there is practically no middle class in McIntosh County from which to secure public officers; the more cultured people do not want the poorly paid and insignificant offices of this poor county; and the poorer whites, without experience in matters of executive responsibility, do not fill the offices with any degre of effectiveness. Nevertheless, the white minority is determined to keep political affairs within its own group.

The jail population by race in McIntosh County suggests that the Negroes at present are more law-abiding than the whites. In 1926 the jail population was 6.6 per thousand for the whites and 7.6 for the Negroes. In 1929, however, the white jail population had climbed to 8.3 per thousand, while the Negro rate had dropped to 6.3 per thousand.

1898 Race Riot Not Forgotten. In 1898, when "white supremacy" was being effected in McIntosh County by commission government and "satisfactory explanations" of the Constitution, a Darien physician was called to a farm house to attend a white mother at childbirth. The baby was a mulatto. The doctor became enraged and threatened to let the mother die unless she told who the father was. Upon fear of death she implicated a prominent Negro, later found to be the wrong man. He was immediately charged with rape, and two undeputized men went to his home to "arrest" him. Finding that they had no warrant, he advised them not to come into his house. Nevertheless they broke in; one received a shotgun volley in his abdomen, and the other was slightly wounded. The Negro helped the slightly wounded man carry the other to their buggy. The latter died before reaching Darien. The Negro was subsequently placed in the county jail. Negroes surrounded it and refused to let the sheriff take the prisoner out or let any white people in. The colored Baptist Church nearby was virtually an arsenal. The Negroes held their vigil until a unit of the National Guard came down from Savannah. Upon their arrival at the railroad station—Darien has no trains today—they shot volleys into the air and the Negroes dispersed. This "race riot" of 1898, though causing no deaths, cost the county $5,400 and demonstrated to the whites that they could not maintain "white supremacy" without the presence of outside help. Prior to 1900, McIntosh County with Darien as the capital, was a possible kingdom for a lesser Emperor Jones.

While among the poorer whites there still persists the lingering fear that the Negroes again may make a demonstration of their strength, the relations are very cordial between many of the propertied Negroes, who have lived in McIntosh County all their lives, and the remaining descendants of the old aristocracy. Even before the trouble of September, 1930, which threatened to take on the proportions of a race riot because of the frantic appeals broadcast by the county sheriff, the Negroes in this county were generally reserved in demeanor, being of the low-country, "Gulla" type. Recent events have made them more inarticulate and now they go about the streets and along the roads almost as silently as shadows.

CHAPTER XII

THE SHERIFF KEEPS FAITH WITH THE MOB
THOMASVILLE, THOMAS COUNTY, GEORGIA

ON THE AFTERNOON of September 24, 1930, an attempted assault on a nine-year-old white girl was reported at Thomasville, Georgia. At eight o'clock next morning the accused Negro, Willie Kirkland, a trusty convict at the county stockade, was taken from the sheriff and his deputies. After being riddled with bullets, his body was dragged through the business section of Thomasville. The members of the mob were unmasked, as were the men in the procession of cars which followed the corpse through the streets. Three days later Lacy Mitchell, Negro, the state's star witness in the case of two white men charged with raping a Negro woman, was shot to death at his rural Thomas County home. There was no connection between the two incidents other than the probability that Kirkland's lynching emboldened Mitchell's white avengers.

THE LYNCHING

Crime Which Resulted in Lynching. On the afternoon of September 24, as a nine-year-old white girl was returning from school, she was dragged from the road and severely bruised about the throat, requiring the care of a physician. She gave a brief description of her assailant; she said he was a Negro, and that he ran with a limp.

The child's home, on a hill opposite the county convict stockade, was within a mile of the city limits of Thomasville. Each day she walked past the stockade on her way to and from the city school.

On the day of the attack she had been sick, and her mother was watching for her. When she saw the child coming down the road from the stockade toward the creek, the mother resumed her house work. After several minutes, however, when the little girl had not come in, the mother became anxious. She feared the child had fainted and fallen by the road. Hurrying out, she heard the little girl screaming. The mother in turn began screaming and ran in her direction. She saw no assailant, but on reaching the child found that her throat was severely bruised. A physician was called immediately. The father, appearing presently, ran to a telephone and reported the incident to his landlord, who in turn notified the county sheriff.

Willie Kirkland Suspected. The father then hurried to the stockade and asked the warden if any of his "trusties" were absent. The warden reported that all were present and assured the father that it could not have been one of his prisoners.

When asked if she had ever seen her assailant before, the girl said that about a week previously she had seen him at a nearby Negro farm cabin where she had gone to buy turnip greens, and that she heard him called "Tom." Several suspects were quickly picked up. In the meantime, a great crowd had gathered. Bloodhounds had been brought from Camilla. From the scene of the crime the bloodhounds circled up the hill to the gate of the stockade barn, which is across the public road and more than a hundred yards from the building which houses the prisoners. The dogs followed the same route to the barn a second time, but did not pick up a trail between the barn and the stockade itself.

Later when the warden learned that the attack had occurred a half hour or more before the father's visit to the stockade, instead of immediately before it, as he first supposed, he reported that a trusty said he had seen Willie Kirkland, another trusty, come in by a side gate about fifteen minutes before the father's appearance. Noticing that Kirkland was wet with sweat the trusty asked him where he had been, whereupon Kirkland is said to have replied, "Out there in the cotton patch," pointing to the field lying between the barn and the stockade. Along with the other suspects, Kirkland was held at the stockade to await further developments.

Death Sentence Precluded by Nature of Crime. People continued to congregate about the stockade and by late afternoon one side of the road was lined with cars for a mile or more. In the meantime a great crowd had gathered at the jail in Thomasville, and demanded to know whether the girl's assailant was there. Officials assured them that he was not. The chief of police further assured them that if the man were there, they would be allowed to take him. This did not satisfy them, and upon their urgent demand the officers permitted a committee of six to go through the entire jail. This committee returned and reported that they found no Negro there answering the girl's description. At about nine o'clock the crowd left the jail to swell the multitude already massed at the county stockade, a mile away.

From nine o'clock until after midnight there were a thousand or more people around the stockade. The fact that attempted rape is not punishable by death was generally discussed. It was assumed, however, that only the unexpected approach of the mother saved the little girl from actual assault. Aware that the Negro, if left to the courts, could get nothing beyond a penitentiary sentence of twenty years, many quite frankly advocated that he be lynched.

Sheriff's Promise to Mob Leaders. From the outset the crowd demanded that the girl see if she could identify her assailant among the suspects. This she tried to do. When she first looked at Kirkland she positively denied that he was the man; upon turning to leave, however, she got a side view and noticed a scar on his face, which she said, was similar to one she had seen on her assailant's face. She later identified him a second time by picking him from a row of suspects placed before her, and again a third time, at about two o'clock in the morning when mob members took him over to her home. The sheriff regained custody of the prisoner only by persuading mob members to let the matter rest until daybreak, that he would have the girl look at Kirkland again at eight o'clock. When someone complained that the sheriff might not keep his promise, he assured them that he was a man of his word. An influential citizen standing by put his hand on the sheriff's shoulder and further assured the crowd of the latter's integrity. Whereupon the mob yielded the Negro to the sheriff and dispersed.

At about this time, two o'clock in the morning, the county health officer was called to relieve the little girl of strangulation caused by the swelling of her bruised throat. The physician stated that she was breathing very heavily, and doubtless could have been heard the distance of two city blocks.

The Unbroken Promise. At six-thirty o'clock that morning a reputable citizen walked into a cafe in Thomasville to get his breakfast. He noticed men sitting informally about the tables, and wondered at their somber appearance. One of the men near him looked at his watch with some such remark as this: "Well, it's nearly seven o'clock, and we were to be back out there by 7:30."

By 7:30 the crowd was reassembling at the stockade. With her mother and father, the latter carrying a shot gun, the girl was brought to the stockade shortly before eight, and for the fourth time identified Kirkland, who this time was with three other suspects. Immediately someone reported to the crowd that she had identified him again. Soon after this the sheriff appeared in the doorway with Kirkland and the three others and started toward a Lincoln car which was at the stockade gate, approximately a hundred yards away. The stockade yard was literally filled with people. The front gate stood open, and the wire fence had been cut. Upon seeing Kirkland, the father raised his gun. A leading citizen called to another, a county commissioner, to knock the barrel up, which he did just as the gun was fired. The load went into the air. "Ah, let the little girl's father have him," was the comment of a Thomasville official. Then the mother screamed, "Get him, get him. Are you men going to let that nigger go?" Immediately the mob surged in and took Willie Kirkland.

The Lynching and Dragging. The pastor of one of Thomasville's largest churches, one of a half dozen leading citizens called there by the sheriff to help uphold the law, stated that the rush happened in an instant, that it looked like a great football scrimmage, that one could see only the backs of people.

As Kirkland was seized by the onrushing mob, the other three suspects disappeared and have not been seen since.

The mob with its prey went directly to Magnolia Park, a beautifully wooded retreat belonging to the Thomasville Woman's Club, a half or three-quarters of a mile away. There Kirkland was riddled with bullets. A white man who heard the shots from his home nearby estimated that about fifty were fired. It was generally reported that Kirkland was told to run, and that the girl's father was given the first shot.

No sooner was Kirkland dead than his body was tied behind a car and dragged from Magnolia Park down Broad Street past the courthouse and the Confederate Monument, then west on Remington Avenue, and thence two blocks north to the west side of the courthouse, where the body was "left for the authorities." Following the body there were several cars in funeral-like procession. A prominent white woman, not knowing what was going on, narrowly missed being struck by the dangling corpse, as she crossed the street. When the procession halted and the body was cut loose, the driver of the car to which it was attached looked round and said, "Huh, I didn't know I had anything back there." A reputable white citizen who operates a business on Remington Avenue, replied, "Well then, you are a fool!" The occupants of all the cars were unmasked and many of them were recognized—some as Thomasville people, some from the rural parts of the county, and some from outside the county.

Unsuccessful Efforts to Prevent Mob Violence. The better element of Thomasville's citizenry frankly acknowledged that the sheriff, his deputies, and the police handled the case very poorly. It should be mentioned here, however, that the sheriff called upon a half dozen or more leading citizens to report at the jail and stockade and help quiet the crowds. Among those who responded were two pastors, a physician, a local member of the state judiciary and four business men, one of them a local Associated Press correspondent and another a county commissioner. These citizens were asked to go through the crowd and help convince the people that it would be best to let the law take its course. Kirkland would doubtless have been lynched earlier had it not been for these efforts.

One Fearless Officer on the Scene. A federal officer who lived in Thomasville virtually saved Willie Kirkland from the mob on the afternoon and evening of the twenty-fourth. Several times when the people surged in and demanded Kirkland, this officer, who has a reputation for courage and bravery, kept them from their purpose. It is believed by many that the Negro would never have gotten into the hands of the mob had this officer remained at the stockade. He was called to Valdosta that night on a federal case and left Thomasville feeling that the crisis had passed. Next day he was greatly surprised to learn of the lynching and expressed regret that he had not remained.

Further Comments on Peace Officers. Grave question might be raised as to the wisdom of permitting a committee from the mob to search the jail. Even less excusable was the police chief's expressed willingness to surrender the prisoner, had he been there. Since the accused person was not in the jail, it may possibly be that these concessions were made only to appease the mob. But while temporarily they may have done so, their ultimate effect could only have been to add to the mob's boldness and determination.

Another doubtful procedure was the repeated identifications, which had the effect of adding successively to the popular frenzy. The sheriff may be condemned also for bargaining with the mob leaders, a procedure which he justified as necessary to provide opportunity for positive identification. Some feel that he should have called the National Guard; others point out that the nearest unit was at Albany, sixty miles away, and that a report of its coming would have precipitated immediate mob action, with three victims instead of one.

Mob's Victim "An Outsider." By local whites and Negroes alike, Willie Kirkland was referred to as "an outsider." Shortly after coming to Thomas County from an adjoining county, he had been sentenced for theft and concealing stolen goods, having accomplished the latter by the unique device of painting a black mule white. It is reported that he had served a sentence in another county for raping a Negro woman. He had been consorting regularly with a local Negro woman who bears a very bad reputation among the Negroes. It was near the scene of their trysting place that the little girl was dragged from the road. Shortly after the crime, this Negro woman was found at their accustomed rendezvous nearby.

REACTION OF THE COMMUNITY TO THE LYNCHING

The fact that Willie Kirkland was taken from the sheriff in broad daylight by a group of unmasked men before one or two of his deputies and a half dozen leading citizens, and that nobody was indicted, indicates the general reaction of the community to the lynching.

Pro-Lynching Position of Local Paper. The local evening paper, the Thomasville *Times-Enterprise*, a daily with a circulation of about 1,500, carried news stories and editorials about the lynching, the coroner's investigation, and grand jury hearings. The editorial position of the paper was one of compromise, with distinct leaning toward the pro-lynching side. The day of the lynching the following "I told you so" editorial pronouncement appeared: ". . . There was an effort made to prevent any drastic and unlawful action. This was carried out on the part of a number of officers, citizens, and ministers of this county. They were futile. . . . It has been said by the *Times-Enterprise* on many occasions that this is the one crime in which there seems to be no possible means of preventing such an affair."

On the day following there was an editorial captioned "A Calm City." It is a perfect example of fence straddling. One sentence is in defense of the lynchers and the next in defense of law and order. Of fourteen sentences, seven were as follows:

"We can truly say that Thomasville seems to be the calmest and most deliberate community that can be found anywhere. . . . The Negro's body was brought to the courthouse and left there for the officers to take the necessary processes. There was no excitement on the streets. People learned that they could do nothing about it and very few sought the morbid reaction that comes from close contact to or actual participation in the scenes of that character. It was no different from any other day or any other time. . . . The fight was over and the battle lost but there was nothing they could do. . . . Thomasville people were not involved or at least very few of them were, if rumor is to be believed. . . ."

And the other seven like this:

". . . Early yesterday a Negro was shot to death at the hands of a crowd of white men seeking to avenge an attempted crime. . . . The general regret over the incident could not be misunderstood. Citizens had volunteered to attempt to stay the hands of the mob. They had worked through the night but unsuccessfully. . . . They have left it in the hands of the law to settle and there must be an accounting. What shall that be? . . . It happened near this city and we cannot as citizens of Thomas County shake the responsibility that rests with us despite the form of crime and the abhorrence that it will eternally create in the minds of all men."

From this on-the-fence position of September 26, we find the following editorial of October 21 on "Judge Thomas' charge:"

"Judge Thomas delivered a very sane, sensible and forcible charge to the grand jury this week. He had a chance to use a lot of pyrotechnics of oratory and legal injunction. He could have created no little comment and publicity. He could have aroused a great deal of feeling and factionalism, if he had desired.

"Instead he left it off but he followed and tracked the law and his duty to the letter. He told of conditions that should exist and he pointed the way of the jury to the solution of the problems that come before them for consideration and action.

"Judge Thomas has always been a practical judge, not a sensationalist. He has always used his judicial power to right wrongs as well as to establish peace and good will. He has been a factor in the limitation of unruly and disordered actions for it is well known that when there is a wilful disregard of decency and order he is relentless in the effort to see that the community shall not suffer as a result thereof and the victim of that disorder shall suffer the full penalty."

The reader's attention may well be focussed on the last sentence of the above editorial, which is consistent with the editor's remark to a lawyer, a friend of his, immediately after hearing Judge Thomas' charge to the grand jury: "Well, they won't dare to indict anybody after that charge."

This Lynching Not Spot News in Georgia. Little attention was given to the Thomasville lynching by the leading papers throughout the state and the South, with the exception of the Macon *Evening News,* which carried a full page red-letter headline, "Negro Attack Suspect Is Lynched." The Atlanta *Constitution* had only a brief news item, while the Atlanta *Journal* devoted but a half-dozen lines to it. It is obvious that by the time of the Thomasville lynching, which was the fourth in Georgia during the year, an ordinary lynching was no longer considered important news.

Only One Witness Before Coroner's Jury. The coroner's jury examined only one witness, the county sheriff, though a number of leading citizens were present when Kirkland was taken. The following statements of the sheriff concern the two o'clock incident, the agreement between the sheriff and the mob leaders to leave final identification until daylight, the futile attempt to move the suspects to a place of safe keeping, and the mob's taking of the prisoner:

"I had quite a time then (two o'clock A.M.) getting them (members of the mob) to turn the Negro back over to me. I promised them that I would keep the Negro in custody until this morning when it was light and the little girl could see better and have a better opportunity of being sure whether this was the right man or not, and this morning at seven o'clock I had three other suspects placed in the stockade with this Negro and sent for the little girl and she came together with her mother and father and they were permitted to go into the building where the four Negroes were and she again did not hesitate to point out Willie Kirkland as being the man. . . .

"The crowd had enlarged quite extensively by this time, but was very orderly, and I did not see any signs of a gun except in the hands of the girl's father. Everything was very quiet and orderly and I decided it would be a good time to transfer the Negro to a place of safe-keeping. I had the doors opened and the four Negroes brought out together, and with my deputies started to my automobile with them. We had gone possibly thirty feet when I turned for a minute toward the girl's father, who was carrying the shot gun to warn him not to make any effort to shoot, then I turned and looked back toward the prisoners when it seemed that possibly fifty men had rushed in and picked out this Negro from the four. We did everything possible to get the Negro to the car without killing someone or getting killed ourselves, but it was impossible. I do not know the party or parties who made the rush or carried the Negro away or who is responsible in any way for his death."

Following is the final paragraph of the report of the coroner's jury:

"We, the jury wish to commend our sheriff for the quiet and orderly manner in which he was able to handle the angry crowd at the jail and stockade, and prevention of other bloodshed. We feel assured that he did his duty in every respect."

No Indictment by Grand Jury. For some reason the grand jury called only a few of the dozen witnesses suggested by a leading citizen who had ascertained the facts about the mob leaders. The foreman of the jury summoned the most prominent men on the list, but later reported that the jury was unable to determine whether the alleged mob leaders named by the witnesses were trying to lynch Kirkland or to help the sheriff protect him. In view of this, he said, the jury thought it needless to summon others. The jury's official presentment said:

"Many investigations not contained on your docket were made by us, we would especially call your attention to our investigation of the killing of one Willie Kirkland, after an examination of many witnesses many of whom were prominent men of Thomas County, it was necessary to close this investigation without an indictment for lack of evidence."

Among those not called were several persons generally believed to have been the actual mob leaders, and certainly eyewitnesses. It was reported about town that the grand jury did not have the power to summons witnesses before it in this kind of case.

The unmasked lynchers and corpse-draggers went free. A few people hung their heads in shame, while a larger number seemed relieved that "their courts" were so "practical."

Some Facts About Eight Probable Mob Leaders. The driver of the car which dragged the corpse through town is an itinerant drunken roustabout who worked in a local garage. His employer, the son of a south European immigrant, who had been arrested on a liquor charge, is known to have taken an active part in cutting the wire fence at the stockade to admit the mob. His brother-in-law is generally reported to have grabbed Willie Kirkland from the sheriff. He lives in a rural section of Thomas County. Some months after the lynching, he was in a liquor-transporting party which wounded the federal officer mentioned above as having stood off the mob.

Two others, a man and his grown son, are reported by neighbors as having been at Magnolia Park. The wife and mother, proud of the fact that her husband and son had participated in the affair, boasted of their participation to neighbors across the street. They are home owners and traders in livestock; neither has more than a common school education. A youth of less than twenty implicated himself by his own statement. He was a problem child in school, and more recently has been involved in several thefts and attempted burglaries about town.

The little girl's father, who was generally reported to have been "honored" with the first shot, came to Thomas County from Mitchell County only a few weeks before the lynching. He arrived too late to put out a crop of his own, and was working as a plantation wage hand. His landlord stated that he had found him a hard-working and honest man of the landless, propertyless, shifting type. His nine-year-old daughter, very much under size, was in the first grade at school.

Several years ago a Negro charged with rape was being returned to Thomasville for trial. At that time Thomasville had a National Guard unit, which was called out to protect the prisoner. This it did. One bayonet drew blood—a man rushed in, grabbed the prisoner, and started off with him, whereupon a member of the National Guard jabbed him in the side. It is reported that this man, still wearing his bayonet scar, was prominent at Magnolia Park. Incidentally, the guardsman who used the bayonet was never able after that time to keep employment in Thomasville. Employers would hire him, but presently the white employees for one reason or another would force him to leave.

According to eye witnesses, something like fifty men went from the stockade to Magnolia Park. Not one of them was masked when he left the stockade, and not one was masked when the body was dragged through the streets. Outside of the persons mentioned above, the identity of the members of the mob was not specifically obtained. In discussing the types who take part in lynchings, Judge Hopkins, referred to later, stated that the mob was made up from the lowest elements of the white population. Then followed this interesting statement: "I'll give anybody a thousand dollars who'll find either a son or a grandson of a slave owner participating in a lynching."

Lynching Deplored and Denounced by a Few. The general run of people, including some of the leading citizens, felt that the lynching was inevitable, and the sooner forgotten the better. A considerable number, however, were shocked and provoked because the body was dragged through the streets.

There were a few who deplored the whole affair. Three prominent white ministers got together soon after the lynching to determine what they would do. They were much distressed and shocked. As time passed, however, there was a tendency on the part of two of them to accept the lynching as inevitable, and to assume that very little, if anything, could be done about it. One of the three was persistent in his efforts to get grand jury indictments. Some of the leading churchmen of Thomasville as individuals were opposed to lynching, but the churches as such merely ignored the matter.

A short time after the lynching, the president of a Columbus men's Bible class, attending the principal men's class in Thomasville, mentioned as his greatest problem his inability to introduce into his class the "point system" of grading. When the visitor sat down the president of the Thomasville class asked his members to pray for the Columbus class on Tuesday night at eight o'clock when the adoption of the point system was again to be discussed. Inquiry revealed the fact, however, that the Thomasville class had taken no notice whatever of the lynching at its door!

Indictments Desired by Leaders of Missionary Society. The Thomasville Woman's Club was greatly disturbed over the affair, and especially because the lynching took place on its property, Magnolia Park. As a gesture of disapproval they discussed closing the gates of the park for a period. Other women's organizations discussed it, among them some of the missionary societies. At one meeting a woman advised that, as wives and mothers, those present should exert their influence to get their husbands and sons to give to the grand jury all possible information about the lynching. The president of the meeting liked the idea, and recommended that the spokesman be encouraged to give a similar message to all missionary societies in town. The president of the W. C. T. U. also made mention of the unfortunate affair.

Anti-Lynching Few Quieted by Pro-Lynching Many. From the very outset, tremendous pressure was brought by the pro-lynching majority upon the anti-lynching few to let the matter drop. One man who was active in protecting the Negro at the two o'clock identification, found himself at once under severe criticism as a "nigger lover," and threatened with boycott, whereupon his expressed attitude was promptly modified. The easiest way for the anti-lynching few to get along in Thomasville was simply to be silent and let the matter drop.

Lynching Justified by Prominent Jurist. But not all of Thomasville's "leading" citizens had to be cowed into acceptance of the situation. Some of them have always defended mob activities. The chief of this group is a prominent jurist who several times before and since Kirkland was lynched has broadcast his convictions that lynchings are inevitable; that when certain crimes are committed by Negroes upon whites there ought to be a lynching, and will be a lynching so long as red blood courses through the veins of courageous men; that the organized courts should prevail, but when the very laws of all creation are wantonly violated good people become insane by reason of their God-given birthright as honorable men; and that as much as godly men might later repent for having done something in a fit of passion, they cannot undo what has been done and by all the rules of civilized and God-fearing people of all times and places such men are accounted champions of all that is pure and good. The above is a brief accurate paraphrase of a lengthy statement made to the investigator. This man, powerful in politics, is also an active religious leader, and a person of great influence in the community.

General Acquiescence of Negroes. It was reported by apologists for the lynching that a leading local Negro said he was glad Kirkland had been lynched and that he would have liked to help do it. How much of this was what the Negro felt and how much of it was what he wanted white people to think he felt, is a pertinent inquiry. Other prominent Negroes of Thomasville, said little or nothing. Certainly those with property, like white people dependent upon the purchasing public, would not carelessly invite their own undoing. The colored ministers voted down a resolution proposed as a protest against the lynching. Negro leaders were dazed by the fact that a lynching had been permitted by the white officers and citizens.

The reaction of the mass of poorer Negroes, as gleaned from the servants, was that Kirkland ought to have known that he would be lynched for such a crime. All elements of the colored population seemed to find some consolation in the fact that he was "an outsider"—obviously they felt more secure than if a local Negro had been lynched. There is, of course, the probability that all of these expressed sentiments are but part of the masks which Negroes wear for their white acquaintances to look at. There was unmistakable evidence that a number of Negroes, while afraid to be openly identified with such a movement, nevertheless sincerely hoped for the indictment and punishment of those who lynched Kirkland.

Some After Effects. What effects will the lynching have along economic, cultural, and ethical lines? The majority of the people feel that there will be no adverse economic results; that it has caused no great disturbance in the community; that the lynching did not violate any of the mores of the community; that it was a passing incident and will soon be forgotten. The more thoughtful people, however, are of the opinion that it will deter Northern people from coming to Thomasville and investing their money in plantations, hunting lodges, and other enterprises. Then, too, some of the most influential Negroes in the community have talked of leaving Thomasville, for they find themselves embarrassed within their own race when referred to as being from a "lynching town."

Thomas County's Second Lynching[1]

On September 28, 1930, three days after the lynching of Kirkland, a second Negro, Lacy Mitchell, was shot to death at his Thomas County farm home by a group of white men, incensed because he had testified against some of their friends in a serious case.

Perhaps an After Effect of the Lynching. A few days before the Kirkland lynching a preliminary hearing was given two

---

[1] Mitchell's death was classified as a lynching by Tuskegee's Department of Research and Records. It should be pointed out here that it was perchance wrongly classified, in that Mitchell's death was accomplished by a few people who executed a conspired plot in secrecy by private methods. In contrast with this secretly planned and gangster-like procedure, nineteen of 1930's lynchings were carried out in a public fashion in open defiance of the law with scores, hundreds, and even thousands of eye-witnesses.

rural Thomas County white men accused of raping a Negro
woman who had a two-weeks-old baby. The two men under
suspicion along with two others were placed before the Negro
woman for identification. Each of the four disguised himself
by the wearing of colored goggles, shaving but parts of his
face, or having all or part of his head clipped. Among the
four were a father and son. The father with a smooth shave
and make-up looked somewhat like a boy, while the son with
several days' growth of beard and make-up had the general
appearance of an older man. The Negro woman failed to
identify her assailants, but Lacy Mitchell, her neighbor, positively identified two of them as men he had seen in the vicinity
of the Negro woman's cabin shortly after the alleged assault.
Several nights later a few masked men went to Mitchell's cabin
to punish him for testifying against white men. Refusing to
submit to a flogging, Mitchell was shot to death in his home.

One Year Sentences for White Rapists. The two white men,
bound over to the Superior Court on the basis of Mitchell's
testimony, were tried at the term of court during which the
grand jury investigated the lynching of Kirkland.

The two white men charged with raping the Negro mother
were brought into court. The witnesses were called, the case
was finished, the jury retired and remained out all night. At
ten o'clock next morning it returned a verdict of guilty, and
recommended sentences of one year each. Two of the jurors
had held out for acquittal, but finally accepted the compromise
of a sentence of one year. Thomasville was in a stir; while some
people were humiliated at the mildness of the sentences, many
more expressed disgust that a white jury should sentence white
men at all on such a charge. At this same term of court Homer
Taylor, Negro, plead guilty of assault with intent to rape a
young Negro girl and received a sentence of twenty years.

Mitchell's Murderers Sent Up for Life. Then came the case
against those accused of murdering Lacy Mitchell. A considerable number of the county's leading citizens were thoroughly
aroused: white rapists getting but one year and lynchers going
unindicted! Too much had been winked at already. Mitchell's
murderers must be dealt with severely. The outcome of the

trial was life sentences for Jack Bradley and O. E. Allen. The former, a brother-in-law of one of the men found guilty of raping the Negro woman, told how he had gone to the home of his wife's father, where the women of the family painted his face and "dressed him up" as a disguise for his visit to Mitchell's home. He admitted that he went into Mitchell's house and was forced to kill him when Mitchell refused to submit to a flogging. Meantime, he said, Allen was at the door with a gun. Allen testified that he was drunk and did not know anything about the murder. His home was in Louisville, Kentucky; he had been in Thomas County but three days. By some it is believed that Bradley "framed" the newcomer to protect some of his own friends. Both had been drinking heavily.

The life sentence of these two white men is serving to some extent, at least, as an expiation of Thomas County's failure to do justice in the other two cases. Faced with these failures, the people of Thomasville are quick to mention that two white men were given life sentences for killing a Negro.

Facts About the Community

Early Population Elements. When Thomas County was laid off from Irwin County in 1826, it was much larger than at present and had a population of less than 3,000, nearly half of whom were Negro slaves. Big cotton plantations had developed along the larger streams as people of means had come in from the older part of Georgia, the Carolinas, and Virginia. Of wealthy planters there were enough to afford a social life among themselves; many of their sons and daughters were educated in England. At the time of the Civil War there were two educational institutions of some repute at Thomasville, the South Georgia College for Males and the Remur Young College for Girls.

Whites of smaller means were coming into the county from the pine hills immediately to the northeast; in Thomas County they lived on the unfertile uplands, owned but little property, followed a self-sufficient farm economy, and maintained a general low plane of living. There was but little social intercourse between the families of wealthy planters and the poorer whites.

In 1850 the population of Thomas County was approximately 8,000, including 5,155 slaves.

By 1890, the county had a little more than 26,000 people, nearly sixty per cent of whom were Negroes. Meantime two additional social classes had come on the scene—the Northern tourist whites, and a scattering of Negroes who had acquired farm lands and other productive properties, enabling them to escape the dependence which characterized the Negro masses.

Negroes Used by Plantation Owners and Northern Tourists. The winter climate of Thomas County early attracted attention, and back in the nineteenth century, with the building of the railroads, vacationists came to Thomasville in great numbers to spend the winter months. Large hotels were hastily erected, and in the years following scores of winter homes were built. Thomasville was a fast-growing town.

Many rich Northern families have bought old plantations, which they now use in a few instances for general farming purposes, but usually for little more than hunting preserves. The general progress of Thomas County has doubtless been retarded considerably by the passing of these most fertile tracts of land into the control of absentee landlords, who, naturally, have had no sustained personal interest in the development of the local people. The wealthy families come to Thomasville to get something for themselves—sunshine, rest, and recreation —and have little interest in the slow and tedious task of developing local human resources. From the outset the wealthiest element of Thomasville and Thomas County, whether Southern planters or Northern game preserve owners, have had more dealings with the Negroes than with the poorer whites, and have been more concerned about them. In 1930, Thomas County had a population of 32,612, 48.6 per cent of whom were Negroes.

A little more than half of the county's people live in eight incorporated towns; Thomasville alone has nearly two-thirds of all town dwellers, the other seven towns being mere agricultural villages. For the most part the remnant of the landed aristocracy live in or near Thomasville, as do also most of the Northern rich. Besides these, Thomasville has shopkeepers, business and professional men, artisans, and a great host of unskilled rural dwellers who have flocked into this urban community to find employment as casual day laborers, domestic servants and home laundresses. Because of rural and urban economic retrenchment caused by low-priced farm products, and a marked decrease in the winter tourist trade, Thomas County's total population decreased by 432 between 1920 and 1930.

Rural Masses Dependent Upon Cotton. Agriculture provides a livelihood for the major portion of the people, for even though approximately one-half of the population is in the incorporated towns, some of the town dwellers own land and many have shops and other business establishments directly and indirectly dependent upon farmers.

Of the crops produced in Thomas County, cotton is the most valuable, and then follow corn, tobacco, watermelons, pecans, and others. In 1929, 36,000 acres were planted in cotton, producing nearly 13,000 bales, while 52,000 acres were in corn, yielding approximately ten bushels per acre. In this same year over one-half million pounds of tobacco were sold at the warehouse in Thomasville, and from the county 2,543 cars of watermelons were shipped. Live stock farming, particularly the raising of hogs, assumes considerable proportions. With the possible exception of Early, Thomas County shipped more hogs than any Georgia county in 1929, forty-five shipments of one or more cars being reported. Cattle raising has been gaining impetus and now there are a few pure bred herds in the county. The watermelon, pecan, and stock raising industries, and to a lesser extent the tobacco industry, are limited to a relatively few of the larger and more closely supervised plantations.

The principal cash income of the typical farmer is secured from cotton alone. This is especially true of tenant farmers, who constitute approximately sixty per cent of all farmers in the county. From 1910-1914 the average annual production was a little over 21,000 bales; from 1925-1929 the average was but 7,240 bales. The number of farmers decreased by one-eighth between 1920 and 1930.

Measures of the County's Economic Rank. In 1924, the per

capita value of farm crops was $41.19, while the value of man-
ufactured products, most of which were lumber and turpentine,
amounted to $104.24, making the total value of farm and
manufactured products $143.43 per capita, as compared with
the state average of $310.78. Another measure is the amount
of money on deposit. Thomas County banks in 1929 showed
an average of $121.77 per capita, while the state as a whole
averaged $155.89.[2] Exclusive of corporation taxes, the per
capita tax valuation in 1930 was slightly greater than for
the state, being $393.86 against the state's $348.03. The taxable property values per person, however, are raised considerably by the generally high real estate values in Thomasville,
and by the vast though unproductive landed estates of the
Northern rich. In 1924, three hundred and seventy-six income
tax returns were made in the county: Three hundred and
twenty-seven for less than $5,000, twenty-nine for $5,000 to
$10,000, and twenty for $10,000 and over. In 1929, two hundred
and eighty returns were filed. It is significant that over ninety-
five per cent of the returns were from persons living in incorporated towns. While there is a considerable element of well-to-
do urban dwellers, the majority of the town dwellers eke out a
living by irregular employment, inevitable because of the season-
al demands of a resort town and the prevalence of former rural
dwellers, accustomed to but little and willing to work for a
very low wage.

Rural Thomas County Now and a Half Century Ago. Except
for an occasional plantation owner who still lives on his land,
the countryside is populated by descendants of the slaves and
the poorer whites. These rural dwellers make a living for the
most part by tilling the soil with one-horse plows, brier hooks,
and long-handled hoes. For getting wood, double-bladed axes
are most common. The agricultural methods and tools of a half
century ago are generally used. In many respects these rural
dwellers have made but little advance since 1880. They produce
but little more now than then; the price of things they buy
has advanced more than the price of things they sell. They
live in poor houses, many of them mere hulls, which when they

---

[2] Two of the town's largest banks were closed in 1931 and 1932.

are a dozen years old have the appearance of having been
built in slave times. The rural people send their children to
one- and two-teacher schools now as in 1880; there were in
1928 eight one-teacher and eleven two-teacher white schools
and thirty-four one-teacher Negro schools in rural Thomas
County. They have preaching but once or twice a month, as
was the case five decades earlier. More than half the rural white
and Negro families are landless farmers and most of them now,
as a half century ago, are dependent upon their landlords or
merchants for the physical necessities of life while producing
a crop, which in most cases does little more than settle the
rent and pay back the "furnishings" advanced. Most of the
rural Negro mothers and many of the poorer whites now, as
a half century ago, are attended at childbirth only by mid-
wives. The major advances made in Thomas County since 1880
have occurred in the incorporated towns, Thomasville in
particular.

The general run of people, however, should not be looked
upon as destitute. The population per automobile dropped
from 13.5 to 7.5 from 1925 to 1929. The need for larger incomes is perhaps no greater than the need for a wiser expenditure of the present small incomes. It is a comment upon
standards when a tenant farmer, white or Negro, with a total
gross income of less than $500 a year, owns and operates an
automobile, not for making a livelihood, but for riding whither
he will, while doing without such things as ceiled houses, fly-
proof privies, screened windows, books, and daily and weekly
papers, to say nothing of doctors. In most rural Georgia
counties the percentage of tenant families who own autos is
higher than the percentage who have doctors to attend their
wives at childbirth.

A Contrast of Urban and Rural Schools by Race. As elsewhere, the children in the largest urban community in Thomas
County have better teachers, better schoolroom equipment, and
longer terms than the open country children. In 1928, the
Thomasville schools cost $78.22 per white child as against
$30.96 for the remainder of the county. The average amount
spent per white child in the eight one-teacher schools and

the eleven two-teachers schools was doubtless below $20.00, for just as Thomasville was much above the remainder of the county, the other seven incorporated towns were far above the average for the open country.

The 1928 expenditure per school census Negro child in Thomasville was $10.24, in contrast with but $3.13 for the remainder of the county. From the above figures, it will be seen that whereas the rural white school child gets a little less than half as much public money as the urban white child, the rural Negro child gets but one-third as much as the urban Negro child, one-tenth as much as the rural white child, and one-twenty-fifth as much as the urban white child. The difference between urban and rural school expenditures by race suggests in a general way the differences in training and pay of teachers and schoolroom equipment.

In Thomasville, where white and Negro schools are quite superior to those in the remainder of the county, and as good as can be found in any Georgia town of its size, the schools are being constantly improved. On September 24, the day before Willie Kirkland was lynched, Thomasville voted $135,000 of bonds for the improvement of schools, something like one-third of which was to be used for Negroes.

School Expenditures Above State Average. In 1928, the total expenditure per school census child in Thomas County was $43.61 for the white child and $5.91 for the Negro child. Both figures were above the state average of $36.88 per white child and $5.07 per Negro child.

The total amount spent by the county for Negro education in 1928 was but three thousand dollars in excess of the amount allocated to it from the State School Fund at the rate of $5.20 per school census child. The total amount spent for the white schools was $190,881.13 more than the state per capita allocation. As poor as this showing is, it is far better than the state average, with one hundred and seventeen counties actually spending less money on Negro education than these counties receive from state funds on the basis of Negro school population.

The Allen Normal School, a private institution for Negroes

with courses from first grade through high school, is supported
by the American Missionary Association and has an enrollment of near three hundred, twenty of whom are boarding
students. The faculty consists of seven white and eight Negro
teachers. Former Mayor Hopkins, one of Thomasville's leading.
citizens, gave the land for the school, when it was moved from
Quitman. Some years ago, the county superintendent of schools
stated that the graduates of this school stood better examinations than the graduates of any white high school in the county.

Town and Country Church Organizations. The Baptists and
Methodists have approximately ninety-five per cent of the
county's total church membership of both races. Of the 3,505
white Baptists in 1926, 3,272 were Southern Baptists, 40 were
Free Will Baptists, and 193 were Primitive or "Hardshell"
Baptists. The Methodist Episcopal Church, South, had a membership of 3,076. The white Baptist church at Thomasville,
with a membership of 1,463 and a total Sunday school enrollment of 1,104, had church property valued at $148,500 and
was served by a full-time pastor who received an annual salary
of $4,000. The other five white Baptist churches reported a
total membership of 954 and a Sunday school enrollment of
474; they had property valued at $12,700, and were served
by pastors who conducted two services a month at three of
the churches, and one service a month at the other two; the
aggregate paid pastors by these five churches is but $1,808 a
year. The county's white Methodist churches present a similar
picture. For example, the amount raised by the Thomasville
Woman's Missionary Society in 1929 was $2,484, as compared
with a total of $297 raised by the societies of all the other
Methodist churches in the county.

The white Presbyterian Church in Thomasville has less than
500 members. The Protestant Episcopal Church has a membership of less than 250, but because of its unusual pastoral
leadership, its select membership and the support of some of
the wealthy Northerners, this church is more closely related
to community welfare projects than either of the other
churches.

The Negro Baptist membership of 4,541 in 1926 constituted

the county's largest denominational group of either race. The
C. M. E. membership was 1,909; the A. M. E., 1,529. The
county's best Negro churches are located in Thomasville. The
Negro ministers of the town have a well-established interde-
nominational union. Many of the rural church houses are
crude structures, some without window sash, many unceiled,
several with benches made of unplaned boards. Only a few have
preaching services more often than once a month.

In 1926, Thomas County had approximately 6,000 people
over fifteen years old who were members of no church. Of this
number nearly thirty-five hundred were whites, a considerable
proportion of whom were farm tenants in the rural sections
where incomes are lowest, schools are poorest, churches are
farthest apart, and community life in general is least organized. These rural slums, along with the urban slums, were
represented at the lynching of Willie Kirkland and the murder
of Lacy Mitchell.

A Revealing Case of a Decade Ago. Because of the light
it throws upon past and present political conditions in the
county a brief résumé is made of a case which occurred nearly
a decade ago. A Thomasville Negro taxi driver by the name
of Smith was hailed late one evening by two white men "from
over the river." He observed that they did not have the appearance of people who rode in taxis; he suspected foul designs,
but feared to refuse their request. Accordingly, he took them
in and, after picking up a Negro friend for protection, started
up the road. Before they had gone ten miles the white men
ordered the driver to stop. When he did so they shot him
down. The second Negro jumped and ran, and although
wounded, fell into a ditch in a nearby thicket. After the men
had searched for him for half an hour they got in the car and
went off. The wounded man made his way back to Thomasville
and reported the incident. Within a few days the white men
were apprehended and brought back to Thomasville. At the
trial the defense lawyers argued that, being a Negro, the taxi
driver was a potential rapist of white women. Capitalizing this
and similar prejudices, they got the murderers off with a sentence of but five years each. One of these lawyers is now a

congressman, while the other holds an important county office.

How the County Votes. In Thomas County there were 2,146 votes cast for governor in the Democratic primary of September 10, 1930. This vote, though nearly twice as large as the combined Democratic and Republican vote for president in either 1920 or 1924, involved less than one-third of the white people of voting age. The vote is usually about ten Democratic to one Republican. In the 1928 presidential election, there were 1,240 Democratic votes, 558 Anti-Smith Democratic, 256 Republican, and one Socialist. The ballot is not attractive to landless, shifting white tenants, and is exercised by only a few Negroes. The latter do not make any aggressive efforts to qualify and participate in general politics, though their support is sought and used in local bond issue elections. Many Negroes voted in the Thomasville school bond election on the day before Willie Kirkland was lynched.

Lawlessness Increasing, Especially Among Whites. The white jail population of Thomas County increased from forty in 1921, which was 2.6 per thousand, to 277, or 16.6 per thousand, in 1929. The Negro jail population increased from 190 in 1921, or 11.4 per thousand, to 401, or 25.4 per thousand. In 1929 the jail population per thousand for the entire state was 12.5 for whites and 25.4 for Negroes. Of the first forty-five felons convicted in Thomas County courts subsequent to January, 1929, twenty-two were whites and twenty-three were Negroes.

The Thomasville jail is old and insecure. There have been several escapes, and the sheriff has had trouble getting an efficient jailer. Some months ago the jailer was discharged for allowing prisoners to escape. Recently a small separate building was erected for women prisoners. Though this may be good within itself, it is given as an excuse by many for delaying the permanent improvement of the old jail. The county stockade from which Kirkland was taken, like the jail, is insecure. It is a wooden structure, with a wire fence about it not strong enough or well enough constructed to hold or delay escaping prisoners. Besides, the gates stand open at all times.

Old Klansman, New Klansmen, and a Penitentiary Crime.

The Ku Klux Klan was active in Thomasville until recently. A few persons were threatened, and in one instance a fake doctor was chased out of town at high noon. However, the Klan failed to enlist some of the leading citizens of the town. Judge Hopkins, ex-mayor and ex-state senator, the only surviving member of the original Ku Klux Klan, was offered honorary membership. He asked who their local members were. When informed by the organizers that the membership was a secret, he firmly declined the proffered "honor."

In connection with the Klan in Thomasville, the following incident is of interest: On Broad Street a Negro chauffeur accidentally struck a white child as she ran from between parked cars. There was considerable excitement. The chauffeur was uneasy. When the child's parents stated that it was not the Negro's fault, things quieted down. Not many days later, however, the chauffeur got a note, signed K. K. K., advising him to put $100 at a certain place or suffer the consequences. The money was put there. A week or ten days later he received a second note demanding $50. Again the money was put on the spot. After a few weeks, a third note, signed K. K. K., was received. The Negro had no more money or credit. Almost frantic, he went to the girl's father asking why he was having to put out so much money, and protesting that he could not meet this last demand. The white man was surprised to hear the Negro's story. He advised that the money be put under the designated rock, while a concealed officer waited. A man reported for the money. It was a Negro. He was tried and is now serving a penitentiary sentence.

Superimposed Welfare Agencies. With the exception of Georgia's counties with the largest cities—Fulton, Chatham, Bibb, Richmond, Muscogee, and Clarke—Thomas County has more welfare agencies and institutions than any county in the state. None of the counties in the southwest part of the state has so many agencies, not even Dougherty, where Albany is located. Thomas County has a Farm Agent, Home Demonstration Agent, full-time health officer, social worker, Y. M. C. A., Salvation Army, county-wide library, and Red Cross.

There is evidence, however, that what seems to be advanced

social thinking is actually to a large extent outside standards superimposed upon the Thomasville community. For example, a few of the Northern people in the community have taken an interest in providing public health nursing and other community services, but without enlisting the coöperation of the local people.

One outstanding public institution in Thomasville, the product of Northern philanthropy, is the Archbold Memorial Hospital. This institution, though serving a great need and patronized extensively by the local people, is not a typical Georgia institution. It is unique, for example, in that it is the only general hospital in the state where a Negro medical student can serve as interne.

Race Relations Modified by Presence of Northerners. Relations between the two races in Thomasville are modified by the presence of the Northern element. Except for this element, the Allen Normal School would doubtless have been lost to South Georgia when it was evicted from Quitman upon the death of its Northern founder, who had established a Negro school in her palatial home in the heart of the little town. Soon after her death the "schoolhouse" burned. The school was without a home. Judge Hopkins, then mayor, offered to the American Missionary Association land on which to relocate the school in Thomasville. Throughout the years, the local citizens who have taken an interest in the Negroes have had the moral and financial support of wealthy Northern residents and visitors.

The Northern owner of one of the big estates not only provides recreational and amusement facilities for the Negroes on her place, but employs both a local Negro doctor and a dentist to care for the health and teeth of her workmen and their families; and, it is reported, pays them well. This is not without meaning, particularly as related to Negro leadership. The Negroes employed as domestics and caretakers by these wealthy people usually occupy a more favorable position than those working for local whites.

Two Native White Classes. The relations between the Negroes and the members of the local landed aristocracy have

been very cordial. The latter look upon the prosperous Negro
with approval: "Why you know, that fellow's grandmother
belonged to my mother's father." A kind of proprietary interest is obvious. Most of Thomasville's best educated and
wealthiest Negroes confessedly move within the pliant wills
of their white benefactors and friends.

The social distance has always been great between the white
people who owned the big plantations and those who lived on
the poorer uplands. Just as there has been a social cleavage
between the cultured and more humble whites, so there has
been a difference in their attitudes toward the Negro. The
descendants of the poor whites take no pride in the creditable
accomplishments of local Negroes. They look with disgust upon
the white teachers at the Allen Normal School, while their
attitude toward the Northerners who exercise most care for
their Negro workmen is dismissed with the reflection that they
are just "yankee nigger lovers," anyhow.

A Number of Prosperous Negroes. Because of the large rural
area it serves commercially, no less than because of the liberal
attitude on race relations of the local landed aristocracy and
the Northerners, Thomasville has a number of prosperous
Negroes. It is the district headquarters of several Negro insurance companies. Three Negro physicians and one Negro
dentist have been very successful. Several own real estate of
value, while an excellent drug store and several restaurants,
pressing clubs, and barber shops are owned and operated by
Negroes. In rural Thomas County there are nearly two hundred Negro farm owners. In all, there are about 500 home-
owning Negro families in the county.

A discerning Negro leader expressed the opinion that the
real cause of the two outbreaks in Thomas County were due to
the hostile attitude which the urban and rural "poor whites"
have developed toward Negroes. A few of the best established
Negroes, he thought, may have aggravated the situation by
"rubbing it in" on the "poor whites."

PART FOUR

LYNCHINGS IN PIEDMONT COUNTIES

In 1930 three lynchings occurred in the Piedmont section: On April 24, that of Allen Green, Negro, at Walhalla, Oconee County, South Carolina; on June 21, that of Dan Jenkins, Negro, near Union, Union County, South Carolina; and on October 1, that of John Willie Clark, Negro, at Cartersville, Georgia. The three occurred within a radius of one hundred miles.

Each of these counties, lying between the Black Belt plantation areas and the mountains, are within the South's textile center. The white population of each has increased rapidly since 1900, whereas the Negro population has either increased but little or has decreased. This, of course, is because the cotton mills use almost no Negro workers.

The population of the textile towns is composed, for the most part, of white tenant farm families from the surrounding areas and small farm owner families from the Appalachian highlands immediately to the northwest. The inhabitants of many a Blue Ridge cove, where rapid erosion precludes successful and continuous hillside farming, have moved practically *en masse* to some mill village in the upper Piedmont. This population movement has been of families rather than of unattached youths, largely because the mills would employ both women and older children, and thus multiply the earnings of the family. Some mills were organized ostensibly to relieve the chronic poverty of the poorer rural and small town whites. One still hears mill executives insisting that out of sheer gratitude the workers are honor bound to keep themselves unspotted from organized labor and other "outside influences" distasteful to the mill owners, who had rescued them from their sorry plight as tenant and hillside farmers. There are still a great number of white tenant farmers in these and other Piedmont counties. One-teacher schools and small Baptist and Methodist churches are the typical rural institutions of both races.

From the standpoint of race relations in these mill villages and environs, there are two distinct white groups. The larger group are descended from poor people who formerly lived in the older plantation belts, but were forced out in great numbers by competition with slave labor. Among this group latent or active antagonism to Negroes is practically universal. On the other hand there are a few representatives of the small slave-holding class, whose relations with their slaves were intimate and personal.[1] Among this latter group the tradition of paternalistic interest in Negroes still survives.

The influence of these diverse backgrounds and attitudes will be seen in the cases that follow, particularly in that of Allen Green at Walhalla.

Within recent decades the Negro's economic opportunities have dwindled appreciably, due in part to his virtual exclusion from the developing textile industry, but more fundamentally to the decrease of cotton farming in the Piedmont counties. Added to this, the colored miners of Bartow and other Piedmont counties are being displaced by whites at a rapid rate. The cotton mill wage scale, though generally low, is high enough to enable many white mothers to hire Negro domestic help, while they themselves work in the mills. In reality this is a comment on the small amount for which a Negro domestic can be had, and upon the Negro's consequent plane of living.

---

[1] The conditions of course were very different on the big slave plantations in the "Black Belt" where the majority of slaves associated only with other slaves and paid overseers.

CHAPTER XIII

"FRAMED" AND LYNCHED
WALHALLA, OCONEE COUNTY, SOUTH CAROLINA

ABOUT MIDNIGHT of April 23-24, 1930, Allen Green, fifty-two-year-old Walhalla Negro, was taken from the Oconee County jail at Walhalla by a mob of a hundred or more, carried two miles into the country, tied to a tree, and shot to death. Accused of having criminally assaulted a young white woman, Green had been arrested and bound over to court at a preliminary hearing. The mob assembled and organized in the adjacent cotton mill village, attacked the jail, clubbed the sheriff into helplessness and secured the keys from his wife.

Special investigators were immediately sent to the scene by Governor Richards, and a firm of local attorneys was engaged by the state to help bring the perpetrators to justice. The investigation was prompt, vigorous, and thorough. Indictments were returned against seventeen men, charged, as principals or accessories, with murder and conspiracy to deprive of life, and assault upon the sheriff with intent to murder. Among those indicted were the mayor and the night policeman of Walhalla.

After two postponements, the cases came to trial. Despite a vigorous and able prosecution, conducted by the solicitor general and special counsel, all the defendants were acquitted, seven as a result of verdicts directed by the judge, and ten declared not guilty by the jury. Two years later one of the seventeen publicly confessed his guilt.*

---

* Walhalla, S. C., Oct. 11.—(AP) Laudy Harris of Walhalla, declaring that "an honest confession is good for the soul," went with his pastor to the Oconee County jail Sunday and confessed to Sheriff John Thomas that he was the leader of a mob that lynched Allen Green, Negro in April, 1930, it became known here today.

THE LYNCHING

An Easter Sunday Morning's Business Errand. About 9:30 on the morning of Easter Sunday, April 20, 1930, a young white man, living on the outskirts of Walhalla, went on foot to the home of Allen Green, well-to-do Negro, located one block off the principal street of the town, in full view from that street and but three or four blocks from the town's business center. He was accompanied by his sister and by his young wife, to whom he had been married only two or three months. Green was married also, but his wife was absent at the time.

The purpose of his visit was to buy or rent from Green a mule to cultivate his crop. He or his father had previously got a mule from Green, but it had died; they were now trying to "trade" for another.

Alleged Rape Under Most Unusual Circumstances. At Green's examining trial the young white man testified that, on arriving at the house, he and his wife went round to the back door and talked with Green about the trade. He had left his sister at the front. Green suggested that he go for his sister, which he did. The distance, so the white man said, was about the length of the courtroom; he was asked to walk up and down the room to demonstrate the length of time he was gone. He did so, and the watches recorded twenty-nine seconds. "It took longer than that," he said, "it took about a minute and a half."

Upon returning to the back door, he found it locked, he said, and his wife nowhere in sight. Going to the window, he looked in and saw her strapped in a chair and Green just completing an assault upon her. He testified that he called to her to "come on out of there!" Green then released her, he

---

Harris returned to Sheriff Thomas the officer's pistol which was snatched from his hand the night of the lynching.

Harris was one of a score of persons tried and acquitted in connection with the lynching. Green had been arrested on a charge of assaulting a white woman.

As the laws of this state do not allow a man to be tried but once for the same crime when his life is in jeopardy, there are no charges to be lodged against Harris.

said, and they came out on the porch, where the party talked together a few minutes longer. Then the white man, with his wife and sister, returned to their home, through the village, but making no outcry or report of the affair.

The testimony given at the examining trial by the young wife was that when her husband turned away to get his sister, Green seized her by the hand, threatened her with a razor, and pulled her into the kitchen. There she saw three belts lying on a table. One of these he bound round her mouth as a gag; then he forced her into a straight chair and strapped her in with the other two. One he placed around her body over her arms and around the back of the chair; the other he strapped tightly across her lap over her dress and under the chair seat. Then he assaulted her as she sat there tightly bound. Having accomplished his purpose, he pulled off one of her shoes, put two little red bows in it, replaced it, gave her a "compact" or powder puff case, and then released her. Asked on the witness stand if all this did not make her very angry she replied, "No, I never even got mad." This evidence is on record in the courthouse and was the only evidence introduced against Green.

Allen Green Arrested. About sundown of the same day of the alleged rape, the young white man's father reported to the sheriff that Allen Green had raped his son's wife. The sheriff immediately went to the white man's house, heard the young wife's story and asked her if Green achieved his purpose. She replied, "No, he only attempted it." This answer she repeated and stood by until her husband said, "That isn't what you told Ma!" Then she replied, "Well, he did then."

The sheriff and a deputy arrested Green, who protested his innocence, at eleven o'clock Sunday night, on his return from church. He was confined in the county jail in Walhalla and on Tuesday morning at a preliminary hearing was bound over to court.

Wanted: 100 Men to Make Lynching Legal. Green was confined in the county jail, the lower floor of which was occupied by the sheriff and his family. On Monday night and again

Tuesday night, groups of men and boys assembled at the mill village ball park and discussed the formation of a lynching party. About seventy were present the second night. They wanted one hundred, some seeming to have the idea that if as many as a hundred participated the lynching would be legal.

Meantime, reports of their plans reached the towns of Westminster and Seneca, also in Oconee County, ten or twelve miles away, and a few adventurous youths drove over on Tuesday night and again Wednesday night to see what was going on. One rumor was that "the Red Men were going to lynch him."

Wednesday night a larger crowd gathered at the park and stood about for several hours waiting for leadership and organization—"a bunch of boys, stragglers, and hill billies," one observer said. A young Walhalla business man, member of a prominent family and an amateur entertainer, heard of the meeting, hurried over to the park, entertained the crowd a while with a dramatic skit, and then tried to persuade them to abandon their purpose. He seemed to be making an impression when somebody called out, "You fellows that haven't got cold feet, get in line here and let's have this thing over." The crowd separated, part of them lining up with the self-constituted leaders. Somebody counted and announced, "We have 108. Let's go." Crowding into a truck and a number of automobiles they prepared to move. It is said that in the party there were fifteen or twenty boys fourteen to eighteen years of age.

Sheriff Struck Down and Green Lynched. Seeing that nothing further could be done with them, the young business man rushed away to the jail just ahead of the mob and awakened the sheriff, who came out into the lower hall just as the mob surged in. The sheriff had a shotgun in his hand and announced that they could not have Green. They argued with him a moment and then somebody felled him with a terrific blow on the head. The gun discharged as he fell, but no one was hit. As he struggled to rise, several men seized him and held him, while others demanded the keys. The sheriff's wife, screaming in mortal fear for her husband's life, secured the keys and handed them over.

Green was immediately taken out and bundled into the waiting truck, and the procession started to the place of execution. Green begged, "White folks, will you let me talk?" to which one of his captors replied, "No, by God! You can't say a damn word!" Someone told him he had better make his peace with God. Green replied, "I am praying now, Captain." Reaching the place for which they were looking, they tied him loosely to a tree; cars were parked around with their lights upon him; a single shot was fired, then a volley, perhaps a hundred shots. The bullet-riddled body slumped to the ground and the crowd hurriedly dispersed.

No Excuse for Lynching. There are cases in which mob violence flames up so rapidly and furiously as to be almost uncontrollable by the local police force. That at Walhalla, however, was not of this character. Plans for the lynching began to take shape three days before the event. So menacing was the sentiment in the mill village on Monday that the pastor of the Methodist Church located there reported the danger to the sheriff and advised him to get Green out of the way. In addition, the night watchman and policeman at the mill warned the sheriff and urged him to take Green away. These warnings the sheriff refused to take seriously. "I couldn't believe anybody really thought Green guilty," he stated later, "and I hadn't the slightest idea that a lynching would be attempted."

On Tuesday or Wednesday, the sheriff could easily have taken his prisoner to a jail where he would have been safe. On the contrary, so confident was he that nothing would be attempted that he did not even take any precautions to guard the jail—no deputies, not even a watchman. When the young business man reached the jail on Wednesday night just ahead of the mob, he found the front door open—according to local citizens it is never locked—and the sheriff asleep. When the latter came out into the hall, he found himself in the midst of the mob. Had he been awake and prepared for the invasion, it is not improbable that single-handed he could have stood them off. Certainly the support of two or three determined deputies would have been quite sufficient to repel a group so heterogeneous and unorganized.

The better element of the community also, unanimous in its condemnation of the lynching, cannot be excused for its failure to realize the danger and take steps to forestall it. Had a half dozen determined men of standing gone down to the ball park on Wednesday night, there is little reason to doubt that they could have dispersed the mob with a sensible appeal. Better yet, had they been awake to the situation they would have insisted that the prisoner be moved while yet there was ample time.

The incident emphasized another characteristic condition— the insecurity of small-town jails. The first floor of the Oconee jail was without bars, as has been pointed out, and the front door was not even locked. With no watchman or guard, the sheriff in such a situation is at the mercy of any organized group that cares to slip in under cover of night. With bars between himself and the Walhalla mob, the sheriff almost certainly would have been able to make an effective defense.

"On This Spot—Parole and—Lynch." Why was it that so large a segment of the community accepted at face value a story so flimsy against Allen Green? Why should others, while frankly discounting this particular charge against Green, nevertheless stoutly justify his lynching? The answer is suggested in part by this grim notice, nailed to the tree where Green met his death:

> "On this spot Allen Green got his
> Parole and here he got his Lynch."

This inscription affords an apt beginning for the study of Green's strange career, and throws significant light on the psychology of his executioners. It refers to the fact that in July, 1915, Allen Green, then thirty-seven years of age, was convicted of "assault with intent to ravish," by the Court of

General Sessions sitting in Walhalla, and was sentenced to thirteen years' imprisonment, and that four years later he was paroled by Governor R. A. Cooper. When released Green was at work on the county chain gang near Walhalla. And to that very spot, as nearly as they could locate it, his self-constituted executioners led him to his death eleven years later.

The first thing the white investigator heard about Green, in conversation with the taxi man who drove him to Walhalla, was, "Oh, yes, no doubt he was guilty. This was his second offense." Every apologist for the lynching—and there were many—referred to Green's previous crime and aborted sentence.

Green's Alleged Crime of 1915. The charge against Green in 1915 was made by a white woman, aged twenty-six, sometimes cotton picker and mill worker who lived second door from Green's mother, and occasionally helped with the washing that the latter took in. She was at the home of Allen Green's mother at the time of the alleged attack, and others were in the house. Green seized her, she said, and tore her clothing, but she succeeded in getting away.

Within three years after his conviction and sentence, repeated petitions for Green's release were sent to the Governor, based largely on doubt of the woman's testimony. "Her reputation for virtue and chastity was exceedingly bad," said one group of seventy-five petitioners. Another wrote concerning her: "I know of no woman in the county who had a worse reputation for illicit traffic with men, both white and black."

Other petitioners said, "There is much doubt as to whether Green laid hands upon her at all," while the district solicitor who prosecuted the case stated that, even assuming that Green did seize the woman, as she alleged, her reputation was such that "defendant's conduct could be construed in the light of solicitation, rather than an attempt to commit a crime."

Here again one meets the question of fact. Did Allen Green assault her, or was the charge a frame up? Evidently even the jurymen were uncertain, since they appended to their verdict a recommendation of mercy, and three years later petitioned the Governor for his pardon.

Conflicting Community Attitudes. In studying the attitudes of the community toward Allen Green, one finds a sharp cleavage along economic and cultural lines. The well-to-do segment of the community—the business and professional people—spoke well of Green, with certain reservations noted below. They liked to employ him. He was "an excellent and competent workman," energetic, versatile, and always busy. He was often employed by the town in the previous administration and sometimes directed white laborers in street and sewer work.

He was thrifty and had saved money. He lived in a neat, well-kept home, owned a truck and some live stock, and was about to develop some sort of Negro park. He was the outstanding Negro of the town, and easily more prosperous than a large proportion of the whites. His chief claim to distinction, however, was his courage and skill as a fire fighter, which was credited with having twice saved the town from threatened destruction.

Another side of the picture was that, though very respectful to well-to-do white people, Green's attitude toward the "poor whites" was distinctly "high hat." That he tended to be a "big talker," "biggity," "overbearing," was reported even by some of those friendly to him. He thought himself "just as good as a white man," if not better than some, and took no pains to conceal it—rather the reverse, it seemed in some cases; he was in his glory as boss of a white crew on the city streets.

All this was bitterly resented by the large element of poorer whites—cotton mill people, tenant farmers, and day laborers. The wage of $7.50 a day paid him by the city for his services and those of his little truck, contrasted with the scant earnings of the less fortunate whites, added nothing to his popularity.

He was generally reported to be "tricky" also. Even his white friends admitted it, and told stories of sharp practices and even of shrewd stealing. "On one occasion he stole fifty gallons of oil from the city," a city official stated, "but was compelled to give it back." The city clerk and others confirmed these general charges of dishonesty.

Hence, when a young lawyer ran for mayor some months before the lynching, his promise that he "would get rid of

Allen Green" became a campaign issue of major importance. It won him a strong following among the mill people and, according to the mayor's own statement, probably accounted for his election. Green, with characteristic alertness immediately resigned. "No sir; Mr. ———— isn't going to fire me," he said; "I resign."

"... *But He Was That Sort.* ... " The bitterest hostility to Green, however, centered around the popular belief that he "had a hankering for white women." Apart from the affair of 1915, for which he was imprisoned, and that of 1930, which cost him his life, one heard many vague rumors and confident assertions to this effect, though definite charges were hard to localize and harder still to confirm. So general was the opinion, however, even among Green's friends, that one could hardly believe it wholly groundless.

The most specific of these charges, oddly enough, came from a Negro neighbor of Green's, one of the most intelligent and prosperous in the community. He stated that Green's interest in white women and his efforts to ingratiate himself with them were well known to the Negroes and deeply resented by them. He told in detail of a case in which one of Green's employers attempted to shoot him because of his attitude toward the employer's wife. Another Negro stated that he had warned Green of his danger; a Negro preacher said of his lynching, "He brought it on himself." It was this deep-seated grudge against Green that validated the immediate incredible charge. "Maybe he wasn't actually guilty in this case," was heard more than once, "but he was that sort of nigger and deserved to die on general principles."

Cause of Allegation an Unsolved Mystery. Of all the persons interviewed who heard or were familiar with the testimony against Green—officials, lawyers, prominent citizens—not one believed the charges. All agreed not only that the crime of rape was not committed, but that it could not have been committed under the circumstances alleged. Whatever its basis in fact, the charge was obviously a "frame up," and a very clumsy one.

But why should the white family have framed Allen Green

with charges of a capital offense? Was it, as some suggested, a cunning scheme to blackmail him into "staking" the family with a mule, as had been done once before? Or did Green on that Sunday morning actually take some liberty with the young woman that infuriated her husband? Or was there something in his attitude or conduct toward her that aroused her husband's suspicion of improper relations? And was there later a scene between husband and wife, eventuating in a plot to get Green out of the picture? All these speculations were seriously advanced by responsible citizens conversant with the case.

Reaction of the Community to the Lynching

"*. . . This Ruthless, Useless, Senseless—and Expensive— Thing. . . .*" Walhalla's weekly paper, the *Keowee Courier*, while carrying a full account of the lynching and lamenting the death of Allen Green as a "ruthless, useless, senseless—and expensive—thing" seemed to find unwarranted satisfaction in the reported participation in the mob of people from adjacent Georgia and North Carolina counties. On April 30 the *Courier* ran a column editorial from which the following extracts are quoted:

"It is regrettable indeed that the early months of the year 1930 brought to Walhalla, to Oconee County, to South Carolina—to the South—the disgrace of a lynching. It is not a local disgrace and shame; its damning effects go far beyond the confines of town, county and state—for there were participants from states other than South Carolina—from both North Carolina and Georgia, we have been informed on apparently good authority.

"The community in which the disgraceful over-riding of the law took place will, of course, in the minds of many, bear the brunt of the disgrace. And yet we doubt if there is a single substantial citizen of Walhalla who does not condemn the act and feel righteous indignation that this ruthless, useless, senseless—and expensive —thing should have occurred at all—more particularly in our town and community, than which there are none to which, ordinarily, we yield place for respect for law and constituted authority. . . ."

Sheriff and District Solicitor Threatened. The following communication appeared on the front page of the *Keowee Courier*, May 14:

"Threatening Letter Received by Sheriff John H. Thomas.

"To the Citizens of Oconee County:

"Since the lynching of Allen Green, numerous rumors and threats have come to us showing a concerted effort on the part of the lawless to scare our courts and law enforcement officers away from their duty. May 9th I received the letter which follows. It was postmarked Seneca at 3 P.M. May 9th, and reads as follows:

"'John you had better go slow. If you dont someone will give yo a cut shell rite in the hart for you ar on a lonsom road But Big Boy Ball got cot in a trap. Luck out no. 10 shoes is very easy to find. Guy if you rattle your tung your hart is going to B shot out. John I dont want to do hit. Yo a sun of abitch or yo would have give oup.'"

"(A picture of a coffin is placed in this space with 'Ded' written on it, and then the letter end:)"

"'Yo are new in this box.   Spunk K K K.'"

"I wish to say I have only tried to do my sworn duty as your Sheriff. I shall continue to do so in spite of all threats. If I must give my life to the lawless as the price of doing my duty, I am ready to make the sacrifice.

"I call on all good citizens to stand for law and order in this dark hour of our county's history.

"J. H. Thomas, Sheriff."

A warning to "lie low," posted at Seneca, was received by Solicitor Leon W. Harris, in which he was told that he would "fare worse" than did the sheriff on the night of the lynching if he continued his efforts to prosecute those who lynched Green. To this threat the Solicitor replied in the papers: "I will heed no warning nor be swayed by any threats or intimidation that run contrary to my duty."

Vigorous Court Investigation—Seventeen Indictments. As the lynching procession moved away from the jail, somebody blew the fire whistle. The warning was too late to prevent the lynching, but it did play an important part in the investigation which followed. Hearing the alarm and suspecting what was happening, a leading attorney drove hurriedly to the jail, where he found the sheriff severely wounded and the prisoner gone. He followed the mob, but could not overtake it. However, he did overtake a car going toward Westminster, and was able to get its number. Next day, through the number, he identified it as belonging to the night policeman of Westminster. On the following day, a special investigator was sent to the scene by Governor Richards and the best local law firm was engaged by the state to assist in the prosecution.

When the Westminster night policeman was subjected to vigorous questioning, he admitted that he had been at the scene of the lynching, and named a number of others who were there. Each of these was questioned and further leads were uncovered. Thus, no less than forty sworn statements were secured from as many persons who knew something about the lynching, including several who admitted their participation in it.

The grand jury, convening on May 26, indicted the following: John Sanders, J. L. Harris,* Dick Craner, Jobe Milbanks, Joe McCall, Jr., Irba Patterson and Pete Epps, Walhalla textile workers; John Stevens and Allen Leard, farmers; Mitch Lee, blacksmith; R. L. Ballentine and Alvin Jones, Walhalla's mayor and night policeman; and, from Westminster, Will Elrod, garage man, William Smith, ice plant employee; Nelson and Harold Matheson, filling station operators, and Grady Lee, textile worker. All were charged with murder, with assault and battery with intent to kill, with robbery, and with conspiracy to rescue prisoner. The mayor and night watchman were charged also with "malfeasance and soliciting crime."

The Indicted Mayor and Night Policeman. It will be recalled that the mayor had been elected largely because of his promise to turn Allen Green out of the town's employ. The deputy who accompanied the sheriff to arrest Green on the night of the alleged crime, stated that they were followed by the mayor,

* See footnote, pp. 263-264.

who practices law, accompanied by his night policeman, and that the two were present when Green was arrested. He stated that the night policeman said to Green, "You need a good lawyer," to which Green replied, "Yes sir, I have just called Mr. ——— and asked him to defend me." "Immediately," said the deputy, "the mayor and night policeman turned round and drove away." His opinion was that if Green had accepted the implied suggestion and retained the lawyer-mayor for his defense the whole story might have been very different.

Certain it is that when the examining trial was called on Tuesday morning the mayor appeared against Green, and made a very inflammatory speech. "If this crime had involved a girl in one of the better families, Allen Green would never have been brought to court," he said. "He would have been shot or strung up to a tree at once." Bitter denunciations of Green and heated appeals to prejudice marked his speech.

Following the lynching, many witnesses testified that the mayor and night policeman had been seen on the streets and at the ball park on Tuesday night and Wednesday night, and that the mayor had talked freely of the probability of a lynching, saying that all the crowd lacked was a leader, and that if anything happened the police would have business at the other end of town. One quoted him as saying: "If my night man interferes I'll take his badge off." Another stated that he said, "If you fellows want him, you can get him." The night watchman at the mill quoted the night policeman as saying that the mayor "wanted the Negro lynched." Eight or ten witnesses agreed substantially on these points. The night policeman admitted that he and the mayor were on the streets at the time of the lynching, and that when the mob came they went after the fire chief instead of to the aid of the sheriff.

The above sworn statements indicated that the mayor not only knew what was likely to occur, but that he approved of it, encouraged it, and took deliberate steps to keep the policeman out of the way. Every man of consequence interviewed was positive that this was so and was severe in condemnation of the mayor's part in the case. A little later, the night policeman was summarily dismissed by the town council, ostensibly because of some infraction of discipline, but really, according to report, because of his connection with the lynching. The night policeman at Westminster, who came over to the affair, was also promptly discharged.

Indicted Textile Worker Justifies Lynching. One of the textile workers indicted as a member of the mob was asked by the investigator how the people who lynched Green justified or excused their act. He replied frankly and in detail: Allen Green was "a mean nigger," they reasoned, always following white women with lecherous eyes; this was his third actual or attempted assault; when previously convicted his "rich" white friends had got him out of it; he had taken advantage of the girl in the present case because she was poor and half-witted; had she belonged to the wealthy group he would have been shot promptly and never brought to trial; as it was, had the mob left him alone, he would have been released again; the law could not be trusted; so they decided it was their duty to put him out of the way once for all. This, when checked by many other interviews, seemed a pretty fair picture of public opinion among those who justified or condoned the lynching.

This confessed mob leader stated that he was a church member and that nearly all of the other men indicted were also church members.

Trials of Indicted Men Twice Postponed. On motion of the counsel for the defense, the cases were postponed from the special May term of court to the July term of court, and the defendants were released on bond of $2,500 each. In July, further postponement was taken until the November term. When the trial began on November 3, Judge M. M. Mann was on the bench, and Solicitor Leon Harris led in the prosecution, ably assisted by a firm of Walhalla lawyers. The jury, according to counsel for the defense, "was composed of good average citizens of the county." The sheriff and his son positively identified two of the indicted men as the leaders of the mob, and apparently strong cases were made against five others. However, most of the witnesses for the prosecution repudiated their written statements in essential details, claiming that they had been made under duress and threat. The court ruled out a number of written statements made by defendants implicating themselves in the crime. One of the most important of these was that of a filling station operator, who had admitted that it was his truck which led the procession to the jail and carried the Negro to the place of execution, and that he himself was the driver.

Nobody Convicted. Seven of the seventeen indicted were freed by directed verdicts from the presiding judge. The remaining ten, including the mayor and night policeman, were freed by an Oconee County jury after an all-night deliberation. Concerning the trial, a leading Walhalla lawyer wrote: "Attorneys for the defense injected all the harrowing, inflammatory race prejudice into the case that was possible and the court's ruling with relation to the written statements was a severe blow to the state's case. However, from expressions of sentiment which we have heard from citizens of the county during the last few months, we doubt if anything would have brought about a verdict of guilty." Solicitor General Harris expressed keen disappointment at the failure to convict, but felt that the vigorous prosecution of the case would have a salutary effect throughout the state.

Change of Venue Needed. The case illustrates the difficulty of securing convictions of persons accused of mob violence, even when the evidence is conclusive. It suggests the importance of a change of venue in such cases, or of some provision by which juries can be drawn from areas unaffected by local public sentiment. The guilt of a number of men tried in this case seemed evident.* Their acquittal can be explained only by personal bias and the pressure of local public sentiment upon jurors drawn from the neighborhood and sharing largely in the prevalent psychology.

One of the Walhalla lawyers assisting in the prosecution was very positive on this point, suggesting the ultimate necessity for national legislation that would throw such cases into the Federal Courts, "away from damn local influence," to use his words. However, he thought the situation might have been met by change of venue or wider selection of juries. He

* See footnote, pp. 263-264.

thought it might be wise also to enact a law that prisoners charged with rape be taken to the state prison immediately on arrest.

Lynchee's Widow Refused Statutory Damages. Under the law of South Carolina, any county in which a lynching occurs is liable for damages of $2,000 payable to the estate of the victim. Allen Green's widow naturally set up a claim in this case, but was unable to make collection. There was no money available for this purpose, she was told by county officials. When the Legislature met, Oconee County's representatives not only refused to approve an appropriation.for this purpose, but one of them introduced a bill, which did not pass, to repeal the law making a county liable in such cases.

When refused the statutory damages, Green's widow resorted to the courts, with the result that the State Supreme Court awarded her a judgment of $2,000 against the county, which, it was reported, would be paid some time during 1932.

General Acquiescence of Religious Leaders. So far as is known, but one of Walhalla's religious leaders, a lawyer who teaches a Bible class in the Presbyterian Church, spoke out publicly against Green's death, roundly denouncing the lynching before his class on the following Sunday. A second positive influence from the religious leaders was the fact that the pastor of the Methodist Church in the mill village sensed the danger on Monday before the lynching and warned the sheriff of it.

Though all the preachers agreed, of course, that the lynching was "an awful affair," not one of the others said or did anything about it publicly. The Methodist pastor, the back windows of whose church look out on Allen Green's house one block away, excused his silence on the ground that he "had but lately come to Walhalla and knew little of local conditions."

Cleavage Along Economic and Cultural Lines. The intelligent and well-to-do people—ministers, officials, lawyers, business men, the editor, the school principal—deplored and condemned the lynching without qualification. They felt it not only as a shocking crime, but as a keen disgrace to a community that had never known such an occurrence before. "It has made me realize that our civilization is the thinnest veneer," said a prominent lawyer. A leading business man was so outspoken in his denunciation of the lynching as to bring upon himself threats of boycott and personal violence.

In the mill village, however, there was a very different sentiment. "So far as I can find out, the public approved of the lynching," said the young employed secretary of the mill village Y. M. C. A. So far as his "public" was concerned he was probably right—nor did he himself indicate to the investigator any personal disapproval of the lynching. A man from Westminster, one of the seventeen indicted, had stated that this same secretary and a textile worker brought him news of the lynching plans the day before. According to the secretary, the defense of the men indicted was provided by popular subscription.

But it was not in the mill community alone that one met approval of the lynching. The stratification of sentiment was not a matter of occupation or location, but of economic and cultural level. "Green ought to have been killed long ago," said a crude but interesting old woman of eighty who conducts a small store in Walhalla. "These big 'Petes' who had him waiting on them liked him," she said, "but everybody else is glad he's gone. The lynching was necessary to keep others from doing the same sort of thing. It will be ten years now before we have another such case." "They should have burned him," said a kind-faced, motherly woman who runs a lunch room in Seneca.

Depressing Effects Upon Negroes. The lynching had a very depressing effect upon the Negro citizens of the community. In at least one case a Negro family, after having received some sort of warning, sold out at a sacrifice and went to Atlanta. The Negroes were greatly surprised and shocked by the occurrence. They did not believe Green guilty, and felt that in any case he should have had a fair trial. The uneasiness felt by Negroes immediately after the lynching was evidenced by the fact that in taking the body of Allen Green to the burying ground they carefully avoided the principal throughfares and went by out-of-the-way and little-used roads.

"A Black Smudge on South Carolina." This was the caption

of the Columbia *State's* editorial on the day following the lynching, two sentences of which were: "The first black smear of lynching to be placed on South Carolina in several years was the work of an Oconee County mob. . . . The mob, having contempt for the state and its courts, seized the prisoner and murdered him."

The Charleston *News and Courier*, also on April 25, said editorially:

". . . The underlying cause of lynching is that there are people in the world, some in South Carolina, who enjoy killing, who have an appetite for murder when their blood is hot, an appetite they indulge when an excuse offers that their fellow citizens may wink at. . . . The men of Oconee who went to the county jail, assaulted the jailer, took out a negro and murdered him, may have the satisfaction of knowing that they have caused humiliation to hundreds of thousands of decent South Carolinians who have had pride that no lynching had occurred in their state in four years.

"Lynchings have occurred rarely in South Carolina of late years," said the Orangeburg *Times and Democrat* on May 1, "and it is terrible that this unnecessary and unfortunate incident has taken place at Walhalla." On May 13, the Newberry *Observer* in an editorial, "A Resurgence of Savagery," said:

"Such utter contempt for law marks the community in which it occurs as still at the mercy of savages. The style of clothes they wear, the vehicles in which they ride, the utensils they use, are the products of a civilization of which they are not a part, but upon which they are a drag. In all communities the highest forces of civilization work side by side with opposing tendencies that range all the way down to primitive animalism. The reflection on a community lies not in the fact that there are present in it such elements of barbarism, but that they are so strong as to get the upper hand."

Lynching Openly Condoned by One Paper. Midway between the textile centers of Greenville and Spartanburg is the town of Greer, with two newspapers and a population of less than

2,500. Both papers commented on the lynching. On May 15 the Greer *Citizen* said editorially: "Texas[1] and South Carolina have recently added more disgraceful records to their histories of lynchings, and if these states do their duty there will be convictions for the partakers of these crimes, not only crimes against individuals but crimes against organized society."

Two weeks later, the town's other paper, the Greer *Tribune*, carried this editorial:

" 'On this spot Allen Green got his parole and here got his lynch.' The mob that lynched a negro at Walhalla some days ago left the above note near-by the body of the dead Negro. The Negro was a convict on a chain gang some years ago and it was while he was at this particular spot that news was brought to him that he had been paroled and given his freedom. The reason he was on the chain gang at that time was because he had been tried and convicted of attacking a white woman. The reason he was lynched years later was because he was accused of attacking another white woman. Draw your own conclusions."

FACTS ABOUT THE COMMUNITY

Settled by German Colonization Society. The town of Walhalla is a bit unique in its history, having been established in 1850 by the German Colonization Society, a group of thirty-seven Germans who came up from Charleston, bought a large tract of land, and laid out the town of Walhalla on a generous scale. Though the German touch would hardly be noticed by the casual observer, a few German names persist, and the Lutheran Church still holds a prominent place in the community.

Today's population of the town, along with the remainder of Oconee County, is about an average cross section of western South Carolina or north Georgia counties—a few substantial white families, mostly of Scotch Irish, English, and German descent, constituting the professional and business leadership, and a much larger number of poor and uncultured people of

---

[1] Reference here is made to the Sherman lynching of May 9. See Sherman case study.

the same racial stock, but who throughout the years have been the victims of the cotton farmer's economic and cultural handicaps. The contrasting interracial attitudes of these two elements, which was suggested above, parallels the situation in most Southern communities. In 1930, Negroes constituted 18.0 per cent of the county's population, in 1920 21.2 per cent. The Negro population dropped from 6,398 in 1920 to 5,999 in 1930; the white population rose from 23,642 to 27,306.

A Distinctly Rural County. Of Oconee County's 33,368 inhabitants in 1930, all but 6,091 lived in the open country. The town dwellers were distributed as follows: Walhalla, 2,388; Seneca, 1,929; Westminster, 1,774. Except for the two cotton mills at Walhalla together employing about 600 "hands," the towns are principally farm trade centers.

From the agricultural standpoint, Oconee ranks well among South Carolina counties: In 1925, 64.0 per cent of its area was in farms, against 54.0 per cent in the whole state; it had 9.0 per cent less tenancy than the state's average; and a $103 per capita value of farm products, against $83 throughout the state. A cotton acreage of 1.9 per bale against 2.8 for the state and an annual milk yield of 375 gallons per cow, against the state's average of 306 gallons go further to indicate the agricultural status of the county.

This relatively good showing does not tell the whole story, for the county's per capita value of manufactured products was less than half that of the 1930 state average, leaving the combined par capita value of farm crops and manufactured products far below the South Carolina average. Added to this generally poor economic situation, at the time of the lynching Walhalla's two cotton mills were running on half time, and some time earlier there was a local bank failure, both of which facts were regarded by some as contributing to the mob psychology which culminated in the lynching of Allen Green. On January 1, 1930, Oconee County's bank deposits amounted to $40.71 per capita while the state average was $105.73.

Excessive White Illiteracy. In 1930, 7.9 per cent of Oconee County's white people over ten years old, and 19.1 per cent of the Negroes of the same age group, were illiterates. The state average for white illiteracy was 5.1 per cent, and for Negroes, 26.9 per cent.

Of the county's fifty-three white schools in 1929, there were twelve one-teacher schools, twenty-four with two teachers; ten with three, and seven with more than three teachers. The average annual salary paid white teachers in Oconee County was $896.90 in contrast with the state average of $1,047.14, and the per capita expenditure for each enrolled white child was $47.65 in the county against $60.06 in the state, The per capita expenditures for the Negro child is scarcely one fifth of that for the white child, and the school term is but ninety-one days for Negroes, against 163 days for the whites.

There is no public library or hospital in the county. The county has a white farm demonstration agent, who claims he works with Negro farmers as earnestly as with whites, and reports that he finds them more appreciative than their white neighbors and quite as intelligent in carrying out projects. The county also has a health unit, consisting of physician and nurse who visit the white schools annually, and extend office and clinical service regularly to any who need it, irrespective of race. The nurse stated, however, that they "had not yet been able to get round to the Negro schools." Though without a hospital, the death rate for the county, for both Negroes and whites, is about twenty per cent lower than for the state at large.

"*An Unlucky Thirteen.*" So mused an observer after looking into the circumstances of the Walhalla lynching and noting the lack of any determined stand for civic righteousness on the part of Walhalla's thirteen churches, ten white and three colored, or a little more than one church to every 200 people. Three of these are in the mill village—Methodist, Baptist, and Church of God. It is reported that the latter does not affiliate with any other and once prayed that the mill Y. M. C. A. might burn down, because it fostered athletics and movies. The uptown white churches—Lutheran, Methodist, Presbyterian, Baptist, Episcopal, Wesleyan Methodist, and Catholic—are all said to have college men as pastors, but needless to say all these churches are struggling for existence, the most prosperous having an annual budget of only $4,200.

The church membership of the whole county numbered 12,-648 in 1926, 9,729 whites and 2,919 Negroes, or about sixty per cent of both races fifteen years old and over. Baptists predominated with 7,257 white members and 2,619 Negroes. Methodists ranked second with 1,423 white members and 300 Negroes.

A Very Democratic County. Of Oconee County's 1,333 votes in the 1928 presidential election, nearly ninety-five per cent were for the Democratic candidate, as compared with ninety-one per cent throughout the state. Even though the county's vote in 1928 was much heavier than common, the total number of votes was scarcely more than one seventh of the white people of voting age. Only a handful of Negroes participate in national elections, while in local and state elections it is reported that but one Negro, Allen Green, was accustomed to register and vote.

On the point of present-day crime, the sheriff stated that the whites were worse than the Negroes. At the time of the investigation of Green's lynching, there were a dozen white men in jail, but only one Negro. According to the sheriff, nearly all of the few crimes involving Negroes are of a minor character, theft and liquor selling being most common.

Races Amicable in Negative Way. Within traditional patterns the relations between the races seem amicable, in a negative way. There is little overt friction; the lynching of Allen Green is the only one recorded against the county.

There was some friction during Reconstruction times, and stories, usually considered humorous, are told of artful expedients by which the Negroes of that era were outwitted and robbed of political power. The original Ku Klux Klan, and later Wade Hampton's "Red Shirts," played parts in that drama, but their rôles, so far as was learned, were spectacular rather than violent. While one talkative "old timer" did credit the Klan with more or less "necessary" violence, one now hears little to indicate that any recognized scars or bitter memories have come down from that period.

With few exceptions, the Negroes are poor and landless, working as tenant farmers, or holding humble jobs in the cities. There are said to be a few well-to-do Negro farmers, but in business circles in Walhalla none has risen above the level of the small barber shop or pressing club.

There is scarcely any Negro leadership. Not only the preachers, but also the school principal, a well-trained college man, are non-residents. The principal knew only one white man in Walhalla, the principal of the white school, who, he said, had manifested interest and helpfulness. The barber, a man of character and intelligence, was nevertheless for business reasons under the constant necessity of "remembering who he is."

In general, the best relations of today conform strictly to the stereotype of subservience on the one hand and condescending patronage on the other. The Oconee County Negro is "all right in his place"—that is so long as he treats every white man with real or simulated respect and does not expect too much in return. Doubtless it was Allen Green's flouting of this inflexible code that formed the background for his lynching and contributed to it in no small degree.

Many of the better type white people, to be sure, have a sense of justice and of obligation toward Negroes, but this sentiment is wholly unorganized and ineffective as a community force. So far as interracial matters are concerned, both races are without leadership, and neither has any collective point of contact with the other. The inevitable result, as in so many similar situations, is that the Negro's community needs remain unknown to the white group and largely neglected by them. For example, when limited funds made it necessary last year to cut the school term in Walhalla, the little, ill-housed, four-teacher Negro school was made to take all the cut, giving up two months of its term, while the white school ran full time. Inquiry revealed the fact that a cut of three days in the budget of the white school would have made it possible for the colored school to run the full time.

CHAPTER XIV

TWENTY MINUTES LATE
UNION, UNION COUNTY, SOUTH CAROLINA

THE BODY of Dan Jenkins, Negro, was riddled with bullets on the afternoon of June 21, 1930, by a mob of more than 150 white men in the Santuc neighborhood, six miles south of Union, the county seat of Union County, South Carolina. The local unit of the National Guard reached the scene twenty minutes after the lynching, having been called out at the request of a private citizen who learned of the imminent danger of mob violence. Jenkins, a laborer with a road construction gang, was accused of having attempted to assault a sixteen-year-old white girl and of having assaulted her older sister-in-law.

THE LYNCHING

Varying Reports on Cause of Lynching. In this, as in many other lynchings, the local white people and the Negroes hold somewhat different views of the cause of the lynching. Among some of the Negroes it was reported that Dan Jenkins had been seeing the older of these two women for some time, and on occasion had given her money. She "squealed," so their story goes, because the community had found out about it. A slightly different story, also current among the Negroes, is that the older woman and Jenkins had met on several occasions on the pretense of his buying milk; that, on the day when the report of the assault was made, the sixteen-year-old sister-in-law saw the two together and, not understanding the situation, told what she saw; and that the older woman accused Jenkins of rape to explain the matter.

In contrast with these reports, the current story is that

the two women were at a local country store in the late after-noon. Jenkins, too, was there and left about the same time that they left. When the women were half way home, Jenkins tepped from a clump of bushes by the side of the road and, with drawn revolver, warned them that he would shoot to kill if they disobeyed his order. According to this story, Jenkins attempted to rape the unmarried girl, and later was successful with the other. The younger girl, running from the scene in spite of Jenkins' threat to shoot, made her escape and reported the affair at home. Her brother reported that, unarmed, he ran immediately to the spot and found his kinswoman in the grasp of the Negro, who fired at him. He fell to the ground, feigning death, to escape further danger. Shortly afterward, his father arrived on the scene and the Negro fled.

Early Arrival of Sheriff. Something like thirty minutes after the alleged crime, the county sheriff was called and told that a man had been shot. Twenty minutes later he was on the scene. When he learned, on arrival, that the Negro was accused of rape, he set out in a quiet way to find the assailant. All night long he and his deputies tried without success to locate Jenkins. By Saturday morning, the people of the community had learned of the case, and several searching parties went out. Apparently, the news was spread only by word of mouth; no evidence was found that a telephone or other rapid means of communication was employed. It was nearly noon before any considerable number of people in the town of Union had heard the report of the alleged assault.

Guard Twenty Minutes Too Late. When the information reached Union, the editor of the *Daily Times*, accompanied by the mayor, went to the home of the young women to learn the truth about the alleged assault. The editor knew the family, having been their pastor some years ago. He stated that, after talking with the mother and making a preliminary investiga-tion, he was convinced that Jenkins had committed the crime of which he was accused. He rushed back to Union to give a news story to the Associated Press. Shortly afterwards, the principal of the white high school rushed into his office and reported that the Negro had been captured at three o'clock, and that unless something was done at once there would be a lynching.

The editor, on his own responsibility, got in touch with Governor Richards at Columbia. Immediately the Governor issued an order for the National Guard of Union to assemble, report to the place where the Negro was held by the mob, and prevent a lynching at all costs. Within forty minutes, the Guard unit came upon the mob six miles southeast of Union. But it arrived twenty minutes too late; the accused Negro had been riddled with bullets.

Fearing that the mob would carry out its threat to burn the victim's body, the Guard accompanied the body back to Union and protected the Negro undertaking establishment where it was kept. On the next afternoon, Sunday, they stood guard while the body of Dan Jenkins was buried in the potter's field. The Guard then dispersed, by order of the Governor.

Efforts to Prevent Lynching. Four white people tried to prevent the lynching. Soon after Jenkins was captured, the high school principal at Union, a recent graduate of Wofford College and a member of the Service Division of the local National Guard, went to the half-dozen men who had captured the Negro and urged them to put the prisoner in a car standing nearby and rush him to the prison at Columbia. The Negro's captors seemed about to act upon this advice, when someone in the crowd said, "You didn't capture him, nohow. Let's take him on and let the girls identify him." The principal was pushed aside as the men milled on with the accused Negro. Down the road a little farther, when other members of the searching party joined the group, the principal again asked them to give the man over, that he might be rushed to a strong jail. He assured them that if the Negro were guilty he would be given the death sentence. His plea was ignored; the mob pushed on. Thereupon, he rushed to Union and informed the editor of the situation, and the local National Guard was called.

Shortly after the school principal left, a city policeman of Union tried to wrest the Negro from the mob, but was curtly told that his own life would be in danger if he interfered further. A local constable and the mayor of Union also made unsuccessful attempt to dissuade the mob from its purpose.

If the National Guard had arrived a little sooner—and it would have if the sheriff had called for it promptly—it is almost certain that there would have been no lynching.

Lynched by Roadside. When the half-dozen men came upon Dan Jenkins shortly after noon, and took him in charge unresisting, news of his capture quickly spread to other armed searching parties, and the accused Negro was soon surrounded by a crowd. Members of the mob first talked of killing him at once, but upon further deliberation decided to let the women identify him. A car was dispatched for the two women; in the meantime, the mob walked the Negro down the road toward their home.

When they had proceeded about half a mile the sheriff came on the scene, having been with one of the numerous searching parties. He requested the custody of the accused Negro, but was repeatedly refused. The mob leaders stated that they had captured the Negro and meant to let the women identify him. A half mile further down the road they met the women, who promptly identified Jenkins as their assailant. Without delay, the mob stood him beside the road, with his face toward the bank, and riddled his body with bullets. The sheriff was looking on, but later testified in court that he could identify none of the participants.

The Victim an Itinerant Laborer. Dan Jenkins, twenty-two years old, born at Beaufort, North Carolina, was an itinerant laborer who had come into Union County with a road construction company. A few days before he was lynched, he had been laid off for insubordination, and shortly before that, in a controversy with a local storekeeper, he had threatened to knife him. None of these things had drawn him into the courts. Being an outsider and a rambler, it was not learned whether Jenkins had a court record elsewhere.

A Negro minister of Batesburg, South Carolina, stated that Jenkins had married a Batesburg woman in 1927. His wife was in Union County when the lynching occurred, but left shortly afterwards.

One of the leading Negroes of the county stated that he

went past the scene immediately after the lynching, and that members of the mob courteously cleared the road for him. He said further that he knows the names of practically all of the persons who took an active part in Jenkins' death, but that he has not divulged their names and does not propose to.

THE REACTION OF THE COMMUNITY

The general community reaction to the lynching is indicated by the fact that no indictments were drawn against the mob leaders. With the exception of the editor, who called for the National Guard and later wrote editorials disapproving the affair, no formal protest against the lynching was made by anybody in Union County.

Lynching Condemned by Local Daily. Immediately after the lynching the following editorial, over the editor's own name, appeared in the Union *Daily Times:*

"Admitting that the case was one of more than ordinary heinousness, admitting that the accused was unmistakably identified, admitting that the strain put upon the citizenship and officers of the law was to the last degree severe, I yet deplore the fact that certain of our citizens took upon themselves the responsibility of acting as judge, jury and executioners in the Dan Jenkins case. If the negro had been fleeing, and shot down, desperate character that he was, it would have been justifiable. If he had been killed outright while resisting arrest, that would have been justifiable. Having been captured, disarmed and safely in the hands of his captors, it is another matter. The sheriff was on hand; several deputies were on hand; the wise course would have been to turn the prisoner over to the officers of the law. As A. M. Jeter and Paul James plead with the captors of the negro, so every law-abiding citizen would have been moved to do. 'Let the law take its course.' That would have been better. Better for the county, the state and for all concerned. Having stood for the law all through the years I could not, at this late day, turn from a lifetime policy and justify a lynching. Having had the lynching we are now forced to be burdened with the humiliation of outside meddlers, paid hirelings and the disruption and friction that will arise among our citizens. Of course the payment of $2,500 to the nearest of kin of the lynched negro, in accordance with federal law (sic) is a small thing, but humiliating, certainly. But that is nothing in comparison to the fact that, in a great crisis our citizens could not rise to the dignity and safety of standing by the law, allowing the law to take its course. . . .

"I telephoned Governor Richards informing him that a lynching was imminent. I have no apologies to make for so doing. It was in line with my lifetime course of conduct. As an editor and as a Christian minister, I have, in season and out of season stood for law enforcement. It would be impossible for me now to desert the stand. And, I believe that even the most violently aroused citizens, even those who participated in the lynching, will upon sober reflection, realize that the better way would have been to allow the law to take its course. Living with my own soul, measuring my own imperfections, thinking soberly, I try to live at peace with my conscience. That is my constant aim, and I do not have to change any stake I have set up."

Denouncement by State Press. The story of the Union lynching was carried in the larger papers of South Carolina and of the Southeast. On June 23, the Greenville *News'* editorial, "Men—or Weaklings," characterized the members of the mob as having "stepped back to the law of the jungle," confessing that "they are a helpless prey to the most primitive passions—unwilling or unable to restrain themselves as befits men who uphold the civilized processes for the punishment of crime."

The Spartanburg *Journal* on June 29 commented editorially: "The forces of law and order were asleep at the switch in Union County when a county-wide search of enraged men was in progress to seize a negro charged with assaulting two young white women. . . . Lynching should be stamped out, and an enlightened, aroused public sentiment alone can accomplish that purpose."

The Charleston *Evening Post* said: "If a fair number of

lynchers are put into penitentiary cells, it will tend to cool men's blood a bit when they are inclined to the sort of heat that leads to mob murder."

The press commended Governor Richards for promptly ordering out the National Guard and expressed regret that the matter had not been brought to the Governor's attention earlier. The news releases carried by the Negro papers were practically the same as those in the white press, except that they generally doubted Jenkins' guilt.

Sheriff's Conduct Termed "Reprehensible" by Governor. The coroner's jury made a preliminary inquest a few hours after Jenkins' death, at which the sheriff testified: "I almost had my hands on the 'nigger' but never succeeded in getting hold of him." Both he and the policeman who had tried to get the accused Negro, assured the jury that they could identify no member of the mob. On the basis of this testimony, the Governor termed the sheriff's conduct "reprehensible."

Solicitor Ibra C. Blackwood, of the district of which Union County is a part, was quoted in the papers as promising a prompt and thorough investigation. He stated, however, that he had left the investigation in the hands of local officers. Apparently doubtful that anything effective would be done by the latter, Governor Richards sent in investigators from his office, among them his private secretary. These special investigators spent some time in Union and then faded from the scene without visible results. No court action has ever been taken beyond a fruitless grand jury investigation.

Although Jenkins' wife made immediate claim against the county for the statutory damages of $2,000 provided in such cases, she had received no settlement as late as April, 1932.

A Thing to be Forgotten. The local editor stands out as the one white person who not only deplored the lynching, but did what he could to prevent it. The attitude of most of the people, including a number of Negroes, is that Jenkins got what was coming to him and that the best thing to do is to forget the affair as soon as possible.

COLE BLEASE ON LYNCHING[1]

"... *To Hell With the Constitution.*" United States Senator Cole L. Blease, in his campaign for re-election in the summer of 1930, toured South Carolina. In Union County, two weeks after the lynching, he delivered himself on the subject of lynching. Some of his statements were:

"Whenever the Constitution comes between me and the virtue of the white women of South Carolina, I say to hell with the Constitution!

"Whenever the negro press and associations are to tell me how I am to vote, I ask my God to deprive me of the right to vote. White supremacy and the protection of the virtue of the white women of the South comes first with me.

"When I was governor of South Carolina you did not hear of me calling out the militia of the State to protect negro assaulters.

"In my South Carolina campaigns you heard me say, 'When you catch the brute that assaults a white woman, wait until the next morning to notify me.'"

".... *Blease's Speech Should Disgust All Decent People.*" No sooner had Senator Blease made this statement, which he doubtless expected to gain votes for him, than the papers of South Carolina and the Southern States, along with the remainder of the nation, burst forth with vigorous denunciations. The Charleston *News and Courier* said editorially: "The issue in the contest for United States Senator is whether or not South Carolina shall endorse lynching. Senator Blease made it the issue in Union. South Carolina Democrats cannot re-nominate Senator Blease this year without endorsing lynching. There is no way of getting out of it. The *News and Courier* regrets that the issue has been made. The people cannot re-elect Mr. Blease without endorsing lynching." The Anderson *Mail* of July 9 quoted this editorial with approval.

---

[1] Because of what Blease said about lynching at Union two weeks after Jenkins was lynched, this discussion is a pertinent supplement.

The Spartanburg *Herald's* editorial of July 10, captioned "Shall South Carolina Endorse Lynchings," closed with: "The miserable cheapness of Blease's speech should disgust all decent people."

Clelia P. McGowan, a distinguished member of one of Charleston's original families, gave a statement to the press soon after this outburst, in which she said:

"Hundreds of thousands of white women in the South feel that the law, as represented by sheriffs, juries, and judges, is their honorable and reliable protection and avenger.

"Through church affiliation with the great religious organizations and the membership of these organizations in the commission on race relations in the South, women have in every state passed resolutions repudiating the use of the name of the white women of the South as a cloak for mob violence.

"They state that they stand for legal protection of all women and lawful execution of those convicted of crime, be it what it will. The women of the South are not afraid to stand by the Constitution of the United States."

"*. . . Protect the Good Name of the South. . . .*" The Winston-Salem *Journal* of July 9 said: "So long as American people allow themselves to be tricked into voting for vaudevillian, flamboyant sensation-seekers and cheap demagogues who stop short of nothing to gain a personal following, so long will Judge Lynch outrage society and the secret terror and open crime stalk through the land."

The Greensboro *News* expressed the hope that South Carolina would honor itself by defeating Blease.

A Macon *Telegraph* editorial, captioned "Two Undesirables," expressed the hope that the spirit of Blease and Heflin would be dethroned.

The Louisville *Leader*, a Negro weekly, had the following to say:

"Tillman is dead and forgotten, Vardaman went crazy, died in an insane asylum and was buried a few days ago without any tears being shed. Heflin is at the end of his road. Blease's sun is setting, and the sooner all of the Cole Blease type are relegated to the past or buried in the ground the sooner we shall be able to stop race prejudice, mob violence, and make all America a fit place for every citizen to live and spread peace and good will over all the earth."

Under the caption, "Why Wake Up Dyer," the Charleston *News and Courier* denounced Blease's statement as likely to encourage the enactment of a Federal anti-lynching law.

". . . *The Intelligent Christian People Do Not Stand for the Foaming and Ravings* . . ." The church papers of the South also voiced vigorous protests. The North Carolina *Christian Advocate* said editorially: "If the people of South Carolina return such a man to the senate they must be classed with Blease in the eyes of the world. If the people of South Carolina repudiate him they will win the respect of all civilized peoples." The *Christian Index*, official organ of the Colored Methodist Episcopal Church, termed Blease a "loud mouthed, coarse political blatherskite, who was common enough to say 'to hell with the Constitution,'" and added: "Thank God the intelligent Christian people of South Carolina do not stand for the foaming and ravings of this political nondescript."

"*Have Senator Blease's Utterances Injured His Candidacy?*" A number of papers in South Carolina and elsewhere watched the effect of this campaign issue. The Greenville *Piedmont* expressed the opinion that he would lose no votes by it.

The High Point *Enterprise*, while deploring Blease's defense of lynching, expressed the opinion that he "seems to know his South Carolina."

But Blease Didn't "Know His South Carolina." Blease's defeat by Byrnes is a matter of history now, and the papers which ventured that "Blease knows his South Carolina" have been proved poor prophets. As a matter of fact, the issue which Blease had raised turned out greatly to his disadvantage. The state press, as seen above, denounced him widely and vigorously, while some of his opponents for the Senate digged up from the days of his governorship a very embarrassing pardon record. They showed that he had pardoned or paroled no less than seventy-seven actual or attempted rapists, many of them Negroes.

FACTS ABOUT THE COMMUNITY

Union County, in the Piedmont section of the state, like adjoining counties, is dependent upon cotton in a two-fold way: The rural dwellers grow it for a livelihood, while cotton manufacturing is the principal urban industry.

Marked Increase of Native-Born Whites. The total population of the county has increased but little since 1890 and scarcely any during the past two decades. It was 25,363 in 1890, 29,924 in 1910, and 30,920 in 1930. Due to the decrease of cotton production and the increase of the textile industry, the county now has 3,091 fewer Negroes than in 1910, while the white population increased from 14,452 to 18,498.

Slightly less than eighty per cent of the people live in the open country. Union, the county seat town, with a population of 7,419, is the only urban community of any size. Approximately three-fourths of the people of the town are white. This is due largely to the presence of cotton mills which employ white labor almost exclusively.

The population of Union County, as of most counties which had lynchings in 1930, is almost solely native-born whites and Negroes, but one in a thousand being foreign-born, whereas for the state three in a thousand belonged to the latter group.

Cotton in Field and Factory. The county's 1930 cotton crop of 17,000 bales was 3,000 bales below the average crop between 1910 and 1914, and a little over 3,000 above the average crop between 1925 and 1929.

Of the county's 2,543 farms in 1930, three-fourths were cultivated by tenants: More than one-half of the county's white farmers and over nine-tenths of the Negro farmers were tenants. A ten per cent decrease in farmers during the past ten years was due for the most part to the unfavorable agricultural conditions which have been prevalent throughout the Southeastern states, and especially in the lower Piedmont counties.

In number of cotton spindles, Union County with 347,100 ranks fourth among the counties of South Carolina. Sheeting, hosiery, yarns, and other staple cotton products are made. For the past three years, Union has ranked sixth in the value of its textile products, which in 1927 totalled $13,724,935. Of the 3,521 cotton mill employees in 1929, one hundred and sixty-eight were Negroes.

The Negro business enterprises in Union consist of three undertaking concerns, a printing establishment operated under the supervision of the Negro high school, and several grocery stores. Besides teachers and preachers, the professional Negroes in the town are limited to one physician and one dentist.

Value of Manufactures High—Bank Deposits Low. In 1924, the value of farm products was $65.57 per capita in Union County, as compared with $83.33 throughout the state. The value of manufactured products for the same year was considerably above the average, being $588.85 per capita, while the state average was $368.76, making the county's combined value of farm and manufactured products more than $200 per capita greater than the state average—due to presence of the textile industry.

Although the value of manufactured products in Union County is relatively high, the people of the county are generally poor; against an income tax return for every 121 persons in South Carolina, Union County made but one for every 242 persons. In 1930 bank deposits amounted to $80.70 per capita in Union County and $105.73 in the state, which further indicates the low economic status of the population.

School Expenditures by Race. In 1929 the Negroes made up forty-six per cent of the county's school population and had thirty per cent of its 251 teachers. For the whites, there were four one-eacher, fourteen two-teacher, two three-teacher schools, and twelve schools with more than three teachers; for Negroes, twenty-eight one-teacher, fourteen two-teacher, four three-teacher schools, and three schools with more than three teachers. The average annual salaries were $1,882.40 for white male teachers, $1,041.97 for white females, $372.23 for Negro males, and $299.96 for Negro female teachers, the salaries for the whites being above and for the Negroes, below the state average. The average term of the white urban schools was 180 days; of the white rural schools, 176 days; of the Negro urban schools, 180 days; and of Negro rural schools, 93 days. The per capita expenditure per white child enrolled in 1930 was $54.72, as compared with $8.54 per Negro enrolled child.

Educational facilities for Negroes in the town of Union are better than in most South Carolina communities of its size. There are two Negro public schools, one a combination elementary-high school, and the other an elementary school. The high school is named in honor of its supervising Negro principal, A. A. Simms, who founded it twenty-five years ago. At present it is one of the three Negro high schools accredited by the state. The elementary-high school is a modern two-story brick structure with eleven classrooms and an auditorium. The faculties of these schools are composed of the supervising principal, an assistant principal, and twenty-three teachers, most of whom are college trained and receive salaries between $50.00 and $75.00 a month. Of the total enrollment in the Negro schools, 171 are high school students, fifty of whom live outside the city limits. There are a half-dozen small Rosenwald schools in the county.

In 1930, the county's percentage of white illiteracy was 6.6 as against 5.1 for the state; that of the Negroes was 24.2 per cent in the county and 26.9 in the state.

Baptists and Methodists. Of the 9,003 white church members in Union County, 4,505, almost one-half, are members of the Southern Baptist Church. The next largest membership is that of the Methodist Episcopal Church, South, with 3,762 members. Besides these two denominations there are 530 Presbyterians, 169 Protestant Episcopalians, 115 Free Will Baptists, twelve Roman Catholics, and other scattered denominations.

The Negro Baptists outnumber all the other Negro denominations combined, there being 3,790.

Some Reconstruction Backgrounds. During Reconstruction, the Negroes gained almost complete control of political affairs in South Carolina. Subsequently the whites re-established their control by force. In his book, *Ousting the Carpetbagger from South Carolina*, Henry T. Thompson says, "From the beginning to the end of carpetbag rule the doctrine which was advocated with the greatest persistency was that of social equality. To attain that end was the height of the Negro's ambition, and his white leaders, who backed him up in it, practiced what they preached." To this a second writer, Reynolds, added: "Most of the white Republicans ate and drank, walked and rode, went to public places, and ostensibly affiliated with Negroes. A prominent white Republican, rather priding himself on his education and refinement, once selected a Negro clergyman to perform the funeral services over the dead body of his child."

The State Legislature between 1868 and 1875, almost entirely Negro, passed civil rights acts for the purpose of enforcing equal accommodations for both races in matters of public service, on railroads, in hotels, and in restaurants and theaters.

In 1873, the Board of Trustees of the State University, composed of whites and Negroes in equal numbers, voted to admit Negroes to the institution. The first to be admitted was Henry E. Haynes, the Secretary of State, who matriculated in the law department. Thomaston, chronicler of this period, wrote, "Negro students entered the University in considerable numbers. As they were unfitted to take collegiate courses, the curriculum was lowered to the standard of a high school. While Negroes controlled the State University many of the young white men of the state refused to attend and the writer of this book, along with thirty-five or forty, matriculated at the Union College, Schenectady, New York, in the year 1876."

Ten Negroes Lynched in 1871. When the white people of the state began to gain control, they endeavored not only to reestablish white rule but to reduce the Negroes to complete subjection. Union County had its share of the original Ku Klux activities. "In January, 1871," wrote Thompson, "a harmless and helpless white man, who had lost an arm in the Confederate army, was brutally murdered by forty Negro militiamen on a highway near the town of Union. The sheriff of the county arrested thirteen of the Negroes and placed them in jail. Two of his posse were badly wounded in the effort to make the arrest. The Ku Klux Klan took two of the prisoners from the jail and shot them to death. Three of the prisoners escaped, and the remaining eight were about to be removed to Columbia by order of the court, when members of the Klan, numbering some one thousand to fifteen hundred, all mounted and disguised, took them from the jail and shot them to death. This bloody work was done quickly and quietly. There was no uproar. The mounted men retired as quietly as they had come, their ranks well kept and their movements marked by a precision which was well-nigh military." This affair created a profound impression upon the Negroes no less than the whites in Union and adjoining counties, and though the Klan continued to operate in Union County it was never again so drastic. At one time lawlessness reached such heights that President Grant declared martial law and suspended the writ of habeas corpus in Union and eight other South Carolina counties.

Though the Ku Klux Klan of recent years was active in the town and county, there were no outstanding demonstrations made against the Negroes. At present the crime situation is more acute among the textile workers and tenant whites than among the Negroes.

Threatened Lynching Prevented in 1927. A threatened lynching was frustrated by the Union National Guard on July 30, 1927, when a mob menaced Albert Simpson, Negro, who had shot a young white man of Union. The sheriff was heralded as having prevented this lynching, with the aid of the local National Guard unit. The case of the sheriff came to the attention of the Commission on Interracial Coöperation, and a medal, "In Defense of Law and Order," was presented to him by the editor of the Union *Daily Times*. It was this same sheriff who failed to get control of the situation in June, 1930.

Overwhelming Democratic Majority. Though perhaps more considerate of Negroes than the people of some other counties, Union countians have not been insensible to political appeals to race prejudice and Reconstruction memories. They always poll a large majority for the Democratic candidates. In the presidential election of 1924, the vote stood 1,826 to 27. In 1928, the presidential vote was Democrat, 2,460; Republican, 60, and Anti-Smith Democrat, 14. The Democratic presidential candidate was much more popular in this county than in South Carolina at large.

Race Relations. The relatively good public schools for Negroes in the town of Union evince a sympathetic attitude on the part of public officials. Another evidence of interracial amity is the Negro hospital at Union, which is operated jointly by members of the two races.

Race relations have been much improved by the persistent efforts of the leading Negro of the town, who for a quarter of a century has waged a fight on miscegenation. This Negro crusader has insisted that a man has no right to be the father of children unless he shares with the mother the responsibility of their rearing.

CHAPTER XV

MOBS—"ORDERLY" AND "DISORDERLY"
CARTERSVILLE, BARTOW COUNTY, GEORGIA

SHORTLY AFTER MIDNIGHT on October 1, 1930, an organized group of men—an "orderly" mob—went to the Bartow County jail, and without opposition from officers, took from his cell Willie Clark, Negro, and carried him to the fair grounds on the eastern edge of town where they swung him up by the neck. According to an elderly resident of Cartersville, who claimed to have seen many Negroes dispatched by mobs, it was the "nicest lynching" he had ever seen.

A few days previously, Clark, alleged slayer of the Chief of Police of Cartersville, had been saved by the National Guard from a spontaneous outbreak—a "disorderly" mob.

THE LYNCHING

Facts of Crime Which Caused the Lynching. One Thursday night in mid-September, 1930, Joe Ben Jenkins, Chief of Police of Cartersville, heard a disturbance in front of his house and went out in his night clothes to investigate. In a parked automobile he found and arrested two Negroes, reported to be John Willie Clark and his brother from Chattanooga. Some men passing at the moment were asked by the Chief to detain the Negroes while he went into the house to dress. As he turned away the Negroes started the car and attempted to escape. They did not make a quick get-away, however, and the Chief overtook them, held them at bay with his gun, and struck John Willie Clark over the head with it. The latter grabbed the butt of the pistol and in the scuffle which followed the gun was discharged and the Chief was mortally wounded. Both Negroes escaped.

Accused Negroes Arrested. Shortly afterward John Willie
Clark's brother was arrested near Cartersville. About ten days
later John Willie himself, driving a stolen car, ran out of gas
near Chatsworth, Murray County. He was recognized by the
warden of Chatsworth Prison, with whom he had served a
sentence some time before. In the attempt to arrest him Clark
was shot, but made his escape. Bloodhounds were put on his
trail and doubtless he would have been taken into custody
had he not made friends with the dogs. After considerable hunting the warden and his associates grew tired and returned to
the prison.

The next morning the warden was in Cartersville and told
some of his friends of his experience with Clark. Three Cartersville white boys immediately decided to try their hands
at catching him. They secured guns and bloodhounds and were
successful in picking up the trail and actually located the
fugitive. One of the two boys wanted to shoot Clark when they
came upon him, but the other two would not agree.

The sheriff of Bartow County was notified that Clark had
been located near Chatsworth, and on Sunday afternoon he
was placed in the Cartersville jail. As soon as it was known,
people began to congregate in great numbers. Besides the
mayor of Cartersville, a leading lawyer and a white minister
plead with the mob to leave the Negro's case with the courts.
In the meantime the crowd was becoming more threatening.

*Negro Educator's Part in Frustrating Threatened Lynch-
ing.* At this time, a Negro educator from central Georgia happened to be motoring through Cartersville. On coming into
town he noticed an unusually large number of people standing
around, and accordingly stopped, ostensibly to buy some gas,
to find the cause of the excitement. He learned of the Negro's
alleged crime and sensed from the commotion that a lynching
was very probable. He immediately got in touch with some
of the leading Negroes in Cartersville whom he knew personally. They were unwilling to take a definite stand in the
matter, feeling that any aggressiveness on their part would
be resented by the white people. One of the local Negroes,
however, did get in touch with the resident judge and a white

lawyer, and was assured by both that the prisoner was in no danger.

Feeling that a lynching would occur unless something definite was done quickly, the Negro educator got into telephonic connection with an outstanding Atlanta lawyer, who, in turn, called Governor Hardman, requesting that he look into the matter at once and if necessary send a National Guard unit. Guardsmen were immediately ordered to Cartersville and the threatened lynching was prevented. The accused Negro was moved to Atlanta for safe keeping.

Change of Venue Refused by Judge. When the trial came up on the last day of September, the presiding judge appointed local counsel for Clark. Much to the surprise of the judge and to the obvious displeasure of the people who jammed the courtroom, three lawyers from Atlanta appeared in court, stating that they were counsel for the Negro. Thereupon, the judge excused the counsel he had appointed for Clark. The first move of these "outside lawyers" was for a change of venue, on the ground that the Negro could not secure a fair trial in Cartersville. The judge accordingly called before the court a number of the leading citizens to ascertain whether they thought the Negro could secure an impartial trial. Without exception they stated that he could. In the deliberations the judge inquired whether the defense lawyers would agree to a change of venue to Murray County (where their client had been captured) or to Cobb County (where Leo Frank was lynched some years ago). The lawyers replied that neither would be agreeable, but insisted that the case go to Floyd, or to Fulton, or some county south of Fulton. The judge ruled that a change of venue was not necessary.

The three lawyers then entered an exception to the judge's action, which automatically delayed the trial until a ruling could be had from the State Supreme Court. Seeing that the defense lawyers had postponed the trial, a court official remarked: "Now, if you'd ask me whether this fellow will be lynched, I'd have to say yes."

Armed Escort for Prisoner Refused. Sensing the increased likelihood of violence to their client, the defense lawyers re-

quested the judge to provide an armed escort for Clark back
to Atlanta for safekeeping. The judge refused to send him
back, stating to the packed courtroom that he knew the people
of Bartow County wanted the prisoner kept in the county,
and that this would be done. The judge added that he always
found it desirable to deal frankly with the local people. He
went on to inform the courtroom that the defense lawyers had
necessitated a postponement of the trial and wanted the defendant sent to Atlanta, but that the people of Cartersville
and Bartow County would demonstrate that the accused Negro
would be looked after. The defense lawyers returned to Atlanta; the accused Negro was lodged in the new county jail
at Cartersville. That night Clark was lynched.

"The Nicest Lynching." Shortly after midnight a group
of masked men went to the jail; without a shot being fired,
Clark was taken from his cell to the fair grounds on the outskirts of the town and hanged to an electric light pole. It is
reported that not more than fifty men were in the mob, and
that they came upon the officers "so unexpectedly" that no
resistance was made. Within five minutes they had the Negro
and were gone. Ten minutes later their victim was dead and
they had dispersed. No shots were fired into the body, and
no mutilations were perpetrated.

The whole thing was carried out with clock-like precision.
The victim's brother, who occupied a cell between the entrance
to the jail and his brother's cell, knew nothing of a mob having
been in the jail during the night, and next morning wondered
why his brother's shoes had been brought to his cell. It was
only after the arrival of the defense lawyer from Atlanta that
he learned of his brother's death.

The sheriff, sleeping in a room adjoining the one occupied
by the deputies in charge, reported that he did not know the
mob had come to the jail until they were leaving with the
prisoner. The judge expressed satisfaction that there had been
no mutilations, and suggested that this indicated the "orderly"
way in which the lynching was effected and the "high class"
of people who did it.

"Outside" Lawyers Highly Resented. Many Cartersville

people resented the presence of the National Guard, feeling that it reflected upon the community's ability to handle its own affairs. They were further irritated by the activities of the three Atlanta lawyers. The mob leaders, upon abandoning their early threat on Clark's life, had been assured by a number of leading citizens that if the case were allowed to go to court, the Negro would be sentenced and electrocuted without delay. In disrupting this tacit agreement, the "outside" lawyers had incurred the active hatred of those whites who insisted upon the court's executing the Negro rather than giving him an impartial trial.

A Washerwoman's Rambling Son. John Willie Clark, born at Vienna, Dooly County, Georgia, October 23, 1907, was one of a family of ten. His father died in 1918. Five years later Clark's mother moved to Chattanooga, where she has lived since, making a living by taking in washing. At the time of the lynching, she was living in two rooms on the ground floor of a dilapidated house on a back street. Clark's mother reported that she had as much washing as she could do.

John Willie attended school but very little. He left home when twelve years old, shortly after his father's death, and since that time had never lived with his mother more than a few weeks at a time. After leaving home he worked around garages. Though his mother heard frequently that he had been in and out of Chattanooga, she had not seen him since November, 1929. Prior to that time he had sent her a little money at irregular intervals; since then she had received no assistance from him. She reported that between the time when the Cartersville Chief of Police was killed and her son lynched, many people came to her cabin inquiring about him. She supposed they were plain clothes men who wanted to capture him in order to collect a reward. She did not know of the lynching until she saw it in the papers. Later when she received a telephone call from Cartersville relative to the disposition of the body, she sent an undertaker for it.

Clark had been in the courts on several occasions, having been arrested a number of times by Cartersville officers on charges of theft and having liquor. As already mentioned, he had been a prisoner in Murray County.

REACTION OF THE COMMUNITY TO THE LYNCHING

"Disorderly Mobs" and "Orderly Mobs." When Clark's threatened lynching in Cartersville was prevented at the time of his arrest, the daily press in Georgia and throughout the South pointed to it as an example of how lynchings could be averted. The Atlanta *Constitution* and other papers commented upon the wise procedure of the officers, as well as upon the "forceful" charge of the presiding judge to the grand jury immediately after the frustrated lynching, in which he insisted that the grand jury indict those who had threatened violence. The *Constitution's* editorial said the judge's charge "sounded very much like a church bell ringing a fire alarm," and closed with this statement:

"It would serve greatly to establish an anti-mob public spirit and courage in every county of this commonwealth if all our judges would deliver to their grand juries law obedience and enforcement charges as that delivered by Judge Pittman. The better people of every community, as a rule, give a respectful and even reverent heed to the calm and solemn utterances of their judges, openly delivered from the bench. So the example of Judge Pittman is worth being repeated all over the state."

After the lynching occurred, however, the people of Cartersville justified it. Elsewhere in the state, on the contrary, many of those who had praised the peace officers and militiamen for the prevention of the earlier threatened lynching, were deeply humiliated. The comment of a disgusted citizen in another Georgia town was: "Well, what's the use to protect a man from a 'disorderly mob' and then have the courts and peace-officers permit, if not invite, an 'orderly mob' to lynch him."

Bartow County's "Practically Unanimous Approval" of Lynching. The Bartow *Herald*, Cartersville weekly paper, carried on October 2, the day after the lynching, a reprint of the Atlanta *Constitution's* church-bell-fire-alarm editorial. The *Herald's* subsequent editorial policy, however, was in conformity with peace officers, court officials, and the general citizenry of the town and county in either condoning or justifying the lynching.

On the day following the lynching one of the county commissioners gave a statement to the press in which he attributed the lynching to the unnecessary delay brought about by the Atlanta lawyers. A part of his statement was:

"Had it not been for the appearance of Atlanta lawyers in this case Tuesday and their actions in filing a bill of exceptions which caused postponement of the trial, there would have been no lynching.

"The people of Cartersville and Bartow County were a unit in agreement that Clark should have a fair and impartial trial, feeling sure that the sentence would have been death in the electric chair.

"However, the action taken by the Atlanta lawyers causing postponement of the hearing for an indefinite period so incensed our people that I believe I am safe in saying the action of the men who took the Negro from the jail is not only condoned, but has met with practically unanimous approval."

Judge and Sheriff Blamed by Atlanta Minister. An Atlanta minister, a member of the National Guard unit sent to protect Clark when first threatened, published a signed statement in the *Wesleyan Christian Advocate* of October 10, parts of which were:

"It is hard to understand how any fair-minded judge could have refused . . . to take judicial cognizance of the true state of affairs . . . and to grant the change of venue sought by the accused. . .

"What is the hardest of all to understand, however, is why the accused was deliberately kept in Cartersville. . . . I am also informed that the learned judge in open court gave a full account of all actions in the case to the assembled throng and told them that the accused would be held in the jail of Bartow County until a decision had been reached by the appellate court. I consider this

to be an almost deliberate invitation to the mob to take the accused
and work their will upon him. . . .

"I am also informed that the sheriff of Bartow County, on Tuesday afternoon, swore under oath that the accused was in no danger
from mob violence and only a few hours later allowed the mob to
'take his prisoner from the jail' and hang him. Again, we witness
the disgusting spectacle of an absent sheriff when it is so convenient for him to be absent."

Concerning the activities of the peace officers and court officials at Cartersville, the *Wesleyan Christian Advocate* said
editorially:

"The most charitable thing that can be said for the authorities
is that they were greatly negligent or grossly incompetent. A man
competent to be judge should have discerned the need to return
the prisoner to safety. The sheriff and his deputies should at least
have made some show of resistance. If an uglier charge than negligence or incompetency should be preferred by any one, he could
make out a fairly good case."

Another Vigorous Letter. In the Atlanta *Constitution* of October 3, appeared this signed letter from John A. Manget:

"Editor Constitution:
"In its sixty years of usefulness *The Constitution* has performed
no greater service than that of fighting against anarchy and
mob rule.

"Thank you for printing today and referring editorially to that
matchless article from the Chattanooga *Times* under the caption
'Georgia Disgraced Again.' It hurts, of course, but Georgia is due
the abuse of all right-thinking people.

"Five brutal murders in one year by mobs in Georgia!

"Has Georgia surrendered to the mob?

"Does the 'sovereignty and authority' of the people of this great
state fail before the murderous lust of a cowardly mob?

"Will the government of this commonwealth continue to 'look
foolish and twiddle its thumbs,' or will it put down anarchy?"

"Cartersville Should Erect a Monument." The editorial from the Chattanooga *Times*, referred to above, chided Cartersville and Bartow County: "Cartersville should erect a monument to itself. And upon this monument should be inscribed the words: 'The people of Cartersville and Bartow County do not agree with lynching in principle, but they heartily approve of it in practice.' "

An Atlanta *Constitution's* editorial of October third said among other things, "We cannot claim a sufferable place in the ranks of civilized people if we are to allow our jails to be invaded by mobs, our courts violently robbed of their jurisdiction and the good name of the state smeared with the gruesome blood of lynch murders. The tendency to such anarchy is intolerable and the fair-minded, conscientious citizens of the state must be as one in demanding that it be quenched by every authority and power that the state possesses."

No Indictments. A coroner's inquest was held over the body with the usual verdict: "We the jury find that John Willie Clark came to his death by hanging by the neck by parties unknown to us, or officers, who were overpowered by masked men."

In mid-January a grand jury investigation was made with the same judge presiding who had refused Clark a change of venue. Note the following sentences from the judge's charge:

"It is my duty to ask that you investigate the recent lynching in our town and make a report of your findings touching the same. It is not within my province to direct the kind or character of investigation you shall make. All I am duty-bound to say and require is investigate, find and report in accordance with the oaths you have taken. I am sure you will do this without other suggestions on the part of the court and I am sure nobody will criticise you for performing a sworn duty. . . .

"You and I did not make these laws, but we are sworn to uphold and enforce them."

The investigation amounted to nothing and was satisfactory to the people of the community.

Local Justification of Lynching. The various local justifica-
tions for the lynching constitute a sorry picture indeed. Doubtless the most prevalent justification was that any Negro who
killed a white man ought to be lynched. The next most common
justification was that the Atlanta lawyers, "outsiders," by
postponing the trial, "broke" the "contract" with the original
mob members that Clark would be tried and electrocuted
without delay if the case were left in the "hands of the law."

Others justified the lynching on the ground that Clark's
money, secured from burglaries and auto thefts, and used to
employ able defense lawyers, should not be permitted to save
him from an immediate death sentence. Another current justification was that Clark had been provided with expert legal
defense by an auto-theft gang with which he operated and of
which he was a productive member. Still another justification
was voiced by an officer of the Georgia W. C. T. U. before
an Atlanta audience, where she expressed the conviction that
Clark was a paid agent of Al Capone's rum ring, and that he
had been sent to Cartersville to get Chief Joe Ben Jenkins out
of the way so Capone's liquor trucks could go unmolested from
the Florida ports to Chicago, for along the whole way only
the Cartersville Chief, she said, had refused to be "bought off"
by the rum runners.

Some Revealing Facts. The defense lawyers stated positively
that the small fee promised them was to be paid by the accused
Negro and his family, and that they had no reason whatever
to believe that any auto theft gang or rum ring was interested
in the case, or that either Clark or any member of his family
had more than the scant earnings of casual laborers, washer-
women, and petty thieves. The Atlanta lawyers became identified with the case when one of them, a member of the National
Guard unit at Cartersville ten days before the lynching, was
asked by Clark to defend him. He and his associates became
intensely interested in the case when upon investigating they
began to doubt that Clark was guilty of first degree murder,
and to fear that he would be "railroaded" to his death.

When the county commissioner gave to the press his statement that the lynching had met with "practically unanimous approval," the public looked in vain to Cartersville for a repudiation of the statement. When none was forthcoming, an effort was made by an Atlantan to get at least a few leading citizens to say publicly that they did not justify the lynching. There were some who disapproved, it was found, but none was willing to say so publicly.

Facts About the Community

Bartow County, fifty miles northwest of Atlanta, in the upper Piedmont section of the state, was laid off in 1832. It was first called Cass, the name being changed to Bartow in 1861 because of the "anti-southern position" taken by General Lewis Cass, for whom the county had been named.

Smaller Population Than Two Decades Ago. When the Indians were driven out of this territory the fertile lands along the streams were much in demand. Valuable mineral deposits attracted a still larger number of white settlers. The earliest inhabitants were from the older counties of Georgia and South Carolina, among them being some of the landed aristocratic group who brought their slaves with them. Ten years after the first settlement, it had a population of 13,000, two thousand of whom were slaves.

The county's population increased steadily until 1890, reaching its highest figure in 1910 with 25,388 inhabitants, which was twenty-four more than that in 1930, when the Negro population amounted to 18.4 per cent of the total against 24.9 per cent in 1920. During this decade the Negro population dropped from 6,348 to 4,569. During the past two decades the white population showed an increase of 1,755. The proportion of foreign-born is less than for the state, being 0.1 per cent against 0.5 per cent throughout the state.

County Seat Town on Historic Railroad. After Cassville had been burned by Federal troops, the county seat was moved to Cartersville, which now has a population of 5,250. More than two-thirds of the county's town dwellers live in this one town, which is bisected by the railroad from Atlanta to Chatta-

nooga over which the "General" made its famous run in the
Civil War. Because of its many minerals, Bartow County early
developed manufactures. The first railroad iron made in Georgia was made there. Cartersville has had its share of prominent
Georgia citizens, chief of whom in recent decades have been
the renowned evangelist, Sam P. Jones, and Rebecca Felton,
first woman member of the United States Senate.

Representative Population Elements. The population elements of Cartersville and Bartow County are much the same
as of the other Piedmont counties treated in this report. Within
recent years there has been a tendency for the more substantial
Negroes of Cartersville to sell out and leave the community.
In the meantime, there has been a considerable influx of less
advanced Negroes from the rural sections round about. These
movements are typical of what has gone on throughout the
smaller towns of the South—Negroes moving from the small
towns into the cities, South and North, and rural Negroes
moving into the small towns. The white population shifts in
Cartersville have also been along the same lines.

Many Minerals Mined. With the exception of the mining
interests, the economic situation in Bartow County is much
the same as that of the other two Piedmont counties studied in
this report. No less than a dozen minerals have been mined
since the county was settled. A soil survey of the county,
made by the Department of Agriculture, lists the following
minerals as occurring there, many of them in paying quantities:
Manganese, iron, limestone, barite, ocher, umber slate, shale,
graphite, gold, bauxite, tripolite, agate, and saltpeter. These
mining industries afford a great deal of employment.

Negro Miners Displaced by Whites. The bulk of the workers
in the mines receive a wage of approximately $2.50 per day.
Until the recent depression, when many white farm tenants
began to seek employment in the mines, practically all the
miners had been Negroes. By 1930, it was estimated that more
than half of them were white.

This transition from Negro to white mine labor is of significance in terms of race relations; for in proportion as the

Negroes are not needed in the mines they lose the active interest of the mine operators, who up until this time have been, with the possible exception of a few large planters, the best friends the Negroes have had.

Below the State's Economic Average. Some comparisons of Bartow's economic conditions with those of the state are: In 1924 the per capita value of farm and manufactured products was $255.62 in Bartow County and $310.78 in Georgia. The per capita tax valuation in 1930 was $278.40 for the county and $348.03 for the state. The per capita bank deposits in 1930 amounted to $75.45 in Bartow County and $155.89 in Georgia. In 1929 an income tax return was filed in this county for every 183.1 persons, as compared with one for each 86.6 throughout the state.

Many Small Schools. In 1928, of Bartow County's fifty-one white schools eighteen were one-teacher schools and an additional eighteen were two-teacher schools. Of the fourteen Negro schools, the one at Cartersville had seven teachers or more, while all of the other thirteen were of the one- and two-teacher type.

The annual expenditures in 1928 per white school child were $33.88, which is $3.00 less than the state average. The expenditures for the Negro school child was $6.95, or $1.88 above the state average. In 1930, the county's white illiteracy rate was 6.2 per cent, against the state rate of 3.3 per cent. The Negro illiteracy rate was 13.2 per cent, against 19.9 per cent for the state.

At Cartersville the Negroes have a junior high school with an agricultural department. The Rosenwald Fund contributed toward the building of the nine-room wooden structure. More than half the teachers in this school are college graduates. The county's second Rosenwald school is located at Cassville. It has two teachers. The principal's salary is $35.00 per month and that of her assistant $25.00.

Nine-Tenths Baptists and Methodists. More than ninety per cent of Bartow County's white church members are Baptists and Methodists, the former being nearly twice as numerous as the latter. In 1926, the total white church membership was 9,288: Southern Baptists 5,837, Southern Methodists 2,676, Presbyterians 263, Primitive Baptists 257, a few score Episcopalians, other denominations with smaller memberships.

There are eleven Southern Baptist churches in the county. The only two with full-time pastors are at Cartersville; two others have preaching twice a month, and the remaining seven have services once a month. Only one Methodist church in the county, also located at Cartersville, has a full-time pastor. The Presbyterians live principally in Cartersville, while most of the Primitive Baptists are in the rural portions of the county.

In 1926, of the county's 3,090 Negro church members, 1,824 were affiliated with the Negro Baptist Church; 1,113, with A. M. E.; and 153, with the Methodist Episcopal. With the exception of the half dozen in Cartersville and other urban communities, the Negro churches are served by preachers who receive salaries of about $150.00 a year for once-a-month preaching. Of the five Negro churches in Cartersville, one is served by a preacher from Atlanta, while the other four have resident pastors.

But Few Negroes Vote. Bartow County nearly always goes Democratic, although the Republican vote is considerable. In 1920 there were 754 Republican votes out of a total of 1,676; in 1924, 482 out of 911; in 1928, 628 out of 1,670. In that year over two hundred votes were polled for the anti-Smith Democratic elector, and two for the Socialist candidate.

The Negroes register and vote in small numbers—usually about sixty in Cartersville. According to local Negroes, the white people have no particular objection to Negroes voting.

In a recent bond issue for the erection of an elementary white school building the Negro vote was needed and was frankly sought by members of the board of education and other white people. As a result, sixty-one Negroes registered and voted for the bonds, and not one voted against them. During the erection of the school plant, however, very few Negroes were employed, and the Negroes protested in vain against this discrimination. They reported also that a number of Negroes formerly employed by the city have been replaced by whites.

White Crime on Increase. In 1921 the jail population of Bartow County was made up of 232 whites and 229 Negroes, in 1929 of 433 whites and 187 Negroes. The white jail population increased from 12.3 per thousand in 1921 to 21.1 per thousand in 1929; the Negro rate was 42.2 in 1921 and 40.1 in 1929[1] The increase of criminality on the part of the whites has been due, for the most part, to an increase of crimes against property.

A Lynching in 1916. Prior to the lynching of John Willie Clark on October 1, 1930, there had been no mob death in Bartow County since February 1, 1916, when Jesse McCorkle, Negro, charged with rape, was lynched. Some years before that a mob gathered and threatened a Negro accused of intimacy with a white woman. However, it was dispersed by a telephone message of protest from the daughter of Evangelist Sam P. Jones. Some years ago, a Negro in the upper end of the county was being hard pressed by a mob. A propertyless white man, a friend of the accused, gave him warning and he left the county.

Negroes Accused of Peeping. During the spring and summer of 1930 the white people of Cartersville had been annoyed by reports charging Negroes with peeping at white women. One suspect was sentenced to twenty years for this offense. Another, an uneducated boy of twenty, was jailed.

The only case which involved any direct racial clash was the rivalry for a swimming hole on the premises of a Negro farmer a short distance from Cartersville. In June, prior to the lynching in October, several Negro boys at the swimming hole were attacked by a group of teen-age whites from a nearby textile center. The Negroes made their escape, some of them without clothing.. Next day the Negro boys, who had armed themselves, wounded two of the whites. One of the Negroes charged with the shooting is now serving a sentence and a second is still at large.

[1] The rapid decrease of the Negro population between 1920 and 1930 was commented upon above.

PART FIVE

MOB OUTBREAKS IN NORTH TEXAS AND
CENTRAL OKLAHOMA

DURING 1930 three mob outbreaks occurred in north Texas and central Oklahoma: Sherman, Grayson County, Texas; Honey Grove, Fannin County, Texas; and Chickasha, Grady County, Oklahoma. These cases have many common factors. They occurred within a radius of one hundred miles, and within three weeks—between May 9 and May 31. In each case the mob numbered more than a thousand. Furthermore, the communities have common backgrounds, and at present social and economic conditions are generally alike; population elements are much the same in the three, with the Negro element small, and race relations strikingly similar.

Concerning race relations, the most distinctive thing about this region, in contrast with other sections of the South, is that the white farm tenant element has been forcing the Negroes to leave many rural trade centers and farm communities. In some instances violence has been employed; in others, threatened. At present most Negroes live in or near the largest towns, there are but few in the open country; the white farm tenant element dominates the rural situation, and the rural institutions are relatively undeveloped when compared with those of the older sections of the South.

In the largest urban communities of the three counties, many business and professional Negroes own comfortable homes and other properties. A considerable proportion of the colored people regularly participate in local and national elections. The leading Negroes here live under fewer restrictions than in the older South: The propertied whites, for example, do not circumscribe the Negro's activity to the same degree as in the Black Belt. On the other hand, the propertyless whites in both areas seem to hold about the same opinions of the

Negro's racial inferiority, and of the absolute necessity of "keeping him in his place."

In north Texas and central Oklahoma, however, the Negro does not occupy an indispensable place in the economic order, as he does in the Black Belt. Consequently he does not receive the same degree of protection from the hostility of the "poor whites." Then, too, the propertyless whites of this region are generally frontier-like and characterized by the virile recklessness best described by their phrase, "rough and ready."

Of 1930's four largest mobs, three were in this relatively newer part of the South, which has been the scene of many of the most relentless and destructive mob outbreaks in recent decades. This is not improbably due to the generally militant attitude of the white farm tenant class toward Negroes.

CHAPTER XVI

BURNING DOWN THE COURTHOUSE
SHERMAN, GRAYSON COUNTY, TEXAS

IN THE AFTERNOON of May 9, 1930, the Grayson County court-house at Sherman, Texas, was on fire and George Hughes, Negro farm hand, was sweltering in the second-story vault. The Negro was accused of assaulting a white woman. After firing the courthouse, the rioters chased the militiamen from the square, blasted open the vault, dragged the Negro's body through the streets, and burned it along with the town's Negro business section.

THE LYNCHING

Alleged Crime Which Caused Lynching. As is frequently the case, there were differences of opinion as to the offense which caused the lynching. The explanation featured by certain Negro newspapers and accepted by many Negroes locally was that Hughes was lynched because he went to his employer's house asking for wages and that the employer, being unwilling to pay him, had his wife to report that she had been assaulted. On the other hand, it was current among the whites that the Negro had raped and mutilated the woman.

The facts seem to be these: About the middle of the forenoon of Saturday, May 3, 1930, George Hughes went to the home of his employer to ask for $6.00 wages due him. His employer, a white farm renter, was not at home; his wife told him that her husband was in Sherman and could be found at the Walnut Street hitching lot, or that he could come back at evening and find him at home. The Negro went away.

About forty-five minutes later, he entered the kitchen with a double-barrel shot gun and demanded the money. The woman backed off from his approach through the hall into a bedroom, whereupon he told her that he meant to lie with her and would kill her if she screamed. Then, placing the shot gun on the bed beside them, he assaulted her. Her five year old child, who had climbed up on the bed, was screaming. This distracted Hughes, so he pushed the crying child into the hall and fastened the door. The woman begged him to quit, and promised him all the money in the house. He tied her hands together above her head and continued the assault, telling her that he knew what he was doing, and knew they would kill him for it, but that he meant to satisfy himself and then kill her and her baby. He told her the white folks hated him and his race, and that was why he was assaulting her. He expressed concern as to the whereabouts of the baby, doubtless fearing that it might attract attention and spread an alarm. Upon leaving the woman he told her he was not through with her and that he would be back in a little while. To make sure that she stayed there, he tied her to the bed posts. Taking his shot gun, he went to find the child.

Accused Negro Arrested Promptly. Seeing Hughes in the yard, the woman managed to get loose; she ran across a field to the nearest neighbor. Upon reaching the house unshod, she fell into a swoon, after having told them that Hughes had tried to kill her and the baby. At once the neighbors went to the scene. They found the Negro walking around the barn looking for the crying baby, whom he could hear but could not see because the child had crawled into the hay-loft and had sunk out of sight in the loose hay. When Hughes saw the men coming he left the barn.

The case was reported to the sheriff, and at once officers went to arrest Hughes, who had been followed by neighbors. The officers reported that he shot at them when they were arresting him. Within a few hours after the assault, the accused was in jail and had made a confession of his crime.

Inflammatory Rumors Circulated. The first report was that the Negro had threatened his employer's wife and child. The accused had been placed in jail and that seemed to be sufficent; and members of the family and friends agreed to leave the case in the hands of the law, with the assurance of officials that there would be an immediate trial.

Intense feeling against Hughes developed rapidly following the afternoon of Monday, May 5. The county attorney, the sheriff, and a deputy had gone to the woman's home that morning to secure a statement from her and get other evidence in the case. It appears that their minutest findings were broadcast to the community in a most inflammatory way.

That afternoon the local paper contained a statement that the three officers had been investigating the case. By late evening, exaggerated versions of the crime were widespread. It was reported that the Negro not only had raped the woman three times in succession, but that he had mutilated her throat and breasts, and that he was diseased.[1]

Early Trial Promised. On Wednesday afternoon the paper carried news of Hughes' indictment on two criminal assault charges, with this headline: "Quick Trial Promised for Negro by Officers, After Jury Acts." The article stated that the trial was set for Friday, May 9, the earliest date on which it could be held under the Texas law.

The principal evidence against Hughes was a written statement secured from the woman by the county attorney. Whatever question there might have been in the minds of the court officials and peace officers with regard to the feasibility of trying Hughes in Sherman was set aside because of the insistence of the woman's family that the trial be held at Sherman. Through the press and otherwise, it was generally known that Hughes would be tried there on Friday morning, May 9.

Publicity and Rain in Abundance. It is reported by some of Sherman's leading citizens that, during the days preceding the trial, "Slim" Jones, later indicted as a mob leader, rode throughout the rural portions of the county and into adjoining counties, telling the people of the case and the time of the trial. Some feel that Jones was the oral agent for a senile Klan

---

[1] The physician who examined the woman, and another who examined Hughes, stated that many of the reports were greatly exaggerated and others were without basis of fact—that the woman's throat and breasts were not mutilated and that the Negro was not diseased.

organization which was making this last effort to demonstrate its importance.

On Monday night a small number of people gathered in the vicinity of the jail, and on Tuesday night a larger crowd. Both gatherings were summarily dispersed by officers on duty there. The next afternoon's paper, feeling that it would not be wise to ignore this group of lawless youths, most of whom were around twenty, held them up before the community as "would-be lynchers." The editor stated he figured that ridicule would tend to make mob efforts unpopular.

By Friday morning people were coming into Sherman from all directions. The fact that it had been raining for several days and that for weeks the ground had been too wet to work added much to the general unrest of the rural masses. A case like that against Hughes always attracts a large crowd; the continued rains, leaving the farmers with little to do, resulted in an unusually large crowd.

George Hughes' Trial. At nine o'clock Friday morning, the judge, a young man newly elevated to the bench, called the court to order. No one was admitted to the courtroom except those concerned in the case. The judge had secured Texas Rangers and depended on them to keep order among the crowds that pushed against the courtroom doors. By eleven o'clock, twelve jurymen had been selected. The woman was then placed on a stretcher and carried into the courtroom. Ostensibly to embarrass her as little as possible, the county attorney read her signed statement to the court.

Because of the commotion in the hall at this time, the judge found it almost impossible to continue the case. With difficulty the Rangers cleared the hall and stairs. No sooner had they returned to the courtroom than the corridors were jammed again. When the first witness was called, the courtroom doors were forced open and the room immediately filled. Upon the request of the judge, the jury retired from the room. At about 12:30 the mob leaders insisted that they be given the Negro, who at this time was in the district clerk's second-floor vault, where the county attorney had taken him to secure a third and final confession to read before the court. The Rangers cleared the courtroom by drawn rifles and tear gas bombs. Firemen were called, and with their ladders took people down from the second-floor courtroom.

Courtroom Overrun by Mob. At 12:58 the mob again surged into the courthouse, up the stairs, and into the courtroom. Ranger Captain Frank Hamer discharged a load of bird shot into the crowd, instructing the other Rangers not to fire without his orders. Tear gas bombs were used as before, and again the firemen took down many, among them women and children. At this time Captain Hamer advised the judge that the trial could not be continued without bloodshed, whereupon the judge and court officials went into conference, stating that a change of venue was being considered. This further enraged the mob, already exasperated by the Rangers' use of tear gas. "Let's get the nigger right now," was heard on all sides.

Attempts to get Hughes from the courtroom had been augmented by a woman, seemingly not known to Sherman people, who, while chiding the men for their "yellowness," had persuaded a group of teen-age boys to take the matter in hand. They tore an American flag from the walls of the south corridor and marched round the courthouse, calling for any to join them who had "enough red blood to do something about a nigger who had raped a white woman." This flag-bearing unit pushed into the courtroom and was among those summarily repulsed by the Rangers' tear gas.

The "Don't Shoot!" Rumor Accepted. About noon when the whole situation was halting between the continuation of the trial and the wild rule of the mob, Captain Hamer was reported to have received a message from Governor Moody telling him to protect the prisoner if possible, but not to shoot anybody. This report was received by the mob members with great glee, and added much to their boldness. This report, sent out in an Associated Press release, was commented upon throughout the nation. The exact origin of the report is not known. After an investigation, the military court declared that there was no basis of truth for it. From the outset,

Captain Hamer stated that he had not received such a message, and the Governor denied sending such a message. The Sherman *Democrat* has traced the "don't shoot" story and is convinced that a reporter from Denison—which, by the way, is Sherman's "rival" town—repeated this rumor in the presence of another reporter who gave it out as a fact. There is a possibility that the Rangers, not wishing to fire into the mob, said something among themselves which gave the impression that they had orders not to shoot. But, however this "don't shoot" story originated, the facts are that the mob was greatly emboldened by it.

Courthouse Fired. While the judge was in conference considering a change of venue, the woman was continuing to brag on the boys for their bravery, the "don't shoot" rumor was being repeated, and the county attorney was getting a final confession from Hughes in the district clerk's vault—while all this was going on, a seventeen year old boy threw a can of gasoline through a courthouse window and another pitched in a match. When it did not take fire, this second boy climbed back up to the window, struck a match, and jumped down, saying, "Now the damned old courthouse is on fire." One of Sherman's old residents who saw the boys set the courthouse on fire stated, "The rosters of the Sherman public schools would show the name of every boy in that group."

Dense smoke spread through the courthouse; for the third time, firemen took people from the courtroom by means of their ladders. The four Rangers escaped from the burning building through a second-floor window and left town immediately. When the county attorney and other local officers were forced to leave the burning courthouse, Hughes was given the choice of running or staying in the district clerk's vault, a steel and concrete fireproof room forty feet square and twenty feet high. He decided to stay in the vault. A bucket of water was left with him. The door to the vault was pushed shut but not locked. While the courthouse burned, there was considerable speculation as to what was happening to Hughes: Some claimed that he would be roasted to death; others thought that with the bucket of water he would live.

Captain Hamer explained that he and his Rangers had left town to get in telephonic communication with Governor Moody; they stopped at Howe, a small town a short distance from Sherman, but upon overhearing inflammatory remarks there they proceeded to McKinney, from which place the Captain talked with the Governor.

According to an eye witness, the firing of the courthouse followed immediately upon an excited bystander's having thumbed a pebble against the tax collector's window pane. Others thumbed larger pebbles, and presently small stones and then larger ones were hurled, the latter crashing through the panes into the office.

Fire Hose Slashed. Efforts of the fire department to save the courthouse were thwarted by members of the mob, particularly by "a great big man" who walked about with a "hack knife" slashing the hose whenever the firemen tried to throw water on the burning courthouse.

Many of Sherman's people were shocked to see the courthouse on fire. Some members of the mob claimed that they as citizens had the right to burn down the county's courthouse if they wanted to; others taking a more active part in the violence are reported to have said, "Let 'er burn down; the taxpayers 'll put 'er back."

By late afternoon the courthouse was gutted. The crowd continued to grow. As night came on, concern was expressed as to whether the accused Negro was really in the vault; so, when the fire had died down enough to permit it, arrangements were made to blast into the vault to see whether he was there.

Militiamen Routed. About six o'clock a small unit of militia arrived from Denison. Because of the crowds, they were scarcely able to march around the courthouse walls. Presently, with brickbats, bottles, and scantlings the mobbers forced the militiamen to retire within the county jail. Other militiamen, fifty-two from Dallas, arrived before seven o'clock; after an attempt to restore order on the courthouse grounds they, too, were forced to retire to the jail. In the forefront of the group which rushed the militia were a number of women, one of whom held her baby high over her head with the challenge: "Shoot it, you yellow nigger lovin' soldiers; shoot it!"

Civilian casualties on the afternoon and evening of May 9, according to the Sherman *Democrat*, included: "J. R. Melton, 18, high school youth of Sherman, hit over head with pistol; Walter Bailey hit over head and back of neck with rifle; Don Shero, Sherman, shot with birdshot while in courthouse; Lynn Scott, 17, high school student, hit over eye with a bottle and seriously cut; Weldon O'Neal, 18, Van Alystyne, hit in the back of the head with a bottle." The last two were wounded by their mob colleagues, the other three by the Rangers and militiamen. Among the militiamen wounded was Albert Sidney Johnston, Dallas attorney and Secretary of the Texas State Democratic Committee.

After the militiamen were driven from the square, the leaders of the mob worked to open the vault. Several unsuccessful attempts had been made with dynamite, when an acetylene torch was carried by ladders to a window on the second floor. After some time a hole was cut through the outer steel casings of the heavy shutters; some concrete filling was dislocated; dynamite was placed in the cavity, and the immense shutter was blown from its hinges. When the vault was entered, Hughes' body was found lying near the window with his head crushed in, apparently by fragments from the explosion. Shortly afterwards the limp body was dumped to the demanding crowd below. The water bucket, left with him, was almost empty. There was every indication that the explosion rather than the fire was the immediate cause of his death.

Some people thought the officers should have given the Negro to the mob and saved the courthouse; others felt that they should have protected him at all costs. As it was, neither the courthouse nor the prisoner was saved; nobody was pleased except those who reveled in the destruction of life and property.

Body Burned and Negro Property Destroyed. No sooner had the corpse been dumped to the ground than a chain was put about the neck; it was dragged down Travis Street to Mulberry Street, and thence to the Smith Hotel property, owned and occupied by Negroes, near the Union Station. What the police officers were doing during this time is commented upon as follows by the local paper: "During the time that the mob was on the streets and on the courthouse grounds, and until late at night, city patrolmen were kept busy directing traffic." The woman who accused Hughes of assaulting her was a niece of one of Sherman's oldest and most popular policemen.

Arriving at the Smith Hotel property, the members of the mob went inside the Negro drug store and other shops for chairs and furniture with which to make a fire under Hughes' body, which had been hanged in a cottonwood tree nearby. The funeral pyre was lighted. About this time mob members set fire to the Smith Hotel property. While the body was roasting and the fire was getting under way in the hotel, everything of value was taken. Chewing gum, drinks, and other confectioneries were passed from the shelves to the folks outside, among whom were a goodly number of women, some with small children and babies in arms.

When the fire at the hotel was dying down, a new fire was started in the Andrews Building, a two-story brick structure belonging to Negroes, half way between the Smith Hotel property and the Methodist Episcopal Church, South, on Travis Street at Mulberry. The crowd left the old fire for the new one. It was rumored that every Negro's home in town would be burned. The mob first went to the nearby residence belonging to a Negro physician. This dwelling was occupied by a white tenant. Members of the mob helped him move out his effects and then fired the house; it burned with a great blaze. Immediately across a narrow driveway was a smaller house belonging to a white man; it suffered no ill effects because the fire department trained water on it.

The Smith Hotel property had been on fire forty-five minutes when the fire department came; no water was thrown on the Andrews Building, and no effort was made to save the Negro physician's property. It should be mentioned also that, though the members of the mob had not permitted the fire department to save the courthouse, they did allow water to be trained upon the buildings on the north side of the courthouse square in the afternoon while the courthouse burned. Most of the Negroes had gone to the homes of white friends, or had left town. Negro property was at the mob's mercy.

Negroes were greatly frightened, and their plight was relieved none by county officers, Texas Rangers, or militiamen. A Negro physician who insisted upon the right to protect his property and threatened those who came near his home was arrested on the next day, but was subsequently released. At midnight when other Negroes called the peace-officers and Rangers and militiamen for protection they were told that nothing could be done for them, that they had better get out of town or stay at the homes of white friends. The threat against Negro properties at Sherman was advertised by a radio message from a Dallas broadcasting station which told of the burning of the courthouse and the rumors that the mob would destroy the whole Negro section of Sherman if Hughes were not found in the vault.

The Negro properties destroyed by the mob included two undertaking establishments, residential property, two cafes, the Odd Fellows Hall, two barber shops, two dentists' offices, two doctors' offices, a lawyer's office, theater, K. of P. Building, hotel, life insurance office, and drug store. The Negroes owned most of this property outright, and suffered a loss between $50,000 and $75,000. Because of riot clauses in policies, no insurance money can be collected to replace these losses.

Additional Troops Sent Out. The mob members were intent on yet other fires, and with gasoline and torches were prepared to carry out their designs. One white man saved a half-dozen Negro dwellings by telling mob members that every house in the block where he lived belonged to him. The Negro schoolhouse, Negro churches, and residences were in danger.

At four o'clock in the morning, over two hundred additional militiamen arrived from Dallas. The howls of the mob died down; and the chorus, "Happy Days Are Here Again," was sung with less enthusiasm. A detachment of troops went to the cottonwood tree near the Union Station and cut down the scorched torso of Hughes and gave it for burial to a Negro funeral director who could not bury it because his undertaking establishment had been burned. As Sherman's other Negro undertaker had been burned out, too, a white undertaker was called upon to take charge.

On the following day, yet other troops and other Rangers came to Sherman. Negroes who had fled the city for safety were brought back to their homes by military authorities. For a time, a detachment of militia was quartered at the Douglass Memorial High School for Negroes.

Martial law was declared on Saturday night, and on Monday morning the military court began collecting information concerning those responsible for the death of Hughes and the destruction of the courthouse and Negro properties. The outcome of this investigation and of other court procedure appears later.

The Victim of the Mob. George Hughes was forty-one years old, was an itinerant, illiterate laborer, and had been living in Grayson County but a few months. He was born and grew up at Petty, near Honey Grove, in Fannin County. Hughes and his wife, Mollie, were said by local Negroes to be denizens of the underworld. He had found Mollie "living with" an old man at Plano, thirty miles south of Sherman. He stole her from this elderly paramour, and, after living with her two years as his common law wife, married her; two children were born. Some weeks before the lynching, Hughes had "quit" her.

In the latter part of April, Hughes had been hired by the white renter whose wife he allegedly assaulted. Hughes' wife's story of the assault is that Saturday morning (May 3) he went to the house to find out whether his employer's wife was there alone, and that he later returned to attack her. Hughes' wife emphatically asserted that he was guilty and that he had commented several times on his victim's physical attractiveness and had indicated what he intended to do.

It is almost unanimously reported that Hughes was mentally unstable, some saying that he was crazy and others that he had "spells." The one differing report was that of the county

attorney who maintained that it is "d— foolishness for any
sensible person to claim that Hughes was feeble-minded; he
had as much sense as any 'nigger'—just a d— beast who knew
what he wanted and meant to have it, hell and hanging notwithstanding." The following appeared in the Honey Grove
Signal Citizen of May 16, 1930: "It came to light here this
week that Hughes had changed his name after leaving Honey
Grove, his former name being George Jackson. He worked for
a number of years on a farm south of Honey Grove, and his
former employer stated Tuesday that he was a hard-working
negro and the best help about the farm he had ever had. He
further stated that he was at that time a trusted employee,
although he did not appear to be bright at all times." Though
known as a half-wit, and considered crazy at times by those
who knew him best, it is well established that Hughes had never
been before the courts.

REACTION OF THE COMMUNITY TO THE LYNCHING

The general reaction to the Sherman disorders of May, 1930,
is suggested in the fact that although fourteen people were
indicted only two have been tried, and that they received sentences of but two years each. Moreover, while no money has
been raised to punish the lynchers or to replace the Negro
properties destroyed, house-to-house canvasses have been made
for funds to assist the defendants.

Martial Law and Military Court. The first small units of
the National Guard were not requested until hours after the
courthouse had been fired. It was noted above that both of
these units retired to the jail for protection soon after their
arrival. As mentioned above, next came the two hundred additional militiamen, at four o'clock Saturday morning. During
the week-end others came, until approximately 450 militiamen and Rangers were in Sherman. At the request of city officials and business and professional men who were hearing
rumors and feared further disturbances Saturday night,
Governor Moody issued a proclamation of martial law for
Sherman effective at 10:30 p.m., Saturday, May 10. Martial
law was lifted May 24.

On Monday morning, May 12, a military court of investigation was set up for the purpose of securing evidence for the grand jury. This court continued its investigations for nearly a week. Of sixty-six men and women questioned by this court, twenty-nine were placed in jail to await action of the grand jury. The evidence secured was transmitted to the district grand jury which convened on May 19.

Against each of fourteen, separate indictments were drawn for rioting, engaging in riot to burn courthouse, burglary of courthouse with explosives to commit arson, engaging in riot to commit arson, and engaging in riot to commit murder. Although two or three women were arrested and taken before the courts, no indictments were drawn against them. The people who drove the automobile dragging the body through the streets were unidentified. The family of the victim of the alleged assault was absolved by the military court from responsibility for the lynching and rioting.

Some Facts About the Fourteen Men Indicted. Jeff "Slim" Jones, forty years old and with but little formal education and frequently before the courts for bootlegging, was a member of no church and made a living by trading in livestock. J. B. McCastland, seventeen years of age, previously before the court for cattle stealing, attended but never finished high school; his father, who died some years ago, was a Mason; his mother now works in a Sherman overall factory.

Jesse Roper of Van Alstyne, forty-four years old, with a wife and several children, was reported to be practically propertyless. Cleo Wolfe, eighteen years old, who had but little schooling, was under suspended sentence for burglary. Web Purdon, twenty-three years of age, with a court record for stealing, had very meager education, and belonged to no church and followed no particular occupation. C. E. Briggs of Van Alstyne, about forty-five years of age, has a wife and several children and is very poor. Negroes report that he had "the nerve" to come to Sherman in the summer months following the May disorder and try to sell watermelons to the colored people.

Leonard O'Neal, Jimmie Arnold, and Roy Allen, of Van

Alstyne, and Alvin Morgan, Leslie Cole, Jim May, and Bill Sofey, of Sherman were the others indicted. It was Bill Sofey's father who saved his Negro neighbors' houses by telling the mob members that all the houses in the block belonged to him.

Horace Reynolds, the fourteenth man indicted, middle aged, is perhaps the highest type man in the group; it was reported that Reynolds, a plumber, assisted in the use of the acetylene torch with which the vault was opened.

With the exception of Reynolds, none of the indicted men owned any taxable property; with the exception of two or three of the younger ones who had attended high school a little, none had had any appreciable amount of education. Though some were members of churches, only Reynolds was active in that capacity. Many had court records. The then secretary of the Sherman Y. M. C. A. expressed the opinion that some of the indictments were brought because guilt had to be placed on somebody and the community would least resent the indictment of those already unpopular.

Curious onlookers made the mob look like thousands instead of hundreds, and made it more difficult for local officers, Rangers, and militiamen to deal directly with the mob leaders. The refined, well-poised, propertied people of Sherman, who pushed in around the square to see what was happening, not only did nothing to curb the mob but got in the way of officers and thus indirectly aided the mob.

Repeated Postponement of Trials. In the latter part of May, a change of venue from Sherman to Dallas was ordered for the fourteen men indicted by the grand jury. Accordingly, thirteen of the mob leaders were transferred to the Dallas jail, the fourteenth, Horace Reynolds, having been released on a $2,000 bond. Bond for each of the other thirteen was placed at $5,000, and the Dallas judge refused to reduce the sum. The trials were deferred from June to September, and further delayed by the county attorney, on the ground that he was too busy to try the cases. In the meantime, all but four of the defendants had secured bond, house-to-house canvasses having been made in Sherman to secure money for bonds and defense lawyers.

When the cases finally came up in mid-November, Judge Pippen publicly stated that sixty out of sixty-eight veniremen declared from the stand that they would not convict the first defendant, Jeff "Slim" Jones, even if the evidence against him were conclusive. Judge Pippen attributed his inability to secure a jury in Dallas to the publicity which had been given the Sherman affair. For this reason, the cases were transferred from Dallas to Austin.

Two Two-year Sentences and the County Attorney. But two of these cases have been called by the Travis County court officials at Austin, the reason given being that the court has been jammed with local cases. The two cases tried resulted in sentences of two years each, on charges of arson and riot rather than murder. It is generally believed that the other cases will not be called, and eventually will be dropped.

After the military court had collected its information and the local district grand jury had acted, Robert Lee Bobbitt, Attorney General of Texas, with his assistant, William A. Wade, went to Sherman and assured the people there that the Texas Attorney General's office would aid in the prosecution of the mob leaders. In a formal statement carried by the press, he said: "It is apparent that responsibility for this disgrace to the state of Texas and Grayson County rests with a small number of individuals. The challenge of a few mob leaders in Grayson County has been definitely and emphatically accepted. Every power and resource possessed by the attorney general will be used in coöperation with the officers and law-abiding people of Grayson County to see that the law is vindicated." Although Assistant Attorney General Wade was assigned to aid in the prosecution, the Grayson County attorney seems to have determined the policy in the case.

Though claiming to desire conviction of those indicted, the county attorney grew heated when he discussed Hughes' crime, and seemed quite satisfied with his fate. It has been noted that the county attorney was too busy to go to Dallas when Judge Pippen first wanted to try the cases. Moreover, contending that it would make it harder to punish the mob leaders, he discouraged the efforts of leading white citizens to make friendly public gestures toward the Negroes who lost their property.

The outstanding member of the Sherman bar regretted the whole affair and regarded it as the result of unwise procedure on the part of the officials. He pointed out that the resident judge is a young man recently elevated to the bench, not experienced in such cases, and over-anxious to please the public.

Attitudes of Mayor and Ex-Mayor. On the morning of May 9, 1930, the mayor sat in his office, which overlooks the square, and noticed the unusually large number of people about the courthouse. To him it was a great crowd of countrymen come to town for the Hughes case. The long wet spell had left them with nothing more interesting to do. The mayor looked upon the matter as an affair of the county rather than of the city. The next day, following the riot, he made a statement to the press explaining that though the affair was "regrettable" Sherman was the victim of circumstances. "The Negro had been in the county only a few weeks," he said, and "only a few of the mobists were Sherman people." He concluded, "Sherman is not under martial law and there is no need for it." Many local citizens thought otherwise, however, and at their request martial law was declared and maintained for two weeks.

An ex-mayor, with a party of business men, left Sherman for Dallas at ten o'clock Friday morning, May 9, to take part in a Shrine celebration. Though they had noticed a large crowd about the courthouse upon leaving, they thought nothing of it and were surprised on reaching Dallas to find extras on the streets featuring the mob outbreak. The ex-mayor left Dallas only when the celebration was over and reached Sherman after midnight. The secretary of the Chamber of Commerce, who was in the party, elected to stay in Dallas all night, not wanting to be at Sherman "in all that mob," he said.

Teachers and Preachers. Sherman, notably a city of churches and colleges is often referred to as "the Athens of Texas."

What did the teachers and preachers do and say about this affair? Although many of them saw the mob in action, no evidence was found that they made any effort to oppose it. They went to the scene, saw something revolting, and left without attempting to organize any opposition, perhaps not even considering the possibility of united resistance. In midafternoon columns of smoke from the burning courthouse curled about the church spires and settled on college campuses, and then in the middle of the night came other columns of smoke laden with fumes from burning Negro barber shops, cafes, funeral establishments, doctors' equipment, lodge paraphernalia, and office supplies—and mixed in with it the acrid smell of burning flesh.

Upon his return from Sherman shortly after the disorders, Dr. W. W. Alexander commented:

"One of the discouraging elements in the situation was the helplessness and ineffectiveness of the ministers of the community. I talked with a number of ministers who were on the square from time to time during the afternoon and one minister told me that he sat on his porch only a few blocks away while the mob was blasting the vault to secure the body. I could find no trace of any efforts on the part of these men to disperse the mob or to urge the officers to do so.

"The affair took place on Friday. There were more than twenty churches in the town. On Sunday, some sort of reference was made to the lynching in four of the churches. On Monday, the ministers were called together by one of the young pastors, a recent graduate of the Vanderbilt School of Religion, and chairman of the Ministers' Alliance. Ten or twelve ministers and the Y. M. C. A. Secretary attended. Of that number, only four felt that the ministers should make any statement. It is to the credit of the pastor emeritus of the Presbyterian Church, Dr. Wharton, that he had started in that congregation an effort to raise money to replace the property belonging to Negroes which had been burned by the mob. The majority of those present at the meeting on Monday, however, thought it was not safe to vote approval and to coöperate in raising this fund."

The four ministers who denounced the mob on Sunday following the burning of the courthouse served the First Baptist, First Methodist, Disciples, and First Presbyterian Churches —the four largest in town. The pastor of the last named church asked for a standing vote as the congregation's condemnation of the lawlessness. Everyone arose. In the smaller churches no mention was made of the matter except in one or two cases, and then the people openly expressed their disapproval of bringing the matter into the church. The pastor of a small church in east Sherman who made bold to denounce the mob was waited upon immediately and told that he must leave off speaking about such matters if he wanted to continue his present work.

Though some headway was being made by the elder Dr. Wharton among his personal friends in raising money to restore the Negro property destroyed, the plan was discontinued at the request of the county attorney who insisted, as already noted, that this procedure would interfere with his chance to convict those under indictment by the grand jury.

Resolutions reaffirming opposition to mob violence and condemning the Sherman affair in particular were adopted by Southern Methodist General Conference, then in session in Dallas.

Mass Meeting Resolutions. A week after the courthouse was burned, two hundred citizens of Sherman met to assist authorities in lifting martial law. At the request of the resident judge, J. C. Dillard presided, and the following resolutions were unanimously adopted:

"Be it resolved by the people of Sherman in meeting assembled:
"1. That we deeply deplore and unreservedly condemn the acts of the mob made up partly of rioters from the city but greatly augmented by others from a distance, which assembled in this city last Friday. No greater outrage could have been perpetrated upon a worthy people.

"2. That we are profoundly grateful for the presence and protection of the National Guard and the Rangers.

"3. That we pledge to all officers, military and civil, all the as-

sistance and co-operation we can render in their efforts to apprehend and punish all guilty participants in the riot.

"4. That we tender our utmost co-operation in safeguarding all
our people and their property, in re-establishing order and banish-
ing all apprehension of danger; and in these efforts we invoke the
support and co-operation of all good citizens of the county and
elsewhere.

"5. We heartily approve the steps now being taken under which
will be promptly organized an efficient force which will act with
the National Guard and Rangers as long as they are with us in
apprehending and bringing to punishment the guilty and in protecting the safety and property of all our citizens, irrespective of
color, and which force will so continue to act after the guards and
Rangers are withdrawn."

A Mother's Letter. Writing to her absent son, a prominent
Sherman woman thus described the affair:

"I'm glad you were not here to witness our terrible disgrace—
indeed I'm glad I had no son to blush for in the midst of a spine-
less population. Were I a man I'd hang my head in shame. As it is
I feel polluted by the contact. Truly it was Sherman's 'Black
Friday.' Twelve good men and true could have quelled the mob—
even one brave man could have organized a defense—but it was
nobody's business. Our Mayor helplessly walked the streets. Our
Rotary and Kiwanis, valiant trenchmen, were not in evidence. . . .

"When word came that a mob was trying to burn the courthouse
my neighbor called me to go with her down town. Black smoke
was rolling from the courthouse. In a few moments it was a mass
of flames and not a drop of water turned on it. The mob, they
said, cut the hose! It was like a circus day crowd looking on a
pageant. I walked on three sides of the square weaving in and out
of the crowd. There was no sign of any mob that I could see. It
was just a curious crowd of men, women, and children. I saw
almost everybody I knew—lawyers, doctors, preachers—nobody
seemed to know what was going on except that the old courthouse
was burning. A policeman, his big silver star glistening on his
breast, walked aimlessly along. I asked him if the Negro was in the

burning building. He insolently replied that he 'didn't know and didn't care.' The indifference of the crowd was amazing. The lawyers were deploring the loss of the records. The preachers, I did not interview. Certainly nobody was trying to get the women and children out of the crowd or to organize the men for defense of law and order. Nobody apparently realizing the gravity of the situation. . . .

" 'It was pitiful to see a whole cityful' passing the buck, for that was what it amounted to. At that time there were no soldiers here. The four rangers were powerless unless they were upheld by citizens and no help was forthcoming. The truth is, son, that the 'white ants' had done their work, undermining the foundation of our civic structure. It crumbled at the touch of lawless hands.

"I heard that the preachers in their pulpits today deplored the horrible tragedy, but if they had lifted their voices against mob law when sheeted figures were sowing the seed that ghastly fruit would never have hung from the court yard tree.

"Judge—— thinks the word went out from deserted Klaverns to come to Sherman for the trial, as a last desperate effort to fan into flames the dying Ku Klux fires. Be that as it may, Oklahoma cars were thick on our streets and strange faces led the attack. However, I saw nothing of any attack, and I was there from 2:30 until 4. Our officers, sheriff, county attorney, and judge, tried to do their duty, I suppose, but you know they could not have used any judgment, they were not able to handle the situation. If they had had their masks and sheets on they might have functioned. As it was, they are criticized on both sides. The most outspoken critic of the mob was ———— ————. White with anger he denounced them, and I thought 'Yes, son, your birds have come home to roost and you don't recognize them.' You know he was a great K. K. Our poor Negroes are panic stricken. For two nights they hid in the woods, cold and rainy as it was, young and old, and infirm and sick.

"Saturday afternoon I went down town and the streets were full of country women, apparently gloating over the outcome. One woman in a group of a dozen declared she wished they had burned every 'nigger' in Sherman. ———— ———— declared she wished she had been allowed to fire the torch that burned him. It is certainly discouraging.

"I understand the matter of taking up a subscription to reimburse the Negroes whose property was burned was broached at the Pastors' Conference by the Presbyterian ministers. The principal pastors were in favor—but the outlying churches—in the poorer districts, cotton mill, Frisco shops, etc., refused. Their pastors said it would be utterly useless to say a word, as their members were greatly in favor of the mob. So far, no steps have been taken. Really it is very discouraging. I wonder what the churches have been teaching in the past twenty years—that their flock should be so savage."

Although there were many women in the Sherman mob, but few of the more cultured women were in sympathy with it. It is reliably reported, however, that one of Sherman's prominent women, on the square at the time of the rioting, advocated the burning of the accused Negro. Equally inexcusable was a Sherman grandmother who got her two grandsons out of bed at midnight and took them some blocks away to see the body of George Hughes roasted. One of the town's leading women in church and civic affairs stated that, though the matter was discussed at various meetings, no public statement was ever made by any organization with which she was connected.

Resentment and Rationalizations. A large proportion of the people of Sherman and rural Grayson County resented the establishment of martial law and the military court investigation. The "nigger," so they felt, got what was coming to him. "Why all the fuss?" Many substantial rural citizens pointed out that the only protection which their wives, sisters, and daughters have against such brutes as Hughes is that a public example be made of one now and then.

From the very outset Sherman people tended to rationalize the affair. Some compensation was found for the destruction of the courthouse in the statement that it was old and in a state of decay—in "a dangerous condition," said the Sherman *Democrat* of May 18.

With regard to the Negro properties destroyed, the common opinion, which was echoed by the press, was that the Smith Hotel had long been a public nuisance—an attitude which tended to justify its destruction.

Riot as Phase of "Battle for Bread." Negroes of Sherman reported that trouble between the races had been threatening for many years. The uncertainty of employment and the slump of farming had further embittered the propertyless whites who openly begrudged the Negroes any evidence of accumulated savings or of regular employment. For example, the bellboys in the Grayson Hotel had been displaced by white boys about 1928, while within the six months previous to the disorders of May, 1930, white people had applied for the places of many Negro janitors. The appearance of Negro business on Mulberry Street further incensed the propertyless whites.

The fact that everything of value was taken out of the Negro buildings before they were burned was interpreted by Negroes as indicating that the mob members wanted what these Negroes had. In a more philosophical mood, the Negroes spoke of the riot as a phase of a long standing "battle for bread" between the poorer whites and the Negroes of this section. A white boy of thirteen years, when asked why the buildings had been burned, replied, "I guess they burned them to get the 'niggers' out of the town; but they didn't leave."

Attitudes of Leading Negroes. One of Sherman's Negro physicians, with a large white practice, rented an office on the edge of the white business section, within a block and a half of the burned courthouse. His office was not molested, but a house belonging to him was burned. When asked why he had made no public protest, his reply was, "Do you think I want to move my office?" Another physician, who saw his office burned and then faced the mob at his home and threatened to kill anyone who entered, was arrested by the military court for carrying a gun and making threats, but was subsequently released. Many of his white friends commended him for protecting his dwelling. A Negro dentist, who lost valuable office equipment in the fire, was unable to collect any insurance, but plans to reopen his office.

The leading negro preachers felt it was fortunate that the mob did not destroy even more property.

Negroes' Doubt of Hughes' Guilt. Many Negroes do not believe that Hughes was guilty of the alleged assaults; their theory of the affair, which has already been set forth, is based on these considerations: Hughes was not openly accused of the assault until after he had been in jail two days; skepticism as to the truth of the officers' charge that Hughes had fired through their windshield; underground reports that members of the police had stated that the charges were greatly exaggerated. The lack of concern for the protection of Negro life and property convinced many Negroes that the guilt or innocence of Hughes was really a matter of no concern to the mob and to the white public.

Fewer Jobs for Negroes. On Tuesday after the courthouse was burned on Friday, typewritten notices were posted in Sherman's Negro section warning them to leave in twenty-four hours. Other notices were sent to employers of Negro laborers in both Sherman and Denison, demanding that they replace them with white help within thirty-six hours. The military court, then in session, requested employers to retain their Negro laborers, which they did for the time being. The Negroes report, however, as does also the secretary of the Chamber of Commerce, that since May, 1930, many Negroes have been replaced by whites.

Sherman Pays the Bill. The mob outbreak cost Sherman many thousands of dollars and will cost a great deal more before the damage is repaired. To build a new courthouse will require at least $100,000, perhaps much more. Other items in the bill are office rent for courthouse officials; expenses for guardsmen and state officers sent to the scene; and the salaries and expenses of the fifty men who served under the Director of Public Safety when martial law was lifted. Other properties destroyed constitute an additional loss of nearly $100,000, for no insurance has been collected due to riot clauses in the policies. The Negroes' equity of about $50,000 in these properties represented their life-time savings. They feel that if the insurance companies are not liable the city and county should be; and suits to determine this issue are possibilities.

The indirect financial losses incident to the riot can only be surmised. Merchants report that the riot has made it more difficult to secure loans on their property and merchandise. Charred courthouse walls are not an inducement to new industries. Through wide publicity concerning the affair, Sherman, lawlessness, and courthouse burning have become synonymous in the public mind.

As great as are the direct and indirect money costs which Sherman is paying for the mob outbreak, it is easily possible that the greatest losses are ethical and moral. Lawlessness was supreme. The people who made this condition by demanding it or by acquiescing in it together stand indicted. The assumptions, hatreds, fears, and evaluations which made this state of lawlessness possible indicate not only views which hold valueless Negro life and property, but give to white people the license to violate their own laws, ignore their own officials, chase their own Rangers and militiamen from the courthouse square, and set fire to their own public buildings. The unwholesome ethical effects of such unrestrained barbarities are too obvious for comment.

Throughout the nation more newspaper space was devoted to the Sherman tragedy than to any other lynching of 1930. That a courthouse, the symbol of law and order and justice, had been burned made the story headline-news everywhere.

Courageous Stand of Sherman's Daily. Sherman's daily paper, the *Democrat*, played a splendid part. Full accounts of the affair appeared each day. When the fourteen men were indicted, the story along with their pictures appeared on the front page. The editor, a young college man, did his part to render dignity to the courts prior to May 9, and to secure adequate punishment of the mob leaders; he wrote numerous

vigorous editorials and reprinted others. The editorial in the
Democrat on the day after the outbreak was:

"Sherman woke up Saturday with her name in every morning
paper in the United States, and over the civilized world where
newspapers are published, and it was not a very complimentary
notice that this city that boasts of her churches, schools, colleges,
beautiful homes and splendid people, received. It does not seem
reasonable that the people of the civilized community should burn
down their courthouse, their temple of justice, where the law is
supreme, and where every citizen, no matter how rich or how
poor, should be able to go and be given a trial on any charge before
twelve of his fellow citizens. . . . The mob is never right. It is
always wrong, and unreasonable, and dangerous, and no half dozen
Texas rangers are able to cope with that number of men gone mad.
Sherman's name has been dishonored by the people of her own
county. It will take a generation to outlive the stain on her honor,
if it can ever be done."

An editorial of May 12, "Martial Law in Sherman," concluded, "It is not a time to say that it is to be regretted that
we are under martial law. The thing to regret is the condition
that has sent martial law here. . . ."

Defensive Attitude of Neighboring Papers. The Denison
Herald, chief competitor of the Sherman *Democrat* in Grayson
and adjoining counties, carried detailed news stories of the disorders. Sherman people reported that this neighboring paper
at first was inclined to make capital of Sherman's misfortune.
After a few days, however, when the press everywhere was
holding Denison along with all of Grayson County and northeast Texas accountable for the Sherman mob activities, the
Herald featured an editorial "Mass Insanity," finding comfort that—

"Out of the deluge of criticism hurled at the South because of
such regrettable occurrences as the recent mobbing at Sherman,
there is occasionally an editorial expression which stands out be-

cause of its fairness and sanity of viewpoint . . . a statement from the New York *Telegram* . . . worthy of reproduction: 'Because these debauches often take the form of Negro lynching, it is mistakenly assumed that this is a racial issue. It is not. The proof is that whites as well as blacks are lynched. Nor is it a sectional issue . . . whether the hysteria destroys a negro in a backward Texas town, or a Sacco and Vanzetti in 'cultured' Boston, the mental disease is essentially the same. There is no reason for the rest of the country to be self-righteous toward Texas.' "

Of all the papers in the vicinity of Sherman, only the *Democrat* has been persistent in deploring the activities of the mob members and in demanding their punishment. Nevertheless, the editor of the *Democrat* on May 18 offered some consolation to the people of Honey Grove, where a mob outbreak had just occurred, by saying, "This is an unfortunate occurrence, but the officers could no more help it than could a single man change the course of the Mississippi river when it gets on a rampage. Sherman knows how to sympathize with the good people of Honey Grove and Fannin County, for Sherman has just gone through a similar experience."

Condemnation From General Press. The rumor of Governor Moody's "Don't Shoot" instructions, the fact that the Texas Rangers had not lived up to their reputation, and the helplessness of the two units of militia were all commented upon widely. The *Daily Oklahoman* pointed out that the Texas militiamen "stand convicted of inefficiency or of poorly disguised sympathy for the mob." The Nashville *Tennessean* said: "It was not the Negro in the courthouse vault who suffered most. It is not the helpless Negroes who fled their homes because of the wild passions of barbarism who were the real victims. No, the real victim of that horrible orgy of crime and violence is our boasted Anglo-Saxon civilization." According to the Fort Worth *Star-Telegram*, "Sherman is the chief sufferer; it is the city and the people of the city who are the chief victims of the mob. The good people of Sherman and of the surrounding country who appeared on the scene out of curiosity during the mob's activity were no part of the mob, but they protected the mob and gave it cover under which to work." An editorial of the El Paso *Times* declared that—

"Friday, May 9, ever will go down in the annals of Sherman, Texas, as 'Black Friday,' the day when the citizens may well put on the sackcloth and ashes and mourn the incident which in a flash stripped them of the veneer of civilization, showing them up worse than the poor black wretch they roasted alive in the vault of their courthouse. The 'roasting' and 'toasting' of Negroes cannot be tolerated no matter what their crime. They must be accorded the right of trial by law. Texans themselves must guarantee that if the Lone Star means anything. We must have no more 'Black Fridays' in Texas."

Scores of papers expressed the hope that the guilty would be punished. "The perfect identification and execution of a few mob leaders," said the Atlanta *Constitution*, "would soon put an almost total end to these damnable savage episodes in our communal life."

Approval of Some Papers. The press was not unanimous in its denunciation of everything that happened at Sherman. In the Fort Worth *Press*, for example:

"From out of the horror and disgrace of the rioting and incendiarism at Sherman recently there came one outstanding performance of merit for which Texans may well be proud. That was the conduct of her National Guardsmen. . . . Possibly the Guardsmen could have laid down a barrage that would have scattered the mob. But such a process undoubtedly would have seen many innocent bystanders killed. At least half of those onlookers were women and children. The mob was not dispersed. Instead many lives were saved. So that's the bright side of the situation."

The Paris, Texas, *News* gave Sherman this word of comfort: "People must realize that the things which happened at Sherman do not serve as an index to the lives and habits of any community, as none are immune to such evidence."

Position of Negro Press. The Negro papers carried volumi-
nous comments on the "Don't Shoot" story, which, it seems,
was taken at face value both before and after its falsity had
been established by the military court. The *Afro-American* on
May 24, a week after the military court had declared the
story unfounded, had an editorial captioned "Lyncher Dan,"
stating that Governor Moody had denied the "Don't Shoot"
story: "The Associated Press which previously quoted Moody
as saying, 'hold them if you can but don't shoot anybody.'
carried a retraction. . . . The first statement of the Associated
Press was, no doubt, correct; and the denial is probably a
lie." In concluding, the editorial asked Governor Moody the
following question: "If you didn't order the militia not to
shoot, why was it that they didn't?"

On May 24 the Houston *Informer* carried a half-column by
William Pickens entitled, "Texas Governor Incites Mob Violence," two sentences of which were "But Dan Moody's wire is
so far the worst outrage committed against law and decency
in the history of mob violence. . . . Old Bill Sherman once said,
'If I owned both hell and Texas, I would rent out Texas.' Well,
Governor Dan Moody is a disgrace even to Texas."

Most unusual of all the reports on the Sherman affair was
that appearing in the Chicago *Defender*, which claimed to copy
an article which appeared in the London (England) *Evening
Standard*. This article purported to carry the exact statements
of Governor Moody as received by a correspondent of the
London paper by direct telephone conversation. The part dealing with the "Don't Shoot" story credits Governor Moody with
the following:

"Texas people go mad if a black touches a white woman. When
they saw Mrs. Farlow lying in that stretcher they went white
hot. . . . Our boys used tear gas and fire hose and drove 'em off.
Then the mob went screaming mad. Women got kerosene and the
men dashed it all around the courthouse and fired it. I got a message
immediately, and so I ordered reinforcements to get to the spot
and gave the commanding officer the order to hold the black man,
but not to shoot one white man. . . ."

Many Negro newspapers throughout the nation carried a story by Roscoe Dunjee in which he said college boys and girls, and women with babies in their arms gleefully sang "Happy Days Are Here Again" while the vault was being dynamited; and Sherman people of both races sitting in the privacy of their homes heard this radio broadcast from a Dallas station: "Vault is now being entered at the courthouse. Mob leaders are rumoring if Negro is not discovered in the vault that they are going to kill every Negro in Sherman and burn their homes."

FACTS ABOUT THE COMMUNITY

Grayson County has been looked upon by Texas as one of the state's leading counties. It will be seen, however, that these claims are for the most part booster phrases which more nearly described the county decades ago, when they were coined, than at present.

Population Growth and Recent Decline. In 1843, Grayson County was laid off from part of the old Peters Colony. The first surveys had been made in this area in 1841-2. By 1850 the county had a population of 2,008. There was a rapid population increase for the next two decades, and in 1870 the county had 14,380 inhabitants. During the next two decades, the population nearly quadrupled, being 52,211 in 1890. For the next thirty years the increase was steady; 74,165 people lived in the county in 1920. The population density was 78.8 persons per square mile and nearly one-half of the people lived in the incorporated towns, the largest of which were Denison and Sherman, with populations of 17,065 and 15,031, respectively.

The 1930 census figures showed 8,322 fewer people living in the county than in 1920; during this decade the population increase of the state was 24.9 per cent. Denison fell to second place, losing nearly one-fifth of its population, while Sherman became the largest town, with a gain of 4.5 per cent. The smaller towns and the rural portions of the county lost nearly 5,000 people in the decade.

Range Lands. During the county's first quarter century,

1845-1870, the land was taken up in open ranges; native grass, growing in profusion, "often reached," according to an old settler, "a man's shoes on a sixteen-hand horse." The fertile soil lent itself to general agricultural purposes, and from the outset small tracts were cultivated.

In 1848 a state legislator, T. J. Sherman, had the county seat moved to his plantation; there it has remained. Decades later, a stone courthouse, one of the best in Texas, was built at a cost of $30,000. This courthouse, later renovated, was burned by the mob of May, 1930. In 1867 the Texas Almanac pointed out that "the county seat town Sherman is a small town with two churches and a fine school, established and equipped by the Odd Fellows."

Slaves in Grayson County. When the county was opened up, settlers came in from everywhere, including many from the slave states who brought their slaves with them. The proportion of Negroes in the total population has decreased from decade to decade. By 1890 the Negro element had dropped to fifteen per cent, and in 1930 it was scarely ten. There were fewer Negroes in the county in 1930 than in 1890.

Throughout the history of Grayson County, which is located on the northwest rim of the slave plantation area, the mass of whites, most of whom are tenants, have openly resented the presence of Negroes. Immediately north of Grayson County in Oklahoma, as in Clay and other Texas counties to the west, scarcely any Negroes are allowed. Within the last few decades, for reasons which we shall discuss later, Negroes have been driven out of several communities in Grayson and adjoining counties.

Railroad Shops and Barbed Wire. The phenomenal increase of population during the second quarter-century of the county's history, 1870-1895, was due in large part to the construction of railroads and the establishment of railroad shops, and also to the introduction of barbed wire, which, in the absence of timber for rail fences, stimulated farming by making it possible to fence cultivated fields without prohibitive expense.

In 1872, Denison, the largest town of Grayson County in 1920, came upon the map. It was built in a cornfield at the terminus of the M. K. and T. Railroad, on a plantation belonging to a Mr. Mitchell, "who had a lot of darkies to cultivate his crops." By 1895 there were well over a hundred miles of railroad in Grayson County, and the shops at Denison employed several hundred people.

During the twenty-five years ending with 1895, Sherman had a population increase of 500 per cent, and with its "elegant opera house," spacious churches, good schools and colleges, and "a community of refined people" had come to be called the "Athens of Texas."

With the increase of population and the extended use of barbed wire, additional lands were put into cultivation. Land was valuable in the county, and to preserve deeds and abstracts about 1890 the county built on the northeast corner of the courthouse what is reported to have been the largest fireproof vault in the world at that time, 40x40x40 feet in size. It was in this vault that George Hughes met his death.

Many Industries. The third quarter-century of Grayson County's history, 1895-1920, was characterized by the development of industry in Sherman, Denison, Van Alstyne, and some of the other smaller towns. In 1909 the railroad shops at Denison had a monthly payroll of $300,000, and by 1920 Sherman had numerous industries, including flour mills, knitting mills, lumber plants, gin and mill machinery manufacturers, nurseries, oil mills, slaughter houses, a tannery, and a pickle factory. The county boasted the largest cotton mill in Texas, the largest peanut factory in the South, and the largest creosoting plant in the world.

The chief industrial concerns in Sherman in 1930 were the Hardwick-Etter Company, manufacturers of fifty different kinds of machinery and by-products; Sherman Manufacturing Company, which consumes 6,500 bales of cotton annually; Sherman Compress, with a daily capacity of 1,000 bales; Emeolake Milk Products Company, with a daily capacity of 110,000 pounds of whole milk plus 5,000 pounds of butter; and four milling companies, with a total daily output of twenty-four carloads of flour, meal, and feeds.

Sherman still refers to herself as a well-balanced city of

industry, agriculture, and schools, with a larger per capita value of manufactured products than any city in the southwest. It is the fifth largest industrial center in Texas. Sherman is well served by railways and bus lines; it has a modern air port and ample electric and natural gas service for home and industry. A healthy relation exists between capital and labor: and 6,300 people are employed in factories, wholesale houses, and Frisco shops. The city is the home of the Red River Valley Fair, has a $150,000 mausoleum, twelve beautiful parks of seventy-eight acres, eighty miles of paved and gravel streets, a modern theater of Italian architecture, splendid newspapers, and "magnificent churches, and a citizenship that believes in progress, law and order." So runs the Sherman Chamber of Commerce publicity.

Urban and Rural Economic Retrenchment. During the last decade, economic conditions in Grayson County have resulted in a loss of population. Though Sherman has been affected to some degree, the real slump has been in Denison and in the rural portions of the county.

The railroad shops at Denison are being absorbed by the shops in the larger cities. Denison's payroll is scarcely one-third what it was fifteen years ago. Its population will doubtless continue to decrease.

The rural areas kept pace with the urban communities during their development between 1870 and 1920. Thousands of acres were transferred from ranch to crops. By 1920, over half the county was in cultivation, with corn and cotton in the lead and oats a distant third. Along with the decrease of urban population in the last decade was a decrease of the rural population, the number of farmers in the county having decreased 7.2 per cent.

White Farm Tenants and Negro Urban Property Owners. There is a large element of propertyless whites in both urban and rural Grayson County. Of the 5,002 farmers in the county in 1925, more than two-thirds were tenants. It is significant, too, that there were but 315 Negro farmers. Rural Grayson County is obviously "whiter" than the urban communities, for in 1930 over ten per cent of the county's population was Negro.

Within the last decade, when the mass of white people in the county have found it more and more difficult to make a living, the Negroes have bought several pieces of Sherman property on Mulberry Street, the leading thoroughfare from the Union Station to the retail district. This was the property which the mob destroyed in May, 1930.

Two physicians, a dentist, and a bishop of the C. M. E. Church are the most prosperous Negroes in Sherman. A number of others own their homes, some of which are in excellent repair and well furnished.

Economic Rank of County. The following data indicate how Grayson County compares with the general Texas average: The per capita assessed value of taxable property in 1930 was $684.34 in this county and $743.07 in Texas; bank deposits per capita were $186.40 compared with $206.05 in the state. In 1928 an income tax return was made for every 66.8 persons in Grayson County, against one for every 51.9 persons in Texas; while for each auto there were 4.7 persons in the county and 4.2 in the state. Although the value of manufactured goods is high, these above data suggest that from the standpoint of material things Grayson does not now hold her former place among Texas counties. The decline of industry and agriculture in the last decade has caused many of the most capable young people to seek their fortunes in Dallas, Houston, and other of the South's rapidly growing cities. A leading lawyer of Dallas, for example, pointed out that the youngest first-rate lawyer in Grayson is sixty years old.

Sherman—"Athens of Texas." Decades ago Sherman was known far and wide for its colleges. Austin College, Presbyterian, established in 1849, is a co-educational institution with an enrollment of over four hundred; it has been among the approved colleges of Texas since 1898. The second oldest, Kidd-Key College of the Methodist Episcopal Church, South, was established in 1871; it has an enrollment of about four hundred, and since 1918 has appeared among the approved Texas colleges. The music department of this school is especially well known and retains the high reputation it gained when it operated independently as the North Texas Conservatory of Music. The St. Joseph Academy, Catholic, was established in 1876; it is a co-educational institution with an enrollment of over a hundred. Another institution of high rank, the Carr-Burdett College of the Christian Church, established in 1894, was discontinued a few years ago. The Sherman Business College provides training comparable to that of business colleges elsewhere.

Relatively Poor Rural Public Schools. In 1930 there were 39 one-teacher and 44 two-teacher white schools in Grayson County. A larger percentage of the rural white children in this county attended one- and two-teacher common schools than for the state as a whole, and the teachers receive a smaller annual salary, the average being $722.62 against $811.42 for similar schools throughout the state. The average salary of the Negro teachers is also below the state average. Grayson County's relatively low illiteracy rates in 1920 and in 1930 for whites and Negroes suggest that the schools in earlier years were relatively better than now.

Throughout the common school districts in this county, a white teacher is provided for each 32.2 children of school age, as compared with a Negro teacher for each 66.2 children.

The independent districts in the county have larger schools, longer terms, and better paid teachers. The public school for Negroes in Sherman, the Fred Douglass Memorial, gives instruction in all grades through high school. This eleven-teacher school is accredited by the state, and is housed in a brick building. The school operates for nine months and the principal is on an annual salary. The high school teachers receive a maximum monthly salary of $90 and the elementary teachers, $80. Two of the teachers have A.B. degrees and two have B.S. degrees. Of the total enrollment of 448, one hundred and twenty are in the high school department. For the last five years sixteen to eighteen of this school's graduates have gone to college annually.

It is generally reported that conditions in the Sherman white high school were most unsatisfactory prior to the mob outbreak, a number of boys had been giving serious trouble in the community. More than one of them, it is reported, had participated in petty thievery, and its logical outgrowth, robbery. It has been observed already that white boys of high school age took an active part in the early stages of the mob activities, including the firing of the courthouse, and several attempts to take the prisoner prior to and during the trial.

Relatively High Church Membership. Among both whites and Negroes, Grayson County's church membership exceeds the rate of the state as a whole. In 1926 the number of white church members in the county was equal to 66.7 per cent of the white populaiton of fifteen years of age and over, in contrast with 59.4 per cent of this age group throughout the state; of the county's Negro population 85.4 per cent were members, whereas for the state the ratio was but 53.7 per cent.

Of the white church membership of the county, 9,398, or nearly one-half, are Southern Baptists; the Methodist Episcopal Church, South, comes second, with 6,538 members; and the Disciples of Christ third, with 2,610; then follow Presbyterians, with 1,849; Roman Catholics, 1,442; American Baptist Association, 830; Protestant Episcopalians, 445, and Primitive Baptists, 146.

Sherman people take pride in their churches. The location there of the Presbyterian, Methodist, Catholic, and Christian colleges grew out of local interest in church affairs. The Negroes, too, have boasted exceptional churches. The C. M. E. Church, with a membership of 412, has a plant which cost $40,000, and a bishop of this church resides in Sherman. The four leading Negro ministers in Sherman receive annual salaries of from $1,200 to $1,800 in addition to parsonages.

The white ministers of Sherman have a Ministers' Alliance, and a spirit of friendly coöperation has existed between the pastors of the various denominations. The Negro pastors, too, have a Ministers' Alliance.

Grayson County at the Polls. Grayson County, generally Democratic by almost two to one, polled a Republican majority of 1,679 in the 1928 presidential election. This shift doubtless resulted in part from the interest of the Baptist and Methodist denominations in the "prohibition issue." The number of votes cast in the county in 1924 and again in 1928 was approximately 35 per cent of the white people of voting age. A number of Negroes vote in all elections; their influence is not great, however, due to their small number and their lack of effective leadership.

Lynch-Law Heritage. One of the oldest and best known citizens of Sherman stated that the county has always been peaceful and has always maintained law and order since the "good people rose up and took affairs in their own hands." This was accomplished in the early days, he stated, when the people who wanted law and order captured a half-dozen horse thieves and swung them up by their necks. That no lynching had occurred in the decades prior to 1930 can be attributed only to courageous officers who since 1890 have frustrated a half-dozen threatened lynchings. Their success in these cases perhaps contributed to the public's over-confidence in the officers' ability to handle the Hughes case.

During the last decade major crime among the industrial white workers of Sherman and Denison and among white farm tenants has increased—perhaps a concomitant of agricultural and industrial depression.

Economical Unattachment of Negroes. Although there are a number of propertied Negroes in Sherman, and although the city provides good educational facilities and sponsors a Negro municipal band, the Negroes do not have any permanent place in Sherman's industries. The Secretary of the Chamber of Commerce does not look upon Negro laborers as of consequence, stating that they should be satisfied with domestic service and such casual labor as they can secure.

Nevertheless, the Negroes have fared much better in Sherman and Denison than in other parts of the county. In recent decades Negroes have been forced out of a half-dozen communities. Something like twenty years ago, when one was accused of assaulting a white woman, they were driven out of Whitesboro. Since then they have been forced out of Bells,

Southmayd, Ruella, Hagermann, Pottsboro, and Saddler. In numerous communities in central southern Oklahoma immediately north of Grayson County and in Texas counties to the west, no Negroes are allowed. "Nigger, don't let the sun go down on you here," is a common phrase in these parts.

CHAPTER XVII

NO PROPERTY DESTROYED
HONEY GROVE, FANNIN COUNTY, TEXAS

CAN A DEAD MAN be lynched? If so, Sam Johnson, Negro, was lynched on the afternoon of May 16, 1930, at Honey Grove, Fannin County, Texas. If a dead man cannot be lynched, Johnson was not lynched, for only his corpse was the victim of the mob. Nevertheless, because of the quick formation and the brutality of the mob of two thousand, the case is presented here.

Honey Grove, in the eastern part of Fannin County, is fifty miles directly east of Sherman. It seems that the Sherman disorders set a new and more terrible standard for lynching, for many of Fannin County's people found consolation in the fact that even though Johnson's corpse was dragged face down through the streets of Honey Grove no property, public or private, was destroyed.

THE MOB OUTBREAK

Size and Intensity of Mob. Three situations taken together resulted in an unusually quick and big mob flare-up at Honey Grove in mid-May, 1930: A Negro farm worker had killed his white overseer; the Sherman mob disorders were but a few days removed; the wet weather which aggravated the Sherman situation had continued.

At about one o'clock on the afternoon of May 16, 1930, a white tenant on a tract of land which Forrest Fortenberry of Honey Grove had sub-rented to him, rushed into town to tell Fortenberry that Sam Johnson, one of his Negro wagehands, was moving away. This made Fortenberry angry; with his informant, he left Honey Grove immediately and, starting toward his rented farm, met the Negro on top of a loaded

wagon. The Negro had "traded" with a planter five miles northeast of Honey Grove and was moving to his place. In his pockets
the Negro had a check, from his new landlord, with which to
pay Fortenberry what he owed him. He asked Fortenberry to
take the check, but the latter would not accept it. In an effort
to force him to return, Fortenberry threatened the Negro, who
retaliated with gunfire. The white tenant rushed back to town
with the fatally wounded man.

Some Honey Grove people had been at Sherman during the
lynching there the week before and had observed with satisfaction the efforts made to run the Negroes out of town.
Throughout north Texas there were rumors that the Negroes
were planning to avenge the destruction of life and property
at Sherman. The mass of whites were determined that there
should be no such retaliation. The killing of Fortenberry was
looked upon by them as a reprisal. In view of this, it is very
probable that Johnson would have been hunted down by a mob,
even if his crime had been less than that of killing a white man.

The constant rain was a third factor contributing to the
size and intensity of the Honey Grove mob. It had created a
rank pessimism and restlessness among the farmers, especially
the tenants. On May 30, when the rains were finally over, the
Honey Grove *Signal-Citizen* discoursed on the "ox was in the
ditch" as follows:

"Quite a few farmers, believing that the 'ox was in the ditch'
last Sunday took advantage of the excellent weather and proceeded
with their farm work. Even though the ground was very soggy for
plowing, considerable work was done, especially south of Honey
Grove. One could hardly be alarmed for taking advantage of the
day, as there is worlds of farm work to be done."

One must be acquainted with the disagreeableness of the
north Texas black mud, and also with the unkempt premises of
the typical tenant farmer in this section before he can fully
appreciate how desperate rain and more rain can make people
—especially when it is mid-May, and each additional shower
means a smaller yield and more tedious hoe work.

Killed Resisting Arrest. No sooner was it known that For-

tenberry had been shot than nearly all the white people of
Honey Grove rushed out to help catch the murderer, who had
jumped from his wagon and run. Word spread rapidly to other
communities, and within an hour and a half hundreds of men
had joined in the search. Within two hours Johnson had been
located in a shack a couple of miles east of Honey Grove, a
Negro tenant having revealed his hiding place. By this time
the sheriff had arrived from the county seat town of Bonham,
and he and a number of regular and special deputies started
toward the cabin. The Negro fired upon them. The sheriff
sent to Honey Grove for high powered rifles. The officers then
took a position outside the range of Johnson's guns and for
two hours fired upon the cabin.

In the meantime the affair had become known throughout
north Texas and even farther away, for only a short time
after Fortenberry's death news of the murder and man-hunt
had been broadcast by the Associated Press. The daily paper
at Paris, in an adjoining county, put out extras with red headlines. This certainly resulted in further swelling the crowd
which was hastily gathering on the hard-surfaced road that
ran within a few hundred yards of the shack where the Negro
had barricaded himself. Concerning the topography of the
"battle field," a news item in the next issue of the *Signal-
Citizen* said:

"It would seem that this scene of the battle was laid for the
advantage of the thousand or more spectators who quickly gathered
on the highway, and who were just out of firing range, but yet
close enough to see every move of the armed posse and also the
lone slayer, as he repeatedly sent hot lead from the cracks of the
shack or from the holes made in the flimsy wall by the high-powered
shells of his pursuers."

At about four o'cock the officers, determined to end the resistance of the Negro, fired almost continuously. When for
some time there had been no return fire, they went to the cabin
and found the Negro dead. Except for a small cook stove in
the cabin which the Negro crouched behind, he doubtless would

have been killed earlier. It is estimated that no less than two thousand shots were fired into the two-room cabin. Most of this ammunition was donated by Honey Grove merchants.

Dragging and Burning of Corpse. The great crowd which had looked on from a safe distance rushed to the cabin when they saw the officers bring out the body. The corpse was snatched up and dragged across a mud-soaked field to the hard-surface road. The body was tied to the back of a truck in such a way as to keep the face down as it dragged. The truck drove off to Honey Grove, other cars following. The procession circled the square in the center of town, then proceeded down the road toward Bonham for more than a mile, back again around the square, and then across the railroad tracks to the Negro section. There the body was hung, head down, from a Bois de Arc tree in front of a Negro church. The body was saturated with gasoline and burned until shortly before nightfall, when heavy rains dispersed the mob and put out the fire. The remainder of the body, the head having burned off, was given to the local Negro undertaker for burial.

There were many women present when the corpse was burned. It is reported that the wife of one white minister rushed to the home of another minister and called to his wife: "Come, I never did see a nigger burned. I mustn't miss this chance!"

The Sheriff's Proud Explanation. The sheriff's own words as to what happened at Honey Grove were approximately these:

I handled the thing the best I knew how, and undoubtedly it suited the people of the county, for I was re-elected by a great majority shortly after the affair. Not only did I get a larger majority in the county than in my previous election, but at Honey Grove, where I got two hundred votes out of eleven hundred in my first race I got six hundred out of nine hundred in the second. Many people of Honey Grove and elsewhere congratulated me on the way the thing was handled: Not a dollar's worth of property was destroyed, not even a piece of weatherboarding was pulled off; no innocent people were hurt; and labor was not disturbed except for a few days. The "nigger" killed a good white man loved by everybody. The white man just wanted to get his money from the "nigger" who was leaving his farm, and the "nigger" killed the man, took his gun, barricaded himself in a cabin and tried to kill all of us officers when we went to arrest him. I got high powered guns, and shot into the cabin until he quit firing at us. When I went to the cabin with my six or eight deputies, some of whom had come from Paris to help us, I found the "nigger" was dead. In the meantime cars had lined the road for at least two miles. People stayed back until they saw us drag the dead "nigger" out; then they rushed in and I tried to get 'em to leave the body alone; I told 'em the man was dead and it was all over; but the crowd wasn't satisfied—they were talking of burning him—and there was no way to keep 'em from their purpose except to shoot, and you nor I nor anybody else would fire upon a group of white people because of a dead "nigger," and so, since I couldn't do anything, off they went with him. Things might have been much worse. A little later when I got to Honey Grove some fellows wanted to get the father of the dead "nigger" and take him to the scene of the burning. I wouldn't let 'em do that. They would have killed him. Someone would have shot him and nobody ever could have told who did it. I handled the case the best I could, but a fellow's got to think quick to take care of that kind of a situation. A false word or move would have resulted in the death of many innocent people—it's hard to tell how many—and the destruction of lots of property.

So goes the explanation of the county sheriff. The sheriff's right-hand deputy stated that Sam Johnson's body was dragged through the streets and burned as a result of Johnson's own stubbornness. The deputy stated that the Negro earned death by killing a white man and earned the dragging and burning by resisting the officers who attempted to arrest him. The deputy added that the whole trouble could have been prevented had they been able to arrest the Negro when they first went to the cabin.

Honey Grove's elderly mayor insisted that Johnson was not lynched, and that there was at no time a mob in Honey Grove. An ex-sheriff stated that the sheriff and his deputies agreed to let the mob have the body on the promise that no property would be destroyed.

The White Victim—"Pistol Totin' Deputy." A leading planter of eastern Fannin County stated that Fortenberry had been a tenant on his plantation for a number of years, and that though he had had no trouble with him, he was very "high strung." He further said that Fortenberry, who at the time of his death was renting about two hundred acres and using wage hands, mostly Negroes, had never been able to get along with his labor except by the "big-stick method," and consequently needed a gun in his business. Courting the favor of public officials, he had been given a special commission with the privilege of carrying a pistol and was referred to as a "pistol totin' deputy."

An ex-sheriff stated that Fortenberry was a very fiery, one-track minded fellow who wanted to show his authority on all occasions, proceeding on the basis that the only way to handle labor was by browbeating and threats. The ex-sheriff went on to tell how about two weeks before the murder, he had seen Fortenberry, all excited, hurrying off to his place to whip a Negro and had remarked to a man standing near: "There goes Fortenberry again! You know, that man's going to get killed."

A Honey Grove taxi owner and operator stated that Fortenberry, who was in the habit of making threats and often "lost his head," virtually committed suicide by going out on the public road and threatening a Negro who was offering to make full settlement of his debt. The taxi man stated that if the case had gone into court the Negro's action might probably have been interpreted as a self-defense killing.

Forrest Fortenberry was fifty years old, had been living in Fannin County for thirty-nine years, and had been a tenant until a few years ago when he began renting larger tracts of land which he worked by means of wage hands or sub-rent tenants. He was a member of the Baptist Church at Honey Grove. Surviving him are his wife and five children, the three youngest of whom are thirteen, twelve, and ten years, respectively. His father and mother live near Petty, a small trading center in Fannin County; his brothers and sisters also live within a few miles of Honey Grove.

Near Illiterate Negro Victim. Sam Johnson was about

twenty-five years old. He had a wife and child and had always made a living either by working as a farm laborer or farm tenant. His father and mother are living. He has a number of brothers and sisters, who like himself and parents, have little or no education. Nevertheless, the Johnsons have been fairly successful farmers and bear a good reputation. The leading Negro in Honey Grove stated that at one time Sam Johnson's father had accumulated a thousand dollars. It is reported that the surviving members of this large Negro family left the Honey Grove community the day of the lynching.

Mob Leaders. According to many of Honey Grove's better citizens, who were eye witnesses of the outbreak, the active members of the mob were limited to a bunch of young fellows, many of them in their teens, and but few over twenty-five years of age. Most of them were said to have been from the white tenant element; and the remainder from the irresponsible, idle town group.

Practically all the white people in Honey Grove, including professional and business men, were interested in the capture of Johnson. The better established whites, though watching the "battle" and doing nothing to help the officers retain the custody of the dead body, referred to the dragging and burning either as inevitable or as inexcusable.

REACTIONS OF THE COMMUNITY TO THE MOB OUTBREAK

Local Paper Called It an "Orderly" Mob. The Honey Grove *Signal-Citizen* made several comments on the Sherman disorders, the most pointed of which suggested that judging by the happenings at Sherman they did not need a courthouse there any way; another comment was to the effect that law and order should have been maintained at Sherman. Both these statements came out in the paper distributed on the morning of Friday, May 16. It was on the afternoon of this same day that the outbreak at Honey Grove occurred. The comments in the *Signal-Citizen* and the brutalities visited upon Sam Johnson's body that same day were discussed as follows by the Garland *News:*

"Right on the heels of an editorial utterance by the Honey Grove *Signal-Citizen* deploring the mob at Sherman, citizens of its town and community shot and killed a barricaded Negro who had killed a white man, and then dragged the body through the streets of the town and hung it up and burned it. Which goes to show that editorial opinion still has influence, though it may be reversed in acceptance."

Honey Grove editorials on the local mob outbreak are not so much in defense of law and order as one might expect from the attitude expressed toward the Sherman affair. Witness these statements:

"The crowd that gathered during the afternoon, and which burned the body of the Negro following his death, was perhaps the most orderly one ever congregated, and at no time during the afternoon or night were they rowdy, noisy, or uncontrollable.

"No attempt whatever was made to do injury to the members of the colored race or to property belonging to that race. No; Honey Grove has not had a lynching, as many of the papers over the country have reported. A vicious Negro shot and killed a splendid white man when the white man asked for payment of money the Negro owed him. Then the Negro took refuge in a shack and, with two pistols and a goodly supply of ammunition, resisted arrest until he was killed by those trying to arrest him. He preferred death to arrest and received what he invited. After the Negro was dead some things were done that were useless, and should not have been done, but there has been no lynching in Honey Grove."

After another week had passed, however, the editorial policy of the local paper had resumed more nearly the position which it held prior to the outbreak:

"Following the recent similar trouble at Sherman this writer gave vent to his opinion in regard to the riot there, and barely before the paper had reached its readers, our little city was face to face with a case of similar nature. . . .

"Honey Grove has received much unsavory publicity since the burning of the body of a colored man here some two weeks ago, publicity of the kind we would rather not have received. Practically every paper in the state has carried editorials condemning the action taken in Honey Grove. Newspapers are fully one hundred per cent against the spirit of mob rule, and never let an opportunity escape to editorially urge its suppression."

Nearby Dailies Usually Alert. The Sherman *Democrat*, less severe on Honey Grove than on Sherman, on May 17 had an editorial captioned "And Now Honey Grove Has Bad Luck," a part of which was:

"Friday afternoon news dispatches from Honey Grove told of the killing of a white farmer by a Negro. The Negro barricaded himself in a house and shot at the posse eight or ten times. . . . The Negro was finally killed.

"And then it was that the mob got busy—the body was chained to an automobile and dragged to Honey Grove . . . and burned. . . .

"Lots of good citizens plead with the mob to prevent this act. But talking to a mob is like throwing the voice on the desert air. Mobs can't be reasoned with, they always are unreasonable, uncontrollable and dangerous."

The Paris *Morning News*, the nearest daily, featured the Honey Grove case by putting out a number of extras during the afternoon of May 16. From the standpoint of immediacy, the work of this paper was most unusual: At 5:25, fifteen minutes after the Negro's body had been dragged from the cabin, an extra carrying this news was on the streets. It has been suggested already that the numerous reports of the Honey Grove affair helped to attract large numbers of people. On the 18th the *Morning News* had an editorial entitled "Aftermath," parts of which were:

"The Negro killed near Honey Grove Friday while resisting arrest paid the penalty due his act. Dragging the body through the streets and then burning it was the act of the mob, and while of lesser degree was of the same character as the occurrence at Sherman just a week ago. . . . For the time we went backward into the age when men lived in caves in the ground and might was called right—a far cry from the civilization that has produced

our schools and churches, our homes and firesides, and every security
that we enjoy and of which we boast."

Reports of the Honey Grove affair went everywhere, largely
because of the intense interest aroused by the Sherman case
one week before. Floyd Gibbons, nationally known radio an-
nouncer for the *Literary Digest*, broadcast the story within
a few hours.

The Negro Press—"Savagery of Cannibals." Primed by the
Sherman outbreak, the Negro papers were most elaborate in
their gruesome details of the Honey Grove outbreak. The
Houston *Informer* said:

"With all the savagery of cannibals and other uncivilized members of the human family, the maniacal white men, women, and
children writhed, twisted, and leaped about the suspended burning
body, shrieking, singing, and howling in ghoulish glee, shouting
defiance to the law, as the body burned in the very shadow of the
temple of God.

"Rain stopped the ceremony here, as it did in Sherman and the
following day 'all was quiet.' Little or no investigation is expected
here, as no public buildings were destroyed by the mob, just another
Negro out of the way."

The *Afro-American* commented that "exactly one week to
the hour after the Sherman, Texas, mob had burned the lifeless
body of George Hughes, the mob again lifted the lynching law
banner by burning the body of Sam Johnson. . . . The lynching,
though lacking the spectacular fire displayed by the Sherman
mob fire, was said to have been perpetrated with unusual
fiendish accomplishment."

A release by the Associated Negro Press appeared in many
Negro papers under the heading of "Texans Lynch Friend of
Hughes Because He Seeks Pay Check; Can't Manufacture
'Rape' Charge," a part of which was:

"Apparently Congress should investigate Texas and send a commission here to study conditions and recommend to the president
that all missionaries now in foreign countries seeking to civilize

and Christianize heathens be returned here for work. So intense is the lynching spirit that in Brownwood a white man, accused of slaying his wife, was spirited away to 'parts unknown' because it was feared that he would be lynched."

"No Law Against It." The courts have done nothing, and most certainly will do nothing. Four months after the outbreak an investigation was made by the Fannin County grand jury. No indictments were brought. Members of the grand jury reported that they were not able to establish whether the body was dragged behind a truck or a touring car. As a matter of fact, it was dragged behind a truck for a while and then behind a touring car for a time. The exchange from the truck to the touring car was made on the town hall square in mid-afternoon in full view of hundreds of people. Nearly everybody in Honey Grove knows the exact facts.

Even more surprising than the attitude of the sheriff and his deputies, who are proud of the way the case was handled, is the position of the present county attorney. He stated that the grand jury indicted no one largely because there are no laws against dragging a corpse through the streets and burning it in front of a church.

Handbills Promising Protection to "Innocent" Negroes. Four days after the mob outbreak, something over one hundred and fifty white people of the community, including the sheriff and other officers, signed a statement assuring "innocent" Negroes that they would be given the protection of the law. This statement was printed in handbill form and distributed widely. The *Signal-Citizen* carried a news item captioned "Colored Folks Assured of Safety," as follows:

"Since the occurrence of last Friday, it has been reported that a number of the colored people of this community were leaving for other sections, having become alarmed that they might be molested or their property destroyed. Some few of the colored population have left the community, and noticing this exodus, on Monday the city officials, officers, business men, citizens and county sheriff signed a statement to the effect that the colored population need have no fear that further violence might be done the race. . . . The white and colored races have always gotten along nicely in this community, and every effort will be made to let similar conditions continue to exist."

No Hiding Place for Negroes. Although leading white citizens feared a general Negro exodus, it did not occur. The assurance given the Negroes by the handbill was a factor in preventing a general movement. A more potent factor, however, was that the Negroes of Honey Grove, like those of Sherman and other places where mob violence had broken out knew of no place where they could go with assurance of protection. In discussing their predicament Negroes ask frankly, "But, where can we go?" The former impression that the North and East were havens for Negroes has been modified as the result of recent experience in those sections. With the exception of Johnson's immediate family, practically no Negroes have left the community.

FACTS ABOUT THE COMMUNITY

Fannin County is immediately east of Grayson County, and since a detailed picture of the general social and economic conditions in rural and urban Grayson has been presented in the case study of Sherman, no detailed discription of Fannin County will be presented. The principal difference in the counties is that Fannin is much more rural than Grayson and without many of the cultural institutions which gave Sherman the title of "Athens of Texas."

Preventing of Lynching Saves White Man. Ten years ago at Honey Grove a lynching was prevented by the sheriff, who faced the mob in front of the jail and saved his prisoner by making ridiculous one of the most vociferous mobbers. A small man near the forefront of the mob kept yelling, "Let's go get him," whereupon the sheriff called him by name, saying, "Here's a gun, you go get the Negro." The loud talker hesitated; the sheriff insisted; the loud talker stepped back. Everybody laughed, and presently the whole crowd dispersed. The Negro, accused of murder, was duly tried and sentenced to hang.

Just before he was executed he confessed not only to the murder for which he was being hanged, but also to the murder of a white woman whose husband, then under death sentence for her murder, had gone mad. The Negro's confession saved the husband from execution, but he did not regain his right mind.

CHAPTER XVIII

DEATH IN CELL BY GUN AND KNIFE
CHICKASHA, GRADY COUNTY, OKLAHOMA

HENRY ARGO, nineteen-year-old Negro, was lynched at Chickasha, Grady County, Oklahoma, on May 31, 1930. He was
accused of having criminally assaulted a white woman at her
"dug out" home in a rural neighborhood near the city. The
lynching occurred just three weeks after the mob disorders
at Sherman, less than two hundred miles to the southeast.
The major events at Chickasha came in rapid succession: It
was about 4:30 P.M. when the alleged assault occurred, and
within an hour the accused man was arrested; at six o'clock
a mob was forming and soon numbered over a thousand; by
eighty-thirty efforts were being made to enter the jail; about
eleven the National Guardsmen were stoned and their truck
burned; at 3:30 A.M. mob leaders shot the accused Negro in his
cell; near seven he was stabbed, and at noon he died.

THE LYNCHING

Uncertainty of Crime Which Caused Lynching. The lynching of Henry Argo was the result of an alleged criminal assault
of a white farm woman about 4:30 o'clock the previous afternoon. Though there are many versions of what took place, the
following details are generally accepted: Henry Argo often
fished in the Washita River near the site of the "dug out"
where his alleged victim lived; on the afternoon of the
reported assault Argo was fishing in this vicinity and the
woman was alone except for her nineteen months old baby;
she had a dog which often attacked people and was in evidence
on the afternoon in question.

Beyond this point there are three different reports. One is

that Argo, while tramping along the river pursuing his fishing, was attacked by the dog, which he struck. This enraged the woman, who started toward Argo with a hoe. The Negro took the hoe away from the woman, and struck her with it. Another report is that Argo, on a fishing tramp, went to the "dug out" by the river's bank, asked for a cigarette, and cursed the woman when she refused to give him one. The woman, in turn, "sicked" her dog on Argo only to see the dog petted and calmed. This irritated the woman, and she started after the Negro with a hoe, which he took away from her. A third report is that Argo went to the "dug out" and assaulted the woman, and that the dog and hoe versions of the case grew up around the methods employed by the woman to defend herself.

Probably just what happened will never be known, for the woman persistently swore that Argo had assaulted her, while the Negro as persistently swore that he had not. The majority opinion, including people of both races, seemed to be that the Negro did not assault the woman, or even attempt it. Several of the woman's neighbors who saw her in ten or fifteen minutes after the alleged assault reported that there were no indications that she had been attacked.

Rapid Succession of Mob Events. Informed of the alleged attack, the woman's husband seized his gun and started in pursuit of the Negro. Failing to overtake him, he called the officers.

Shortly before five o'clock Argo was observed by a deputy sheriff crossing a field south of Chickasha. This deputy stated that when he asked Argo where he was going he replied that he was on his way from Oklahoma City to Texas with two other Negroes. The deputy arrested Argo as a suspicious character, placed him in the county jail, and shortly afterwards took him to the "dug out," where the woman positively identified him as her assailant. Argo was returned to the county jail.

In a short time news of the alleged crime had spread throughout Chickasha and surrounding country. The deputy stated that he observed a half-dozen men following him as he took Argo back to the jail. By 8:30, a crowd of approximately two thousand had assembled in the immediate vicinity of the jail and began an attack upon it, using sledge hammers, poles, and planks.

At nine o'clock Adjutant General Barrett issued an order for the mobilization of the local National Guard unit, and an hour later it appeared on the scene; a machine gun was planted on the sidewalk at the entrance to the jail door. For a short time the mob wavered. Several speeches were made in defense of law and order.

By eleven o'clock the mob had regained its morale. A government truck, used for transporting the troops, was burned and six guardsmen were injured by stones hurled at them. Mobbers dragged the burning truck from the jail door. A chain, fastened to the battered door, was hitched to a truck and the door was jerked from its hinges.

Guardsmen and police inside the jail kept the mob from going upstairs until firebrands thrown through the windows ignited the jailer's bedroom and kitchen. After about an hour, suffocating smoke forced the guardsmen to abandon the jail; the mob permitted all prisoners except Argo to be removed and allowed the fire department to work, once the officers had been forced to abandon the jail. Five wounded guardsmen were permitted to pass through the mob to get treatment for their injuries at a local hospital. About three o'clock in the morning the county sheriff arrived.

Death in Cell by Gun and Knife. By this time the jail had been abandoned to the mob. The outer door was off its hinges, and an effort was being made to break into the Negro's second-floor cell. Unable to break open the cell door, the mob chiseled a hole through the wall. Not able to make a hole sufficiently large to get Argo out, the mob leaders shot him in his cell. This happened about 3:30 A.M., but was not generally reported until about five o'clock.

After seven o'clock spectators moved at will through the jail; one of these, said to have been the husband of the woman, slipped into the Negro's cell and stabbed him near the heart.

At ten o'clock the Negro was placed in an automobile and taken to a hospital in Oklahoma City, where he died shortly before one o'clock.

Peace Officers and Their Explanations. The sheriff, who was very late in arriving at the jail, asserted that he had gone to Purcell, thirty miles away, in an effort to apprehend the Negro. General reports, however, are that he was at home. Officers of the National Guard claimed that they received little or no aid from the county officers who were present. The latter, in turn, stated that the guardsmen offered but little material assistance to them. Though the rioting was staged within two blocks of city police headquarters, the police are not known to have done anything to help ave the prisoner or disperse the mob. They explained that since the alleged assault occurred outside the corporate limits of Chickasha and was, therefore, a county case, they allowed the county officers to handle the mob as they saw fit.

Many leading Negroes, some of whom had worked persistently to get the officers and citizens to disperse the mob, feel that the sheriff's Negro deputy could have prevented the lynching had he coöperated with the local Negroes in requesting additional assistance. When the sheriff was defeated at the election following the lynching, the Negro deputy was dismissed.

Influential citizens interviewed were practically unanimous in stating that the sheriff failed woefully in his duty and that the other officers showed no skill in keeping the mob from its purpose. According to reports, the mob was practically unarmed; mob leaders were said to have called for a gun with which to shoot the Negro in his cell.

Illiterate Negro Victim. Henry Argo, illiterate, generally thought to be feeble-minded and termed a "half-wit" by local Negroes, was nineteen years old. The father left the mother before young Argo was born, and all knowledge of the mother had been lost since shortly after Argo's birth.

The boy, with unwholesome home surroundings, early came into conflict with the law and was sent to an Arkansas reformatory. Neither his age nor his exact offense could be definitely ascertained, but it is generally reported that he was in his early teens, and that he was charged with a sex offense.

Dan Argo, father of the boy, after deserting his wife in Arkansas, came to Chickasha where he and a brother went into the garage business. The men lived in the garage. The father, anxious to have his son with him again, secured his parole from the Arkansas reformatory in March, 1930. Young Argo had been in Chickasha but ten weeks when he was lynched.

On April 24, a little more than a month before he was lynched, Henry Argo was arrested and charged with assault, on complaint of a Negro girl in Chickasha. When the case was brought before the police court the accuser failed to appear and Argo was released.

The surviving members of the Argo family evidently felt insecure in Chickasha after the lynching, for they moved to Wichita, Kansas, where they are continuing in the garage business.

Reaction of the Community to the Lynching

The fact that there have been no convictions of mob leaders serves as an index of Grady County's general reaction to the outbreak.

"Savagery" says Chickasha's Only Daily. On the morning afer the lynching, Chickasha's daily paper, the *Express*, said editorially:

"Savagery flared up in Chickasha Friday night as it did in Sherman, Texas, a few weeks ago. The law of the jungle asserted itself and in the early hours of Saturday morning it circumvented the law of the land.

"Sheriff Sankey and national guardsmen under Captain Smith battled bravely to maintain the majesty of the law, but infuriated passions triumphed over reason, and soon the shameful news of mob rule in Chickasha was spread from one end of the land to the other.

"It matters little that the group of enraged youths and a few men constituted only an infinitesimal part of our citizenry; the country at large will hold the entire community responsible for the tragic and disgraceful affair. Let it be remembered that a number of our best citizens plead in vain for reason to prevail. It is certain that the overwhelming majority of our people were painfully shocked by the whole horrible proceeding. . . ."

As forceful as the editorial is in some respects, it should be observed that the sheriff and other officers were exonerated, and that the mob was made up of a "group of enraged youths and a few men" who constituted only an "infinitesimal part of our citizenry."

"What is Grady County Going to do About it?" A second editorial in the local paper on June 4 was more detailed, pointing out the officers' mistake in leaving the accused Negro in the county jail and asking what Grady County and Oklahoma were going to do about it; "Proceed with the probe until the bed rock facts are ferreted out," the editor concluded.

Indictments but No Trials. Charges of felony were filed by the state against twenty-three men for personal violence and for destruction of county property. Bonds were fixed at $1,500 each. Seven made bond at once and the others within a few days.

The trial was first set for June 17. The complaint filed against the twenty-three accused persons by the county attorney appeared in the Chickasha *Daily Express* on June 6 as follows:

"Now come B. F. Holding, and upon oath says that Jud Brown, A. C. Walker, John Gooch, Cobe Donaldson, ——— Walker, Harry Miller, Leonard Davis, Red Johnson, Red McWhorter, Tom Johnson, Red Hale, James Hedgecock, John Lee, Dr. Anderson, George W. Skinner, John Roberts, T. A. Vernon and Richard Roe, late of the County of Grady and State of Oklahoma, on or about the thirty-first day of May, in the year of our Lord, one thousand nine hundred and thirty, at and within said county and state, did commit the crime of riot, by then and there wilfully and unlawfully, feloniously and riotously, and without authority of law, and with a premeditated design upon the part of them and each of them to effect the death of one Henry Argo, and each and all of them, by then and there committing a felonious assault upon the person of the said Henry Argo, and they did riotously assemble to commit a felonious assault upon the person of him, the said Henry Argo, and the said defendants, and each of them, by use of force and violence, and while acting together and in concert with each other, did then and there assault, strike, shoot, stab, beat and wound the said Henry Argo, and all of said defendants and each of them, being then and there armed with dangerous and deadly weapons, to wit, certain pistols and knives, which they and each of them then and there had and held in their hands, did shoot and stab, with the intent aforesaid, the said Henry Argo, with the intent, to unlawfully, wilfully and feloniously kill, and that the said defendants, and each of them, while so riotously assembled together, and acting in concert with each other, did counsel, advise, encourage and solicit each other to participate in said riot, and that the said defendants and each of them, while so acting together and in concert with each other, and with the premeditated intent then and there, upon the part of them and each of them to effect the death of said Henry Argo, did then and there, wilfully, unlawfully and feloniously and riotously, shoot the said Henry Argo with a pistol loaded with powder and leaden bullets, which said pistol they and each of them, then and there held in their hands, then and there and thereby inflicting upon the head and body of the said Henry Argo, certain mortal wounds from which the said Henry Argo did die on the thirty-first day of May, A.D. 1930, as was intended by the said defendants and each of them.

"That the said defendants and each of them, while so riotously assembled, did then and there unlawfully, wilfully and maliciously, feloniously and riotously, set fire to and burn the county jail of Grady County, Oklahoma, with the malicious intent then and there, upon the part of them and each of them, to injure and destroy said property.

"And that the said defendants and each of them did then and there while so riotously assembled and acting together and in concert with each other, and with the felonious, wilful, unlawful and malicious intent to injure the county jail of Grady County, Oklahoma, they and each of them, did then and there wilfully, riotously, feloniously and maliciously, with a large piece of timber, batter down the outer and inner doors of the said county jail of

Grady County, Oklahoma, contrary to the form of the statutes in such cases made and provided and against the peace and dignity of the State of Oklahoma."

The hearing set for June 17 was postponed until July 2, on request of the county attorney, who stated that other arrests were contemplated and that it would facilitate matters to have all the hearings at one time. On July 3 the local paper reported "Date for Riot Trial Changed—Will be Held Sometime after July 21." This second postponement, for which no reason was given, was reported to have been agreed upon by the prosecution and defense counsel.

Since the announcement of the second postponement, no further steps have been taken toward bringing the cases to trial. Apparently the cases will never be carried through the courts, for the public opinion which demanded the indictments at the outset does not now demand trials.

No Results From State or Federal Action. At the governor's request the Attorney General of Oklahoma detailed a member of his staff to assist the county authorities with the prosecution. This state officer obviously has been content to offer his services only when called upon, with the result that neither state nor county officers have brought the cases to trial. An interview revealed that this state official had no record of the case in his office. It is evident that the state officers have moved within the wishes of the local prosecuting attorney.

Since a truck belonging to the United States Government was burned, federal charges were brought against each of the twenty-three men indicted by the local grand jury. The hearing was set for June 23. When the state first postponed its trials, federal agents postponed theirs. The federal hearing took place before the district court at Muscogee, July 16. The grand jury, having failed to indict in any of the twenty-three cases investigated, the presiding judge accused its members of allowing race prejudice to enter into their decision and asked for further consideration of the case. As a result, bills were returned against two men. Bonds placed at $2,000 each were raised immediately. September 1 was set by federal authorities for further consideration of the Chickasha affair. The case was postponed, and to date (July, 1932) no further action has been taken.

Most Mob Members From Lower Classes. The responsible citizens in the community felt they had been disgraced, and forthwith endeavored to place the full responsibility upon the farmers living near the scene of the crime and the lower social classes in town. One of the Chickasha ministers, among the spectators on the night of the lynching, stated that "only the poorer element of Chickasha's citizens, and a few farmers from the neighborhood where the criminal assault was committed" took active part in the rioting and lynching. A college professor stated very emphatically that "the lower class was responsible for the whole situation." Members of the city and county police forces stated that the leaders were a "bunch of rowdy young fellows" in Chickasha and a "few farmers from the nearby neighborhood."

Twenty-three men were indicted by the courts for participating in destroying public property, rioting, and lynching. Whereas probably all of the twenty-three and others were instrumental in accomplishing the death of Argo, the real leadership of the mob seemed to have been furnished by two men. The husband of the woman complainant, who was one of those indicted, is generally reported to have been one of the two main mob leaders and the one who stabbed the accused Negro in his cell. The other, also among those indicted, was a man with professional training. According to reports it was he who held the mob together at ten o'clock on the night of the rioting when it wavered upon the appearance of the National Guardsmen.

" 'Vigorous Investigation'—Shall We Applaud or Merely Yawn?" In commenting upon the state Attorney General's announcement that his office would assist in a "vigorous investigation" of the Chickasha disorders, on June 2 the *Daily Oklahoman*, after some discerning comments on the affair, editorially inquired: "Shall we applaud or merely yawn?"

An editorial on the afternoon of June 2 in the Oklahoma City *Times* was frankly skeptical about the punishment of the mob leaders, but suggested that there was hope in stronger prisons and more capable officers.

Editorial comment on the lynching was confined largely to the local Chickasha paper and to the dailies in the state's two largest cities. Out of eleven white state dailies examined for editorial comment during the months of June and July following the lynching, six carried no editorial comments on any phase of it. Similarly, most weekly and semi-weekly papers in the state made no editorial comment.

The Negro papers of Oklahoma and throughout the country put out big headlines and wrote scathing editorials about the incident.

FACTS ABOUT THE COMMUNITY

Population Increase With "Dry Farming." Grady County is in west central Oklahoma. In 1930 it had a population of 47,638, over sixty per cent of whom lived in the open country. It has a population density of 42.8 persons per square mile, as compared to 34.5 for the state. The population, almost constant from 1910 to 1920, increased 40.3 per cent from 1920 to 1930, while that of the entire state increased but 18.1 per cent.

Agricultural prosperity accounts mainly for the last decade's population increase. For in spite of the discovery of oil and gas, a larger proportion of the people live on farms now than ten years ago. "Dry farming," a system of deep plowing for utilization of moisture, has made cotton growing profitable in this area with less than thirty inches annual rainfall. Prior to 1920 the agricultural lands were largely devoted to the growing of wheat, while an even greater acreage was used as range lands. The increase of Grady County's cotton crop from an annual average of 15,472 bales from 1910-1914 to an average of 57,291 bales since 1925 is a measure of the transition from wheat farming and cattle ranging, which require but little labor, to cotton farming and its inevitable hand picking.

Some attention is devoted to the dairy industry. The area now comprised by this and adjoining counties formerly was much desired by Texas cattlemen who sometimes tarried weeks, grazing their cattle on the tall prairie grass, while on their way to the Kansas City cattle market.

One Town and Many White Farm Tenants. In 1930 Chickasha had a population of 14,099; the other six incorporated places in the county had a combined population of but a little over four thousand. The Rock Island Railroad shops and two cotton compresses in Chickasha—which is primarily a farm trading center—are the only concerns which employ any considerable number of people.

More than three-fifths of Grady County's people live on farms in the open country, and of the rural population almost two-thirds are of the tenant farmer class. The county is more rural than the state average, and a larger proportion of its rural people are tenants than of the state's rural people. In rural parts of this county as in rural Grayson and Fannin counties, Texas, where mob outbreaks occurred shortly before, the white tenant element predominates.

Almost No Negroes in Open Country. Grady County has a larger proportion of native-born whites than the state as a whole. Of the county's people, 4.7 per cent are Negroes, 1.2 per cent are Indians, and 0.6 per cent are foreign-born whites, while of Oklahoma's total population 7.2 per cent are Negroes, 2.8 per cent are Indians, and 1.1 per cent are foreign-born whites.

Nearly three-fourths of Grady County's 2,247 Negroes live inside Chickasha's city limits; one-ninth of Chickasha's inhabitants are Negroes, as compared with one-sixtieth of the county's rural dwellers.

In Chickasha, as in Sherman and Honey Grove, there is a small group of Negroes reasonably well-to-do: Three physicians, one dentist, one theater owner, ten ministers, a dozen school teachers, seven carpenters, three grocerymen, six barbers, and ten plasterers.

For the most part the Negroes are unskilled laborers and are employed at the Rock Island shops, the two cotton compresses, the hotels and stores, and as domestics and casual laborers about town. For street cleaning and other politically controlled menial work, white workmen are generally used.

Grady County on the Highway. When observed from its railroad connections and highway system, Chickasha is by no means an isolated community. The Chicago and Rock Island Railroad traverses the county from north to south. The St. Louis and San Francisco Railroad crosses the county from northeast to southwest; a branch line of the Santa Fe Railroad enters the county from the east and terminates at Chickasha.

Travel by bus is offering serious competition to the railroads. United States Highway 81 from Canada to the Gulf of Mexico passes through this county; the state maintains an east-west highway. Grady County has 9,979 motor cars, or one to every 4.9 persons; throughout the state there is one to every 4.6 persons.

Schools Slightly Above State Average. When compared with the other counties in the state, educational facilities in Grady are slightly above the average. The county has relatively fewer illiterates and relatively better paid teachers than the state as a whole. For the white children, Chickasha provides five grade schools, a junior high school, and a senior high school. There are only five schools for Negroes, four of them one-teacher schools. The largest, at Chickasha, is part of the city school system. It has twelve grades, a well-equipped building and a fair library. A small building is available for shop work. About one hundred students are enrolled in high school, and each year since 1925 there have been about ten graduates, most of whom have gone to college for one or more years.

The difference between the average expenditures per white and Negro child, though marked, is much less than in most Southern communities: In Chickasha $47.20 and $37.23 for each white and Negro child, respectively; the small enrollment per Negro school in the remainder of the county resulted in $37.65 being spent for the Negro child as compared with $34.36 for the white child. All schools for both races have eight-month terms. Of the county's population over ten years old, 2.2 per cent are illiterate as compared with the state rate of 2.8 per cent.

The Oklahoma College for Women, a state institution for white girls, is located in Chickasha. The usual courses of instruction given in women's colleges are offered. The enrollment of approximately one thousand is drawn almost entirely from the state.

But Few Churches in Rural Communities. The open country church in Grady County, as elsewhere in Oklahoma, does not play so important a part in the rural situation as it does in the older states. In fact, there are but few open country churches in rural Oklahoma. Of Grady County's 10,141 white church members in 1926, 2,966 were Southern Baptists; 2,439, Southern Methodists; 1,218, Disciples of Christ; 705, American Baptists; 747, Church of Christ; 540, Roman Catholics, and a few score Presbyterians and Protestant Episcopalians. The chief contrasts of church membership in this county as compared with the state is that, whereas the Southern Baptists and Southern Methodists are relatively more numerous in this county, the Roman Catholics and Presbyterians are relatively less numerous.

Nearly three-fourths of Grady County's Negroes over fifteen years of age were reported as church members in 1926, as compared with less than one-third of the whites of the same age group. Of the Negro members, 767 were Baptists; the remaining 285 were about equally divided between the Methodist Episcopal, African Methodist Episcopal, and Colored Methodist Episcopal. Chickasha's 1,625 total Negro population supports eleven Negro churches and ten full-time pastors. There is no Negro church building in the rural portions of the county; two one-teacher Negro schoolhouses are used as places of worship.

One-Party Politics. Though the Republican presidential candidate in 1928 received a majority, Grady County's election machinery is controlled by the Democrats. In the 1930 county primary, when the unusually large number of 9,094 people participated in nominating the sheriff, but 39.2 per cent of those of voting age took part. This relatively large vote was a product of the lynching in May, 1930: Sheriff Sankey, the real political "boss" of the county for ten years, was not a popular candidate for reëlection, because of the commonly prevailing impression that he had failed utterly in his duty in connection with the lynching. The outcome was the defeat of Sankey by approximately two thousand majority.

There have been no efforts to exclude Negroes as a class from voting. This fact is significant when it is remembered that the county is overwhelmingly Democratic, having been settled in the main by Southern people. Of the county's twelve thousand registered voters in 1930, approximately five hundred were Negroes, nine-tenths of whom lived in Chickasha. As a matter of expediency, the Negro vote in Chickasha is usually Democratic. The Negro voters usually agree on their choice of Democratic candidates and vote practically solidly for them. "Remember Henry Argo" was the slogan of the Negroes as they went to the 1930 Democratic primary and cast their votes against Sheriff Sankey. His unsuccessful attempts to rid himself of their opposition in the last election is the first record of any efforts being made to keep Negroes from voting.

Most Murders in Open Country. Grady County has no system of organized public welfare. A small county poor fund is set aside each year from the tax revenues; this fund is administered by the chairman of the board of county commissioners. In Chickasha there are two private social agencies: The Salvation Army maintains a post, but its resources are very small; the United Charities administer some relief; in 1929-30 a total of $2,000 was raised by the annual community fund drive.

The Chickasha police register shows 4,400 arrests between May 1929 and January 1931, of which number 2,020 were analyzed for this case study. It was found that Negroes accounted for only 7.3 per cent of all arrests, whereas Negroes make up approximately nine per cent of the town's population.

The most striking thing gleaned from the court records was that in the twenty months ending with January 1931, one murder occurred in Chickasha, while ten occurred in the remainder of the county.

In so far as is known, Grady County had no lynching prior to that of Henry Argo. Some years ago a tense racial situation existed in Chickasha. According to local reports, a young Negro undertaker who had a wife and child, developed an intimate acquaintance with a white girl. After repeated rumored irregularities on the part of the two, feeling became aroused to such a point that the Negro undertaker was spirited out of town to prevent a threatened lynching.

"Negroes Not Wanted Here." The proportion of Negroes in Grady County is less than in Oklahoma, which state has a smaller Negro element than any other Southern State, and smaller than the United States as a whole. There are, however, obvious evidences of Negro segregation in the county. Negroes are excluded from many communities. "We don't want Negroes here, and they know it!" is the explanation. In turn, there are exclusive Negro towns throughout central and western Oklahoma. In Cleveland County, where the state university is located, Negroes are restricted to one small rural locality. They have never been allowed to reside in Norman.

Negro Voters in "Their Place." Race relations in Chickasha seem to be generally satisfactory to the people of both races. The Negroes vote without molestation, and at intervals Negroes have served as police officers in the colored section. The white people of Chickasha generally report that the local Negroes are on the whole responsible and law-abiding. It seems, however, that matters of race relations largely revolve about the orthodox Southern pattern. For example, a Chickasha police officer, stating that the town has "a good bunch of Negroes," elaborated upon their willingness to "stay in their places."

PART VI

LYNCHINGS OUTSIDE THE SOUTH

IN THE twenty-eight months ending with April, 1932, eight of the thirty-eight lynchings in the United States occurred outside the South: At Marion, Indiana, two Negro men, August 7, 1930; at Maryville, Missouri, a Negro, January 12, 1931; at Schafer, North Dakota, a white man, January 29, 1931; at Salisbury, Maryland, a Negro, December 4, 1931; at Lewisburg, West Virginia, two Negroes, December 4, 1931; and at St. Francis, Kansas, a white man, April 18, 1932.

Seven of these lynchings occurred in counties where the Negro and foreign-born elements were relatively smaller than in their respective states. The mobs at Marion, Maryville, Salisbury, and St. Francis had thousands of members, while at Schafer and Lewisburg the mobs numbered about eighty and sixty, respectively. Each of the eight lynched persons were taken from jails or from peace officers, and in no case did the officials or the general public make any serious effort to protect the prisoners.

In view of the larger proportion of lynchings outside the South since 1930 than during that year, we have presented the case study of the lynchings at Marion, Indiana, and Maryville, Missouri. It will be seen that the latter community had suffered many bank failures and that the former was characterized by excessive industrial retrenchment. In both instances the general plans for the lynchings were common knowledge well in advance, and in each the activities of the mob continued for hours. The militia was called into action at Marion, but not until after the lynchings, when the sheriff was frightened by threatened reprisals. Similarly, at Maryville, no show of determination from the peace officers was in evidence until the sheriff was frightened by rumors that Kansas City and Omaha Negroes were moving on Maryville to avenge the lynching.

Special newspaper reporters and photographers hurried to Marion and Maryville to get first-hand stories and pictures for the press. While a few people in each community roundly denounced the affairs, the majority, along with most of the officials, seemed to have assumed that they were inevitable. No member of either mob has been sentenced by the courts. Many Southern papers referred to these lynchings as proof that mob violence knows no geography, and many Northern Negro papers expressed concern lest such outbreaks become more frequent outside the South.

CHAPTER XIX

A PUBLIC AFFAIR
MARION, GRANT COUNTY, INDIANA

ON THE night of August 7, 1930, Tom Shipp and Abe Smith, two nineteen-year-old Negroes, were taken from the Grant County jail in Marion, Indiana, and lynched. The mob victims were accused of murdering a young white man and raping his woman companion.

THE DOUBLE LYNCHING

Cause of Lynching Obscure. As in most of the cases covered by these studies, the evidence as to just what lay back of the lynching is far from conclusive. The mob, of course, accepted the rape story at face value, but there were many who doubted it. Discussing the matter before the Ministers' Evangelical Union of Marion, one of its white members expressed the confident opinion that the affair grew out of the operations of a gang who made a practice of robbing roadside couples at night—a gang composed at first of white boys only, but later enlarged to include the white girl involved in this case, and two or three young Negro men. The girl, he stated, acted as a decoy, taking her male companions to a designated spot where her confederates robbed them. These holdups, he said, had been going on for some time, but had not been brought to the attention of officers because of the compromising circumstances in which the victims found themselves.

It was reported further, from other sources, that the girl belonged to one of Marion's "black and tan" social groups, that she and Abe Smith were on friendly terms, and that she was wearing his wrist watch on the night when Deeter was shot. Some believe that the tragedy really grew out of a controversy between the girl and the two Negro men over the division of spoils from previous robberies.

The story of the affair as given by most of the white people is that Tom Shipp, Abe Smith, and another Negro, named Cameron, came upon Claud Deeter and his girl companion on a lonely road a few miles out of Marion—a place known locally as "lovers' lane"—and that one of the Negroes at the point of a gun forced Deeter to leave his companion, while the second held the girl and the third raped her; and that Deeter was killed when he heard her screaming and tried to come to her rescue.

The crime, it is said, was at once reported to the officers by a "respectable" white woman, who, with a male companion, was nearby at the time. The information which she furnished, on promise that her name would not be divulged, led to the prompt arrest of Shipp and Smith. Officers went immediately to Shipp's house and found his automobile engine warm. Abe Smith was arrested at a party later in the night. The next morning, which was Saturday, August 9, white people in Marion talked about lynching the Negroes—especially if Deeter should die. Deeter died shortly after noon that day.

Storming the Jail. Upon hearing of the death of Deeter, a crowd gathered immediately about the jail. The sheriff was notified by several Negroes that a lynching was imminent. He scouted the idea, stating that the jail was impregnable. The crowd continued to grow, and when night came on there was much shouting and threatening. It was evident that trouble was impending. From the outset the local newspaper reporters were on hand, and saw everything that happened.

At first the sheriff armed his deputies, and reported that he could take care of the situation. As time passed, however, he decided upon other methods, and taking all the guns from the deputies, retired with the latter inside the jail with a small supply of tear gas bombs.

After 6:30 the crowd increased rapidly. The active mob leaders at this time numbered not more than a score, many of them in their teens, and practically all under twenty-five years of age. They were urged on by young girls and women, some of whom held babies in arms. By eight o'clock the active mob had grown to 150 or 200, and the number of onlookers to not less than 5,000. From the jail windows officers begged the mob to disperse, but were answered only by "cat calls" and demands for the keys.

Beginning at 8:30, with crow bars and sledge hammers secured from the Marion Foundry, the mob labored diligently to open the outside jail door. Shortly after ten o'clock the large stones around the outside door had been dislocated. The door, facing and all, was jerked out of the wall.

In the meantime officers had momentarily frustrated the mob with tear gas bombs. However, the rioters soon learned to throw water on the bombs, or to hurl them back through the windows at the officers.

As soon as the door was down, the members of the mob entered and proceeded to the turnkey's door. Here they again faced tear gas bombs and retired for a few minutes. Quickly returning, however, they battered open the inside doors and secured entrance to the cells. Demanding to know where Shipp and Smith were, they threatened to lynch all the prisoners if they were not told.

Shipp and Smith Lynched. Shipp had managed to climb into an opening on the top of a cell, and was out of sight except one foot. He was pulled down. At first he begged for mercy; then he fought ferociously, and bit the ear of a white barber so severely that the wound required treatment. The barber is no longer in Marion. Some of the Negroes reported that he died from his infected ear. Shipp was taken outside the jail where a rope, tied to the grating of the jail window, was fastened about his neck. He delayed strangulation by getting his hands on the rope above his head. This momentary delay enraged his self-appointed executioners; they climbed into the window and, by kicks in the face, rendered him unconscious. While this was going on a white girl, about eighteen years old, was on top of a nearby automobile screaming, "Hang that nigger!" The Negro died of strangulation; shortly afterwards the girl fainted and was carried away by friends.

In the meantime Abe Smith had been taken from the jail to the courthouse square. His clothes were torn off; he was draped in a large cloth; a rope was tied around his neck, and he was pulled up into a tree, his head coming alongside a second floor window which opens into the courtroom. In a few minutes Shipp's limp body was brought to the courthouse square and hanged beside Smith's.

Many informed local people feel that the sheriff and his deputies had every opportunity to protect their prisoners, even after the mob had torn away the outside door. The construction of the jail is such that two or three men with rifles at either of two places inside the jail could have kept back a mob of thousands, for the passageway from the outside entrance to the cells makes three right angle turns. If the foremost leader of the mob, upon coming into one of these elbows, had been shot down, it is highly probable that the other rioters would have turned back.

Grewsome "Object Lessons." Shortly before midnight the coroner gave orders for the bodies to be cut down. The mob, however, demanded that they be left swinging as "object lessons" to Negroes. Accordingly, the bodies were left dangling from the tree until nearly six o'clock next morning, when they were cut down and taken to an undertaking establishment in Muncie. Upon learning of this the mayor of Muncie, who was out of town, wired back demanding that the corpses be taken out of Muncie. Accordingly they were returned to Marion.

After Shipp and Smith had been lynched, the mob returned to the jail and got Cameron, the third Negro arrested in the case, who steadfastly asserted that he had been placed in jail for hoboing. In this deception he was supported by the prosecuting attorney, the sheriff, and other officers. The mob cuffed Cameron about for a time and then returned him to jail.

Late Arrival of Militiamen. The double lynching was broadcast immediately by the newspaper reporters on the scene. Upon hearing of the outbreak, officers from Anderson, Huntington, and Wabash rushed to Marion.

When the sheriff failed to take effective steps to prevent the imminent lynching, local Negroes, chief among them the wife of a physician, telephoned to the Governor and asked for a National Guard unit. It is reported that this request, in the absence of Governor Leslie was received by his secretary, a former resident of Marion, and that on hearing the Negroes' request he discourteously hung up the receiver. It is reported that this secretary also refused an appeal for troops made a little later by the mayor of Marion.

Troops were finally sent, however, when requested by the sheriff, who had received threats for permitting the lynchings. Before the Guard arrived he retired to the jail and placed armed officers at all entrances. It is obvious that he called for the troops out of fear of reprisals upon himself, rather than for the protection of Negroes against further mob activities. The commander of the local unit of the Guard, who was away at the time of the sheriff's request, rushed back to Marion by airplane, reaching there the day following the lynchings; two National Guard companies arrived at five o'clock on the second morning after the lynchings. Most of the troops were stationed near Johnstown, a slum community from which threatening rumors had been coming. They remained in town until the mob's victims were buried on Sunday afternoon.

Victims—White and Black. Claud Deeter, the white murder victim, was twenty-four years old and unmarried. He was a laborer in a Marion foundry. His father and mother lived on a farm near the Quaker community of Fairmont, south of Marion. Young Deeter's Quaker parents took no part in the double lynching; they were surprised and displeased when the news of it came to them on the following morning. They emphatically denied that the girl who was with their son on the fatal night was his fiancée.

The girl, eighteen years old, lived with her father, a trader in old race horses, in a shack on the outskirts of Marion. As noted already, she was reported to be a member of a gang which specialized in robbing couples parked along lonely roads.

Tom Shipp, nineteen years old, was employed regularly as a laborer in the Malleable Iron Works, having worked there the day before Deeter was shot. About ten years before, he had come to Grant County from Kentucky. What schooling he had was secured before coming North. He attended Sunday School regularly until a few Sundays before his death. His parents were poor but respectable, and were especially active in church work. They lived in a five-room house in Weaver, an all-Negro farm community on the old "underground railroad" nine miles southeast of Marion. Because his father was an invalid, young Shipp was the main support of the family. He was without court record.

Abram (Abe) Smith, also nineteen years old, lived in Marion with his grandparents. His parents had been separated for years. When he was lynched his father was facing liquor charges, and his mother was living in a distant city. The teachers of the school where Smith finished the sixth grade reported that he was above the average in his studies, but was unruly when angry. Soon after quitting school he began stealing automobiles and pay checks. He was sentenced to the penal farm, but escaped, and was never retaken. Smith, it seems, was looked upon by local people as something of a minor gang leader.

Herbert Cameron, the third Negro arrested in the case, was sixteen years old. He was reared in Marion and attended a local Negro school. Cameron's mother lives in a dilapidated shack. His stepfather is now in the penitentiary, charged with the shooting of Cameron's brother and a peace officer. Accused of having held the girl while his confederate assaulted her, Cameron has been removed to another jail for safe keeping. According to the prosecuting officer he will be charged with the capital offenses of rape and murder.

THE REACTION OF THE COMMUNITY TO THE LYNCHINGS

The general feeling in Marion is that mob violence is likely to happen anywhere when certain crimes are committed. The actions of the Indiana courts have been very similar to those of Walhalla, Sherman, and Chickasha.

Local Papers Condone Dual Lynching. The local press did not take a determined position against the lynchings, the explanation being that the Marion *Leader Tribune* and the Marion *Chronicle* had just been consolidated and that the new management was anxious to say nothing which would displease the community.

The local news reporters were aware that something spectacular was apt to happen and, as indicated already, were close at hand to report developments. One of these reporters who interviewed the girl with Deeter on the night he was shot, was threatened by her father; and later when his reports concerning her were carried in the papers, her father threatened the editor of the *Leader Tribune*. Taking the threats seriously, he left town for three days.

"Mob Psychology" was the *Chronicle's* editorial the morning following the lynchings; parts were:

"Marion is about the last place on earth where we should have expected to witness a lynching. Yet, this very thing happened here. The lynching was done not by men of violent and lawless dispositions. These men are ordinarily good citizens, but they were stung to the quick by an atrocious crime, and spurred on to their violent act by a want of confidence in the processes of the courts. Enraged by the dastardly and murderous deed of the two criminals, the lynchers for the time were obsessed with one idea and that one idea they put into execution, never stopping to reflect either on the criminality of their own act or the effect of it on the good name of their community. Today we wake up to a sense of the great shame and humiliation the lynching has brought upon us. Never have we had a feeling of so great sadness as we felt last night as we looked helplessly on that seething mass of humanity milling around the jail, knowing all the while that a great humiliation and sorrow were coming upon our fair city in this unfortunate and distressing affair. It is sad to reflect that, human nature being what it is, and social conditions being what they are, what has taken place here in Marion is not unlikely to befall any community. Mob psychology may break out anywhere."

The other daily paper, the *Leader Tribune*, had an editorial, "Let Us Go Forward," a part of which was:

"We cannot recall the past. Regretful as was the very unfortunate occurrence of Thursday night, it cannot be recalled.
That event constitutes a sorrowful chapter in the history of this city.
The discussion of it, much less the rehashing of the events that led
up to it, can get us nowhere."

No Conviction—Sheriff Exonerated. The local prosecuting
attorney, who was present in the jail when the mob took the
third Negro from his cell, announced at the outset that an
investigation of mob activities would be made in September
by the regular session of the grand jury. In addition to
making no indictments, the grand jury exonerated the sheriff
and all other peace officers. The case was then transferred to
the State Attorney General's office. Though continuously urged
to action by a group of Marion Negroes, it was only after considerable delay that the Attorney General appointed attorneys
Wall and Stroup to handle the case. Warrants were issued for
eight men alleged to have been active members of the mob,
they were arrested and subsequently released on bonds of $2,000
each. The arrests produced much local bitterness against the
state authorities. No charges were made against the sheriff for
failure to perform his duty.

The judge who presided when the first of those arrested was
up for trial expressed the desire to absent himself from the
courtroom during the closing arguments, but his request was
refused by the prosecution. It required two days to secure a
jury for this trial, 150 veniremen having been called before
twelve jurors were selected.

Throughout the trial the crowd which jammed the courtroom was orderly, but plainly in sympathy with the defendant.
When a verdict of "not guilty" was announced, there were
cheers of approval. The second case, in which the jurors remained out twenty-one hours, resulted in an acquittal, also.
Newspaper reporters and other witnesses testified that the
defendant had taken an active part in breaking into the jail.
Since neither of these defendants, against whom the evidence
seemed most conclusive, was convicted, it is the consensus of
opinion that the other six cases will never be tried.

A Wandering Turk, a Musician, and Two Taxi Drivers.
One of the people arrested as a leader of the mob was a
thirty-eight year old wandering Turk, who some years before
had come to Marion almost penniless, and at the time of
the outbreak was operating a pool room and quick-lunch stand
in the main part of town. He had never taken out his last
citizenship papers. It is reported that, being of dark complexion, he was struck over the head during the mob demonstration
by one of his fellow rioters who mistook him for a Negro.
He had been taken into court on a liquor charge, and had been
arrested some years before for operating a gambling house.

A musician, under thirty-five years of age, who has taught
both Negro and white pupils, was another of the men arrested
charged with being a member of the mob. At the time of the
lynchings he lived in a Marion hotel and directed a local
orchestra.

Another of the accused, a thirty year old taxi driver, left
Marion immediately after the lynching, but was arrested when
he came back to see relatives. A second taxi driver also was
arrested.

Mob Leaders Under Twenty. A teen-age farm hand, who
lived with a local livestock farmer, was also arrested and
charged with an active part in the mob. As an itinerant farm
laborer, he had come to Grant County only a year prior to the
lynchings.

A second boy of sixteen or seventeen years of age arrested
was the son of an ex-city-fireman and blacksmith who owns a
modest home. He quit high school a couple of years before the
lynchings and became a mechanic in a local motorcycle shop.
Two other boys under twenty were arrested.

The Determined Efforts of the N. A. A. C. P. As indicated
already, a group of Marion Negroes openly and aggressively
worked to prevent the lynchings and later to secure punishment of the mob leaders. The wife of Marion's leading Negro
physician was president of the local chapter of the National
Association for the Advancement of Colored People; she was
also president of the state organization. A committee from
the Marion chapter waited on the Governor, demanding the

discharge of the sheriff for failure to perform his duties. Walter White, of the National Headquarters of the N. A. A. C. P., went to Marion about two weeks after the lynchings and made an investigation. As a result he reported that he sent to the State Attorney General's office the names of twenty-seven persons reported as participants in the lynchings, together with evidence against them.

In the mind of many Marion white people and some Negroes there is a question as to the wisdom of the methods employed by the N. A. A. C. P. in this case. It is not unnatural, of course, that local and state officers should refer to the "unwarranted demands" of this organization when trying to defend themselves. Be that as it may, it is a fact that the Marion N. A. A. C. P. was the only local organization that waged an open and direct fight in any case of a lynching in 1930.

Prosecuting Attorney and Sheriff Not Reëlected. The prosecuting attorney, whose grand jury returned no indictments against the mob and exonerated the sheriff, was defeated for re-election a few months after the lynchings.

When reminded that the mob's seizure of his prisoners made him subject to an investigation by the State Attorney General's office, the sheriff simply replied: "I knew that statute was on the books, but I believe I did the best thing." He too, was defeated in the subsequent election.

Before and since the lynchings, Marion's young mayor has been most cordial with the Negroes, seemingly bidding definitely for their votes. He sent flowers to the funerals of the mob victims, and, it is said, has promised a Negro fire department unit in the near future.

The Factor of Racial Antagonism. While there were individuals who differed, the general reaction of the local people to the double lynching was that a mob outbreak like that in Marion was likely to take place anywhere under similar circumstances, and that the lynchings were in no wise the result of racial antagonism.

The pastor of the largest church in town stated positively that the lynchings were not due to racial factors. He suggested that the relations between the races in Marion have always been cordial, and while there had been considerable antagonism in Muncie and other sections of north Indiana, this had not been true in Marion. He pointed out that, while Muncie would tolerate no Negro athlete on the high school teams, the most popular Marion high school athlete in 1930 was a Negro.

Another pastor of the same denomination, with an outlying church, took the opposite view. He stated that there was every reason to believe that the lynchings occurred only because the accused persons were Negroes. He pointed out that shortly before Shipp and Smith were lynched, a number of white men had been arrested in Grant County for criminal assault upon white women, and that shortly after the double lynchings two white boys were arrested for the same offense. White people had also murdered other whites, but in no instance had there been any evidence of mob action.

While there were many white persons in Marion who looked upon the mob outbreak as an evidence of lawlessness and barbarity, and as absolutely inexcusable, no group of white people made an organized effort to prevent the lynchings or to secure conviction of the lynchers. The white people who desired conviction of the mob leaders either had little influence in the community or did not use such influence as they had.

Some After Effects. Whereas many of Marion's leading Negroes coöperated in the efforts of the N. A. A. C. P., and others worked individually, the whole Negro population has let it be known that they have prepared to protect themselves against future mob outbreaks, some of them quietly and with dignified restraint, but others somewhat defiantly. If there were no racial antagonism in Marion before the lynching, one can hardly say as much since.

Another effect is that the Negroes of the North have become apprehensive lest lynchings become more prevalent in that section. On this point Walter White, after personally investigating the Marion case, referred to the mob deaths of Shipp and Smith as "among the most horrible and brutal in the whole history of lynching," and pointed out that the "Marion lynchings are a challenge to every decent citizen and especially to Negroes, in that they were an invasion by lynching mobs of a Northern state. Certain officers in Marion claim that these mob murders were not racial in character. This seems somewhat difficult to believe in view of the fact that there were in the jail at the time of the lynchings two white men charged with rape, while two others charged with the same offense were at liberty on bail. Also in the jail at the time of the lynchings was another white man charged with one of the most brutal crimes in the history of Grant County. He had hacked off the head, arms, and legs of another white man in a disturbance over a woman. None of these white persons was molested by a mob."

"... *Largely Pro-Southern* ...." While white Northern papers universally deplored the Marion affair without devoting a great deal of space to it, the leading Negro papers, most of which are in the North, featured it conspicuously. An Associated Negro Press' news release of August 13th, under the heading of "Indiana's Klan Spirit Culminates in Lynching of Two Men," said in part:

"Despite the presence of the sheriff's forces and the police strength of this city of 23,000 the mob was permitted to enter the jail and to batter down cell doors with sledge hammers without the firing of a single shot by the police officers, either to protect the public property under their care, to save the lives of the prisoners and guarantee them a fair trial, or to uphold the majesty of the law. . . .

"News of the incarceration of these boys was the signal for the klan-spirited citizens of the county to assemble and demand their lives. The mob grew quickly from one hundred, who came to this city from Deeter's home town, Fairmount, to several thousands. . . .

"Although Indiana has a considerable colored population, its sympathies regarding the Negro, despite its geographical location in the north, have always been a matter of question. It was largely pro-southern before and after the Civil War. Since the World War, it has been a hot bed of Ku Klux Klan activity, association with this intolerant and un-American organization having been charged against many of the most prominent officials in the state.

"The Negroes of Marion stayed quietly in their homes while Shipp and Smith were being murdered."

"There Is No Disposition to Gloat. . . ." The story of the lynching was carried widely in the white papers of the South and seemed to be welcomed by many of the editors as proof that mob violence is liable to break out anywhere.

Some of the Southern papers made of Deeter's girl companion a most exemplary young woman. A news item in a Sumter (S. C.) paper, for example, said: "This young woman was to have selected her engagement ring today; instead she will attend the funeral of her fiancé at his father's home at Fairmount."

The *Times-Enterprise* of Thomasville, Georgia, on August 14th, which was a little more than a month before a Negro was lynched there, significantly said:

"There is no disposition to gloat. . . .

"Revolting crimes have about the same effect everywhere and only in rare instances is it aroused to such an extent. Yet it has happened before and we can see no assurance that it will not happen again. There is but one thing that will bring on a lynching if such a thing is possible and that is the attack by a Negro on a white woman."

On August 7, the Valdosta (Ga.) *Times* had an editorial, "Indiana Gets Angry," the last sentence of which was: "In all seriousness, the incident in Marion should prove to the people of that section that there is no geography involved in indignation." In its next issue, this south Georgia weekly reprinted this from the New York *World:*

"The outbreak in Indiana was on a par with recent mob performances in Georgia and Texas and forces the reluctant conclusion that lynching is still more than a local problem. . . .

"The only real difference between the sections in this matter which is visible to the unprejudiced observer is that the crimes usually leading to lynching are necessarily more frequent in the sections where the Negro population is congested than in sections where that population is relatively small."

Another south Georgia paper, the daily Albany *Herald* of August 9th said: "The Marion, Ind., mob was wrong, of course. It should have permitted the law to take its course, but it didn't. . . . Given the same provocation, a mob above the Mason and Dixon line is not different from a mob below."

A north Georgia daily suggested: "The double lynching in Marion, Indiana, prove little beyond the fact that human nature is pretty much the same, North, South, East and West. The only reason why there are more lynchings in the South than in the balance of the country is because there are more Negroes in the South."

One of the sanest editorials appearing in Georgia came from *Progress*, a small rural weekly paper, published at Jasper, Pickens County:

"When Friday's newspapers arrived with the news of the lynching we were surprised to see some people, who ordinarily are strongly opposed to mob law inclined to exult in it, simply because it occurred in the North. That kind of spirit will never get us anywhere and every expression of sympathy with mobs in other sections helps breed a mob spirit at home."

Editorials in other Southern States commented upon the affair in much the same fashion, emphasizing that the mob spirit is "not sectional."

FACTS ABOUT THE COMMUNITY

Grant County, seventy miles northeast of Indianapolis, lies within a fertile farming section, which until ten years ago was also a prosperous industrial region. The county was laid off in 1831.

Many Public Services. A county-wide public school system was established in Grant County soon after it was formed.

Funds for a county library were authorized by an act of the Legislature which provided that ten per cent of the sale price of county seat lots should be set aside for this purpose. In 856 a township library system was established. In 1834 an overseer for paupers was named. In 1848 the Grant County Medical Society was organized, with nine charter members— a year earlier than the organization of the State Medical Society and only a year later than that of the National Association.

The county fair was organized in 1874, a development which grew out of a number of Grant County farmers' organizations, many of which were established prior to 1860. In 1869 gravel road building was begun and the Marion and Liberty Gravel Road Company was organized. In the last quarter of the past century Taylor University, a Methodist Episcopal institution, was established at Upland, a small urban community of Grant County, and the Marion Normal School was located in the suburbs of Marion. These facts indicate that the people have had considerable interest in community welfare matters from the outset.

Most of the early inhabitants were from the northeastern and central Atlantic states, with a goodly number from as far South as Virginia and North Carolina. In 1840 the county had a population of 4,875. During the next decade the population rose to 11,092, and regularly increased by four or five thousand with each census until 1920, when a total population of 51,353 was reached. In 1930, however, the population of the county was 287 less than in 1920, due primarily to the fact that certain industrial plants had been moved from Marion during the decade.

Quaker Influence a Factor. The Society of Friends, or Quakers, settled early in Grant County, and throughout its history has been a very important cultural factor. Largely because of their concern about Negro slavery in the South, there was in Grant County a terminus of the underground railroad, and several Negroes had settled in the county before 1860. From the outset Negroes have maintained two distinct farming communities. One of these is in the suburbs of

Marion; the other, Weaver by name, the terminus of the old underground railroad, is nine miles southeast of Marion. It will be recalled that one of the lynched Negroes was from the latter community and the other from the former.

Although Grant County is in the northern part of the state, 3.1 per cent of its population was colored in 1920 against 2.8 per cent in the entire state. During the following decade, however, the county lost 200 Negroes and the state gained 30,000, making the percentage of Negroes in the state greater than that in the county.

In common with most Southern counties with lynchings in 1930, Grant County had a smaller foreign-born population than the state as a whole—1.6 per cent against 4.2 per cent for the state.

The population density of the county in 1920 was 121.4 persons per square mile, compared to 81.3 per square mile throughout the state. More than two-thirds of the people live in five towns; Marion, the county seat, with 24,130, is more than three times as large as either of the other four.

Local Industrial Retrenchment. In the last decade several large industrial concerns have moved from Marion, with a small loss of population resulting. Most of the Negroes have been employed as foundry mechanics, unskilled iron workers, janitors, porters, domestic servants, and hotel employees. Some few hold political appointments: two policemen and two firemen. At the time of the lynching there was considerable unemployment among both races. The rural sections of the county compare very favorably with other parts of the state. The principal crops are corn, small grains and vegetables, with livestock much in evidence.

Compared with Southern counties with lynchings in 1930, Grant County ranked high in per capita income, taxable property, bank deposits, etc. When compared to Indiana as a whole, however, it falls below the state average in nearly every instance. In 1920 the per capita value of farm and manufactured products combined was $747.51 against $817.65 for the state. The loss of several industrial concerns since 1920 has probably further lowered the county's relative standing. In 1930, the county's per capita assessed value of taxable property was $1,386.20 against $1,595.61 in Indiana. In 1928, an income tax return was filed for every seventy people in the county as compared with one return for every 42.2 persons in the state. In bank deposits alone the per capita showing for the county was better than for Indiana, $237.30 against the state average of $207.43.

Negro Business and Professions. Among the business enterprises owned by Negroes in Marion are two restaurants, a pool room, a barber shop, and a tailoring establishment which does high grade work and is well patronized. The leading Negro business man in Marion is a contractor and road builder, who with modern equipment competes with the most up-to-date concerns. He has done work in many Indiana cities, having put down practically all the pavement in Anderson, midway between Marion and Indianapolis. The wife of a leading Negro minister has built up a small insurance business for an Indiana Company.

Besides a dozen preachers and three school teachers, the Negro professional group is limited to one physician, a lawyer, and a chiropodist. The physician is a specialist in venereal diseases, and many white people go to him for treatment. Though without formal training in law, the colored lawyer practices in the Grant County courts and more than three-fourths of his clients are white. For nearly a score of years he worked as clerk in the county tax collector's office. At present he has some influence in county and state politics and is president of the state Masonic organization for Negroes.

Theoretically No Racial Segregation in Schools. While theoretically there is no racial segregation in Grant County, there is an all-Negro school in South Marion and another in Weaver. Except the three who teach in these two schools, no Negro teachers are employed. The other Negro children in the county attend school along with the whites. Of the twenty-eight Negroes in the Marion high school in 1930, five were in the senior class.

White and Negro Churches. Throughout the years, the whites and Negroes of the county have maintained separate

churches. A Negro church was established at Weaver prior
to the Civil War. Like Sherman, Texas, Marion is a great.
church community, and the leading church people did not
believe that a lynching was possible there. Afterward, however, they were inclined to forget the affair as soon as possible.

In 1926, the Methodist Episcopal Church had a total membership of 5,476 in the county. The Society of Friends, or
Quakers, was the next largest denomination with 2,519 members, which was approximately ten per cent of the state's
membership of this religious body. Other white denominations
in the county had memberships as follows: Disciples of Christ,
2,314; United Brethren in Christ, 1,313; Roman Catholics,
1,311; Presbyterians, 882; Church of Christ, 842; Baptists,
701; and Protestant Episcopalians, 214.

Of the 680 Negro church members in the county, 320 were
members of the A. M. E. church; 188, of the M. E. church;
and 172, of the Negro Baptist church. The Negro church
members, especially the Baptists, have been in conflict among
themselves throughout the years, and at present there are
five Baptist churches in Marion, averaging less than thirty-
five members each. There is a Ministers' Evangelical Union
at Marion made up of both Negro and white ministers.

Parties of About Equal Strength. In the 1928 presidential
election an exceptionally large number of votes was cast,
14,659 Republican and 7,273 Democratic. The regular Democratic vote usually accounts for between thirty-five and forty-
five per cent of the total. Because of this close division, the
Negroes often hold the balance of power.

In the recent county election, for example, almost all Negroes voted with the Democrats to defeat the sheriff and
solicitor who were holding office when the lynchings occurred.
It is rumored that the Negroes will next unite to defeat the
resident Judge who tried the lynching cases.

Courts in Bad Repute. During the past few years there
has been much lawlessness in Grant County, and local people
said that the police and the courts have done very little about
it. It was pointed out on every hand that the courts' failure

to deal effectively with recent cases was one of the principal factors leading to the mob outbreak.

One heard repeatedly of a middle-aged Fairmount couple accused of poisoning a twelve-year-old foster child. The woman was acquitted; the man was given a short sentence, and within a year was released. Another case complained of was that of a Marion Negro garage worker who shot a local white boy, and received a relatively light sentence.

Added to these cases, Marion has had repeated bombings. One October 2, 1929, when the mold makers in Marion foundry were on a strike, a bomb exploded in the local labor temple, killing three people. Four weeks later a union laborer was killed when he stepped on the starter of his car and set off a bomb. On February 3, 1930, another bomb was attached to a car starter, but was observed in time to prevent an explosion. When the local officers failed to ferret out the culprits, private detectives were put on the cases but no arrests were made.

Crimes By Race. According to the 1930 report of the Superior Court Clerk, offences against the family, such as failure to provide, neglect and non-support, lead all others with seventy-nine cases, partly due doubtless to industrial retrenchment. Forty-seven persons were charged with larceny and forty-two with embezzlement and fraud. The criminal court records showed five indictments for murder and fifteen for rape. At the time of lynching, it will be recalled, there were in the jail five white men charged with rape, and that a few months later two more were jailed charged with the same offense.

Threatened Lynching in 1885. The double lynching of 1930 was the first on record in the county. In 1885 a lynching was threatened in the case of a Negro alleged to have frightened two white girls. The mob dispersed, however, when Sheriff Orange Holman shot and killed its leader, James Keley.

Race Relations Generally Harmonious. Prior to the lynchings of 1930 race relations had been very harmonious in Marion and Grant County. Negroes and whites lived in the

same communities, the more wealthy Negroes living alongside the wealthier whites and the poorer Negroes sharing the
slums with the poorer whites. In 1930 one of Marion's most
popular high school athletes, the captain of both the football
and basket ball teams, was a Negro. He and a few other
younger Negroes of the more cultured group mingled with
the youth of the town quite oblivious of race.

Race relations are generally harmonious, too, on the lower
levels, and throughout the years there have been "black and
tan" parties, in some places called "gorilla" parties, in which
the members of the two races associate on intimate terms. It
was reported that mixed couples went regularly to a Marion
theatre, and at one performance an investigator observed
four such couples. A white usher seated them in a
matter-of-fact way, but in a gallery reserved for colored people. Eight mixed couples, legally married, were living in
Marion in 1930, and many "common law" unions were reported. In a section of Marion known as Johnston, unions of
the latter type are not uncommon. After the lynching, the
mob threatened to burn this section, and might have done so
had not the residents armed themselves for defense. On the
arrival of the troops part of them were stationed in this
section. We have here then this situation: Between
the low types of whites and Negroes, a very intimate relation;
between those at the upper cultural levels, a cordial relation;
and on the part of certain laboring class whites who live in
communities apart from the Negroes, a definite antagonism
toward them.

CHAPTER XX

CHAINED TO RIDGE-POLE AND BURNED
MARYVILLE, NODAWAY COUNTY, MISSOURI

ON JANUARY 12, 1931, occurred the first lynching of the year in the United States, that of Raymond Gunn, Negro, twenty-seven years old, accused of the rape and murder of a young white woman school teacher about three miles from Maryville, Missouri. Suspicion fell upon Gunn; he was arrested and placed in jail. When a threatening mob gathered, he was taken to St. Joseph for safe-keeping and the St. Joseph National Guard was called out to prevent mob violence. Some days later, at Maryville the sheriff and his deputies permitted a mob to take Gunn without offering resistance or calling on the assembled Guard. Gunn was marched to the schoolhouse where the crime had been committed, and was chained to the ridge-pole and burned to death as the schoolhouse itself was consumed.

THE CRIME AND THE LYNCHING

Raymond Gunn's Family Background. The victim of the Maryville mob came of a family for the most part highly respected in the community. A representative of Nodaway County in the legislature stated that he had known Gunn's great grandmother, and that the family bore the reputation of being hard-working and law-abiding, except that Raymond's mother, though an industrious and careful domestic servant, "went bad" on occasions—moral lapses—but had never been in the courts.

Many expressed the opinion that Raymond was simply born "with a bad streak." Certain it is that he showed criminal tendencies early. Born in Maryville, and reared there, he was employed at odd jobs by various citizens and business houses after completing the seventh grade. He stayed in Maryville until he began leaving town to get work elsewhere.

Convicted of Attempted Rape in 1925. In September, 1925, Raymond Gunn fell into his first serious trouble. A young woman college student, whose home was in an adjoining county, was walking toward town from the Maryville Teachers' College one evening near dusk. As she came to a little ravine near the edge of the campus, she saw a young Negro man standing there, apparently waiting. She hesitated, somewhat frightened, until he called to her not to be afraid. She proceeded, but after she had passed the Negro, heard him following close behind. In a moment he had seized her, dragged her into the nearby bushes, and was about to assault her, when the woman told him that she expected her escort to pass that way in a moment and he would surely kill him. The Negro became frightened and hurried away.

Gunn, arrested almost immediately, was positively identified by the young woman as her assailant. He was convicted of assault with intent to rape, and was sentenced to four years in the state penitentiary. Officials made strong attempts to force Gunn to confess this crime, but he would not do so. He began serving his sentence November 8, 1925.

His Record at the Penitentiary. He was recorded at the penitentiary as No. 28,882; age 21, nativity, Missouri; trade, cook and houseman; height, 5 feet 6⅛ inches; length of foot, 10½ inches; hair, black; eyes, maroon; complexion, maroon brown; religion, none; education, 7th grade; former imprisonment, none. No mental tests are made at the Missouri penitentiary, but it is reported that Gunn was generally considered a "smart nigger." Prison officials stated that he was much quicker and brighter than most colored prisoners. This bears out the opinion of numerous Maryville people, who maintained stoutly that the reports of Gunn's mental subnormality were untrue; that he was, in fact, keen-minded.

Notations were made showing that he made "merit time" of 20 days, and was given jail time of 16 days, so that he was released from prison January 28, 1928.

Bad Reputation Following His Release. While Gunn's prison record is clear, his record after being released is far from good. In fact, it was generally stated that he seemed to harbor a grudge against college girls, and made at least two attempts at assault during the year following his release from the penitentiary. At any rate, he was under strong suspicion as the man who seized a college girl and attempted to drag her away near the campus; the girl refused to push the case because of the notoriety to her that would result; shortly after the incident, Gunn left town for Omaha. By that time he had married a Maryville mulatto girl, whom he took with him.

It is known that his wife died some months before the lynching, ostensibly from pneumonia, but common rumor has it that Gunn beat her badly and otherwise mistreated her, finally kicking her in the chest so that she died really from wounds. Most of the county officials of Nodaway are of this opinion. Some of the other unsubstantiated rumors of Gunn's criminal career in Omaha include his guilt of the famous axe murders of that city.

Along in 1930 Gunn came back, although he left town for frequent trips to Kansas City and Omaha. In the early fall of 1930 he took out hunting and trapping licenses, and trapped and hunted small game north of Maryville. On the evening of December 15, 1930, a farmer living about four miles north of Maryville was motoring into town, and overtook Gunn walking along the road. He started to pick him up, but seeing who it was, decided that he might as well walk. It was near the Garrett schoolhouse, and this fact was an important link in the chain of evidence that led to the arrest of Gunn following the crime of the next day.

Young School Teacher Murdered. The one teacher at the Garrett schoolhouse was born and reared on a farm about seven miles from Maryville, in the Clearmont neighborhood of Nodaway County. Her father is a farmer of moderate means. She attended the State Teachers' College in Maryville for two years, and in the fall of 1930 obtained a position teaching school at the Garrett schoolhouse, located about three miles from town and five miles from her home. She obtained board and room at the home of a farm family living near the school.

On the evening of Tuesday, December 16, the teacher did not return from school at the usual time; after an hour or so, the family with whom she lived became alarmed. The man started out to search for her, and went first to the school. There he found her body lying on the floor, near the center of the room, her head in a pool of blood from gaping scalp wounds.

Intense excitement followed the report of the crime. The coroner took charge of the body, assembled a jury for an immediate inquest, and brought the body to the office of a Maryville physician who performed an examination.

Raymond Gunn Immediately Suspected. The local prosecuting attorney, whose office was to expire December 31, at once suspected Raymond Gunn because of his former conviction and the persistent stories of his later attempts at rape. The only tangible clue was a plain heel-print, near a window of the schoolhouse. This print was preserved.

The prosecuting attorney sent out requests to sheriffs far and near to apprehend a Negro answering the description of Gunn. Many arrests were made. The next morning a farmer living near the school told of having seen a young Negro loitering about the lane near the school on the evening before the crime; the farmer who passed Gunn on the road on the same afternoon reported having seen him returning to town. No one apparently had seen Gunn on the afternoon or evening of the crime.

In the meantime, however, he was close at hand. He had attended a frolic of young colored people in town the night of the crime, and had explained the blood on his clothes by saying that he had gotten rabbit blood on his shirt while hunting.

His Arrest and Confession. On the 18th he was found in hiding, was arrested, and taken to the prosecuting attorney's office to be grilled. He still had on the clothes he had worn, with the blood on his shirt. The heel-print fitted his shoe perfectly. The officials tried to make him confess, at first without success. The prosecuting attorney stated that Gunn had been beaten badly during his questioning before the previous trial that sent him to the penitentiary, and yet no confession was obtained, so different tactics were decided upon this time. For most of the afternoon the questioning went on, the evidence weaving more tightly about the prisoner. Then they "tried religion on him." He was told that they were sure he was guilty, and he might as well make his peace with his God. This brought a complete confession, according to the prosecuting attorney and others who were present. The town was full of newspaper correspondents from St. Joseph, Kansas City, and other points, and some of them heard at least parts of the confession.

Gunn told of being in the neighborhood the day before, passing that way to look at some traps, and thinking over the idea that had occurred to him some time before, of raping the school teacher. Accordingly on the next day along in the afternoon he hid himself close by, and after the children had gone home, he crept to a window and watched the teacher as she was closing the building. She took the coal bucket outside and filled it, and just as she was re-entering, he appeared at the door. She was frightened and ran inside, he following. He carried a hedge club in his hand.

Gunn related in detail the struggle, and said that as he tried to seize the girl she bit his thumb badly. (Officials recalled that the girl who figured in his former crime testified that he had placed both thumbs in her mouth and tried to hold her in such a manner that she could not scream.) This tallied with his thumb's being bitten almost to the bone. He said that the pain of the bite caused him to swing his club and strike the girl over the head. She seized the coal bucket and swung it to strike him, whereupon he struck her again, a blow that knocked her down. She fell between two desks, and he dragged her out into the center aisle.

At this point, Gunn said, he thought he heard a noise outside and went to the window to look, and saw a girl on a bay horse with a grey nose, riding down the lane in front of the schoolhouse. He said he watched her until she passed. Then he returned to the girl, and proceeded to tear off part of her clothing. As he did so she revived and asked him to get her some water. He said he picked up his club, hit her over the head, and again hit her head after it struck the floor. In the opinion of the examining doctor, it was this last blow that fractured the skull and caused death.

Gunn maintained that he did not perform the rape. He said that he heard another noise, and became frightened at it and at what he had done, and ran out of the building, carrying the club, which he discarded in the nearby field as he hurried away.

Some Untrue Reports. Although news reports were almost unanimous in saying that the examining physician had reported that an assault had been made, the examining physician stated that there positively had not been a rape, and that he had never announced there had been. This fact illustrates how reporters close to the crime and to its confession can lend exaggeration.

One heard the wildest tales of how the girl had been butchered. The minister who preached the funeral of the victim related horrible tales of how Gunn had cut her body. A local representative in the State legislature, who so vigorously and successfully opposed the resolution condemning the lynching, wrote news articles which the editors were obliged to leave out because of his childish delineations of the butchery of the girl.

The Correctness of Gunn's Confession. The physician who examined Gunn's victim and the prosecuting attorney in separate statements agreed on every particular, and coincided with Gunn's confession: They found the girl who rode the horse Gunn described; they found the club on the spot where he said he had thrown it; the coal bucket showed evidences of having been used by the girl in trying to defend herself; her torn clothing was found in the condition he described; and the wounds on her head tallied exactly with the blows he said he gave her. The minutest examinations failed to show any evidences of rape. No knife or other sharp instrument had been used on the victim at all. She had bled profusely from head wounds.

From Maryville to St. Joseph. From this point on, the sheriff of Nodaway County figures prominently. Immediately after Gunn's confession on Thursday night, December 18, the sheriff put Gunn into a car, took two deputies, and hastened to St. Joseph. Feeling was high and doubtless Gunn would have been lynched that night had he been left in Maryville. An incident which occurred on the trip illustrates the sheriff's attitude: The party was going along through the night at a rapid rate, when ahead they saw a car drawn up, with a fire built nearby, and what appeared to be a party of men standing round. The sheriff was alarmed, and said it was likely a party bent on taking the prisoner away from them, and if so, they should let them have him without a struggle. Certainly he would want no one to get hurt. They slowed down for the parked car, and found it only a group repairing a tire!

Mounted Machine Guns at St. Joseph. All next day, Friday, crowds milled around Maryville, talking lynching. A Nodaway County official, whose attitude toward lynching was a curious mixture of regretting that it "had to happen" and a feeling that it would best be over with, stated that the men who wanted a lynching had held a conference in his office that day, and outlined plans to go to St. Joseph and storm the jail, providing it was not too strong and the sheriff did not put up too much opposition. At any rate, it would not hurt to try to get the "nigger" at once and have it over with. When the county official told them he could not go with them because of his position, they advised him to keep quiet and left his office.

Fearing trouble, the adjutant general of Missouri hurried to St. Joseph. That afternoon, Saturday, the mob came. But St. Joseph was prepared. "It just proves what a determined sheriff can do," a state official said. "He asked for the mobilization of the local National Guard. They were on the job at once. A machine gun truck was backed up squarely against the jail door. Another gun was mounted on the roof. Others

were placed about the jail yard. The guard had several rounds
of tear bombs, besides their side arms and machine guns."

The mob swarmed around the jail. The sheriff came out
and told the leaders he would protect the prisoner to the utmost. The mob howled and stormed—vocally. "About that
time," the state official said, "an amusing thing happened. The
boys in charge of the machine gun on the roof were oiling
it up. One of them swung it back and forth as though to get
range of the crowd below. He was not really aiming the gun,
but the crowd thought so, and they melted away as though
you had touched a snow drift with a hot poker!" After milling
about awhile, the crowd returned to Maryville. Late that night
Gunn was moved to Kansas City.

The Newly Elected Prosecuting Attorney. On the night
following Christmas day, shortly after midnight, a party composed of the sheriff, two deputies, and the local prosecuting
attorney took Gunn from Kansas City to Maryville for arraignment in the justice court, according to law. They reached
town about 3:30 A.M., and took the prisoner into the court.
The charge was read to him; he was docketed as waiving preliminary hearing, and bound over to circuit court for trial.
Immediately thereafter the party sped out of town with him,
and by daylight he was back in the Kansas City jail. No one
except the officials in charge knew of the trip.

On January 1, the newly elected prosecuting attorney took
office. He had kept in close touch with all developments, of
course, as the crime happened after his election. The incoming
prosecutor was a young man, and had been practicing law in
Maryville since his graduation from the University of Missouri in 1924. One of his first acts was to announce, publicly,
that Gunn would have a fair and open trial. The editor of
the Maryville *Forum* related how the prosecutor early in
January brought over several statements with the request that
news stories be run about them to the effect that "Gunn would
be tried just like anybody else." The editor at first refused
to carry the statements, but finally ran a condensed story
which set forth the prosecutor's determination to see that
Gunn had a fair trial. Just what was in the prosecutor's mind

in thus advertising the case is a matter of conjecture. As will be seen later, he did not demonstrate any intelligent interest in preventing the lynching.

A Maryville lawyer, paid a fee of $500 in advance, was selected to aid the prosecution. Just why is a mystery, since the attorney general of the state had offered to send an assistant for the trial. This offer, however, the prosecuting attorney had curtly refused.

Forthcoming Lynching Widely Advertised. The fact that Monday, January 12, would be opening day of the court which would try Raymond Gunn was given wide publicity in practically every paper in the section. It is curious to note how even the papers which condemned the lynching editorially, had earlier run news stories calculated to arouse—or at least to mirror—interest in the trial.

A week before the opening of the court, preparations for a lynching were going forward. No quick flare-up of mob spirit, this—on the scene of a crime just committed. One is amazed at the deliberate planning back of the event; of the widespread understanding that the Negro would be lynched. A county official stated: "Such a crime would have meant a lynching anywhere. Even if it had been a white man, the prisoner would have been lynched. There seemed nothing else to do. That is the best explanation of it. Of course, I refused again to join in the plans. The leaders were local men, or rather, they were for the most part men of Maryville or in the country nearby. They came here and discussed their plans: They were to seize the Negro at the courthouse. Even if the sheriff tried to protect him, which they did not expect, one of the crowd was to pick the prisoner off with a gun. The main point of agreement was that the Negro was not to come to trial." This official added: "I went to the sheriff repeatedly and told him what was to happen. He would not listen to me. He said there wouldn't be any trouble."

The mother of the murdered girl had repeatedly said that she would not attend the trial, and would not testify in any way, as she could not bear to do it. Her statement was given the significance that the family did not want Gunn tried, but

wanted summary death. At any rate there was great sympathy
for the mother. Her oldest son had been killed fighting in
France. Her murdered daughter was buried by his side.

So generally was it "in the air" that Gunn would be lynched
that a conductor on a Burlington train, taking the ticket of
a Maryville woman on Saturday before the fatal Monday,
remarked to her: "Getting back home just in time; they are
going to lynch that nigger Monday." Various newspapers
sent their reporters over on Saturday and Sunday with instructions to get all the good pictures of the lynching possible. The St. Joseph *News-Press* sent up a star reporter
and staff photographer Sunday evening. These two men covered the event as thoroughly, perhaps, as any lynching was
ever covered. A business man stated that early Monday morning a reporter from somewhere in Nebraska came into his
place of business: "What's going to happen here this morning?" "Nothing," the business man answered, "the Negro will
be tried." "Pshaw," he grumbled, "I thought I would get to
see a lynching."

Troops Assembled at Maryville. In the meantime, the mayor
of Maryville, who has served the city for the last 12 years,
honored and respected by all, wrote to the governor of Missouri and begged that he use all his power to prevent Maryville
the disgrace of a lynching. The mayor insisted that there
would be a mob outbreak if the local authorities were not
strengthened. A number of business men likewise wrote the
governor, as did members of the bar. On Saturday evening
the governor wired the adjutant general, ordering him to proceed at once to Maryville,—as the adjutant general said, "to
assist the local authorities in any way they may need."

Here was the setting for what later happened: Under the
laws of Missouri the National Guard units may be called out
to assist in preserving peace and order "at the written request
of the sheriff or other local authorities." Had the governor
given the adjutant general specific orders to "prevent the
mob," undoubtedly the officer would have gone ahead without
reference to what the sheriff did or did not do. But the governor, of course, did not know that the sheriff would refuse

positively to accept the aid of the state troops. The adjutant general arrived at Maryville Sunday noon. On the way he wired the captain of the local battery of National Guard to arrange a conference with the prosecuting attorney and the sheriff. The captain met the adjutant general and they talked over the situation. After lunch they went into conference with the sheriff, the prosecuting attorney, and the latter's special assistant. Just what transpired in that conference is the key to the whole tragedy, and will be given its special place in this report.

The Cars Kept Coming. The adjutant general noticed that the town was full of people on that Sunday afternoon. And still the cars kept coming. "I made a trip about the square just at dark," he said, "and noticed that every parking place about the square was filled. Every third or fourth car had three or four men in it. They were just quietly sitting there, wrapped in overcoats and robes, for it was quite cold."

All night long the cars came. The night clerk at the Bainum Hotel, facing the courthouse, said men filled the lobby that night, standing or sitting around, and discussing the plans for the lynching. Most of them were strangers, he said. All Sunday evening the rural 'phones were ringing, and each was given this message: "Be at the courthouse at eight o'clock. You know the rest."

The reporter for the St. Joseph *News-Press* stated that plans for taking the Negro to the schoolhouse for the lynching were openly discussed Sunday night by the milling crowds.

All Prepared—Mobbers and Guardsmen. The morning of Monday, January 12, dawned cold but clear, and found hundreds of men, many of them dressed in mackinaws and wearing laced boots, with caps pulled down just about their eyes, milling about the square, filling the courthouse corridors, and looking expectantly toward the jail, a block away. A county official who arrived at his office on the first floor of the courthouse stated that he heard the discussions going on, with such remarks as, "You fellows watch over here at this door; you watch here . . ." and the like.

When the adjutant general left the conference on Sunday

afternoon, he told the captain of the local battery, in the hearing of the sheriff and the prosecuting attorney, to mobilize his men and have them in uniform and armed at 7:30 Monday morning. They were at the armory, and side arms and ammunition, including a round of tear bombs, were issued them. About eight o'clock the adjutant general went to the battery and found it ready for action. The captain put the boys through a drill for the next half hour, and then they waited.

"Prisoner Taken Straight Into the Mob." When the judge entered the courthouse shortly before nine o'clock, he had to push his way through the crowds both in the hallways and in the courtroom itself. The sheriff and the prosecuting attorney entered closely behind him. The judge opened court, and after the short formality sat down, and said: "Call the first arraignment." "State vs. Gunn," the clerk read. "The sheriff will bring in the prisoner," said the judge. He leaned back with his hands clasped behind his head and waited. The sheriff walked back through the crowds, and to the jail. Two deputies were waiting in his car, and in a moment he had placed Gunn in the back seat beside one of them. The car started up the street, turned at the corner of the square, and headed directly into the crowd massed about the courthouse door on the south side.

"It was an amazing sight," the *News-Press* reporter related. "Here was the prisoner being taken straight into a mob waiting for him. I was standing with the editor of the local paper. We ran toward the car, and the crowd nearly beat us to it. 'Here he is!' they yelled, and crowded around the car as it came to a stop just opposite the courthouse entrance on that side. 'Grab him!' several men yelled. I saw the sheriff open his door, and a big man put an arm around him and pulled him over. Another leader opened the back door in the meantime, and held the deputy, while a third reached in and seized the Negro. A dozen men swarmed around the prisoner, and pulled him out into the street. The sheriff picked himself up, dusted off his coat, and walked back toward the jail. I don't know what happened to the deputies. They just sort of melted away."

Miles Down the Road. One block north from the courthouse square is the armory. As though by agreement not to pass by the armory, the crowd surged with the Negro into the street leading east. Halfway down the block they paused. And here the "man in the red coat" took command. No one knows who he was, apparently. This man, wearing a bright red-and-brown mackinaw, mounted the running board of a car parked nearby, and addressed the crowd. They would take the prisoner to the schoolhouse and burn him, he said. The crowd yelled approval. Should they get cars? No, they would march. "Don't go down by the armory where those toy soldiers are!" some one said. So the crowd moved on westward to the corner, turned north, passed a block from the armory, tramped the eight or ten blocks down one of the main residential streets, and out into a country road leading toward the school.

In the meantime the *News-Press'* photographer was taking pictures. He got views of the crowd just as they seized the Negro; as they started the march, as the "man in the red coat" addressed them; and as they went on the march out of town. The reporter, with a number of others, got in a car and rode out to the schoolhouse. The roadway was filled with cars, all headed that way. When he got to the schoolhouse a big crowd had gathered, and the whole countryside was pouring in, men, women and children. "They've got him and are on the way!" was the word that went over the 'phone wires then. Many came from ten and fifteen miles away to witness the burning after the march had begun.

Arrival at the Schoolhouse. The *News-Press* reporter went back and met the mobbers about a mile from the schoolhouse. They moved in close formation, with the Negro held by a chain packed in the center of a group. His ears and nose had been badly cut. The leader was out in front, directing the way. They halted before the schoolhouse. The march had taken about an hour and a half. Long before the mob reached its destination, a number of those already on the ground had begun to move out the furnishings of the small building. When the mob arrived, the work of clearing the building was completed. The chairs, desks, the table, the piano—even some of the blackboards had been taken out and stacked together.

Then the leaders took Gunn inside the schoolhouse. Besides the prisoner only twelve men were admitted. One of the twelve wrote the *News-Press* reporter (in an unsigned letter) that since he had so much information on the lynching, he might want to know what went on inside, so he would tell him. The writer related that they got a piece of paper, wrote a confession for Gunn, read it to him, and asked him if it were true. He said it was, but that another Negro helped in the crime, and implicated "Shike" Smith, formerly of Maryville and more recently of Omaha. "Now what are you going to do with me?" Gunn asked. "Well, nigger, we're going to burn you," the leader said.

The party came out. By a small ladder, two of them climbed up on the roof of the schoolhouse, and pulled Gunn up after them. The *News-Press* photographer's collection included pictures of the mob around the building, and of the two men on the roof pulling the Negro up after them. Then the "man in the red coat" saw him, rushed angrily at him, called for some men to assist, and they seized the camera. The rolls inside were destroyed, and the photographer had difficulty in getting them not to smash the camera itself. Several pictures were made by other photographers, however, showing the fire in progress.

Chained to Ridgepole and Burned. One of the men on the roof tore away some shingles on either side of the ridgepole, and then ordered the Negro to lie prone across the ridge. They passed a chain over his legs and around under the rafters, securing his arms likewise. Gasoline was sent up in cans, and poured over the Negro and about the top of the roof. Other men drained off gasoline from cars, and poured it in through the windows, throwing it all about the walls and floor. Then the leader ordered the crowd to get back, lit a paper and sent it flying through a window. In a flash the interior was in flames. In a moment more the roof burst in flames about the victim.

For five minutes the flames raged, and then they died down somewhat, as the gasoline had burned out. The clothing quickly burned off the Negro, who writhed about on the roof. He was silent except for one long scream. After eleven minutes he was still. In sixteen minutes the roof fell in. It was 11:30.

Before the fire had been set, while the crowds were still jamming in, the cars were being parked in some sort of fashion by the direction of a member of the police force of Maryville. While the building was in flames, the *News-Press* reporter saw standing by his side, intently watching the burning, one of the deputies who had brought the prisoner to the courthouse and to the mob. "Isn't this an awful thing to watch?" the reporter commented. "Yes," the deputy responded, "but it just had to be!"

Souvenirs for Men, Women, and Children. The crowd that witnessed the lynching has been variously estimated at from 2,000 to 4,000. The former figure is likely more nearly correct. But it took three hours longer for the cars finally to disentangle themselves. About one-fourth of the crowd were women, and there were hundreds of children. One woman held her little girl up so she could get a better view of the naked Negro blazing on the roof. The leaders took poles and poked the timbers into the blaze, so that everything would be consumed. "We don't want the expense of a funeral," was said repeatedly. All the afternoon the crowds milled about, poking in the ashes for souvenirs. The charred remains of the victim were divided piece by piece. The piano was dismembered and literally carried away in pieces as souvenirs.

If the Sheriff Had Wanted to Prevent the Lynching. A threatened lynching can be prevented, "if." The lynching was prevented at St. Joseph by the display of just ordinary intelligence and determination on the part of the sheriff, cooperating with the National Guard of the state. That the disgrace of Maryville could have been spared if the sheriff had used the same intelligence and determination is beyond question.

Here is the story of the conference of Sunday afternoon: When the adjutant general and the captain of the local National Guard unit went into the courthouse office of the prosecuting attorney, three men were there. They shook hands with the adjutant general, but the captain had failed to introduce them. Whereupon the "most important looking man" among them (whom the adjutant general thought must be the sheriff), said: "General, I am glad we can have this conference, as I am convinced there will be trouble tomorrow. The town is filling up with men intent on a lynching." He went ahead to outline the danger, and the necessity for National Guard assistance. Then he said: "Of course, the matter lies in the hands of the sheriff here—" (motioning to another of the group).

"I turned about then toward the sheriff," said the adjutant general, "who sat against the wall. He made no move to say anything. I suggested that I would be glad to coöperate, and he said: 'Well, I don't think we'll need you. There'll be no trouble.' Beyond that I could hardly get him to talk. He seemed to resent outside interference. The prosecuting attorney had nothing to advise, except that he agreed with the sheriff. I finally laid out a plan for the sheriff. I reminded him that he would have to request any help in writing, according to the state law. 'I am familiar with that,' he said. I proposed that he write me a letter then and there, asking for assistance from the National Guard and then let me take charge. I assured him I would turn the active command over to the captain, a local man, who could be trusted by the citizens to do what was right. He responded that he would not agree to that, and would not need any help.

" 'Are you going to use any deputies?' I asked.

" 'Yes,' he said, 'I'll handle the matter with my own deputies. We won't have any trouble.' "

Continuing, the adjutant general said: "We stayed in conference for an hour and a half. I simply could not overcome the apparent antagonism of the sheriff and the prosecuting attorney. I asked again that the sheriff write a notice asking for assistance, and give it to me. If I did not need it, then I would hand it back to him the next day, and he could just consider that he had never written it. He refused to do it. As we left the office, I told the captain to mobilize the battery anyhow, so that if we were needed we would be ready."

Should the Adjutant General Have Acted Anyhow? That is a question that has had endless discussion by lawyers and laymen all over the state. There is no doubt the lynching could have been prevented. Another battery of the same regiment is in Burlington Junction, in the same county; in an adjoining county is a company of infantry; and beyond these, a hundred men could have been called in from the St. Joseph company. In all, 250 troops could have been in town by Sunday night. The streets could have been patrolled, the cars moved, crowds dispersed, and the prisoner amply protected. Here enters a pertinent query: Why didn't the adjutant general get in touch with the governor after the conference, and get orders to proceed independently of the sheriff? He could have taken orders directly from the governor. He has said that he was under orders to coöperate with the sheriff and that he could not do so, legally, without written request. All academic questions aside, there resulted one of the most unusual spectacles in the history of lynching—men armed to prevent a lynching rendered impotent by the red tape of a legal provision.

After the crowd had left town with the prisoner, the adjutant general went to the courthouse and met the judge, who had adjourned court for the day, and was "feeling pretty badly." The prosecuting attorney was there, but had nothing to say. He found one of the deputies—apparently the one who didn't go out to see the burning—and asked where the sheriff was. "He's at home, and has a broken arm," the deputy answered. But the investigator found at the home of the sheriff the curt information that, though the sheriff's arm was not broken, he was "all shaken up" over the affair and couldn't see him or anybody else.

More About the Sheriff. Immediately after the lynching, the sheriff talked freely. He didn't call on the guard for fear "somebody would get hurt." The sheriff said to a local editor, "The governor needn't blame the adjutant general that the guardsmen weren't called out. He can blame me, if he feels that anybody must be blamed. Most of the members of the guard are young men, 18 to 20, and I knew that if they were turned loose in that crowd with their automatic pistols somebody would be killed or badly injured, and probably it would be the guardsmen. I feel that lives were saved by leaving those young men in the armory and not sending them against the crowd. I heard people in the crowd say that they would make short work of 'those tin soldiers' if they came out with their popguns." It is nothing short of bewildering that a sheriff should assume that guardsmen are ever "turned loose" in a crowd.

When specifically asked whether the adjutant general was sent to Maryville with orders to prevent the lynching, or to place himself at the disposal of the local officials, the sheriff replied: "I was not advised why he was sent here." When asked whether he thought bloodshed would have resulted if the National Guard had been called out, he said that most certainly it would if the guardsmen had been sent against the crowds any time after 8 o'clock that morning. Then, to the heart of the matter, he was asked whether he thought the lynching could have been prevented without bloodshed if the National Guard had taken charge sometime Sunday afternoon. "There was no occasion for them being called out at that time," he contended. When it was suggested that the adjutant general and the National Guard might have been given authority to proceed as they saw fit, he answered: "My understanding was that there was not to be any trouble. And of course when the crowd started, there was not any time to notify anyone." How can one reconcile the sheriff's own statements?

Nevertheless, that the sheriff feels himself justified is obvious; that he appreciates the approbation of the admirers and supporters of his actions is likewise obvious—as shown by the collection of letters, names, and editorials tacked on his office wall, described later in this report.

REACTION OF THE COMMUNITY TO THE LYNCHING

That the community generally justified or condoned the lynching is evinced by the fact that the courts have punished no one.

Many Men of Many Minds. As wide a divergence of private reactions and opinions on the matter as can be imagined was found in Maryville and the surrounding community. For example, within the circle of the local Teachers' College faculty one official was a member of the mob, at least to the extent of interested observation, and came back to a group of his fellow faculty members with glowing countenance and happy expression, with the remark: "Well, we got him!" Two professors carried on such a heated discussion of the rightness and wrongness of the mob that both were ordered to cease talking about it for the good of the school. By far the majority of the faculty members stood out against lawlessness. One college official assisted materially in securing information for this case study. A professor opened a column in the Maryville *Forum* for clear and open discussion of the evils of mob violence. Another professor, reared in Nodaway County, and, one of the oldest of the faculty members in years and point of service, has been recognized as the leader in matters of racial coöperation in the community. He gave a number of special lectures to the junior and senior students after the lynching; they were frank, powerful addresses on the shame of lynch law.

The sentiment of the people generally seemed to have crystallized along these lines: Those who unqualifiedly condemn the lynching; those who regret the affair, but feel that "under the circumstances" no one should be blamed—not even the sheriff—and that it all should be forgotten as quickly as possible; and those who frankly uphold the actions of the mob.

The first group is in the decided minority. Opinions of the last group have been harder to elicit, of course. The second group seems to include the great majority of Maryville citizens, including the officials, the ministers—except one—and most of the business and professional men. As the deputy said to the reporter as they witnessed the burning, "it just had to be."

A county official well expressed the case of those who felt that the lynching "had to be" when he said: "That crime would

have meant lynching anywhere. If anyone had tried to prevent it, we'd still be burying the bodies!" It is of interest that
several witnesses to the burning recalled seeing this official and
his wife.

Preparing For Negro Avengers. Intense anxiety and fear
were in evidence for a week following the lynching. On the Saturday following there occurred a big hoax which put a terrible
fright into Maryville's citizens. Word was 'phoned in from
Kansas City that about 2,000 Negroes from that city, and
from other nearby points, were arming and preparing to in-
vade Maryville to avenge the lynching. So widely was the story
circulated that the local papers in Springfield on that evening
carried large scare-heads to the effect that a race war in
Maryville was imminent. It has never been learned just who
started the rumor. Maryville people speak somewhat apolo-
getically of the affair now, but they admit practically the
whole town stayed awake during that night. "Every man in
town was armed, and on the streets," said a white minister
who believed the rumor. "We were sure we were going to have
to protect ourselves in blood. The sheriff deputized numerous
men to help with the defense. The streets were crowded all
night. It was particularly trying to hold church the next
morning."

By night the story had been augmented to include an invasion from Omaha, to lend reinforcements to the Kansas
City Negroes. Efforts were being made to hold them at the
bridge across the Missouri River, reports said. The sheriff,
recovered from his shock of the Monday before, was now out
fearlessly on the streets, giving orders right and left, depu-
tizing and officially arming men and 'phoning for help from
other counties.

Attitudes of White Ministers. Among those who held that
the mob was excusable under the circumstances must be placed
at least three of the white ministers. Smarting under the
criticisms of a former Maryville minister, who made an investigation of the mob outbreak, each of them made elaborate
explanation of why he did not preach against the mob. One
complained that the former minister "accuses us of entering

into a conspiracy of silence. No, there was no conspiracy. We just decided it would be better to preach on other subjects. I 'phoned the other brethren, and asked them what they intended to say. They said they would not mention the affair. I said I would not either. Of course, Brother————, said he would preach against it. But the rest of us were in agreement."

"I felt it was no time to mention the mob," said another. The third minister's comment was: "I did tell my people, at the request of the minister of the colored church, that the colored people appreciated the efforts of Christian white people to restore and maintain friendly relations. Beyond that, I did not feel that I should mention the matter."

A fourth minister, this one outspoken against the mob, said: "When I found that the other ministers had agreed not to mention the lynching, I told them I could not agree with them; that I had hoped to have their coöperation in condemning it; that I would act independently. At our communion service that Sunday morning, I took twelve or fifteen minutes to make a quiet but earnest appeal that the Christian people of the community atone in every manner possible for such an outrage as the lynching had been." The local Catholic priest stated: "There were no communicants of my church in the mob; at least if they were, they knew they were going counter to the teachings of their church."

Dispersion of Maryville Negroes. There was almost a complete exodus of colored people from town following the lynching, and for most of the week they remained away. The Negro teacher and the Negro minister stayed in town to help smooth the way for those who wished to return. In the meantime, the mayor met with the Negro minister and a committee of white business men, and assured the colored people that there would be no trouble for those who wanted to come back and were law-abiding. They drew up for the Negro minister a list of about ten Negroes that were branded as undesirable, and he was requested to ask these never to return. This he did.

The Negro minister stated that the affair had so broken into his work that he did not see how he could carry on, but would do so as long as he did not starve. His people were without money, without spirit, and rapidly moving away. Several weeks after the lynching the teacher found herself with only six pupils, and fearful of losing two or three of these.

The white citizens with the most money and influence took the lead in making it plain that they did not want their colored people to leave, and would give them work and support them. Of course there was the usual renewed activity of the hoodlum element, who insisted, so some business men stated, that all the Negroes be run out permanently. This effort failed in part, for leading business men refused to dismiss their Negro janitors.

The Fight in the Legislature. The morning after the lynching, the atmosphere about the halls of the legislature seethed with talk of what action should be taken by that body. The session was but a few days old. The Democrats were in control of both houses, for the first time since 1922.

Several Kansas City members of the house, all of them Democrats, introduced a resolution officially condemning the affair and calling on the proper authorities to bring the leaders of the mob to justice. The resolution precipitated a real fight. Leading the forces against its passage was a Nodaway County representative who told of the horrors of Gunn's crime, and begged his colleagues to let the local folks handle the matter in their own way. There was no party alignment on the issue. Most of the Kansas City and St. Louis delegations, the latter all Republican, voted for the resolution and the majority of the rural members voted against it. It was lost.

No One Indicted. Immediately after the lynching, the governor announced that he would make no statement until he had received the report of the adjutant general. Since then he has been quoted as favorable to an investigation, but the latest reports are that he is waiting for the action of the local authorities.

In his first statement to the press, the county sheriff stated that he knew the mob leaders by their first names, and would give the information to the authorities. Presently, however, the sheriff and local prosecuting attorney seemed determined to let the matter drop. When questioned about his plans, the prosecuting attorney was non-committal, with such answers as, "Well, I really don't know about that." Or, "I can't say; I don't know." When an effort was made to get him to explain the actions of the sheriff in not calling for the guard, he seemed to resent the suggestion. He had nothing to say about his plans for the punishment of the mob leaders. As to a special grand jury he said one was not necessary, for a regular grand jury was meeting in three months. And so nothing was done by the local authorities immediately after the lynching, or three months later, or since.

But One Unknown Mob Leader. Save one, all of the mob leaders were well known to the sheriff and other officials and citizens of Maryville. One citizen called the names of the following mob leaders—the man who knocked the sheriff down, the man who opened the car door, the man who first seized the Negro, and the man who first climbed on the roof. Many of the mob leaders came from a distance. On the night before, about half the cars parked about the square bore Iowa tags. Many Kansas and Nebraska cars were present next morning.

Just what part the Klan played in the matter is not known, although many stated that it had a big part. Then there were stories of the participation of other organizations—some of them new. While doubtless the Klan and similar organizations were well represented, yet it is obvious that some men follow prospective lynchings just as some men like to attend fox hunts and turkey shoots. For this type, the Maryville situation was too good a chance to miss. Illustrative of such men must have been the group that sat about one of the cafés, following the lynching, counting up their expenses, so they could collect from their buddies back home.

Who was the one unknown mob leader, the "man in the red coat"? He was positively a stranger to Maryville and the community. All they knew was that he "came in here to help out." Among the cars from a distance was one with a Louisiana license. The story persists that a noted Shreveport busi-

ness man sent this unknown leader. If court pressure would
be put upon the local mob leaders, the identity of this stranger
would doubtless be revealed.

Spot News for the Papers. The reaction in the newspapers
to the Maryville lynching was almost unanimously that of
severe condemnation. From one end of the country to the other
the editorial columns broke forth in bitter comments. It is likely
that this lynching got more "news space" and more editorial
inches than the average two or three lynchings combined, and
for several reasons. It was not in the typical "lynching belt,"
as some papers call the Southern States; the enormity of the
crime had attracted much attention; the deliberate preparations for the lynching were almost without parallel; and the
fact that the National Guard stood ready within a block of the
courthouse where the Negro was turned over to the mob.

Only Condemnation From Missouri Dailies. Maryville's
daily paper, the *Forum* and the *Weekly Tribune*, both sturdily
deplored and condemned the mob and its leaders. Especially
did the *Forum* speak out against the disorders. From its office
went the first news flash that the Negro had been taken
by the mob, and with the story went the complete statement
of the actions of the sheriff in refusing the help of the National
Guard.

Equally severe in condemnation was the *News-Press* of St.
Joseph, only 45 miles from Maryville, and the dominant city
of northwest Missouri. All the St. Louis papers united in deploring the outrage, the *Post-Dispatch* continuing in this
respect the crusade for better race relationships it has always
carried on, sometimes independently and sometimes in co-
operation with its "big sister" in New York, the now departed
World. In Springfield, metropolis of southwest Missouri and
fourth city in the state, the two daily papers, the *Leader* and
the *Press*, vied with each other in condemnation of Missouri's
shame. So did the two daily papers in Joplin, fifth city; and
for that matter, no daily paper in the state made any defense
of the affair.

*". . . The More Deplorable Because It Easily Could Have
Been Prevented."* Outstanding in influence and prestige in the

Middle West is the Kansas City *Star*, a successful newspaper from every standpoint of modern journalism, and retaining that fine flavor of leadership in civic and public affairs instilled into it by its founder. A study of the *Star* for the week following the first break of the news is a chronicle of how relentlessly a paper with courage and ability in news and editorial expression can portray the facts about and the effects of a lynching such as at Maryville. A complete condemnation of the mob was given in this paper, with discussions also of the blame that should rest on the local officials, the adjutant general, the citizens, and the mob leaders.

"Missouri in Shame," ran the heading of its first editorial on the subject, followed by these words: "The lynching at Maryville was about as horrible as such a thing can be. Lynching in itself is a fearful reproach to American civilization. Lynching by fire is the vengeance of a savage past. Public opinion against mob law has grown to such weight that the number of such crimes has been greatly reduced in recent years. Now Missouri enters the list of states where such crimes are still possible. The sickening outrage in the more deplorable because it easily could have been prevented. . . ."

Reaction of the Southern Press. Every conceivable angle of the case was attacked with similar vigor and in like vein by the press everywhere, with but few exceptions. Comments from large newspapers in the South were especially interesting. The Atlanta *Constitution* said: "How much oftener must it be proclaimed from court, press and pulpit that there is no case anywhere in civilized America that justifies lynching? It is a fiendish and indefensible crime of crimes, committed first against the peace and honor of the community and then with brute rage against a helpless victim. Without exception every lynching is an exhibition and confession of cowardice and cruelty."

In some of the Southern papers there were traces of a feeling of "geographical vindication," that mobs could be staged elsewhere. One of the most vivid of a wave of cartoons that followed the lynching was one displaying the hand of the "Maryville lyncher" holding aloft a torch; in the distance are the smoking embers of the schoolhouse. The cartoon was captioned, "The Torch of Civilization in Missouri."

The most bitter of all the comments, in both news portrayal and editorials, came from the Negro press. The Kansas City *Call*, and the St. Louis *Argus* are the leading Negro newspapers in the state; both papers augmented their own editorial comment with clippings from other papers, white and colored alike.

Sheriff Praised by Some Missouri Weeklies. There were numbers of papers that "toned down" the shamefulness of the mob action, and played up the crime that Gunn had committed, to imply that in some instances mob violence is quite explainable, if not excusable. A few papers, notably some weekly papers of Missouri and the Middle West, came out in support of the sheriff. On the wall of the sheriff's office is an astonishing collection. There are six or eight editorials pasted end to end. "Instilling the fear into the hearts of niggers is the only way to handle them," says one of the editorials, while the others run in similar vein. Nearby on the wall are several lists of signatures of citizens commending the sheriff for not calling out the militia against the mob; one list is of "Holt County citizens," and another "Nodaway County citizens." Then there are several letters—all of them anonymous—telling the sheriff what a wonderful man and "American citizen" he is for letting the mob take the prisoner.

FACTS ABOUT THE COMMUNITY

Unexcelled Agricultural Section. Maryville lies at the heart of the most fertile farm land in the Middle West. It is the home of one of the five State Teachers' Colleges of Missouri, and the county itself leads in adequate rural schools.

Nodaway County adjoins the Iowa line and is the next to the last county in the northwest tip of Missouri. This section is known as the Platte Purchase of 1837, comprising fourteen counties.

The Platte Purchase was not originally included in the boundaries of Missouri, this triangle being "infested" with troublesome Indians. The white settlers organized a movement to have this territory included in the state, and as a result the Indians moved across the Missouri River.

The secretary of the Missouri State Board of Agriculture, sets forth that "these Northwest Missouri counties are in the center of the very best agricultural section, not only in the United States, but in the whole world. As proof of this, there has never been known a crop failure in this section. Hogs, cattle and lambs shipped from the feed lots of these counties to the markets are of heaviest weight and finest quality to be found."

Earliest Settlers from Kentucky and Tennessee. Immigrants pushed into this fertile country as soon as the purchase was made. Mostly from Kentucky and Tennessee, they came overland, or by boat to the "turn of the river" near what later became Kansas City, from which landing the great wagon trains for the far west were made up. During the late Thirties and early Forties these Southern people came, bringing with them their slaves. They rapidly settled what are now the three counties immediately north of Kansas City.

It is about a hundred and twenty miles, however, from the Missouri River to the Iowa line. By 1845 enough settlers had pushed up to the Nodaway County territory to form a town, and they called it Maryville. While these settlers, like those to the south of them, came largely from Southern states, yet this fact must be noticed: Many families came in from the eastern sections of Tennessee and Kentucky, and these did not own slaves. They went on beyond the slave sections just north of the river, and settled in the counties joining the Iowa line. Thus Nodaway County cannot be called one of the "slave counties" of Missouri, and, in fact, there have never been more than 250 Negroes in the county.

The first store was opened in Maryville in 1845; the first lawyer set up practice in 1847, the first school was built in the same year, and next year the first bank was chartered; the first flour mill was opened in 1848, and the first brick building was erected in 1852. The first Masonic Lodge was instituted in 1856.

Later Settlers from Ohio, Indiana, and Illinois. Immigration and settlement slowed down considerably during the years immediately preceding the Civil War, but started again with a boom when peace was declared. And now came people, mostly from Ohio, Indiana, and Illinois. Nodaway County, then, is a blend of Southern and Northern people. The unusual productivity of the soil naturally attracted high class farmers.

In 1930 the population was 26,371, of which only 95 are Negroes. More than ninety-six per cent are native American born. As have practically all rural counties of Missouri and of most of the agricultural states, Nodaway has steadily lost population in recent decades: 32,809 in 1900, 30,000 in 1910, 27,774 in 1920; and 26,371 in 1930.

King of Agriculture Among Missouri Counties. Farms in the county average 123.9 acres, and are valued at about $18,000,-000 on a normal rating. The soil is an even, fertile, black prairie loam, and most of the lands are farmed by their owners. From this magnificent setting for agricultural productivity Nodaway rules as King of Agriculture among Missouri Counties.

Particularly does the county lead in corn, heading all in crop volume, producing in 1929 over three million bushels. In 1929, the average acreage for all counties in Missouri planted to corn was 48,777; Nodaway planted 152,260 acres. It produces more corn than the combined production of Arizona, Idaho, Maine, Nevada, New Hampshire, Oregon, Rhode Island, Utah and Wyoming.

In hog production the county also leads, with 158,070 for last year, as compared with an average county production of 37,833. In cattle raising, the county leads with a figure of 50,880 to a general average of 20,035 for the state. The county census showed 14,870 milk cows at the first of last year, to an average for the state of 7,254. Poultry numbered 513,190 last year, as compared to 276,786 for the state average. In all other products usually grown in the middle-western area this county ranks high. In the days when horse and mule raising was much more profitable than now, Nodaway led in production of horses and ranked near the top in mules.

Maryville, with a population of 5,200, has the usual number

of people engaged in the businesses and professions. The chief
unit industry of the town associated with the handling of
agricultural products is the creamery. The town has two
modern hotels, one large hardware store, five first-class mercantile establishments, one grocery store, as up-to-date as can
be found, and two large chain stores. In all there are ten
blocks devoted to retail business, cafes and hotels, including
the four sides of the square and the adjoining streets of the
business section. The usual professions are represented—
doctors, lawyers, dentists; there are two chiropractors, and an
osteopathic physician.

Significant Educational Institutions. The State Teachers'
College at Maryville and the large Catholic Abbey at Conception are important economic factors. The former institution
was founded in 1905 by a special act of the Missouri legislature, as a part of the state system of five colleges for the
training of teachers and other students. Its territory is the
entire northwest area of the state. It offers the full four-year
course, with appropriate degrees. There are modern buildings
and equipment, and 166 acres of land for the campus. The
faculty, with fifty-five members, has been assembled from various
graduate schools. The enrollment runs to about 1,000 students.

Maryville's Public Schools. Maryville's public schools include
one senior high school, a Teachers' College high school, a
central grade school for white children, and a grade school
for colored children. The senior high school is housed in a
new building, well equipped and a model of latest improvements.
The Teachers' College high school is a practice school for
student teachers at the college. There are 1,100 children in
the grade school of the city, with eight grades, fully approved,
and far above the average of small-city schools in equipment
and teaching force.

The one colored school (in Missouri there must be a school
provided for colored children wherever there are any of school
age) is a small but well built structure, modern in every respect,
with provisions for two class rooms and a small auditorium.
A large basement provides space for recreational activities.
The Negro teacher is a capable person, does good work, and

is highly respected. A few years ago there were 35 Negro pupils enrolled. Within the two years prior to the lynching several colored families moved away to place their boys and girls in high schools, and the enrollment dropped to 16 in 1930. In the spring of 1931, the enrollment was only six, a telling comment on the dispersion of Maryville's Negroes following the lynching.

Eighteen Rural High Schools. Outside of Maryville, there are eighteen high schools in Nodaway County, fifteen of them approved as first-class; 1,257 students are in these high schools. There are thirty-eight first-class rural schools, with an enrollment of 4,029. Here again the county leads, Nodaway being first in the number of first-class rural schools. The buildings are for the most part well heated, lighted, and provided with sanitary toilets; with piano, pictures, a library, and other needed equipment. The salary schedule for rural teachers runs far above the average for Missouri. For the high standing of the rural schools, much credit is given the county superintendent, who has held office since 1923.

The Catholic Schools. About one-fourth of the county's people are Catholics; there are two divisions, the Irish and German. Maryville has two Catholic schools, St. Patrick's and St. Mary's. At Conception, some miles southeast of Maryville, is the great Catholic center, with a magnificent cathedral building and various schools for the training of priests and nuns. In 1873 the institution was founded as a monastery and some years later was made an abbey.

Maryville's Churches. There are five white Protestant churches and one colored Protestant church in Maryville, two Catholic churches and a small Christian Science congregation. The Protestant churches are of the usual denominations found in a county-seat city of the Middle West—Baptist, Methodist Episcopal, Methodist Episcopal South, Christian and Presbyterian. In membership and influence the Christian Church with about 950 members leads. The next strongest is the Methodist Episcopal, with 800 members. All five denominations have good church buildings. There are nearly 350 Baptists, 300 Methodist Episcopalians and about 200

Presbyterians. In each of the Protestant churches is a Sunday school, with enrollments comparable to church memberships. Reference has been made already to the fact that of these ministers, but one stood up boldly against the lynching. The church leadership as represented by these pastors seems to be static, stereotyped, and unprogressive. Dynamic leadership seems sadly lacking.

There were two colored churches in town until a year or so ago, when the Baptist congregation dwindled and the meetings were given up. The Methodist Episcopal Church survives, but quite feebly, for the depression and the removal of families after the lynching have weakened it. As indicated earlier in the report, the Negro minister was the one constant point of contact between the colored people and the white people of Maryville in the days following the lynching.

Two Strong Parties. Nodaway County, politically, has long been considered one of the "normally Republican" counties of Missouri, carrying it by about 500. But the county has also been noted for "scratching" its ballots, so that often both Republicans and Democrats have won county offices at the same elections. The county is in a congressional district with the parties equally strong, and party work is carried on actively during the political campaigns. In the election of 1928, the Republican presidential candidate received 7,160 votes out of the county's 12,660; in this election most of the Republican county ticket was elected. The 1930 election saw the Democratic state representative elected by 1,409 majority, along with most of the Democratic ticket.

The circuit court of the judicial district of which Nodaway County is a part meets three times a year in Maryville. The present judge, elected by a majority of fifteen votes, is the first Republican judge this district has elected. The county bears the reputation of being one of the most law-abiding in the state. There are seldom more than half a dozen prisoners in the county jail, and usually the majority of these are transients. Of course, there are some "bad families" in the county, whose members get into jail on minor offenses. Crimes of violence have been few. Undesirables repeatedly have been asked to leave Maryville in an effort to keep the town free from prospective criminals.

Many Civic and Public Welfare Agencies. Maryville is amply supplied with civic and public welfare agencies, due in part to the added culture which the Teachers' College brings to the community. There is a Rotary Club; a Monday Forum Club, popularly referred to by some citizens as the "highbrow bunch" and containing a number of the college faculty members; a Business Men's Club, composed of the leading business and professional men; a Chamber of Commerce, with convenient and active headquarters and regular meetings; and a country club with the usual features. Outstanding among the women's clubs is the Twentieth Century Club. There is also a small Business and Professional Women's Club.

There is a good-sized Carnegie Public Library, with an active circulation. A large, modern hospital is sponsored by the Catholic Church.

In matters of public welfare, Maryville has prided itself on prompt performance of duty. There is practically no problem of abject poverty; since the depression only a few families have been in need. Red Cross and other relief organizations are supported fully; even during the winter of 1930-31 the Red Cross roll call quota was reached with no public solicitors at work; only recently the town sent a carload of food stuffs to a drought area in southern Missouri.

"No Race Prejudice Here!" This phrase summarizes the remark of Maryville citizens on their estimate of the relations between the races. In 1930, of Nodaway County's 95 Negroes, all but eleven lived inside Maryville. Practically all the Negroes are descendants of slaves brought in by the original settlers. Ministers of the churches were unanimous in the report that never before had there been an expression of ill-feeling between the races. Various members of the Teachers' College faculty reiterated it, although several of them modified the statement somewhat to mean "no race prejudice, on the basis of the usual treatment of Negroes by whites." Especially did the professor of the social science department emphasize that while there is no race prejudice as generally understood, there could

have been closer coöperation betwen the races and a greater spirit of helpfulness on the part of white citizens in assisting the underprivileged, in recreation and other public welfare matters.

Depression, Bank Failure, Unrest. In the study of the situation at Maryville, no background for the lynching would be complete without mention of the effects of the severe depression. There has developed in Maryville and environs a spirit of restlessness and anxiety, as well as dissatisfaction with public officials and the courts, which helped bring about conditions under which the lynching could be possible.

During the World War, good farming land was at a premium. Prices on Nodaway County land went up and up and in value. Then came the slump of 1921. While business generally recovered and rose to the prosperity era of 1924 to 1928, it is common knowledge that farm lands and farm products have never recovered in any way comparable to other basic industries. The slump and depression that began in 1929 and carried on through 1930 pushed the farm situation into the abject depths of pessimism. While diversification of crops has furnished enough to eat and some marketable products in Nodaway, and there has been no hunger, yet the big homes, massive barns and silos, the herds, the fertile soil, have become symbols for low values, debt, and failure. The situation has fostered a pessimism previously unknown in Nodaway.

With the depression have come bank failures. Nodaway County presents a sad list of them, reaching back to 1926. In that year the Real Estate Bank of Maryville closed its doors. Two years later the bank at Clearmont and the bank at Skidmore failed. In 1929 both the banks at Burlington Junction went under. An official in one of these was convicted of embezzlement. Early in 1930 the bank of Wilcox failed. On April 7, 1930, occurred the big crash of the Farmer's Trust Company of Maryville, with a million and a half on deposit. This failure was a staggering blow to the community. Many men were left penniless. Four of the churches of the city had their deposits there. The outlook for credit and money among the business houses was decidedly gloomy. Shortly after that the bank at a small town, Hopkins, closed its doors, and the president committed suicide. Early in 1931 the bank of Quitman and the bank at Parnell both failed.

The number of foreclosures on farm property grew steadily throughout 1930, with the largest number ever carried in the county paper appearing in January 1931, on the twelfth day of which month Raymond Gunn was burned.

PART SEVEN

FOILING THE MOB

NEARLY FORTY reported threatened lynchings, involving over sixty accused persons, were prevented in 1930. While it would be interesting to have a case study of each of these, as of each of the lynchings, five representative case studies are presented: Port Arthur-Beaumont, centers of oil refining and commercial activities in southeast Texas; Shamrock, a new town in sparsely settled northwest Texas; LaGrange, a textile town in the west Georgia plantation area; Sylvania, a village in an east Georgia rural plantation county; and Huntsville, a farm-trade and textile town in north Alabama. In one case the National Guard was called into action; in two the state police assisted the local peace officers; in two the local officers alone prevented the threatened lynchings. In three instances the accused persons were removed to distant prisons for safe keeping; in all five there was close coöperation between peace officers and court officials.

Of the five Negroes saved from mobs, two were charged with capital crimes, and were tried, given death sentences and executed; two, charged with attempted rape, were tried and given sentences of thirty and forty years each; the fifth one, accused of murder, was released when a thorough investigation had established his innocence. The presence of mobs before and during the trials of the four convicted accused persons doubtless resulted in the court's giving more severe sentences than would have been forthcoming under normal circumstances.

At Scottsboro, Alabama, and Elberton, Georgia, where the National Guard prevented lynchings in the first half of 1931, death sentences were imposed in courtrooms overflowing with and surrounded by mobs openly demanding speedy conviction and execution. In both cases troops had to be called out to protect the accused prisoners, both before and during trial. By so doing, the lives of the accused were saved; relative to the mobs, however, the troops only forcibly restrained would-be killers from becoming actual killers.

Lynch prevention is a constructive measure in so far as it discourages the formation of mobs in the future. The five cases below are presented as illustrating the means by which peace officers, court officials, and private citizens have restrained mobs from their murderous purposes. Stricter law enforcement must be accompanied, however, by a general rise of economic and cultural levels before the mob can be banished from the scene.

CHAPTER XXI

PROTECTING THEIR PRISONERS

THE CASE STUDIES below of the threatened lynchings prevented at Port Arthur-Beaumont, and Shamrock, Texas, will further set forth specific ways by which officers have kept mobs from their murderous purposes. It will be observed that whereas court officials coöperated in both cases, the greater credit for foiling the mobs clearly belonged to the peace officers.

PORT ARTHUR-BEAUMONT, JEFFERSON COUNTY, TEXAS

In late June, 1930, a Negro, accused of numerous assaults upon women—one of whom was colored—was arrested and placed in jail at Port Arthur, Jefferson County, Texas. A mob gathered immediately; the prisoner was transferred to the county jail at Beaumont, and on subsequent nights attempts were made to take him. Except for the courage and common sense displayed by the chief of police at Port Arthur, and later by the sheriff of Jefferson County at Beaumont, he would doubtless have been lynched

Alleged Crimes of the Accused. For several weeks a Negro was alleged to have followed the practice of descending upon couples parked in the vicinity of Port Arthur, and at the point of a gun forcing the man to leave and then assaulting his woman companion. The first case reported to the police was that of a woman who had to be treated at the local hospital for severe scalp wounds. She alleged that a Negro had come upon her and her companion and at the point of a gun had forced them to get out of their car. Thereupon he grabbed her and ordered the man to leave. When she began screaming, the Negro struck her over the head and cursed her. In the meantime her companion had made his way to a nearby telephone and called the police. When the latter arrived shortly afterwards, the Negro had fled.

Unable that night to find the prowler, on the next night plain-clothes officers parked where the couple was parked the night before. Sometime after they had turned off their lights, Rainey Williams, 38-year-old local Negro, approached the parked car. He was arrested and placed in jail at Port Arthur. In his confession, he is reported to have admitted that it was he who had molested the couple on the night before, and that on several other occasions he had committed similar offenses. According to police reports, his confessed earlier crimes were presently verified.

Precautions Taken by Chief of Police. When it was known around town that a Negro had been arrested charged with numerous assaults, a large crowd gathered at the jail. Port Arthur's chief of police immediately dispatched guards to protect the accused man. Threatening shouts were heard from all sides. Mob leaders went to the police chief, demanding that they be given the keys to the jail. His reply was that the keys were locked in the safe. Remembering Sherman, the members of the mob quite naturally talked of burning the jail if Williams could not be had otherwise.

The preliminary trial was set for eleven o'clock Friday, June 27. Hours ahead, the streets surrounding the jail and police station were jammed. Fifteen minutes before eleven, clearing the way by the use of tear gas bombs, the chief of police took the Negro from his cell on the second floor across into the second floor of the fire station adjoining, whence upon instructions, the Negro slid down the brass pole to the side of the fire chief's automobile. Officers threw him into the rumble seat; members of the mob rushed in and jerked him out; the officers exploded tear gas bombs and pushed the Negro back in the rumble seat as the automobile roared off to Beaumont, making the twenty-two mile run in about fifteen minutes. A car full of peace officers next sped off in another direction, and the mob followed the second car.

Sheriff Mingled with Mob Members. Soon after Williams

had been placed in the county jail at Beaumont, crowds began to gather. Shortly after midnight a mob of over two hundred men and a few women, most of them said to have been from Port Arthur, attempted to take the Negro from the jail. They had an acetylene torch, and on several occasions the sheriff extinguished it. Tear gas bombs were finally used to disperse the crowd. Two young women in the mob ridiculed the men; one of them shouted. "What's the matter with you men, why don't you go in and get him?"

The county sheriff mixed with the crowd, and more than a half dozen times was thrown from his feet by members of the mob. His pistol was knocked from his hands more than once, but each time he regained control of it. The sheriff stated that he put his deputies inside the locked jail with guns, and instructed them to protect the prisoner, and that he went outside to talk with the men, feeling that this was the best way to keep them from storming the jail. He further stated that he threatened to shoot nobody, and in a friendly way urged them to refrain from violence.

Mob's Lack of Leadership. There was little evidence of leadership in the mob. Without results, two young men about twenty-five years of age did what they could to whip the crowd into concerted action. When forty volunteers were called to storm the jail, several men responded and retired across the street to perfect plans. Without difficulty, plain clothes policemen dissipated this developing nucleus by arresting a few of the leaders. The two young women who were taunting the men for being "yellow," one of them reported to have been assaulted by a Negro on one occasion, were not long in evidence, for they too were lodged in jail for the remainder of the night.

Again on the next night the mob congregated. Anticipating this move, the sheriff had placed electric lights in the jail yard; also he had an additional number of deputies, and was in close touch with the fire department. Someone in the mob remarked that the county jail might just as well be knocked down or burned, since it was to be pulled down in a few months preparatory to the erection on the same site of a new million-dollar courthouse. While the mob was endeavoring to develop sufficient momentum to storm the jail, several inmates of the building shouted encouragement. One prisoner yelled, "Why don't you dynamite de joint?" This resulted in a big laugh and relieved the mob of much of its tenseness.

The Sheriff's Effective Technique. In the meantime the grand jury's investigations had been started. Feeling that the mob would approve of the state's expressed plans to seek the death sentence for Williams, the sheriff sent for the court stenographer who, at two o'clock in the morning, appeared at the jail and read to the mob the proceedings of the court. Convinced by this that the court was developing a "hanging case," the crowd dispersed slowly.

With each night the mob had grown weaker; by the next night the demonstrations about the jail had practically ceased. When a report came to the sheriff that the sailors from a ship in port were going to lead another attack on the jail, he went immediately to the docks. Coming upon the doughty sailor boy who was organizing the affair, the sheriff nipped the demonstration in the bud by rendering the leader a hefty blow which knocked him from his feet.

One of the leaders of the mob, so the sheriff stated, was a man who had been a peace officer, and at the time of the threatened lynching was working at one of the refineries; another was a man who had run against the sheriff for a minor city office years earlier; a third, also formerly an officer, was quieted when the sheriff reminded him that his own sheet was far from clean, since he had once killed a man. While some of the mob members were from Beaumont, most were from the oil refineries near Port Arthur. "I saw no cutthroats or professional lynchers in the crowd," said the sheriff. "All I saw were working men; I understood their position, knew they were excited. But I meant for them to understand my position, too: Under no circumstances would I have permitted them to take away from me that prisoner, or any other prisoner." The sheriff was presented with the Interracial Commission's bronze medal for having prevented a threatened lynching.

Factors in Preventing Threatened Lynching. The prevention of the threatened lynching seemed in part a by-product of long-standing rivalry between the chief of police at Port Arthur and the sheriff at Beaumont. The Port Arthur Chief insisted that the real crisis came when the mob threatened to take the Negro from the insecure Port Arthur city jail, and that there was no possibility of a lynching once the prisoner was in the "strong" county jail at Beaumont.

On the other hand, the sheriff at Beaumont stated that the Port Arthur chief had done nothing especially deserving, for there was no real danger of a lynching at Port Arthur. The sheriff added, however, that many Port Arthur people were determined to lynch the Negro at Beaumont, in order to disgrace his record as sheriff, and that he was determined that the prisoner should not be lynched on his hands.

Another element in the situation was the fact that the sheriff was running for reëlection. When he went among the mob members about the jail, he plead with them not to lynch the Negro, because if they did it would mean a grand jury investigation and a lot of publicity, and would ruin his chances of reëlection. A further factor tending to stiffen the sheriff's attitude was that he was soon to be the host of the district peace officers' association. The coöperation of the fire departments of the two cities was also a helpful factor. Perhaps most significant of all was the announcement by officials of the two largest oil refineries that they would discharge any employees participating in a mob outbreak.

Death Sentence in Eighteen Minutes. Although six indictments were brought against Williams, the principal one upon which the state made its case was the accusation of Joyce Keller, Negro, who stated that Rainey Williams came upon her and her companion parked at night, and that Williams shot her companion when he would not leave. She testified that Williams claimed to be an officer of the law and had a right to shoot anyone who did not do as he instructed. He then tried to drag her into a ditch, she said, and when she struggled he shot her through the shoulder and later assaulted her. The case was strengthened by the testimony of three white women, who accused Williams of similar assaults. After eighteen minutes of deliberation the jury returned a verdict of guilty and the sentence of death was imposed.

Jail and $250 Fine for Defendant's Lawyer. The Negro's counsel, appointed by the court, was a 29 year-old Port Arthur lawyer. At first he refused to serve. As a result, he was charged with contempt of court and was fined $250 and placed in jail, where he remained an hour and forty minutes. He was conscientiously opposed to defending the Negro, it seems, but reconsidered and accepted the assignment. He asked for a change of venue, which was denied, and filed exceptions to some of the evidence, but did not appeal the case. Williams was promptly executed.

Throughout the trial, every precaution was taken by the officers to see that no demonstrations occurred. Every person who went into the courtroom was searched; the shades of the corridor doors were pulled down, and armed officers were stationed there; when the Negro had been sentenced, an armed escort took him from the courtroom.

Oil in Abundance. In recent years Jefferson County, on the Gulf of Mexico near the Louisiana state line, has been widely known as an oil refining center. Besides local fields, oil is piped in from points in Texas and Oklahoma to be refined. It is also a commercial center of importance. Beaumont has a population of 58,000, while Port Arthur has nearly 51,000. The county's population increased from 73,120 in 1920 to 133,391 in 1930. Approximately one-fourth of the population is Negro.

Beaumont, the county seat, was laid out in 1838; in 1900 it had a population of 9,427. Up to that time the people of the county lived principally by sawmilling, cattle raising, and rice growing. In January 1901 the Lucas oil well, in the Spindle Top Field, lying between Beaumont and Port Arthur, burst forth at the rate of 70,000 barrels a day, a record then without precedent. Twenty thousand people rushed to Beaumont, ten thousand in one week. At present there are 12,000 wells in this one field, and, though the flow is not so great as formerly, there is still a substantial output.

Port Arthur came on the map as the terminus of the Kansas City Southern Railroad in the last decade of the last century. In 1900 it had a population of but 900. From the outset it has been a cotton shipping and oil refining center. By 1909 the value of cotton and oil products shipped from this port amounted to over seventeen million dollars.

All of Jefferson County, and especially Beaumont and Port Arthur, is dominated by the oil boom psychology, and human relations, along with everything else, have been affected. The Negroes, the majority of whom live in Port Arthur and Beaumont, are employed as domestics and as workers in the oil refineries. Due to the shrinkage of general employment during recent months, some of the white employees of the refineries have been suggesting that the Negroes be laid off to make places for their unemployed white friends. So far, however, there has been no displacement of Negro labor. Should the general depression continue, there are indications that a united effort may be made by the whites to make a white man's job of the oil refinery work.

County's High Economic Rating. There was an automobile for every 4.0 persons in Jefferson County against one for every 4.2 persons in Texas. The per capita value of taxable property was $981.34 compared with $743.07 in the state. The county's bank deposits per capita were $252.18 against $206.05, while an income tax return was made for every 34.4 persons in Jefferson County and one for every 51.9 in Texas.

The schools of Beaumont and Port Arthur, both white and colored, are good. In Beaumont there are one high school and five elementary schools for Negroes. The school expenditures for both white and Negro children in this county are above the state average.

Church Membership, Votes by Parties, Lynchings. A little less than fifty per cent of Jefferson County's white people over fifteen years of age were church members; throughout Texas 59.4 per cent were members. The Negro church membership, too, was below the state average, 41.5 per cent, against the Texas average of 54.0 per cent.

Although the county usually goes Democratic, of 16,222

votes in the 1928 presidential election, 9,216 were for the Republican candidate. Relatively few Negroes vote. The total number of votes cast was equal to 32.0 per cent of the white population of twenty-one years of age and over, while the state's total vote was equal to but 27.9 per cent of the state's white population of voting age.

Although there have been no lynchings in Jefferson County since 1910, four are reported between 1900 and 1910: On February 11, 1900, Joseph Sweeney, Negro, accused of murder, was lynched at Port Arthur; on July 23, 1903, Mooney Allen, Negro, accused of murder, was lynched at Beaumont; on July 15, 1908, an unnamed Negro was lynched at Beaumont, it being a case of mistaken identity; on February 2, 1910, another unknown Negro, accused of rape, was lynched at Beaumont. In the meantime, a number of threatened lynchings have been prevented by official action.

COLLINGSWORTH AND WHEELER COUNTIES, TEXAS

Alleged Crime. In mid-July, 1930, Jesse Lee Washington, Negro, was accused of assaulting and killing the wife of a white planter living in a rural community near the Texas-Oklahoma border twelve miles southeast of Shamrock, Wheeler County. People hurriedly gathered to run down the murderer and the sheriffs of Wheeler and Collingsworth Counties soon arrived and joined in the search.

Washington, who later confessed the crime, was arrested and questioned. It is reported that the murdered woman's husband, whether by official connivance or otherwise, had every opportunity to kill the Negro at the time of his arrest, and surprise was generally expressed that he did not do so. When the accused had been taken into custody, the sheriff of Collingsworth County drove off toward Oklahoma with the prisoner and three of those reported as most determined to lynch him.

How Two Sheriffs Prevented Mob Violence. After riding several miles the sheriff, upon approaching a country store, asked the men in his car if they wanted something to drink. They answered that they did. He stopped. No sooner had they climbed out of the car than the sheriff sped off with only the

Negro, whom he rushed to a strong prison in Oklahoma.

A special session of the Wheeler County grand jury was called and the accused was promptly indicted. On a change of venue the trial was held at Miami, in an adjoining county. The Negro was sentenced to die and executed without delay.

Meantime a certain element in Shamrock was threatening the Negro section of the town. For two days and nights the Wheeler County sheriff stood between the town's small Negro section and a group of men persistently demanding and threatening "to burn the niggers out." He also called for State Rangers and five were sent to his aid.

Determined Texas Rangers. The Rangers came upon the scene with an air of determination. At Shamrock there could be no "don't shoot" rumor, such as came out of the Sherman mob outbreak.[1] They were now under specific instructions from the Governor to keep complete control of the situation, to protect the accused Negro, and to prevent any mob demonstrations against the colored people.

The following statement to the Governor, protesting against his vigorous instructions, was signed by forty Shamrock white women:

"Big newspaper display of your instructions to Texas Rangers to kill our fathers, husbands and brothers in order to protect confessed Negro rapist and murderer who so brutally attacked and killed Ruth Vaughan, one of the sweetest characters of our community, horrified us, for it has two effects.

"First, it leads Negro fiends to believe that the law will protect them to the extent of white lives, and, second, it leads them to believe that our husbands, fathers, and brothers are not permitted to protect us. Such highly advertised instructions leave us at the mercy of any Negro fiend who runs amuck and we protest such instructions in behalf of all the white women of Texas."

On the other hand, some weeks after the trouble the Shamrock Methodist Woman's Missionary Society sent a resolution to the sheriff commending him for his action.

---

[1] See Sherman case study above.

One Sheriff Defeated—The Other Reëlected. In the following fall the sheriff of Wheeler County was defeated for re-
election, as the result, he thinks, of his protection of Negro
property. Many of the leading citizens, however, discount this
explanation and assign other causes, chief among which was the
sheriff's defense of his deputy, who was charged with and
sentenced for two felonies.

The sheriff of Collingsworth County, on the other hand, was
reëlected by a large majority.

Two Texas Pan-Handle Counties. Wheeler and Collingsworth counties, in the pan-handle section of north Texas, have
been settled within recent years, and are still frontier-like. In
the towns the churches, schools and other institutions are
well established. In the rural sections, the institutions are much
weaker than in the older Southern communities. Shamrock, in
Wheeler County, is the trade and cultural center of this and
adjoining counties. It is a wide-awake thriving town with paved
streets, civic organizations, and better than average weekly
papers.

"White Man's Country!" Until recently Shamrock was an
all-white town and Wheeler County an all-white county. As
one man put it, Negroes were not even permitted "to stick
their heads out of the train coaches." Negroes first came into
Shamrock about 1926, when an out-of-town construction company paved the streets. About the same time "dry farming"
cotton cultivation was successfully introduced into the pan-
handle, and Negroes were brought in to pick cotton. Most of
them left when their work was over, but some remained. Each
year a few new residents were added. Incited by Jesse Lee
Washington's crimes in the summer of 1930, a considerable
element of the white people insisted upon running all the
Negroes out of this "white man's country."[2]

These counties fall below the state average economically:
In 1930, the assessed value of taxable property was $581.71
per capita in Wheeler County against $743.70 in Texas. The

---

[2] Note evidences of this "white man's country" complex in the case studies
of Sherman and Honey Grove, Texas, which are in the Red River basin,
300 miles below Collingsworth and Wheeler counties.

per capita bank deposits were $135.39 in the county and $206.05 in the state. An income tax return was made for every 68.4 persons in the county and for every 51.9 persons throughout the state.

Collingsworth County's rating was below that of Wheeler in taxable property, bank deposits, and income tax returns.

The political situation in both counties is similar. Like the State both went Democratic in the 1924 presidential election and Republican in that of 1928.

CHAPTER XXII

COOPERATION OF POLICE AND COURTS

MOST LYNCHINGS occur either soon after the accused persons are apprehended, or days later when they are brought before the courts. The arresting officers usually can frustrate mobs which flare up immediately after a reported crime. Against those that form later, which are more deliberate and better organized, the close coöperation of police and court officials is essential if the accused are to be protected. The following case studies of LaGrange and Sylvania, Georgia, and Huntsville, Alabama, set forth the methods by which threatened lynchings were prevented at each of these critical times.

LaGrange, Troup County, Georgia

Alleged Crime. On April 5, 1930, Leonard Philpot, Negro, was accused of attempted rape upon two women at LaGrange. Both women were of influential white families, and neither did anything to precipitate or encourage the formation of a mob. Feeling was intense, nevertheless, and mob action was threatened by several hundred people who gathered about the jail.

Threatened Lynching Prevented by Coöperating Officials. Upon noting the excitement, the chief of police got in touch with the mayor, who went immediately to the jail where Philpot was being held and persuaded the crowd to leave, telling them they were not sure they had the guilty man. Just as soon as the crowd dispersed the county sheriff and other officers placed the accused Negro in an automobile and rushed him to the Fulton Tower in Atlanta, where he remained until his trial.

The district judge and prosecuting attorney, realizing the danger of having the trial in LaGrange, ordered a change of venue to Newnan, in an adjoining county, and some weeks later when the time of the trial arrived, an armed escort was provided for Philpot from the Atlanta prison to the Newnan courtroom. Philpot was tried, convicted, and given a sentence of twenty years in each case.

Though there was a considerable element of white people in Troup County who felt that Philpot should have been lynched, the effective majority took pride in the way the case was handled.

The Accused Negro. Leonard Philpot, fifty-one years of age, was born in Heard County, immediately north of Troup. He had been married twice, and had deserted both wives. Some years earlier he had served a six-months chaingang sentence in Troup County for shooting at the sheriff in a liquor case. He is reported to have been a heavy drinker, and a ready fighter. It was said by officers that he carried a pistol regularly and that he was drinking on the afternoon of the alleged attempted assaults.

Philpot persistently denied his guilt. His sister-in-law, with whom he lived in LaGrange, expressed doubt as to his guilt, saying that he was in a barber shop when arrested and had been there all afternoon. Convicting evidence, however, was secured; both of the white women identified him.

Cotton Farmers and Cotton Manufacturers. Until forty years ago Troup County, on the Alabama line, was predominantly rural; it was also predominantly Negro, being on the northern border of the plantation belt. In 1890, the population of the county was 20,723, of which number sixty per cent were Negroes; in 1930 the population was 36,752, 46.6 per cent Negro. The increase in population has been in response to the development of the textile industry in and near LaGrange, and here, as in most Southern communities, the mills employ practically all white workers. In 1930 more than two-thirds of the county's population lived in four towns, and two-thirds of all town dwellers lived in LaGrange, the county seat, located on the main railroad and highway between Atlanta and Montgomery.

The textile industry, with its ready cash wages, has recruited its workers chiefly from the tenant white class of Troup and adjoining counties. In the meantime the growing of cotton, chief crop of this locality, has become less profitable because of the low price and the increased expense of fighting the boll weevil. The average annual crop of 22,209 bales between 1910 and 1914 dropped to 13,031 bales between 1925 and 1929. Since 1900, these combined factors have resulted in a 34.4 per cent decrease of farms in the county. At present approximately three-fourths of the farmers are tenants.

County Above State Average Economically. In 1924 the value of farm products in Troup County was $11.29 per capita below the state average, while the value of manufactured products was approximately $1,000 above, making the combined per capita value of farm and manufactured products, $1,285.55 in the county against $310.78 in the state. As with cotton mills everywhere, however, even though the value of production per employee was high, the wage scale was low, the average weekly wage for men being a little over $12.00 and for women a little less than $10.00. In 1930 the tax valuation per capita was $351.29 in Troup and $348.03 for Georgia; the number of persons per automobile was practically the same for the county and state. In bank deposits per capita the county fell below the state average, $75.63 compared to $155.89.

Taking the county as a whole, the public schol expenditures are a little above the state average for the whites, and a little below for the Negroes. This is due largely to the fact that a disproportionate number of the whites live in the towns, about the mills, while most of the Negroes are farm tenants. The Negroes in LaGrange have one of the best Negro schools in the state, maintained in part by the Presbyterian Mission Board. The plant is a modern brick structure with twenty-one rooms. One-third of the 450 students are in the high school department and more than half of its recent graduates have gone to college. Of the thirty-eight one-teacher and four two-teacher Negro schools in the rural sections of the county, many are housed in lodge halls and churches. There is no Rosenwald

school in the county. The white schools have been consolidated
to the point that there are no one-teacher white schools.

White Baptists, Methodists, and Democrats. The white
church membership is made up largely of Southern Baptists
and Southern Methodists, with small but significant groups of
Presbyterians and Protestant Episcopalians. The Negro membership is more than two-thirds Baptists, with the remaining
one-third divided almost equally between the M. E. and C. M. E.
churches. In the county, there are forty-five Negro Baptist
churches, which means that the farm tenants of each one-
teacher school district maintain a Baptist Church and part of
a Methodist Church. This in turn means crude buildings and
equipment and a small salary for non-resident ministers with
little training.

Troup County always goes Democratic. In the 1920 presidential election four-fifths of the votes were cast for the
Democratic nominee; in 1924, eight-ninths. In 1928, nearly
two-thirds were for the regular Democratic candidate, while
one-fifth were for the Anti-Smith Democratic electors. A local
Negro politician stated that of the county's 150 regular Republicans all but a few are Negroes. Practically all of the
voting Negroes live in LaGrange.

Crime by Race. So far as known, there has been but one
lynching in Troup County. This occurred during Reconstruction days, when a Negro was accused of living with a white
woman. About four years ago a controversy arose between
the son of a plantation owner and his Negro tenants; the
owner's son was fired upon. The planter, with a group of white
men, went to investigate the matter and reprimand the Negroes.
Officers and other white men got the news and followed. The
crowd fired upon the cabin occupied by the accused Negro
and his family, and he was killed. Many of the Negroes looked
upon this as a lynching, but officers reported that the victim
was killed while resisting arrest. The dead man's mother, two
sisters, and a son were convicted of aiding and abetting him
in resisting arrest. The women received sentences of one year

each, and the son, who was barely sixteen, was sentenced to ten to fifteen years on the chaingang.

Between 1921 and 1929 the county's white jail population increased from 4.1 to 9.9 per thousand, and the Negro jail population decreased from 16.5 to 10.4 per thousand.

Sylvania, Screven County, Georgia

The Case in Brief. On the afternoon of April 21, 1930, a Negro boy was alleged to have entered a white man's farm home near Sylvania. The man was absent, and the Negro was said to have struck the wife over the head with an axe, and to have attempted to assault the eighteen-year-old daughter.

For days, officers from a half-dozen counties and large groups of undeputized men searched for the assailant. At length LeRoy Scott, a seventeen-year-old Negro boy employed by the family as a farm wage hand, was arrested. Except for the skillful maneuvers of the sheriff and the judge's coöperation, the boy would probably have been lynched.

How the Situation Was Handled. When LeRoy Scott was arrested, and it was reported that he had confessed the crimes, the Screven County Sheriff removed him to a strong prison in an adjoining county. Later he was moved to an Augusta prison. These steps were taken to avoid threatened mob violence.

The Negro remained in the Augusta prison until time for his trial. Then one evening about eight o'clock, he was brought unannounced before the district court judge at Sylvania. Having plead guilty to the crimes in a written confession, he was sentenced to thirty years in prison. Immediately after the sentence was passed, he was taken by an armed escort to another county to await consignment to a Georgia prison. The cautious action of the sheriff in this case, together with the coöperation of the district judge, is believed to have prevented mob violence either prior to or at the trial. From day to day during the court session crowds had jammed the courtroom, eagerly awaiting Scott's appearance. The sheriff persistently pretended ignorance of the date Scott would be tried. Hardly a dozen people knew of the trial until sentence had been passed and the Negro removed. Many persons expressed open criticism of the sheriff for not letting "the people" know when Scott would be brought before the court. The sheriff stated his belief that if a public trial had been attempted, the Negro would have been lynched.

Unusual Conduct of the Husband and Father. In spite of the fact that officers brought before the court a confession from the Negro, throughout the excitement and the trial the husband of the injured woman and father of the girl contended that Scott was not guilty. Indeed, while the Negro was being held as a suspect, he did what he could to get him out of jail, and took such an active part that some of the whites were indignant, and demanded an explanation. The sheriff, well acquainted with the husband and father for years, explained his behavior by saying that he had a "single track" mind, and having once decided that Scott was not guilty had held doggedly to that opinion.

The Confessions. The amount of pressure brought upon Scott to get his confession is not known. However, soon after his arrest several officers questioned him for a considerable time, and he finally elected to tell the Screven County Sheriff "just what happened." A little later when Scott was in the Richmond County jail, the officers there got another confession from him, in which he alleged that the farmer had hired him to kill the wife. But the sheriff thought that this second confession was secured by methods which invalidated it. Hence it was not brought into court. According to the sheriff, Scott claimed that the Richmond County officers frightened him, and he was afraid not to say what they told him to say. Though sentenced on his own confession, Scott was not identified by the girl he is alleged to have attempted to assault, or by the woman he was accused of striking. From the outset the girl declared that she could positively identify her assailant, yet she never did implicate LeRoy Scott, the Negro boy who for several weeks had eaten regularly in the kitchen of her home.

According to his earliest confession, which was brought before the court by the sheriff and upon which he was sentenced, Scott got the "notion" of assaulting the girl when he saw her moving about the kitchen while he was eating his meals. The confession went on to state how he and his employer were together in a field plowing. Thus he knew that no one was at home but the employer's wife and daughter. Accordingly, he said, he left the field, committed the crimes, and returned to work.

The employer reported that he did not know Scott had left the field during the afternoon. A Negro tenant, working on an adjoining farm, is reported to have said that in the early afternoon of the day the crimes were committed, Scott was away from the field for something like an hour.

An Illiterate Negro Farm Wage Hand. LeRoy Scott, seventeen-year-old Negro boy, was born and reared in Screven County near Sylvania. For several years he had earned his livelihood as a farm wage hand. For some months he had been employed at the place of his alleged crimes, at a wage of $7.00 a month and board. He was illiterate, but without court record, and the sheriff spoke of him as being more intelligent than the average Negro. His immediate family and many other kinsmen were living in Screven County near Sylvania.

The Reaction of the Community. A small element of the better people in Sylvania and environs are proud of the sheriff for having prevented a threatened lynching. Another element, seemingly much more numerous, "wanted the nigger." For months afterward they voiced the feeling that the sheriff should have "let the boys have him," openly resenting the fact that the sheriff had kept their "rightful prey" from them. This feeling gradually subsided, however, and the sheriff was reëlected.

A Rural and Poor County. Throughout its history Screven, one of Georgia's oldest counties, has been almost wholly rural. In 1930 more than 85 per cent of the people lived in the open country. This county is in the old slave plantation belt, and more than half the population has been and is made up of Negroes, who in 1930 constituted 56.7 per cent of the total.

Sylvania, its largest town, had a population in 1930 of 1,781, a smaller figure than ten years before. During the decade the population of the entire county decreased by one-eighth. It is one of the most completely rural and generally least developed counties in the Georgia black belt. The county had had its last lynching on July 27, 1910, when Evan Ralent, Negro, was burned to death near Sylvania by a mob of several hundred. He was accused of attempted rape.

Screven County's yield of cotton per acre is much better than the state average, and the county's value of farm products per farm family in 1924 was $941.08, as compared to $831.75 for the state. None the less, the people of the county are generally poorer than the state average. The lack of manufactures and commercial pursuits leaves the whole economic structure dependent upon farming, and nearly three-fourths of the county's farmers are propertyless tenants. In 1930 the county's per capita tax valuation was $130.75, in contrast with the state average of $348.03. Its per capita bank deposit was $20.34 against the state average of $155.89.

Screven County's general public school facilities are far below the state average. In 1930 the county's white illiteracy rate was 5.3 per cent, as compared with the state rate of 3.3 per cent, while that of Negroes was 27.4 per cent against 19.9 for the state. In Sylvania itself, however, the schools for both whites and Negroes are unusually good. Indeed, the latter is one of Georgia's half-dozen best small town Negro schools. The white church membership of the county is made up almost entirely of Southern Baptists and Southern Methodists. The majority of the Negro church members are Baptists.

The county Democratic candidates are always elected, though there is a larger proportion of Republican votes in Screven than in most Georgia black belt counties. In 1920, approximately one-fourth of the votes were for the Republican presidential candidate. In 1928 the Republican electors received 370 votes, the anti-Smith Democratic electors 336 votes, and the Democratic electors but 300 votes, which was the first time in decades that the Democratic presidential candidate had failed to get a majority vote.

In general, the economic indices place Screven in the type of county where lynchings have most frequently occurred. Except for the precautions taken by sheriff and judge, refusing to tell where the Negro was held prior to the trial or when he would be brought into court, there is every reason to believe that a lynching would have occurred there in April, 1930.

But Was Impartial Justice Achieved? Here is admittedly a method that was effective in preventing mob violence in this particular case and in others more recent. It may be questioned, however, whether the mob spirit did not at last defeat the ends of impartial justice. The sole evidence against the Negro was his two "confessions." Both of these were made under official pressure, and the sheriff himself excluded one of them as having probably been secured by questionable means. The Wickersham Commission devotes a whole volume to the common practice of third degree methods by which prisoners are sometimes "persuaded" to confess things they never did. Courts may well view critically all evidence secured in this "star chamber" manner.

In this particular case, moreover, how shall one explain the attitude of his employer; how explain the failure of either the mother or the daughter to identify and accuse him, though for weeks he had taken his meals in their kitchen? The best that can be said is that the Negro was saved from the mob. The worst is that, though unaccused by his alleged victims, he was sentenced to thirty years imprisonment. This case clearly demonstrates that it is the mob, rather than any one particular activity of the mob, which must be eliminated, before impartial justice can be achieved.

HUNTSVILLE, MADISON COUNTY, ALABAMA

Shortly before midnight on September 28, 1930, a prominent business man of Huntsville, Alabama, was murdered in his home. His wife, who was in the room when her husband was killed, reported that the murderer was a Negro. Police were notified, and a widespread and intensive search was begun. On the following day, Gus Henderson, Negro, was taken from a freight train at Decatur, thirty miles away, and under cross examination admitted that he had just come from Huntsville.

The bloodhounds' trail from the scene of the crime toward the depot further placed suspicion upon the arrested Negro.

Threatened Lynching Frustrated by National Guard. The Negro was taken to Huntsville and put in jail. A mob formed to lynch him. Influential citizens advised the Governor of the case and requested the National Guard. The troops were ordered out at once. When they came on the scene, a small demonstration occurred at the jail; the troops threw tear gas bombs in the crowd; the fire department was called out. The members of the mob retaliated with stones and other missiles.

When the leaders of the rioting had refused to retreat and several guardsmen had received minor wounds a guardsman, with the butt of his gun, struck down one of the mob's leaders. With this and other evidences of serious purpose, the mob was driven back more than a block; there were no further demonstrations. At the hospital, the wounded mob leader was identified as a local light-weight boxer.

The mob continued to grow and, at the request of the commanding officer, additional troops came on the scene on the afternoon of the next day. The mob then dispersed. Adequate National Guard strength was on hand in Huntsville because of the alertness of local officials and private citizens.

Investigation Suggested Inside Job. The Huntsville officers were uncertain of the accused Negro's guilt, and accordingly every angle of the case was thoroughly investigated. The murdered man's wife did not identify Henderson. A member of the State Enforcement Department came to help with the investigation. When the officers learned that the telephone had been "dead" since the early evening of the murder, they investigated and found that the small wires inside the insulation had been cut. They noticed, too, that an electric bulb in the hall, in line with the door to the room where the murdered man slept, was seemingly "burned out." Upon further observation it was seen that the bulb had been unscrewed just enough to break the connection.

When asked specifically concerning the person who killed her husband, the widow, who was in the room at the time of the crime, stated that the murderer was a heavy, broad-shouldered, thick-chested man, and that she thought he had a black neck. She reported that the murderer at all times kept his back to her, although she had moved all about the room. She further stated that he seemed to have been well dressed, except for his hat, which did not conform with his other apparel. No valuables were missing. These facts, convinced the officers that the man had not been killed by a night prowler, but rather by someone inside the house who had made preparation for the murder.

Arrest of Son and White Employee. Furthermore, it was learned by the officers that the murdered man's son had gone to a local "U-Drive-It" garage two or three days after the murder, and had asked for a contract he had signed in obtaining a car on the night of the crime. He was informed that he could not get it, and was told that it was an unprecedented request. This with other evidence subsequently secured, led to his arrest and that of one of the white employees of the deceased.

Gus Henderson was released soon after the two white men were arrested.

Three of the leaders of the mob which came near lynching Henderson were a farmer with almost no education; a cotton mill employee; and the light-weight boxer who, as mentioned already, was struck down by one of the guardsmen. These three, arrested for interfering with public officers, were later released on bonds of $1,000 each.

A Rural Cotton County. Madison County, Alabama, on the Tennessee line is in the north-eastern part of the state. It is essentially rural: In 1930 nearly four-fifths of its 64,623 people lived in the open country. The population has increased nearly ten per cent in the last decade. Approximately thirty per cent of the people are Negroes. The foreign-born element is negligible, being three per thousand population, as compared with eight per thousand in the state.

In recent years Madison County has become one of the leading cotton producing counties of Alabama: The average annual crop between 1910 and 1914 was 30,095 bales; between 1925 and 1929, 54,434 bales; the 1929 crop was 57,243 bales.

The per acre yield of cotton in this county is a little better than the state average. In 1930, with a 16.5 per cent increase of farms during the decade, the county had 7,174 farmers, seventy per cent of whom were tenants.

For a town of 11,554 inhabitants, Huntsville, the county seat, has a large number of well established Negro business and professional men. Negroes own two good grocery stores, two undertaking establishments, and a drug store. There are four Negro physicians, two dentists, and one lawyer. The county's most unusual Negro business enterprise is a coöperative cotton gin.

Fair Economic Rating. In 1924 Madison County's per capita value of farm crops and manufactured products was well in advance of the state average, $389.56 against $286.93. In 1930 the county's per capita bank deposits amounted to $74.94 against $107.07 throughout the state. In 1927 there was an income tax return made for every 159.0 persons in the county and one for every 94.6 persons in the state.

The public schools are much the same as in most Alabama rural counties, perhaps a little above the average. The Huntsville Negro high school has twelve grades and fifteen teachers. It is reported, however, that but few of the Negro graduates go to college.

"Slavery Ordained of God." In 1926, nearly three-fourths of the white church membership of Madison County were either Southern Baptists or Southern Methodists, there being 3,678 of the latter and 3,390 of the former. The Presbyterian and Episcopal denominations have a little less than 500 members each. The Negro church membership is made up largely of Baptists, nearly one-half of whom are Colored Primitive Baptists. The M. E., C. M. E., and A. M. E. Churches have small memberships.

In 1857 Rev. Fred Ross, D.D., pastor of the Huntsville Presbyterian Church, published a book entitled, *Slavery Ordained of God.* This treatise, pointing out wherein, according to the Scriptures, "slavery is of God," was dedicated to "the men North and South who honor the Word of God and love their country."

But Few Negro Voters. Usually, more than four-fifths of the votes of Madison County are cast for the Democratic presidential candidate. In 1928, however, the Republican nominee received a half-dozen more votes than the Democratic nominee, 2,697 against 2,691. The total number of votes was scarcely one-fourth of the whites of voting age. The Negroes are virtually excluded from voting. A Negro property owner and business man, who has lived in Huntsville for twenty-five years, reported that he was mistreated some years ago when he attempted to register, and finally was registered only when he threatened legal action. Huntsville's Negro attorney reported that members of his race who expressed interest in politics have been insulted and mistreated so persistently that they had just about quit trying to vote.

There has been no lynching in Madison County since September 7, 1904, when Horace Maples, accused of murder, was lynched at Huntsville. Before this, on July 23, 1900, Elijah Clarke, accused of rape, was lynched there.

Threats Against Negroes. In recent years a united effort has been made by some of the poorer whites to run certain Negroes out of Huntsville. One of these was a Negro grocer who had bought a store from a white man and was able to do more business than the white man had done. Moreover, many of the poorer whites felt that the Negro grocer was "living too good for a 'nigger.' "

During the recent threatened mob violence, most of the better established Negroes of Huntsville left their homes for more than a week. One of them, however, sent word to officials that there was no reason why he should leave his home, that he was a tax payer and should be protected, that if the police did not protect him he would protect himself, and that any group that came to "scare him out" could count on three or four being killed, even if he was one of them. It is reported that after receiving this statement the officers provided the Negro community with more adequate police protection.

In Conclusion. The threatened lynching of an innocent Negro at Huntsville was prevented by peace officers, city officials, and guardsmen. Interested citizens in Alabama and adjoining states watched the case and expressed satisfaction with the way it was handled. Governor Graves played his part well, as did also the State Enforcement Department which assisted in ferreting out the evidence which resulted in the arrest of the two white men. The significant thing about this case is that, except for the immediate protection of the National Guard and the thorough investigation on the part of local and state officials, an innocent man doubtless would have been lynched or else given the death sentence by the courts. In either case an innocent man would have suffered, and his fate would doubtless have protected the real murderers from suspicion and punishment.

APPENDIX A

THE TWENTY-ONE LYNCHINGS IN 1930*

February 1—Ocilla, Irwin County, Georgia; James Irwin, colored; accusation, rape and murder; taken from officers of the law and burned to death.

April 23—Rosedale, Bolivar County, Mississippi; David Harris, colored; accusation, murder; shot to death; did not come into the hands of the law.

April 24—Walhalla, Oconee County, South Carolina; Allen Green, colored; accusation, rape; taken from jail and shot to death.

April 28—Plant City, Hillsborough County, Florida; John Houdaz, white; accusation, bombing houses; taken from officer of the law and shot to death.

May 9—Sherman, Grayson County, Texas; George Hughes, colored; accusation, rape; Hughes placed in vault at courthouse for protection from mob; courthouse burned; body blasted from vault, and dragged into Negro section of town where it was burned.

May 18—Honey Grove, Fannin County, Texas; George Johnson, colored; accusation, slaying farm overseer in altercation over a debt; shot to death by a sheriff's posse after he had barricaded himself in a cabin; his body was tied to an automobile and dragged through the town and later burned in front of a Negro church.

May 31—Chickasha, Grady County, Oklahoma; Henry Argo, colored; accusation, rape; mob broke into jail and prisoner was shot in the head; later while lying on a cot, he was fatally stabbed in the chest.

---

* Data from the Department of Records and Research, Tuskegee Institute, have been used throughout this report. These data, compiled largely from newspaper reports, have in the main been found quite satisfactory. Question might be raised, however, as to the correctness of classifying as lynchings the deaths at Honey Grove, Texas; Ailey, Georgia, and Thomas County, Georgia.

June 17—Bryan, Brazos County, Texas; William Roane, colored; accusation, attempted rape; shot to death; did not come into hands of law.

June 21—Union, Union County, South Carolina; Daniel Jenkins, colored; accusation, rape; shot to death; did not come into hands of law, though sheriff was present.

July 4—Emelle, Sumter County, Alabama; Esau Robinson, colored; accusation, killing man in altercation over automobile battery; Robinson came into hands of the law, but was left unguarded; taken by mob and body riddled with bullets; five other persons, two white men, two Negro men, and one Negro woman, were killed.

July 29—Ailey, Montgomery County, Georgia; S. S. Mincey, colored; accused of no crime; beaten to death.

August 7—Marion, Grant County, Indiana; Thomas Shipp and Abraham Smith, colored; accusation, rape and murderous assault; taken from jail and hanged.

August 15—Raymond, Hinds County, Mississippi; George Robinson, colored; accusation, resisting officer of the law; shot to death.

August 19—Tarboro, Edgecombe County, North Carolina; Oliver Moore, colored; accusation, rape; taken from jail and shot to death.

September 8—Darien, McIntosh County, Georgia; George Grant, colored; accusation, killing officer of the law; shot to death in jail.

September 10—Scooba, Kemper County, Mississippi; Pigg Lockett and Holly White, colored; accusation, robbing two tourists, a man and his wife; taken from officers of the law and hanged.

At Honey Grove the accused Negro was killed by a deputized posse while resisting arrest. The fact that a mob of a thousand was present when he was killed and that his corpse was dragged, face down, for miles and then burned in front of a Negro church probably justify its classification as a lynching.

Question might be raised also as to the proper classification of the deaths of S. S. Mincey, of Ailey, and Lacy Mitchell, of Thomas County, in that both were lacking in that general public participation which characterized the other lynchings of 1930. The deaths of Mincey and Mitchell, premeditated and executed by a small group of people employing private and secret means, were in many respects not unlike the gang murders in the large cities.

September 25—Thomasville, Thomas County, Georgia; William Kirkland, colored; accusation, attempted rape; taken from officers of the law and shot.

September 28—Thomas County, Georgia; Lacy Mitchell, colored; accused of no crime; star witness in case against two white men charged with raping a Negro woman; was shot to death in his own home.

October 1—Cartersville, Bartow County, Georgia; John Willie Clark, colored; accusation, killing officer of the law; taken from jail and hanged.

LYNCHINGS IN 1931

January 12—Maryville, Nodaway County, Missouri; Raymond Gunn, colored; accusation, murder; taken from jail.

January 29—Schafer, McKenzie County, North Dakota; Charles Bannon, white; accusation, murder; taken from jail and hanged.

March 22—Inverness, Sunflower County, Mississippi; Steve Wiley, colored; accusation, attempted rape.

March 29—Vicksburg, Warren County, Mississippi; Elijah Johnson, colored; accusation, attempted rape.

April 17—Union City, Obion County, Tennessee; George Smith, colored; accusation, attempted rape.

August 2—Point a la Hache, Plaquemines Parish, Louisiana; Oscar Livingston, colored; accusation, attempted rape.

August 5—Haynesville, Lowndes County, Alabama; Neal Guinn, colored; accusation, attempted rape.

August 28—Blountstown, Calhoun County, Florida; Richard and Charles Smoke, father and son, colored; accusation, attacking and beating a forest ranger.

November 7—Columbus, Lowndes County, Mississippi; Coleman Franks, colored; accusation, wounding white farmer during previous month; taken from convict road camp and hanged.

December 4—Salisbury, Wicomico County, Maryland; Mack Williams, colored; accusation, murder, taken from hospital cot and hanged in yard of Wicomico County courthouse.

December 10—Lewisburg, Greenbrier County, West Virginia; Tom Jackson and George Banks, colored; accusation, murder; taken from jail where they were awaiting trial and hanged, bodies riddled with bullets.

LYNCHINGS IN 1932

April 1—Crockett, Houston County, Texas; Dave Tillis, colored; accusation, attempted rape; hanged, did not come into the hands of the law.

April 18—St. Francis, Cheyenne County, Kansas; Richard Read, white; accusation, rape and murder; taken from jail and hanged.

May 31—Princeton, Caldwell County, Kentucky; Walter Merrick, white; accusation, dynamiting store; taken from jail and hanged.

June 6—Jasper, Hamilton County, Florida; Henry Woods, colored; accusation, robbery and murder; body riddled with bullets, then burned; reported to have been killed by an arresting posse.

June 11—Ironton, Lawrence County, Ohio; Luke Murray, colored; accusation, threatening men with knife; taken from jail, body later found floating in Ohio River.

September 15—Crossett, Ashley County, Arkansas; Frank Tucker, colored; accusation, wounding officer of the law; taken from jail and hanged.

September 15—Warrenton, Fauquier County, Virginia; Shadrick Thompson, colored; he had been sought for an alleged rape of July 12; on September 15 his body was found, near Linden, hanging from a tree.

November 19—Wisner, Franklin Parish, Louisiana; William House, colored; accusation, insult to two white women; placed in Franklin Parish jail; taken from officers en route to trial and hanged.

Helena, September 25, 1930, Negro, attempted rape, removed to distant jail.

Batesville, April 9, 1931, white man, murder, removed to distant jail.

Pine Bluff, August 10, 1931, Negro, shooting into picnic party, removed.

McGhee, September 12, 1931, Negro, murder, removed to distant jail.

Little Rock, April, 1932, Negro, murder, removed to distant jail.

Poplar Bluff, August, 1932, Negro, attempted rape, removed to distant jail.

Blytheville, November, 1932, Negro, attempted rape, removed to distant jail.

CALIFORNIA—

Los Angeles, December 29, 1930, two white men, rape, force used to repel mob.

COLORADO—

Pueblo, September 1, 1930, three Negroes, rape, removed to distant jail.

FLORIDA—

Gadsden County, January 1, 1930, Negro, rape, removed to distant jail.

Blountstown, April 21, 1930, Negro, killing officer, removed to distant jail.

Cassia, March 21, 1931, Negro, murder, removed.

Ocala, March 25, 1931, Negro, rape, removed.

Palatka, June 2, 1931, white man, murder, removed.

Bartow, January 23, 1932, white man, rape, removed.

Lakeland, March 27, 1932, four white men, killing officer of law, force used to repel mob.

GEORGIA—

LaGrange, April 8, 1930, Negro, attempted rape, removed.

Sylvania, April 27, 1930, Negro, attempted rape, removed.

Dublin, August 15, 1930, Negro, auto collision, force used to repel mob.

Cartersville, September 15, 1930, Negro, killing officer, Guard used and prisoner removed, but subsequently lynched.

APPENDIX B

THREATENED LYNCHINGS PREVENTED

JANUARY 1, 1930, TO JANUARY 1, 1933*

PLACE, DATE, ACCUSATION, NUMBER AND RACE OF PERSONS THRE- ENED AND STEPS TAKEN TO PREVENT LYNCHING

ALABAMA—

Troy, April 2, 1930, Negro, rape, force used to repel mob.

Luverne, April 5, 1930, Negro, wounding boy, removed to tant jail.

Huntsville, September 29, 1930, two Negroes, murder, Nat Guard used.

Mobile, October 22, 1930, Negro, murder, removed to di jail.

Scottsboro, March 25, 1931, nine Negroes, attempted rape, tional Guard used.

Mobile, April 30, 1931, Negro, rape, force used to repel m

Talladega, April 6, 1932, Negro, attempted rape, remove distant jail.

Ashland, April 6, 1932, Negro, attempted rape, remove distant jail.

ARIZONA—

Yuma, December 20, 1932, Negro, suspected of murder, rer to distant jail.

ARKANSAS—

Devall Bluff, March 23, 1930, Negro, attempted rape, rer to distant jail.

---

* Data from newspaper reports compiled by Department of Record Research, Tuskegee Institute.

Waycross, October 20, 1930, Negro man and Negro woman, murder, removed.

Rome, February, 2, 1931, Negro, murder, removed.

Campbell County, April 5, 1931, Negro, murder, removed.

Elberton, May 19, 1931, six Negroes, rape, Guards called out.

Douglas, August 20, 1931, Negro, murder, removed.

Moultrie, December 5, 1931, Negro, rape, guards augmented.

Alpharetta, December 25, 1931, white, wounding man, removed.

Albany, May 15, 1932, Negro, attempted rape, force used to repel mob.

Bainbridge, June 18, 1932, Negro, murder, removed.

Rome, August 7, 1932, Negro, wounding woman, removed.

Damascus, October 9, 1932, Negro, murder, removed.

INDIANA—

Evansville, January 23, 1930, Negro, murder, removed to distant jail.

Anderson, July 8, 1931, two Negroes, murder and robbery, removed.

Marion, May 19, 1932, Negro, rape, force used to repel mob.

KENTUCKY—

Fulton, May 14, 1930, white, murder, Guards augmented.

Mayfield, January 20, 1931, two Negroes, robbery, removed.

Hopkinsville, January 21, 1931, Negro, murder, force used to repel mob.

Hickman, April 20, 1931, Negro, rape, removed.

Elizabethtown, April 28, 1931, Negro, murder, force used to repel mob.

Richmond, December 26, 1931, Negro, murder, removed.

Hiseville, February 19, 1932, Negro, wounding man, forced used to repel mob.

Jenkins, February 27, 1932, Negro, murder, removed.

Manchester, August, 1932, white, murder, force used to repel mob.

LOUISIANA—

Caddo Parish, March 12, 1931, Negro, rape, removed to distant jail.

Shreveport, January 18, 1931, Negro, murder, Guard used.

Bogalusa, January 26, 1931, Negro, murder, removed.

East Felica Parish, August 27, 1931, Negro murder, removed.
Coushatta, May, 1932, Negro, murder, force used to repel mob.
Lake Charles, August 8, 1932, Negro, murder, removed.

MARYLAND—

Snowhill, October 13, 1931, Negro, murder, removed for safety.
Snowhill, November 5, 1931, two white men and one white woman, legal defense of a Negro accused of murder, all three removed for safety.
Elkton, January 5, 1932, Negro, attempted rape, removed.

MICHIGAN—

Ludington, August 4, 1932, white, murder, Guards augmented.

MINNESOTA—

Anoka, September 7, 1931, Negro, attacking girl, removed.

MISSISSIPPI—

Vicksburg, January 6, 1930, three Negroes, wounding officer, removed.
Laurel, February 20, 1930, Negro, rape, removed.
Clarksdale, October 20, 1930, Negro, rape, National Guard used.
Quitman, January 2, 1931, Negro, murder, removed.
Water Valley, May 6, 1931, Negro, murder, force used to repel mob.
Ocean Springs, February 24, 1931, Negro, rape, removed.
Quitman, August 18, 1931, Negro, robbery and wounding of man, removed.
Oxford, August 26, 1931, white, murder, removed.
Liberty, October 22, 1931, Negro, murder, force used.
Rawls Springs, April 20, 1932, Negro, threatening woman, removed.
Amory, June 20, 1932, Negro, rape, removed.
Philadelphia, September 23, 1932, Negro, murder, removed.
McComb, October 8, 1932, Negro, rape, removed.
Crystal Springs, October 18, 1932, Negro, wounding man, removed.

MISSOURI—

Ironton, January 28, 1930, white, murder, prisoner removed.
St. Genevieve, October 15, 1930, two Negro men and one Negro woman, murder, prisoners removed.
Poplar Bluff, March, 1931, Negro, attempted rape, removed.
New Madrid, August 9, 1932, Negro, attempted rape, removed.

NORTH CAROLINA—

Wallace, January 19, 1930, Negro, murder, removed.
Concord, June 28, 1930, seven Negroes, rape, Guard used.
Greenville, September 18, 1930, white, murder, removed.
Southport, March, 1931, Negro, rape, removed.
Greensboro, October 1, 1931, Negro, murder, removed to distant jail.
Gastonia, May 7, 1932, two Negro men, murder, removed.
Waynesville, September 7, 1932, Negro, insulting woman and killing officer of the law, force used to repel mob.

OHIO—

Bucyrus, January, 1931, three Negroes, murder, Guard used.
Massilon, February 13, 1932, two Negro men, attempted rape, removed.

OKLAHOMA—

Pawnee, December 7, 1930, Negro, murder, force used to repel mob.
Wetonja, June 25, 1931, Negro, murder, Guard used.

OREGON—

Medford, January 24, 1931, white, murder, Guard used.

PENNSYLVANIA—

West Chester, January 14, 1931, Negro, murder, Guard used.

SOUTH CAROLINA—

Graniteville, May 18, 1930, two Negroes, rape, removed.
Edgefield, June 10, 1930, Negro, rape, removed.
Lexington, January 5, 1931, Negro, murder, removed.

Lexington, January 9, 1931, three whites, murder, prisoners removed.

Lexington, January 20, 1931, six Negroes, murder, Guard used.

Anderson, January 18, 1931, Negro, murder, removed.

Georgetown, January 31, 1931, two whites, killing man in auto accident, prisoners removed to distant jail.

Lockhart, September 14, 1931, Negro, murder, force used to repel mob.

Hampton, July 22, 1931, Negro, wounding man, force used to repel mob.

York, November 15, 1931, three Negro men, accused of murder, attempted rape, improper advance to white woman, respectively, all three removed.

Walterboro, May 24, 1932, Negro, rape, removed.

TENNESSEE—

Bolivar, January 28, 1930, Negro, rape, force used to repel mob.

Union City, April, 1930, Negro, rape, National Guard used.

Lawrenceburg, September, 1930, Negro, rape, removed.

Trenton, April 19, 1931, Negro, murder, removed.

Bolivar, February 20, 1930, Negro, murder, removed.

Tiptonville, June 1, 1931, white, rape, National Guard used.

Springfield, July 21, 1931, Negro, wounding officer, force used to repel mob.

Lebanon, September 5, 1932, three Negro men and two Negro women, killing two officers of the law, force used to repel mob.

TEXAS—

Brownwood, May 16, 1930, white, murder, prisoner removed to distant jail.

Granbury, May 22, 1930, Negro, wounding man, removed.

Port Arthur, June 27, 1930, Negro, rape, removed to strong jail.

Shamrock, July 14, 1930, Negro, murder, removed.

Arlington, December 7, 1930, Negro, murder, removed.

Mount Pleasant, January 31, 1931, Negro, murder, Guard used.

Marshall, March 17, 1931, Negro, attempted rape, Guard used.

Conroe, August 17, 1931, two Negroes, murder, Guard used.

Greenville, November 8, 1931, Negro, rape, removed.

Texarkana, August 29, 1932, Negro, rape, removed.

VIRGINIA—

Alexandria, January 1, 1930, Negro, killing officer, Guard used.

Radford, July, 1932, Negro, rape, Guard augmented.

WEST VIRGINIA—

Clarksburg, September 20, 1931, white, murder, force used to repel mob.

APPENDIX C

TABLE I

Lynchings, Whites and Negroes—1889-1932*

Year	Whites	Negroes	Total
1889	81	95	176
1890	37	90	127
1891	71	121	192
1892	100	155	255
1893	46	155	201
1894	56	134	190
1895	59	112	171
1896	51	80	131
1897	44	122	166
1898	25	102	127
1899	23	84	107
1900	8	107	115
1901	28	107	135
1902	11	86	97
1903	17	86	103
1904	4	83	87
1905	5	61	66
1906	8	65	73
1907	3	60	63
1908	7	93	100
1909	14	73	87
1910	9	65	74
1911	8	63	71
1912	4	61	65

* Data secured from "The Negro Year Book, 1931-1932," page 293, and from materials subsequently secured from the Department of Records and Research, Tuskegee Institute.

The deaths from the race riots in Atlanta, Chicago, Tulsa, and other places are not classified as lynchings; neither are gang murders in cities South or North. As popularly defined, a chief distinction between a lynching and a gang murder is that, whereas the latter is premeditated and carried out by a few people in conspired secrecy from constituted authorities, the former is usually spontaneous and carried out in a public fashion with scores, hundreds, and not uncommonly thousands of eye-witnesses. Gang murderers—like other murderers—operate in secrecy to evade the law; lynchers operate in the open and publicly defy the law.

Year	Whites	Negroes	Total
1913	1	50	51
1914	3	49	52
1915	13	54	67
1916	4	50	54
1917	2	36	38
1918	4	60	64
1919	7	76	83
1920	8	53	61
1921	5	59	64
1922	6	51	57
1923	4	29	33
1924	0	16	16
1925	0	17	17
1926	7	23	30
1927	0	16	16
1928	1	10	11
1929	3	7	10
1930	1	20	21
1931	1	12	13
1932	2	6	8
Grand Total	791	2,954	3,745

TABLE II

Accusations Against Persons Lynched—1889-1932*

Year	Homicide	Felonious Assault	Rape	Attempted Rape	Rob'ry & Theft	Insult to Whites	All Other Causes
1889	51	5	34	4	19	....	63
1890	25	2	26	2	5	....	67
1891	52	2	38	2	28	....	70
1892	88	4	37	12	38	2	74
1893	56	2	34	4	10	2	92
1894	73	2	42	10	16	6	41
1895	71	1	29	13	20	1	36
1896	42	9	29	6	14	....	31
1897	68	5	25	9	23	2	34
1898	74	5	11	7	8	2	20
1899	56	....	5	6	6	....	34
1900	43	10	18	13	7	....	24
1901	48	9	21	8	21	1	27
1902	43	7	19	11	1	....	15
1903	53	8	16	7	....	1	19
1904	36	4	14	6	1	2	24
1905	34	4	15	4	2	....	7
1906	24	7	16	14	1	1	9
1907	20	7	13	11	4	1	7
1908	50	10	14	6	4	3	32
1909	28	12	3	18	1	3	5
1910	38	6	16	8	2	2	2
1911	37	4	9	6	1	4	10
1912	37	6	10	2	1	3	5
1913	20	11	5	5	2	1	8
1914	30	8	6	1	1	....	6
1915	26	10	11	....	9	3	8
1916	20	7	3	9	8	2	5
1917	6	2	7	5	2	2	14
1918	28	2	10	6	2	....	16
1919	28	3	9	10	1	6	26
1920	22	9	15	3	....	3	9
1921	19	7	16	3	....	3	16
1922	15	5	14	5	4	2	12
1923	5	5	6	1	1	1	14
1924	4	2	5	2	....	3	....
1925	8	1	4	2	....	1	1
1926	13	3	2	3	1	1	7
1927	7	2	2	3	....	....	2
1928	5	3	2	....	....	....	1
1929	1	3	3	....	....	2	1

*Data secured from "The Negro Year Book, 1931-1932," page 294, and from materials subsequently secured from the Department of Records and Research, Tuskegee Institute.

Year	Homicide	Felonious Assault	Rape	Attempted Rape	Rob'ry & Theft	Insult to Whites	All Other Causes
1930	5	....	8	2	3	....	3
1931	5	....	....	5	....	....	3
1932	2	1	1	1	....	1	2
Total	1,406	215	623	255	267	67	902

TABLE III

LYNCHINGS PER TEN THOUSAND POPULATION—1900-1929*

	LYNCHINGS PER TEN THOUSAND NEGRO POPULATION				Lynchings Per Ten Thousand White Population†	Lynchings Per Ten Thousand Total Population†
	Black Belt Counties	Counties With ¼ to ½ Negroes	Counties With Less Than ¼ Negroes	State		
Florida	3.51	4.34	5.77	4.46	2.22	1.48
Oklahoma	......	......	......	3.87	.29	.27
Arkansas	2.12	2.18	6.28	2.88	1.03	.76
Texas	3.79	1.82	1.94	2.47	.51	.43
Georgia	2.24	2.83	2.25	2.45	1.71	1.01
Mississippi	2.11	2.91	3.87	2.4?	2.82	1.29
Kentucky	......	1.47	2.40	2.23	.27	.24
Louisiana	2.02	2.12	2.96	2.11	1.45	.87
Missouri	......	......	......	2.10	.13	.12
Alabama	1.10	1.18	2.57	1.31	.86	.52
Tennessee	.52	1.09	2.35	1.05	.39	.32
South Carolina	.79	.80	.00	.78	.81	.41
North Carolina	.43	.40	.69	.46	.21	.14
Virginia	.40	.47	.27	.38	.17	.11
Totals	1.64	1.71	2.44	1.84	.69	.51

*Data compiled from detailed record of lynchings by counties from the Department of Records and Research, Tuskegee Institute, and average population by states and counties for 1900 to 1930 from U. S. Census publications.

† It will be observed in Table I that approximately nine-tenths of the persons lynched since 1900 have been Negroes. The only reason for presenting the number of lynchings per ten thousand total population and per ten thousand white population is to give a measure of the degree in which the general public and the white populace of each of the Southern States have shared in the guilt of lynching Negroes.

TABLE IV

Lynchings and Preventions of Reported Threatened Lynchings—1914-1932*

Year	No. Persons Lynched	No. Lynchings Prevented
1914	52	16
1915	67	19
1916	54	18
1917	38	18
1918	64	13
1919	83	37
1920	61	56
1921	64	72
1922	57	58
1923	33	52
1924	16	45
1925	17	39
1926	30	33
1927	16	42
1928	11	24
1929	10	27
1930	21	40
1931	13	62
1932	8	33
Total	715	704

* Data secured from "The Negro Year Book, 1931-1932," page 294, and from materials subsequently secured from the Department of Records and Research, Tuskegee Institute.

INDEX

Irwin, James, 4, 6, 141 ff.
Irwinville, Ga., 141, 168.
Italians, 130, 132 ff.
Italy, 130.
Israelites, 23.

Jack, Guy, 90, 91, 92-93.
Jackson, Andrew, 98.
Jails, 7, 13, 32, 44, 52, 86, 107, 108,
109, 137, 138, 143, 203, 205 ff., 214,
218, 231, 232, 238, 257, 263, 265 ff.,
288, 300, 303, 305, 308, 310, 320,
322, 326, 367, 369 ff., 387 ff., 394,
413, 418, 444 ff., 454, 459, 463.
Jail population, by race, 170, 202,
231, 257, 284, 316, 437, 438.
Jailers, 109, 110, 207, 235, 236, 266,
305, 322, 371, 388-389, 418.
James, Paul, 290.
Jenkins, Dan, 261, 286 ff.
Jenkins, Joe Ben, 302, 311.
Jeter, A. M., 290.
Jews, 82, 103.
Johnston, Albert Sidney, 326.
Johnson, Red, 374.
Johnson, Sam G., 7, 256 ff.
Johnson, Tom, 374.
Jones, Alvin, 274.
Jones, Sam P., 313, 316.
Jones, "Slim," 321, 331, 333.
Jones, Winston, 59, 63, 65.
Journal (Atlanta), 241.
Journal (Homer, Ga.), 158.
Journal (Pelham, Ga.), 160.
Journal (Spartanburg, S. C.), 291.
Journal (Winston-Salem, N. C.),
116, 294.
Journal and Guide (Norfolk, Va.),
97.
Judge censured, 186, 187, 308-309.
Judge, condoned lynching, 153.
Judge's charge, 150-152, 310; *see
also, Judges.*
Judges, 17, 19, 109, 111, 150-152, 153,
186, 240, 304-306, 309, 322 ff., 324,
334, 344, 418, 423, 454-455, 458-459.
"Judicial murders," 46; *see also
"Legal Lynchings."*
Jurist, defends lynching, 246.
Jurors, attitudes of, 18-19.

Kansas, 27.
Kansas City, Mo., 409, 426.

Keley, James, 405.
Kemper County, Miss., *see Scooba.*
Kemper Herald (Scooba, Miss.),
88, 89.
Kentucky, 27, 43, 392, 433.
Keowee Courier (Walhalla, S. C.),
272, 273.
Kirkland, Willie, 233 ff.
Kilby prison, 64, 70.
Kidd-Key College, 351.
Ku Klux Klan, 124, 183, 186, 196,
199, 200-201, 257-258, 284, 299, 300,
338, 373, 398, 429.

"Labor bruiser," 127.
Labor, disorganization of, 2, 41, 62-
63, 341, 366-367, 427-428, 466.
Labor trouble, 125.
Labor matter, 56.
LaGrange, Ga., 441, 454-458.
Landed Aristocracy, 56-58, 62-63, 80,
95, 126-127, 193, 225, 250, 259-260.
Lanier, A. L., 183.
Laws, needed, 50-51.
Lawyers, 19, 56, 183, 206, 256, 305-
306, 338.
Leader (Louisville, Ky.), 294.
Leader (Springfield, Mo.), 430.
Leader Tribune (Marion, Ind.), 393.
Leard, Allen, 274.
Lee, Grady, 274.
Lee, John, 374.
Lee, Mitch, 274.
Lee-Grant Hotel, 162.
"Legal lynching," 19, 33, 46, 137-138;
see also, Promises to mob.
Leslie, Harry G., 391.
"Let 'er burn," 325.
Lewis, W. M., 183.
Lewisburg, West Va., 385.
Life sentences, 36, 105, 219.
Lightweight boxer, 463.
"Lily White" Republicans, 172-175,
186.
Liquor, 63, 94, 95, 186, 210, 307,
395; *see also, Intoxication.*
Literary Digest, 365.
Livestock, 77, 121, 192, 251, 378-379,
433, 434.
Livingston, Ala., 71, 74, 77 ff.
Livingston State Normal School for
Girls, 78.
Local (Sylvester, Ga.), 156, 158.
Lockett, "Pig," 85, 86, 88, 90.

DATE DUE

AUG 2 1 1990			
il:5513663			
5-18-84			
APR 1 9 1991			
FEB 2 2 1993			
FEB 0 2 2000			
NOV 2 6 2003			
DEC 1 7 2006			